Choreographing Mexico

Joe R. and Teresa Lozano Long Series in Latin American and Latino Art and Culture

Choreographing Mexico

Festive Performances and Dancing
Histories of a Nation

MANUEL R. CUELLAR

University of Texas Press ⟨⟩ *Austin*

Requests for permission to reproduce material from this work should be
sent to:
Permissions
University of Texas Press
P.O. Box 7819
Austin, TX 78713-7819
utpress.utexas.edu/rp-form

⊛ The paper used in this book meets the minimum requirements of ANSI/NISO
Z39.48-1992 (R1997) (Permanence of Paper).

Library of Congress Cataloging-in-Publication Data

Names: Cuellar, Manuel R., author.
Title: Choreographing Mexico : festive performances and dancing histories of a
    nation / Manuel R. Cuellar.
Description: First edition. | Austin : University of Texas Press, 2022. | Includes
    bibliographical references and index.
Identifiers:
LCCN 2022002144
ISBN 978-1-4773-2516-2 (cloth)
ISBN 978-1-4773-2517-9 (PDF)
ISBN 978-1-4773-2518-6 (ePub)
Subjects: LCSH: Folk dancing—Political aspects—Mexico—History. | Folk dancing—
    Mexico—Influence. | Folk dancing—Social aspects—Mexico—History. |
    Dance in motion pictures, television, etc.—Mexico—History. | Festivals—
    Political aspects—Mexico—History. | Mexico—Centennial celebrations, etc.—
    Political aspects—History.
Classification: LCC GV1627 .C84 2022 | DDC 793.3/19810972—dc23/
    eng/20220125
LC record available at https://lccn.loc.gov/2022002144

doi:10.7560/325162

A mis eternos maestros: María Adelaida y Víctor, mis padres.
A mi familia, gracias a la cual soy y estoy.

Contents

Preface   **ix**

Acknowledgments   **xv**

Introduction. Choreographing a Festive Nation:
Performance, Dance, and Embodied Histories in Mexico   **1**

1. Rehearsals of a Cosmopolitan Modernity: The Porfirian
    Centennial Celebrations of Mexican Independence in 1910   **39**

2. La Noche Mexicana and the Staging of a Festive Mexico   **74**

3. Nellie Campobello: The Choreographer of Dancing Histories
    in Mexico   **117**

4. Cinematic Renditions of a Dancing Mexico: *Folklórico*
    Dance in Mexican Film   **164**

Epilogue. Queering Mexico's Archive: Ephemerality, Movement,
    and Kinesthetic Imaginings   **224**

Notes   **233**

Bibliography   **279**

Index   **301**

Preface

The year was 1995, and I had been chosen to audition for the local prestigious and popular *folklórico* group—the current state champions among federal middle schools in Chihuahua, Mexico. I had officially started learning folklórico dance, or Mexican regional and traditional dance, only the year before in one of my regular classes, *educación artística* (artistic education). But in a way, I had been dancing folklórico all my life.

I began dancing folklórico in kindergarten, when I first learned a simple choreography of "La raspa," a traditional Mexican tune. "La raspa yo bailé" (I danced La raspa), and ever since I have been dancing. When I started middle school in 1994, I participated in the parade commemorating the Mexican Revolution dancing *sones* from the Ixtapa-Soyaló region of Chiapas, the southern Mexican border. Folklórico dance was an integral part of my elementary and secondary education. It enabled me to learn a regional and national expressive repertoire. I was in disbelief, then, when I was asked to be part of my middle school's highly selective folklórico group, which had won multiple state championships. This dance group managed to bring much pride and recognition to the small, easily overlooked community of Saucillo, Chihuahua. And yet, my middle school was located less than a kilometer away from one of the few federal teacher training schools for women, Escuela Normal Rural "Ricardo Flores Magón." This meant that our folklórico instructor, José Alfredo López Minjarez, was also training future educators, teaching them Mexican dance as an integral part of their curriculum. In high school, I continued to dance with Kórima, a group that had recently been created by the same director, while I also attended a summer folklórico training school in the state's capital, Escuela Superior de Danza Folklórica Mexicana. For five consecutive summers, I continued with my formal folklórico education and eventually did my *prácticas profesionales* (professional practices) teaching folklórico in rural and urban elementary schools in Guanajuato, Mexico, where I performed with a local folklórico group, Zihua-Temachtiani, which had been founded by elementary school teachers in Irapuato, Mexico.

My life changed drastically in the summer of 2000 when I migrated to Los Angeles. I stopped dancing for a while. As a migrant, I was struggling to find a sense of self and adapt to my new reality. Soon, thanks to my mother's initiative, I found myself volunteering at a local middle school in Glendale, California, teaching folklórico in an after-school program for youth considered "at risk." This experience led me to join Mosaico Mexican Folk Ensemble, where I danced during my years in community college and at the University of California, Los Angeles, until I finally moved to Berkeley to pursue my doctoral studies in Hispanic literature. At Berkeley, I first joined and then became the artistic director of Reflejos de México, the university's folklórico group. And after two years, I decided to join Ensambles Ballet Folklórico de San Francisco, where I found a welcoming community and acquired more experience as a dancer and as an instructor while performing choreographies of Mexican nationalism. Now, almost three decades after that first audition, I am still an active member, instructor, and artistic advisor of yet another group, Corazón Folklórico Dance Company in Washington, DC.

Each of these dance companies exposed me to different ways of engaging, creating, and performing the vast and complex network of Indigenous, Afro-mestizo, and popular expressive cultures throughout Mexico. Each artistic director and dance instructor choreographed his or her own vision of Mexico, and yet each one cited the same corporeal genealogy and embodied culture that characterizes Mexican folklórico dance. As the Mexican dance scholar and choreographer Juan Carlos Palma Velasco points out, despite the singular iterations, methodological differences, and representations of Mexican regional and traditional dances, a shared movement vocabulary, embodied history, and body culture inform and sustain Mexican folklórico as a well-established discipline across different aesthetic and political manifestations.[1] At home and abroad, as my own dance trajectory demonstrates, folklórico is a vital mechanism for expressing Mexican popular culture, and, as a result, this dance form is a generative site of political enunciation. After all, dancing the nation has long been part of the construction of a festive Mexico.

Choreographing Mexico: Festive Performances and Dancing Histories of a Nation reveals the complexities, trajectories, and slippery attachments of my embodied history of dancing and researching Mexican dance while performing and at times critiquing the nation. I have approached this academic project and journey as a dancer, choreographer, and scholar, which allows me to research, teach, and write from a unique perspective across disciplines, institutional units, and community organizations. While I have studied and received training in other dance forms, such as tango, modern dance, and Afro-Latin rhythms, my research as a cultural studies scholar is informed by almost thirty years of experience and training in folklórico dance in Mexico and the United States. My strong background in Mexican traditional and regional dance is what has led me to explore dance's role in identity formation, gender, indigeneity, and queerness in Mexico and the United States. In this book about the role of dance, movement, and other public displays and choreographies of Mexican nationalism, I seek to complicate the discursive formulation of *lo mexicano* (Mexicanness), while also examining how knowledge was produced and circulated, focusing on moving bodies in the early part of the twentieth century in Mexico, from the 1910s through the 1940s.

As an instructor and dancer of Mexican folklórico, I wrote *Choreographing Mexico* from a commitment not to separate my academic endeavors from my strong connections with the communities to which I belong, both within and outside the academy. The historian María Elena Martínez challenges us to examine how we understand and write about history by attending to "the experiential knowledge lodged in our bodies and minds" while we engage in archival work.[2] Part of the archival work I have conducted these years involved my imagination and body as someone who, like many other students in Mexico and folklórico dancers, performed iconic dances such as *El jarabe tapatío*, *La bamba*, or *Jesusita en Chihuahua* as part of my kinesthetic formation as a Mexican subject, particularly during the commemorations of Mexican Independence and the Revolution. Each performance, each distinct *zapateado* (footwork), engaged in a mode of storytelling that created a space for others to kinesthetically feel, imagine, and respond to my body as an expression and even an extension of a collective imaginary across time, space, and borders. In this work, I use queerness as a methodological intervention. In this capacity, queerness allows me to frame movement as an embodied, though ephemeral, trace that has systematically and historically been negated, erased, or simply excluded in discussions of Mexican nationalism. Each one of the examples I analyze constitutes a concrete materialization and rehearsal of a national identity, but it also demonstrates individual and collective responses to stagings and choreographies of Mexican nationalism.

Folklórico is certainly complicit with normative and hegemonic renditions of the nation, but it has historically been much more than that;

it has made, remade, and unmade the nation. Folklórico is a corporeal modality that makes it possible to access, interpellate, and recognize collective imaginaries of Mexican nationalism. As a contested terrain, folklórico enacts an embodied sociality with which to grapple with our histories, geographies, and bodies as well as our political and affective investments while we perform the nation at home and abroad. After all, dance, like any other form of embodied expression, brings together our creative, cultural, political, and intellectual endeavors, allowing us to reflect and act on our cultural practices, political alliances, and power dynamics and their complex relationship to local communities. By examining the complicated and contradictory displays of Mexican nationalism before and during the postrevolutionary period, I draw attention to the historical, cultural, and theoretical significance of movement and embodied experience.

I could have never imagined I would be writing this book during a pandemic, an attempted coup, and a highly policed transfer of power in the United States. The insurrection on January 6, 2021, revealed how bodies in motion can destabilize power. The displays of white supremacy forced us to grapple with the differentiated deployments of national symbols and the colonizing and dangerous repercussions of enactments of imperial whiteness. Indeed, embodied white supremacy characterized the traumatic and taxing presidency of Donald Trump. And yet, while anxiously awaiting the election results on that very long night of November 3, 2020, I found myself dancing with my partner and a dear friend in front of the US Capitol to a song I heard for the first time that night. Staying still is not always an option. There was something generative and even healing in that improvised dance, in that gesture of occupying an empty area that symbolized so much and that had not been designed for us, for our physical presence and experiences.

The absence of crowds during the inauguration, symbolically replaced by US flags, reminded us that such displays of nationalism could never reproduce the meaning-making power of bodies in motion. After the insurrection, the small apartment where I wrote and revised this book became a limited and limiting space, part of a neighborhood that was heavily securitized by the presence of thousands of members of the National Guard, police, and even the border patrol, a neighborhood where brown bodies like mine and my partner's needed to be careful. I felt unsafe. Our brown bodies needed to not be too much, for we were being policed. We had to occupy as little space as possible and ask for permission to return home. There were days when I did not leave my apartment, but there were others when I felt compelled to move.

The pandemic had already forced us to stay mostly indoors. It significantly restricted our mobility and our ability to interact corporeally with others. I went from dancing weekly to dancing virtually and eventually to just imagining dancing again. During these months, close family members and friends became infected. Covid-19 took the lives of Marco and Martha, part of my chosen/queer family. I tried to occupy this wounded space, to draw strength from it, and to heal. By inhabiting my wounds and mourning the lives of those lost, I sought to wrest back certain forms of knowing and relating to others, embracing a shared vulnerability as a way to begin a collective process of healing. Covid laid bare the precarity and vulnerability that condition our interactions, and yet it also revealed the very intimate ways we are all interconnected. The pandemic has forced us to grapple with meaning-making processes that demand that moving bodies be together, sharing affinities and complicities. Bodies in motion capture, even fleetingly, traces of lived experience: we relate to others through stories recounted through our bodies, affirming and creating spaces of belonging.

Dance allows for restorative and resistive possibilities of occupying, enacting, and reimagining public spaces, while shedding light on the precariousness, fragilities, and alliances shared by dancing communities and amateur and professional dancers on and off the stage. The dance theorist Judith Hamera, proposing that dance is a form of "communication infrastructure," asks us to think of aesthetics as "inherently social" and as a form of "communicative currency" that fosters "interpretative communities."[3] In this way, dance reveals the social work of aesthetic practices and generates socialities beyond the performance event—reshaping possibilities for intimacy. By thinking of Mexican dance as an embodied sociality, as a "relational infrastructure," I invite the reader to view the relationship between bodies, histories, spaces, and imaginaries as a cultural and political intervention, an archival site, and an aesthetic practice that was foundational to the consolidation of a festive Mexico, of lo mexicano. Mexican regional and traditional dance functions as a meaningful public cultural discourse. Through this discourse, dancers and spectators explore social arrangements and sociopolitical landscapes that reveal the slipperiness of Mexican civic life and attachments to a shared sense of belonging.

This project began when I noticed a certain dissonance between the scholarship (or lack thereof) on the role of dance and movement in the consolidation of Mexican nationalism and my own experience as a trained folklórico dancer and instructor. The project grew as I questioned my intellectual, physical, and affective investment in the creation of a body of work about a communal practice. Most important, it has led me to recognize how Mexican dance has made it possible to relate to others, to identify with others, to embody being-with-others, to foster intercommunal solidarities, to perform justice, to enact alternative socialities, to affirm ourselves, and, during these months of lockdowns, violence, and loss, to heal with others.

And so, here we are. *¡A bailar!*

Acknowledgments

Esta también es una práctica de comunalidad. Como todos los textos, éste también fue escrito junto con y a partir del trabajo imaginativo de otros, justo en el horizonte de esa mutua pertenencia al lenguaje que nos vuelve a veces, con suerte, parte de un estar-en-común que es crítico y festivo. Aquí también, pues, su devoción. Aquí su tiempo. Y el nuestro.

CRISTINA RIVERA GARZA

This project could not have been possible without the love, care, courage, and friendship of many people—a testament of the community that nourishes me. I am forever thankful to each one of you for writing it with me, for I did not do it on my own. I am blessed to have the love and support from many people from different walks of life, particularly during this pandemic. *Gracias.*

Choreographing Mexico started as a dissertation at the University of California, Berkeley. Estelle Tarica, my adviser—a generous and demanding reader—challenged me intellectually to be clear, concise, and assertive, and wholeheartedly supported me in this intellectual and personal endeavor: *gracias por tu voto de confianza*, Estelle. Ivonne del Valle's insightful questions and suggestions significantly expanded the breadth of this project: *por las risas, las protestas, las charlas y las cenas—gracias Ivonne.* Juana María Rodríguez always motivated me to pursue my passion for dance, to write owning my claims, and to cross borders, whenever necessary: *muchas gracias Juana querida* for helping me embrace my queer *latinidad* and for dancing along with me. Finally, Robert McKee Irwin inspired me to pursue this interdisciplinary project and not to be afraid of crossing disciplinary boundaries; like Juana, he always knew that my project was about dance: *¡mil gracias Robert!* Angela Marino also inspired me to embark on this festive intellectual endeavor with much guidance and support. My sincere gratitude also goes to Natalia Brizuela, Francine Masiello, Emilie Bergmann, José Rabasa, and Ignacio Navarrete for enriching my academic journey in the Department of Spanish and Portuguese. Verónica López deserves a special mention for creating such a welcoming and nurturing space: *gracias de corazón*. Carla Trujillo, Heather Asfan, and particularly Josephine Moreno were my first introduction to Berkeley and continued to be strong mentors and supporters.

At Berkeley, I was privileged to be able to learn from and interact with incredible individuals, who remain lifelong friends. But there are two people without whom I would have never made it: Ricardo López and Ivett López Malagamba; each literally had to endure living with me, which was not always easy or simple, to say the least. *Gracias; son mi familia*. Anna Cruz and I stumbled upon each other—that simple, that profound, *¡gracias azizam!* *No tengo palabras para expresar mi agradecimiento y cariño a* Krista Brune, for the long walks, sustained intellectual dialogue, and regular check-ins, *muito obrigado*; Julia Chang, for the dancing, radical care, and feminist friendship; Julie Wesp, for her love, enthusiasm, and dancing energy; Giancarlo Cornejo, for the life-changing conversations about queerness and academia; Ashley Brock, for her encouragement, support, and writing companionship; Julie Ward, for sharing her joy of writing, the laughter, and the motivation. Special thanks also go to Camilo Jaramillo, Silvia López, Jax Bialostozky, Tara Daly, Iván Ramos, Ianna Owens, Rob Medina, Dexter Zavalza, Danae Valenzuela, Camilo Lund, Emilia Cordero, Richard Grijalva, John Mundell, Michelle Velasquez Potts, Heather Rastovac, Juan Manuel Adalpe, Naomi Bragin, Azucena Hernández, Ariel Wind, Mayra Bottaro, Sujey Reynoso, Daniela Milián, and Tricia Sarmiento for all their support, laughs, long talks, coffee, drinks, and nourishment. Carlos Macías, Jessica Stair, and John Sullivan: thank you for sharing your love and passion for Nahuatl with me!

At George Washington University, I have found a welcoming and stimulating space for developing this book and creating a community. I am particularly indebted to Heather Bamford, Christopher Britt, Kathryn Kleppinger, and Sergio Waisman for their encouragement, mentorship, and generous feedback. Antonio López provided invaluable guidance, feedback, and unwavering enthusiasm to draft this manuscript; *gracias compadre*. I thank Pauline Goul, Masha Belenky, and Lynn Westwater for their steadfast support and for facilitating rich intellectual exchanges in our department. My gratitude also goes to my departmental colleagues,

Yvonne Captain, Abdou Waberi, Margaret Gonglewski, Mary Beth Stein, Richard Robin, Peter Rollberg, and Bradford Marshall, as well as Dolores Perillán, Alicia Suárez Touzón, Tania Leyva, and María José de la Fuente. Special thanks go to Ariadna Pichs and Víctor Valdvia, *mis vecis, por el café, los tragos, las comidas y las risas.* Carliss Parker-Smith deserves a special mention for her warm welcome to and enthusiasm (and patience!) for the department and Tyana Butler for her support. I am very fortunate to have a vibrant community across campus. I thank Elizabeth Vaquera, Elaine Peña, and Wendy Wagner for making George Washington University a welcoming and thriving space of growth. I also thank my colleagues Amy Cohen, David Mitchell, Kavita Daiya, Elizabeth Rule, Daniel DeWispelare, Elisabeth Anker, Francesco Sinatora, and Gayle Wald for creating such an intellectually rich community. Carol Hayes and Eiko Strader became a lifeline this past year, creating a community that provided the peer support, accountability, and space I needed to prioritize my research in such a complex academic year. My heartfelt thanks also go to my students Will Hoadley-Brill and Vivian Kong, my research assistants, whose meticulous work, patience, and enthusiasm significantly improved and facilitated the completion of this project.

I am very grateful to have found a vibrant network of colleagues across the larger DMV area; their work, friendship, and mentorship have substantially enriched my life. Special thanks to Eyda Merediz, Mariela Méndez, Álvaro Kaempfer, Núria Vilanova, Laura Demaria, Gwen Kirkpatrick, Jason Bartles, Griselda Zuffi, Brenda Werth, Tania Gentic, Silvia Kurlat, Rocío Gordon, Todd Garth, Ricardo Ortiz, Jim Maffie, Ryan Long, David Sartorius, and Rosa Aurora Chávez. Anna Deeny has opened up her home multiple times to build a strong community and celebrate life. Thanks to her, I participated in the production of La Paloma at the Wall, directed by Nick Olcott in 2019, her adaptation of the zarzuela, *La verbena de la paloma*, a creative work that profoundly impacted me as a scholar and dancer. I also thank Alberto Fierro, Beatriz Nava, Ix-Nic Iruegas, and Enrique Quiroz at the Mexican Cultural Institute for creating such a vital space of cultural and intellectual exchange in DC. And I want to thank Eduardo Díaz, Suzanne Schadl, Catalina Gomez, and Jesse Garcia for their support and collaboration in various projects. María Thurber deserves a special mention for her invaluable support at the Library of Congress; *muchas gracias.*

I have been blessed to find life-affirming and sustaining relationships that have made DC home. Thank you, Mireya Loza, Mike Amezcua,

Perla Guerrero, Sharada Balachandran, and Kali Cyrus for the many days of laughter, meals, drinks, impromptu trips, and loving companionship. *¡Salud por eso!* Robert McRuer welcomed me to DC by sharing his brilliance, generosity, and queer/crip world, including the joyful friendships of Santy Rodelo, Joseph Choueike, and Andrew Glaspie. Juliana Martínez, *con esa casa de brazos abiertos*, offered critical insights throughout the process but most importantly a space to keep dancing and singing, experiencing healing and transformative connections, together with Steve Dudley and Salvador Vidal Ortiz (*¡y la Marisol!*)—*¡a seguir cantando y bailando chicxs!* Juan Sebastián Ospina León gave me incredible suggestions for my chapter on film and has been a true friend since we first met applying to graduate programs; it's been an honor sharing this process with you. Lakshmi Krishnan, Jay Butler, and Jonathan Yuen created an intimate space to commune, a space of compassion that was vital during my first years in DC. David Tenorio has been a queer, loving, and radical presence in my life and I have been blessed to have crossed paths with them in California, México, and DC; *queride, ya sabes todo*. Diana Pardo has been an enthusiastic force in this last push, and I am so thankful for the community we have created.

I have met many friends that are now like family in academia. Guadalupe Caro Cocotle and Armando García radically transformed my life during a summer in Tepoztlán and have filled it with much joy, laughter, and love; *¡mil gracias queridas comas!* Kelly McDonough drastically changed my relationship to writing one day at a time; these past years she became a great friend and mentor, encouraging me and inspiring me through radical gestures of care to continue to do the work I love. Mónica García Blizzard gave me invaluable suggestions for my chapters on film and became a motivating companion in this last stretch. Sarah Smith probably read all of my shitty first drafts but most importantly became an indispensable sounding board and friend for this project. Deborah Vargas saw something in me and has become an indispensable supporter and advocate during this journey; *¡gracias por todo Deb!* Laura Gutiérrez has become a valued and inspiring interlocutor and mentor, who has provided critical feedback along the way. Nanci Buiza provided a welcoming space of respite and friendship, particularly during this pandemic. Special thanks to Valeria Valencia, Vanessa Fernández, Marco Martínez, Judith Sierra, Leticia Robles, Edward Chauca, Vicki Garrett, Ariel Tumbaga, Sara Townsend, Angel González, Sandra Sotelo, Sandra Ruiz, Román Luján, Chase Raymond, Sarah Moody, Rocío Ferreira, Karla González, María Fernanda Díaz, Carmen Valdivia, Claudia

Salazar, Alicia Vargas, Pablo García, Kathleen Long, Iván Eusebio Aguirre, Xiomara Cervantes-Gómez, Miguel García, Wilfredo José Burgos Matos, Julia Morales, Stephanie Sherman, and Regina Mills (who wrote with me every week), for their friendship and support.

Writing is always a dialogue, an interaction with others. I am very grateful for the community of scholars who make my work possible: Diana Taylor, Ramón Rivera Servera, Maricruz Castro Ricalde, Oswaldo Estrada, Michelle Clayton, Ignacio Sánchez Prado, Alejandro Madrid, Sergio de la Mora, Natasha Varner, Patricia Aulestia, Sophie Bidault, and Melissa Blanco. Chrissy Arce deserves a special mention because she introduced me to Nellie Campobello; it was her work that inspired me to become an academic in our discipline. Margarita Tortajada's work has been foundational for Mexican dance studies; she became a steadfast supporter, valued interlocutor, and friend in the realization of this project. Mitchell Snow's work is also an obligatory reference for Mexican dance studies; his generosity and insights significantly enriched this project. José Luis Reynoso, a pioneer of Mexican dance studies in the US, became an indispensable interlocutor and encouraging colleague; *¡muchas gracias José Luis!* Juan Carlos Palma shared his tremendous knowledge of Mexican folklórico and talent with me, leaving an indelible mark in my understanding of this discipline that has transformed my life—*¡estoy en deuda!* Claudia Carbajal kindly shared her pioneering work with me, enhancing my understanding of massive spectacles and the trajectory of the Campobellos. Román Santillán significantly enriched my understanding of this time period, offering critical insights and comments, and sharing his encyclopedic knowledge of Mexico with me; *¡quedo en deuda contigo!* Jesús Vargas and Flor García's work on the Campobello sisters was crucial in the writing of this book; I thank Jesús Vargas for sharing with me the transcript of Nellie's interview with Patricia Aulestia. Thank you, Luis Martín Ulloa and Antonio Marquet, for your friendship and radical work. At UCLA, Claudia Parodi, John Skirius, Makela Brizuela, and Adriana Bergero supported my academic journey in Mexican studies. At Glendale Community College, Lin Griffith, Flavio Frontini, and Laura Chambers opened the first doors and gave me the confidence I needed to get moving when I had just arrived. Thank you to James Ramey, Mauricio Calderón, and Maricruz Castro for inviting me to participate in the edited volume, *Mexican Transnational Cinema and Literature*, where portions of chapter 2 first appeared: "La escenificación de lo mexicano y la interpelación de un público nacional: la Noche Mexicana de 1921" in *Mexican Transnational Cinema and*

Literature. Eds. Maricruz Castro Ricalde, Mauricio Díaz Calderón, and James Ramey (Peter Lang, 2017): 123–140.

I have no words to express my gratitude to Kerry Webb at the University of Texas Press for her patience and support though this difficult journey. Thank you, Kerry, for believing in this project and in me. I also thank Andrew Hnatow, Tammy Rastoder, and the rest of the editorial team at UT Press for their help with this manuscript. Thank you to the anonymous reviewers for your questions, suggestions, and support of this book. Your insightful comments substantially improved the scope and breadth of this project. I would also like to thank Cathy Hannabach and Morgan Genevieve Blue from Ideas on Fire for an extraordinary interdisciplinary index.

Katelyn Knox's program, coaching, and mentorship offered me the ultimate roadmap to pursue this journey. I could not have completed this book without her guidance and the supportive community she has created. Special thanks also go to the incredible Allison Van Deventer, whose extraordinary editing skills substantially improved this project. I am very grateful for the loving and welcoming virtual community of Writing Every Day, whose members became caring supporters, keeping me accountable during these last difficult months during the pandemic. Thank you, Juana, for inviting me to join this wonderful community! And I also thank the various members of the National Center for Faculty Development and Diversity for helping me find the best balance between life and work.

This manuscript was written with the support of generous grants, fellowships, and research funds. Summer and travel funds from the Department of Spanish and Portuguese and the normative time and dissertation completion fellowships from the Graduate Division of the University of California, Berkeley, allowed me to conduct the initial research in Mexico for chapters 2 and 3. A University Facilitating Fund, Columbian College Facilitating Fund, and Humanities Facilitating Fund grants from GWU provided much-needed support to travel to Mexico regularly to conduct research at a number of libraries and national archives. A summer fellowship at the National Humanities Center in 2019 allowed me to write the first version of chapter 4. I am extremely grateful for the invaluable support of the incredible librarians and staff members, particularly Brooke Andrade, Lynn Miller, Joe Milillo, and Sarah Harris and my fellow colleagues during the program. I was able to present and discuss my work at Swarthmore College, Catholic University, Gettysburg College, and the Mexican Cultural Institute. I thank Nanci Buiza, Juan Sebastián Ospina León, Álvaro Kaempfer, and Alberto Fierro for their invitation to share my work.

In Mexico, I would like to express my sincere gratitude to the librarians, archivists, and staff members of multiple libraries and archives who supported my research throughout various stages of this project. I would not have been able to conduct my research without the generous access to periodicals and archival materials at the Biblioteca Miguel Lerdo de Tejada; special thanks go to Lydia Ortiz and Mario Rebollo for their invaluable support and patience in the realization of this project. At the Escuela Nacional de Danza de Nellie y Gloria Campobello, Fernando Aragón (the former director) and Dafne Domínguez (the archivist and librarian) allowed me to look at original documents and generously welcomed me to the institution multiple times; thank you to current director Jessica Adriana Lezama and librarian and archivist Dafne Domínguez for their support with the images for chapter 2. At the Archivo Histórico de la Universidad Nacional Autónoma de México, Cuitlahuac Oropeza helped me secure the images from the Fondo Martín Luis Guzmán for chapter 2; I thank the art historian Nieves Rodríguez for sharing her knowledge about this incredible archive. I thank Antonia Rojas and Nahún Calleros at the Filmoteca de la UNAM for their generous support. I would also like to thank the Centro Nacional de Investigación, Documentación e Información de la Danza José Limón for their support with my research as well as the staff and librarians at the Archivo General de la Nación, the Biblioteca Nacional, and the Hemeroteca Nacional. Thanks also to the staff at the UC Library System, George Washington University, and the Library of Congress.

My folklórico family deserves a special mention. My understanding of dance derives greatly from the privilege and joy of having danced folklórico for almost thirty years with incredible human beings—too many to mention. It is thanks to my folklórico family that I can call any place I reside home. Thank you for welcoming me into each group, for all the shows we performed together, for the parties, the laughter, and the love. *Mis ensamblinxs*: Zenón Barrón, Lupe Flores, Priscilla Lopez, Mayra Cuevas, Jeanette Quintana, May Belany, María Anaya, Vanessa Orr, Linda Gamino, Mario Sosa, Raúl Ramos, Jesús Gómez, David Martínez, Christian Ortega, Alex Ledesma, Alberto Morales, and of course, *mis queridos* Marco Castellanos and Luis Rodríguez, in San Francisco. Thanks to folklórico I met Arturo Flores and Javier Valdovinos; *gracias a ambos por enseñarme a querer la persona que soy, por ayudarme a forjarla, por su sinceridad brutal y cariño.* My heartfelt gratitude to Joti Singh for teaching me Bhangra and the rest of the members of Duniya Dance and Drum Company for inviting me to move otherwise. In DC, *mis corazones*: Alejandro Góngora, Diana Alexanderson, Imelda García, Ariel Ruiz, Laura Bohorquez, Paulette Chavira, Sofía Galván, Cynthia Hernandez, James Hernandez, César Sotelo, Alfredo García, Óscar Holguín, María Eugenia de la Peña, Rosalba Ruíz, Lupita Rodríguez, Ana Paula López, Angelina Romualdo, Christine Cortez, Liz Cordova, Vicky Estevez, Sara García, Deborah Membreno, Ale Tristan, Odette Maciel, Enrique Nahucatl, Luis Pacheco, Natalia Bogdanova, Lucero Ortiz, Besher Lunachick, Katie Aragón, Karina Herrera, Ana María Rivera, and Covadonga Soto.

Outside the academy, I am indebted to the generosity and friendship of incredible humans that fill my world with love and joy. José Luis Gutiérrez and Luis Díaz deserve a special mention for welcoming me into their home time and again in Mexico City; without their love and support, I would not have been able to conduct research in Mexico: *su ejemplo y apoyo me dan la confianza de que es posible construir otros mundos*. In Mexico, I also thank Marina Domínguez, *siempre presente*; Claudia Alcocer, *por compartir tu mundo conmigo*; Sofía Blanco, *por la fortaleza trasmitida y el cariño incondicional*; Raquel Agraz, *parce que* all you need is love; Javier Eduardo Ramírez, *por los intercambios de saberes, tacos y libros*; Saby Cruz, *tlahuel nimitztlazcamatilia*; Andrés Méndez, *por tu sincera amistad y entusiasmo*; Nieves Rodríguez, *por compartir tus conocimientos, tus recursos y tiempo*; *mil gracias a* Luz Elena Montes. *Gracias infinitas a la gran familia* Gutiérrez: *mis tías, tíos, primas y primos por esos brazos siempre abiertos y su cariño incondicional. Tlazcamati miac* Eduardo de la Cruz and Santos Cruz. Thank you to my dear friends Anibal Rosario, Javier Vargas, and Christian Cruz for making my life full of joy. Luca Bertieri, *ti tengo vicino*. In Los Angeles, I would be forever grateful to have crossed paths with Ángeles Flores, *mi "Shiquia,"* Nivardo Valenzuela, and Luis Mares. Your presence has enriched my life in ways I cannot express.

José Luis Mares and I crossed paths almost by chance, but his presence has radically transformed my life. I learned to heal with him and inhabit our wounds to grow together and become *un nosotros*. I am always in awe and blessed for his capacity to love and his immense patience. His fortitude, courage, and nurturing love kept me, us, afloat. *Gracias por ser y estar, Chaparro*.

Este trabajo y proyecto de vida se lo dedico a mi familia, pero en especial a mamá y papá, María Adelaida y Víctor—mis eternos maestros. Su

ética de trabajo, su perseverancia, su visión de familia, su fortaleza y sus muestras de amor me han dado las lecciones más importantes en mi vida y me han forjado como individuo. A ellos me debo, como me debo a mis hermanos y hermanas: Claudia, Rosy, Fernando, Carlos y Víctor. Me tocó ser el del medio. Con admiración, he sido testigo de sus esfuerzos y he sido partícipe de sus logros como ahora comparto con ellos éste que es el mío. Soy un tío orgulloso y feliz gracias a la presencia de mis sobrinas y sobrinos: Adrián, Paulina, Emiliano, Gabriel, Daniel, Carlett, Benjamin, Brianna, Victor, Fernando, Lizbeth, Karen e Ian. This is for you too! *Mi familia dista mucho de ser perfecta, pero ha sido su fortaleza la que me ha dado el sustento para estar aquí. "Aquí su tiempo." Aquí su amor.*
    Gracias.

Choreographing Mexico

Introduction
Choreographing a Festive Nation: Performance, Dance, and Embodied Histories in Mexico

In January 1919, the world-famous Russian ballerina Anna Pavlova arrived at the port of Veracruz after a long tour through South America
and a complicated stay in Cuba. The arrival of her renowned company
in Mexico was an important event for the government of Venustriano
Carranza, who had been elected president in 1917. Two hundred soldiers were assigned to ride on the train that transported Pavlova and her
company from the port of Veracruz to the nation's capital to ensure their
security. Her visit validated the importance of Mexico City as part of the
international dance circuit. At the time, Pavlova was one of the leading
exponents of the dynamic world dance scene, epitomizing knowledge,
beauty, and technique.[1] In Mexico, audiences immediately fell under her
spell. Her success had such an impact that matinees were offered in *plazas
de toros* (bullrings), where Pavlova performed for up to 30,000 people.[2]
Both there and in local theaters, she debuted a set of "Mexican dances"
that her massive audiences immediately acclaimed. The performance
of these "Mexican dances" signaled both the incorporation of regional
Mexican dances into an international repertoire and the "elevation" of
such dances to the place of ballet, the predominant international dance
form at the turn of the century. Specifically, Anna Pavlova incorporated
into her repertoire the traditional dance *El jarabe tapatío* (known in the
United States as the Mexican hat dance) and offered it back to Mexicans
with a twist: *bailado en puntas*, danced *en pointe* as part of her piece
Fantasía mexicana.[3] Though performed en pointe and balleticized, El
jarabe tapatío corporeally evoked Mexico, highlighting the appeal of its
traditional and popular dances to a national and international audience
(see fig. I.1).

Pavlova's acclaimed performances of Mexican dances in the debut of
Fantasía mexicana at the Teatro Arbeu on March 18, 1919, inserted Mexican regional dance into the transnational sphere of modernist dance.[4]

1

What comedians, clowns, and local dancers had performed for over a century suddenly became the quintessential representation of Mexican people. Jaime Martínez del Río created this popular divertissement, with Eva Pérez Caro as the choreographer of the Mexican dances, Adolfo Best Maugard as the set designer, and Manuel Castro Padilla as the music director.[5] The plot was simple: a group of women selling flowers falls in love with a group of *charros*. In the festive finale, Anna Pavlova dressed as a *china poblana*[6] danced El jarabe tapatío en pointe with either Mieczyslaw Pianowski, the ballet master, or Alexandre Volinine, the leading male dancer, dressed as a *charro* (a traditional horseman in Mexico, whose attire consisted of an embroidered or decorated short jacket and pants, a bright tie, and a wide-brimmed, decorated hat).[7] El jarabe tapatío is, after all, a courtship dance between men and women. This bucolic Mexican scene was accentuated by Best Maugard's costumes and scenography: a black backdrop with a colorful floral clay jug (or *jícara*) from Uruapan, Michoacán, a clear reference to Indigenous arts and crafts.

The premier of *Fantasía mexicana* was such an immediate success that Pavlova and her company continued to perform it each time they danced

Figure I.1. "Anna Pavlowa," *El Universal Ilustrado*, April 4, 1919. Courtesy of the Biblioteca Miguel Lerdo de Tejada de la Secretaría de Hacienda y Crédito Público.

during their stay in Mexico. El jarabe tapatío ceased to be exclusively a dance from rural Mexico and became a symbol of modernity, refined dance technique, and cosmopolitanism. In his description of the popular debut in *El Universal Ilustrado*, Luis A. Rodríguez captures Pavlova's transformative performance:

> Consuela ver que nuestros bailes nacionales, que hasta ahora sólo se cultivaban en teatros de barriada, mañana en la peregrinación artística de Anna Pavlowa [*sic*], serán exportados, y que públicos extranjeros al aplaudirlos conocerán que México, el país de maravillosa vitalidad, tiene su arte propio. . . . Con el milagroso don de espiritualizar todos los bailes, Anna Pavlowa [*sic*] ha descifrado el secreto de nuestra alma ancestral, ha comprendido nuestra emotividad, y ha desprendido los detalles más vivos de nuestro clásico baile nacional.

> (It is consoling to see that our national dances, which until now were only cultivated in neighborhood theaters, will tomorrow be exported through the artistic pilgrimage of Anna Pavlova, and that foreign audiences, upon applauding them, will realize that Mexico, the country of marvelous vitality, has an art of its own. . . . With the miraculous gift of spiritualizing all dances, Anna Pavlova has deciphered the secret of our ancestral soul, has understood our profound emotions, and has extracted the most vital details from our classical national dance.)[8]

Rodríguez captures the radical transformation of Mexican vernacular dance into a balleticized dance as executed by Anna Pavlova. Whereas previously Mexican regional and traditional dances had been disdained as expressions of "teatros de barriada," they now represented the vitality of Mexico's national art. Even as she dazzled Mexican elite and international audiences with her modernist aesthetics, Pavlova interpellated the masses through her bodily movements, corporeally interacting with them.[9] This iteration of the popular dance was easy to export once "refined" (or "spiritualized," to use Rodríguez's term) through Pavlova's impeccable dance technique. Mexican dance offered the "secret to our ancestral soul," serving as a platform to express Mexico's profound emotions. As the perfect combination of tradition and modernity, Pavlova's balleticized rendition of El jarabe tapatío took Mexico's art to an international stage.

It is not surprising, then, that the inauguration of Mexico's first National Stadium in 1924 featured one thousand dancers performing El jarabe tapatío. Modeled after the stadium in Athens built for the 1896

Olympics, the National Stadium was inaugurated on May 5, 1924.[10] One of the most ambitious structural projects of José Vasconcelos, the minister of public education and a key intellectual of the postrevolutionary period in Mexico, the *teatro y estadio* (theater and stadium) served as a massive stage for public ceremonies, cultural events, and sports tournaments, with a capacity of sixty thousand spectators (not including the thousands of performers who could fit on the field). As the commemorative plaque read, the teatro y estadio "se dedica a la gimnasia y al arte para el bien y la cultura del pueblo mexicano" (is dedicated to gymnastics and art for the good and the culture of the Mexican people).[11] Vasconcelos orchestrated a spectacular program for the stadium's inauguration: 12,000 schoolgirls sang the Mexican national anthem and Mexican and Spanish songs such as "La Pajarera," "La Norteña," and "La Chaparrita"; 2,500 students executed gymnastic exercises; 1,000 schoolgirls performed El jarabe tapatío dressed as chinas poblanas; hundreds of athletes paraded with their physical strength on display; teams competed against each other with a giant balloon; and military cadets formed human pyramids while the cavalry executed various formations with precision.[12] As figure I.2 shows, Vasconcelos's program deployed the masses to stage a monumental choreography of modern Mexico. In this way, the National Stadium materialized one of the major ideals of the postrevolutionary presidency of Álvaro Obregón: the symbolic and metaphorical unification of Mexican citizens, whose that bodies were perfectly aligned, whether they were sitting down, marching, or dancing.

The classical but modern architecture decorated with murals by Diego Rivera was the ideal aesthetic and political stage for the new national body. In his inaugural speech delivered at the opening ceremony and later published by the popular newspaper *El Universal* for those who were not present at the stadium, Vasconcelos highlighted its significance: "En el estadio balbuce una raza que anhela originalidad, expresada en la más alta belleza. Canta coros, ejercita deportes, y así se adiestra buscando la verdad" (In the stadium a race mumbles longing for originality, expressed in the highest form of beauty. It chants and plays sports and in so doing becomes more adept in the search for truth).[13] Rehearsing some of his key ideas regarding the emergence of a cosmic race (discussed in the next section), Vasconcelos emphasized the importance of cultivating physical strength and performance arts as a way to experience beauty.[14] He placed particular emphasis on the role of dance at the stadium: "Se verán danzas colectivas, derroches de vida y amor, bailables patrióticos . . . ritos simbólicos, suntuosos, acompañados de músicas

Figure I.2. "Con un grandioso festival se inauguró ayer el Estadio Nacional," *El Universal*, May 6, 1924. Courtesy of the Biblioteca Miguel Lerdo de Tejada de la Secretaría de Hacienda y Crédito Público.

cósmicas" (Collective dances will be seen, tremendous displays of life and love, patriotic dances . . . symbolic, sumptuous rites, accompanied by cosmic music).[15] By 1924, El jarabe tapatío had already come to play a central role in demonstrations of Mexican nationalism. Vasconcelos imbued this embodied expression with an aesthetic revolutionary ideal, characteristic of his cultural and educational agenda. After all, the one thousand performers were schoolgirls educated by the institutions he had so vehemently supported. In doing so, he helped elevate Mexican regional and traditional dance to a national stage and to the complex political arena of Mexican nationalism.

Mexican regional and traditional dance—known today as folklórico dance—and its attendant aesthetic practices have been central to the creation of Mexicanness (which names the complex interplay between nation and identity), offering a window into the conflicts, frictions, and failures of this contested formulation. Folklórico dance is also one of the primary modes of expressive culture in Mexico and across the Mexican diaspora. And yet this vital practice remains surprisingly underexplored in analyses of Mexican cultural production. In the following pages, I examine written, photographic, cinematographic, and choreographic renderings of a festive Mexico, highlighting the role dance and movement have played in citizen formation and national belonging from the late Porfirian regime to the immediate postrevolutionary era (1910–1940). I contend that public cultural performances of dance, such as El jarabe tapatío executed by Anna Pavlova and by the thousand schoolgirls at the National Stadium, reveal the contradictory interaction between representations of national identity, representations of Mexicanness, and the dance's embodiment—that is, its symbolic, material, and physical production. By focusing on the images and the language used to represent Mexico during the festivities of the centenary in 1910 and 1921, in massive choreographies in stadiums in the 1930s, and in films of the Golden Age in the 1930s and 1940s, I chart the contradictory, contingent, and yet concrete ways that bodies in movement signify within specific contexts of Mexican nationalism.

Festive cultural performances create a sense of corporeal expression by influencing the ideas, aesthetic practices, and institutions that have shaped cultural and political formations of a Mexican national identity at home and abroad. With the term *festive*, I refer to what David Guss has called "festive forms," or public expressive practices that have the potential to produce new meanings and social imaginaries while responding to specific local realities and historical junctures.[16] The embodied cultural performances and dances I examine show how state-sponsored cultural projects attempted to instruct and model the nation, even as they were exceeded and contested through the bodily actions of Mexican citizens. I cast Mexicanness, or lo mexicano, as a performance in an effort to posit the body and embodied cultural performances as critical sites for subject formation, knowledge production, and collective action.[17] My emphasis on the embodied practices, dance, and movement of a diverse population helps unpack the ways race, gender, and sexuality unsettle the homogeneity attributed to displays of national identity. Foregrounding embodied performances of lo mexicano reveals the contradictory ways Mexican nationalism has been experienced. By attending to festive cultural performances and their concomitant performativity of power, we can understand the roles of embodiment, movement, and choreography in configuring the political and cultural ideologies of modern Mexico.

As will become evident in the pages that follow, bodies in motion at once activate and challenge scenarios of Mexican nationalism and its representations. The one thousand girls dancing El jarabe tapatío during the inauguration of the National Stadium mobilized gendered imaginaries of normative Mexican femininity, with their china poblana outfits and their markedly feminine comportment, bodily movements, and dance steps. Such choreographed embodied experiences codified Mexican mestizo aesthetics and solidified a sense of modernity and national belonging. In this book, I call attention to the ways movement and the awareness of that movement—kinesthesia—function as archival practices that reveal power dynamics and forms of sense making that have often been neglected in the official archive and in the dominant history of Mexican nationalism. The young girls dressed as chinas poblanas performed more than a traditional dance. Their movement and choreography simultaneously summoned Pavlova's balleticized rendition of the dance, performed the fusion of tradition and modernity, and enacted an alternative sociality in which young girls were at the forefront, experiencing their own sense of agency and belonging.

I use a methodological approach that centers on the embodied performances of lo mexicano and the cultural and corporeal configurations they summon, which are always contingent and contextual. This book treats performance as an aesthetic, embodied, and political practice and as a methodology to account for the conflicting social systems at play in Mexico. Indeed, it is at the center of the aesthetic, the political, and the personal that I position the body, which opens possibilities beyond textual and visual analysis. In the festive performances discussed in this book, Mexican citizens rehearsed contested ideas of the nation since the Porfirian regime but particularly during the postrevolutionary period. Festive instances are an opportunity not only to symbolically negotiate tensions between the quotidian and the possibility of imagining ourselves otherwise but also to feel and experience the world differently, to embody an "elsewhere" within our own reality, and to expand and reeducate our senses.[18] How does a performing body conjure other imaginaries and embody a different sensorial reality through festive dances such as El jarabe tapatío? What is at stake in the (re)visualization of normative paradigms of lo mexicano through cultural performances of the nation? How can our understanding of festive forms help us comprehend the roles played by kinesthetic memory, intelligence, and empathy in configuring symbolic and national normative realms?

I draw from extensive archival sources, including periodicals, historical photographs, and footage from the 1910s to the 1940s, as well as classic films from the Golden Age of Mexican cinema (particularly during the

1930s and 1940s), to study both discursive and visual modes of representing a dancing Mexico. The language and images used to represent Mexico, I argue, are performatively undone by the actual embodiment of the people whom they aim to represent. Rather than resorting to the common approach of highlighting Mexicanness as the embodiment of a monumental but static mestizo masculinity, I construct a genealogy of key moments in which the public performance of bodies reveals a nuanced articulation of female, Indigenous, Black, and at times even queer renditions of the nation. These moments show how meaning in motion is created, how it can be produced and sensed in the archive, and how it can be accounted for in our intellectual endeavors. The festive performances I explore ultimately draw attention to the multiple ways Mexican citizens experienced and embodied the nation before and during the postrevolutionary period, from the 1910s through the 1940s.

On the Cultural Politics of lo mexicano and the Mestizo State

The active promotion and celebration of a performative nationalistic ritualized behavior is perhaps best exemplified by the Porfirian regime between 1876 and 1911. The *Porfiriato*, as this period is known, consolidated what has since become the primary means of performing lo mexicano and Mexican history. It inaugurated the co-optation by elites and intellectuals of certain aspects of Indigenous material culture and the establishment of an indigenist narrative to tell its past. Nationalist claims to the legacy of the Aztecs inaugurated a "neoindigenist style" that became central to the configuration of (creole) nationalism during the Porfiriato. According to Barbara A. Tenenbaum, the erection of monuments such as the statue of the last Aztec emperor, Cuauhtémoc, and other structures, along with their attendant discourses, led historians not only to appeal to the symbolism of the Aztecs to justify Porfirio Díaz's rulership but also to mobilize the official "veneration of the 'Aztecs'" as a means of asserting the power of Mexico City.[19] Claims to Aztec imperial legacy helped to promote the centralization of the state. However, the Porfirian elite also turned to France for inspiration and legitimation. Reforma Avenue, for instance, was aimed at impressing foreign capital by imitating Baron Georges-Eugène Haussmann's restructuring of the Champs Élysées, which contrasted with the Alameda or the Zócalo, a space for the people. Díaz's regime was therefore characterized by two fronts: the Francophile progressives and the nationalist mythologizers.[20]

Indeed, Reforma Avenue became the epitome of the cosmopolitan, modern city, while showcasing the monumental Indigenous history of Mexico's past. The Aztec Palace in 1889 at the Paris Universal Exposition and later the centennial celebrations of Mexican Independence in 1910 were certainly intended to display Mexico's rich Indigenous cultural heritage as a means of staking a claim to a cosmopolitan modernity while grappling with the increasingly visible presence of displaced Indigenous people, as I discuss in chapter 1.

Díaz's regime attempted to unify the ethnoracial diversity of Mexico. The result was the emergence of a racialized and modern mestizo state.[21] This process was characterized by a double bind: although Mexico's Indigenous peoples and cultures became the bearers of cultural authenticity and uniqueness, they needed to be modernized and racialized as mestizo; that is, the state had to integrate their difference into the idea of a homogenized but mestizo nation. This conflict brought to the fore the so-called "problema del indio" (the Indian Problem) that became the racial trademark of Mexican nationalism, a framing that portrayed Indigenous peoples as backward and antimodern. The assimilation of Mexican Indigenous populations became an imperative of the state, and cultural and political projects led to a conflation between racial identity and modernity.[22] The Mexican Revolution continued the construction of a mestizo nationalistic narrative, consolidating it as the metadiscourse that articulated the nation. This process systematically erased and collapsed the vast diversity of Indigenous groups. Even though it rhetorically aimed to recognize the contributions of the diverse ethnic and popular sectors of the population, the postrevolutionary government resorted to *mestizaje* as a national fiction, thereby erasing and excluding other ethnoracial configurations, including the historical presence of Afro-descendants and Asians, to mention two prominent examples.[23]

Postrevolutionary Mexico then launched a cultural campaign to produce, circulate, and unify the nation. Two important works consolidated lo mexicano as mestizo: *Forjando patria* by Manuel Gamio in 1916 and the Constitution, promulgated in 1917. Ignacio Sánchez Prado argues that, unlike the thinkers who proposed colonial Mexico—both "criollo" and Catholic—as the ideal nation, Gamio's seminal study articulated the integration of the Indigenous populations into the project of mestizaje and attended to the "secularizing spirit" of the Constitution of 1917 by "synthesizing" the values and demands of a movement that had until then lacked a "clear intellectual guidance."[24] The emergence of mestizaje was, in effect, the result of a cultural and political enterprise. In *Forjando patria*, Gamio gestured toward the incorporation of Indigenous populations as a strategy for dealing with numerous multifaceted Indigenous groups. He maintained that a national culture could only be derived from an "intermediate" or mestizo culture, which would homogenize Indigenous populations into one. The emergence of a national culture, however, presumed the seamless integration of complex Indigenous cultures with European values. Despite insisting on the "Indianization" of Mexican society, Gamio clearly believed that the "Prehispanic" cultures needed to be acculturated in order to partake in the future of mestizaje as the metaphor, discourse, and mechanism that was to define the Mexican nation.[25]

José Vasconcelos was the other great ideologue of the philosophy of mestizaje. In 1925, he published *La raza cósmica* (*The Cosmic Race*), in which he advanced a theory of Pan-Americanism that celebrated the fusion of multiple races. Vasconcelos embraced an "assimilationist" stance in regard to the emergence of a "cosmic race," which would be the product of the synthesis of diverse racial configurations and would integrate all peoples into a true universal vision.[26] Whereas Gamio proposed to think of mestizaje as the future of Mexico, Vasconcelos took it a step further: he suggested that mestizaje was the future of not just Latin America but the entire human race. His notion of mestizaje encompassed a merging of all races that would engender the "cosmic race," or the "race of bronze." At the national level, the racial ideology of mestizaje privileged the mestizo as the principal marker of Mexican nationalism, subsuming indigeneity once again into a colonial racial paradigm.

Members of the intellectual, cultural, and political elites constantly marked Indigenous people as noncontemporaneous, "pre-Hispanic," and therefore outside a shared spatiotemporal historical conjunction. The Indigenous groups' ambivalent role revealed the contradictory consequences of the process of colonization and modernization: on the one hand, they purportedly represented the "essence" of lo mexicano; on the other, they needed to be assimilated and modernized to be part of the nation. This was the same double bind they had faced during the Porfiriato. Alan Knight argues that postrevolutionary leaders understood the armed Indigenous mobilizations during the Mexican Revolution as a commitment to the state and to the process of nation-building. Such Indigenous agency, however, needed to be coordinated and directed by the state, which operated as a "social arbiter" among the various ethnic groups that formed the Mexican nation.[27] Once the armed conflict stopped, the "social arbitration" was carried out by the political and intellectual elites.

uses it to foreground the kinesthetic dimension of the cultural history of Mexico. The following chapters investigate the tensions and contradictions as well as the complicities and affinities of the embodied iterations of Mexican mestizo nationalism, moving from the realm of the visual and the discursive to that of the kinesthetic. Although the mestizo state operates as the primary frame of reference for the enactments of lo mexicano, I ultimately show that its embodiment allows for the possibility of imagining and even inhabiting it otherwise.

In these pages, I trace the relationship between embodied performances and knowledge production, between public performances of dance and discourses around national identity in Mexico. By analyzing staged instances of lo mexicano as festive practices that create contested, polyphonic fields of action, this approach centers on embodied iterations of Mexican cultural productions. In so doing, it contributes to ongoing discussions of lo mexicano as a trope that has been privileged in the analysis of Mexican nationalism, particularly as these discussions engage questions about discursive and visual modes of representation, such as muralism and the novel of the Mexican Revolution. In focusing on embodied expressions of Mexican nationalism, I examine how such practices become intimately intertwined with the consolidation of mestizaje as an intellectual and political project.

Indeed, lo mexicano as a trope has been rigorously examined in Mexican historiography.[40] The Mexican Revolution triggered the creation of a symbolic order that fostered the configuration of lo mexicano. The so-called organic intellectuals of the Revolution made it possible for the ideology of mestizaje to become public policy, as they worked for the state. José Vasconcelos played a prominent role in this undertaking, especially through the consolidation of public education in Mexico. Nevertheless, as Pedro Ángel Palou astutely contends, mestizaje ultimately became a state-sponsored, legitimatizing discourse that established cultural, political, and economic practices exemplified by the "mestizo," a biopolitical construct that aimed at modernizing the figure of the Indian, deterritorializing it from its nonurban and hence nonmodern state.[41] Through the discourse of mestizaje, then, the state established an ideology not only to reproduce and legitimate itself but also to dominate.

This process led to the production of a "mestizo habitus," an embodied occurrence that reproduces the system of which it is a product.[42] As Gareth Williams observes, the Revolution changed the way people perceived reality; it transformed artistic practices, translating them from the realm of the aesthetic to that of the social.[43] By exploring the implications and repercussions of the embodiment of a mestizo nation, I, too, think about social praxis in order to explore the shift of cultural practices from aesthetics to the social and hence to the body. My study foregrounds the complex and messy intersections among the corporeal, the sociopolitical, and the aesthetic. It asks: How did the aesthetics of Mexican nationalism become choreographed into an embodied experience of the nation?

By focusing on the aesthetic experience of the people who not only consume but also create forms of artistic expression, we can expand the realm of the aesthetic and dialogically engage with the limits and possibilities of art. As expressive gestures of a collectivity, popular aesthetic manifestations like the regional dances in this study defy hegemonic and stereotypical representations of the popular that invisibilize and silence the knowledge and symbolic production of a community. My understanding of the aesthetic is indebted to B. Christine Arce's reformulation of Jacques Rancière's notions of the "distribution of the sensible" and the "emancipated spectator" for the Mexican context. In *México's Nobodies: The Cultural Legacy of the Soldadera and Afro-Mexican Women*, Arce claims that "the symbolic producer and community are mutually constituted, that knowledge is produced through the creation and consumption of the aesthetic, and that this invokes a generative space of multiple possibilities."[44] Arce's reformulation of the aesthetic invites us to consider the instances in which the artist and participants may be one and the same in order to contemplate the complexities of the consumption and production of art by individuals who are at once spectators and performers, members of the same community.[45] The aesthetic experience and the concomitant consciousness derived from the creation of collective artistic expressions can lead to a more dynamic engagement with the sensible. Moreover, because art allows individuals and communities to feel, imagine, and inhabit alternative spaces, reducing popular expressions and experiences to fetishes, common tropes, and stereotypes "impoverishes" and even "violates" the legacy of otherwise ignored, silenced, and invisibilized communities.[46] Arce's generative approach to the aesthetic asks that we attend to the contradictions, denials, and refusals it produces as well as to the affinities, connections, and knowledge circulation it invites and creates. In this sense, the affective reception of spectators can contest and disrupt knowledge creation, circulation, and consumption. In so doing, it can participate in the relational production of truth.

An active engagement with the aesthetic, then, requires returning to the body and its experience. My use of this definition of the aesthetic relies on understanding bodies relationally. I investigate how some bodies make other bodies feel as part of an aesthetic sociality that the various iterations of lo mexicano in the following chapters bring forth, rehearse, and perform. Tobin Siebers posits that "aesthetics tracks the sensations that some bodies feel in the presence of other bodies."[47] Such an approach requires that we reposition the body as the primary means of grappling with the aesthetic.[48] Corporality and bodily experience shape and are simultaneously shaped by the aesthetic. Therefore, the aesthetic is a site in which "social possibilities are both rehearsed and performed."[49] Understanding aesthetics as rooted in bodily experience brings into focus the embodied intimacies, affinities, and affiliations that instances of lo mexicano reveal, however negatively, thereby revaluing what would otherwise be considered too minor, complicit, or unimportant.

Reframing aesthetics in terms of an embodied relationality allows me to reconsider the complex and contradictory nature of the emergence of a nationalistic mestizo aesthetics. Studies of Mexican nationalism often draw attention to the relationship between the consolidation of a mestizo aesthetics and the role of education in disseminating and instilling it. Ricardo Pérez Montfort, for instance, examines the emergence of state-sponsored nationalistic expressions as invented, mythified, and imaginary creations of the urban artistic and intellectual elites, used to unify and legitimize the government. As Pérez Montfort notes, despite the presence of an aestheticized and discursive nationalism present in the cultural and political activities of the Porfirian regime, a "popular" tone became "medullar" for the political discourse of the postrevolutionary government, thereby "inventing" a series of stereotypical representations of lo mexicano.[50] El pueblo, which vaguely referred to the peasants and marginal groups that had fought during the Revolution, became less a material reference than a mythical abstraction.[51] This process of abstraction and mythification also responded to the consolidation of the mass media and to the establishment of a public educational apparatus in Mexico, thanks to the work of the so-called "cultural caudillo" José Vasconcelos, as explored in the later chapters of this book.

Postrevolutionary Mexico intensified the expansion of the realm of the national and the inclusion of the popular sectors. In effect, the emergence of Mexico as a modern nation mobilized a series of discursive tactics that emphasized the "performance" of the nation as a whole. However, postrevolutionary Mexico sought to incorporate its contemporary citizens into an idealized version not of the past but of the future. It had to create its own national public. In his detailed analysis of the emergence of a nationalistic aesthetics and cultural politics in postrevolutionary Mexico, Rick López also draws attention to the ways their consolidation was part of a complex web of transnational intellectual, economic, and artistic discourses that significantly transformed the sociopolitical, economic, and cultural spheres in rural and urban communities across Mexico.[52] For López, the political and intellectual elite of postrevolutionary Mexico, unlike their predecessors, posited "the living indigenous heritage as a vital component, even the foundation, of Mexico's authentic national identity."[53] The network that allowed for the production and circulation of cultural projects and products changed with the transformation of the national cultural politics and their concomitant aesthetics. This phenomenon had a tremendous impact at the local level. The new cultural, economic, and political developments required the assimilation, integration, and transformation of Indigenous peoples and their culture.

Here lies the importance of reconsidering the aesthetic project of Mexican nationalism as an experience intimately and relationally connected to the body. Positing aesthetics as intertwined with bodily experience demands that we become attuned to the ways it enables the rehearsal and performance of social possibilities. In this process, its political valence relies on the reformulation of the coconstitutive nature of aesthetics as that through which lo mexicano is imagined, mythified, and abstracted (i.e., represented) and also embodied (i.e., rehearsed, performed, enacted, and resignified). In these pages, I chart the messy networks of the repetitive iterations of Mexican nationalism. This nationalism's slippery nature reveals that such collective expressions cannot be reduced to hegemonic and stereotypical renditions of lo mexicano.[54] On the contrary, its continuous performance uncovers the trajectories of its resignification, local instantiations, and differentiated knowledge circulation. The following chapters investigate how the consolidation of a national aesthetics and its attendant embodied cultural performances transformed communities and individuals and their respective understandings of power dynamics.

State Rituals, Power, and Festive Performances

Embodied cultural performances, such as rituals, dance, celebrations, and other manifestations, have dominated the public scene since pre-Columbian times in Mexico. Mesoamerican rituals, especially among the Nahua communities, structured daily Indigenous lives. Nahuas, for instance, conceptualized their world as being in constant movement, which affected their understandings of religion, ethics, politics, and aesthetics as well as their everyday practices.[55] Indigenous communities engaged in ritualistic celebrations in order to form and organize spatial and temporal references and mark key moments in their collective lives and sacred cosmologies. The arrival of the Spanish and eventual conquest of the Triple Alliance, or the so-called Aztec Empire (Tenochtitlan, Texcoco, and Tlacopan), affected the Mesoamerican populations' relationship to their environments, their gods, and themselves. This traumatic episode drastically changed how they perceived and understood time, space, and embodied expressive culture.[56] In fact, there was a radical difference between native and European ritual manifestations: Indigenous ritualistic performances were "both a representation *of* and a presentation *to* the gods." Diana Taylor and Sarah J. Townsend remind us of the importance that cultural performances held in Mexico and in other parts of Latin America, where they operated as an epistemological means for both groups to make sense of each other and as a critical mechanism to maintain and contest social authority.[57] They were, however, fraught, functioning as slippery sites of contact that often led both groups to ascribe to each other mistaken values and wrong identifications.[58]

Although the Spaniards held power, Indigenous people actively participated in ceremonies and rituals. Their bodily movements continuously offered the possibility of resignifying such practices and creating alternative meanings. With the arrival of other groups, particularly enslaved Africans and Asians, embodied cultural performances also created contingent and precarious spaces that contributed to the formation of extraordinarily diverse communities in colonial Mexico. Festive cultural performances in particular "create[d] a unique opportunity to both reinforce and challenge the conception and enactment of power" while operating as alternative forms of knowledge production and circulation.[59] At the same time, the Spanish sought to legitimate their power through language and ceremony.[60] Accordingly, as Eric Van Young points out, the transfer of "sacrality from systems of religious ideas and forms of worship to the cult of the nation-state marks the passage of Mexico from colony to nation." Van Young, for his part, notes that the "state regulation of public life" in Mexico after its independence also meant the regulation of public ritual and ceremonies, as both aimed to assert the legitimacy of state power and reinforce the "affective loyalty to a nation," ideally fostering a sense of belonging and improved material conditions.[61] Public performances functioned as sites of cultural translations and transculturation that enabled communities to negotiate and contest colonial and state power. As meaning-making systems, these cultural performances also reconfigured the "cultural memories and political identities" of differing ethnoracial communities, and, in so doing, they served "as a means of physically and symbolically incorporating audiences into the national framework."[62]

Embodied cultural expressions allow people to transmit knowledge, create communities, and question power. These corporeal forms of "local knowledges" shape intimate understandings of the sociocultural and politico-economic processes at play in the configuration of a given community and nation.[63] At stake, then, is the relation between hegemonic structures of community making through embodied performances and their local workings. One of the key features of the consolidation of the Mexican nation-state is its performative character, for state rituals have long marked its formation. A ritualistic organization of social structures facilitated the transmission and policing of symbolic and material culture and knowledge. In effect, a ritualistic mode of presenting and representing lo mexicano characterized its circulation as symbolic and material culture. Public rituals have been intimately intertwined with the formation of political communities within a national space. As the staging of a massive historical parade in 1910 and the massive celebration of a *Noche Mexicana* (Mexican Night) in 1921 illustrate in the following chapters, public rituals have served as sites in which to negotiate and dispute the political relations between the state and local actors and communities. Claudio Lomnitz points out that rituals made it possible to claim and engage with the state while simultaneously creating a hegemonic order.[64] Rituals contributed to the configuration of a Mexican polity, allowing collective expressions to take place within legible and legitimate cultural and political spheres. Their importance derives from the construction of an arena that positions "a collectivity vis-à-vis the state" and the creation of a discursive space in which "subjectivities [are formed] by the state" and "state institutions are locally appropriated."[65] Embodied cultural performances functioned as rehearsals of often-contradictory renderings of the nation, highlighting the significance of the hegemonic representational framework of lo mexicano with respect to its local and eventually national iterations.

Mexican regional and traditional dance, which became folklórico dance, underscored the contradictions of establishing a national imaginary based on the insistence on a homogenized and sanitized notion of cultural difference. Throughout the following chapters, I show how embodied cultural performances and Mexican dance point toward cultural activities that insist on difference as a marker of national unity—from historical parades and festive celebrations to massive ballets and moving images of Mexican popular dances.[66] Folklórico dance, I argue, has operated as a ritualistic cultural arena in which to negotiate the tensions between the production of cultural difference and its local and national iterations and appropriations. I use the term *folklórico* in Spanish to allude to its specificity as an established dance practice and movement vocabulary in Mexico and in the global Mexican diaspora.[67] I contend that folklórico dance is not just another modality of representation. Rather, it systematizes the kinetic and the eventual kinesthetic formation of Mexican national subjects—that is, the formation of national subjects through movement and through their awareness of movement, or kinesthesia. As such, folklórico dance is a contested, slippery site for controlling and normalizing national bodies, for summoning individuals to corporeally recognize themselves as Mexican. Through state rituals aimed at imposing a hegemonic frame of reference (for instance, through the performance of El jarabe tapatío at official events), local iterations facilitated the incorporation of local knowledges, thereby revealing the power of local agency vis-à-vis the state. Each rendition of El jarabe tapatío may have been citing an idea of the nation, yet there were always competing interests at play; performing the so-called national dance in a city such as Guadalajara was not the same as performing it in a rural community in the north or south of the republic. How did Mexican dance, such as El jarabe tapatío, interpellate audiences and Mexican citizens? What was at stake in corporeally citing the nation as an Indigenous woman or a rural campesino as opposed to a bourgeois woman or a Hacienda man? In these pages, I explore how embodied performances of the nation negotiated the tensions and excesses between the production of cultural difference and its ambivalent and contradictory stagings, focusing on moving bodies in public spaces. I argue that the performance of Mexican regional and traditional dances allows us to expand our understanding of the aesthetic and material practices of lo mexicano—its conception and representation—as well as its embodiment.

Focusing on cultural performances also draws attention to the unstable meanings and functions of embodied practices of nationalism. The cultural anthropologist David Guss emphasizes the role that festive forms play in the construction of new national imaginings but warns us not to take them to represent "the uniform expression of a collective consciousness." By approaching these festive practices as "cultural performances," however, we can ask how they enact a specific sociopolitical reality.[68] Each individual experiences these events differently, since multiple factors influence the enactment and reception of each performative rendition of the nation. But these performances also capture the changing nature of the nation's sociopolitical reality, as they must be continuously cited and renewed. Cultural performances are, after all, "sites of social action where identities and relations are continually being reconfigured." Analyzing festive behaviors as cultural performances, as Guss proposes, helps us juxtapose notions of authenticity and tradition vis-à-vis "the socially constructed and contingent nature of festive practice."[69] His work makes it possible to ask how aesthetic practices, both "modern" and "traditional," are coconstitutive and respond to various social realities. For instance, Nellie and Gloria Campobello's interpretation of El jarabe tapatío, as I show in chapter 3, challenged conventional understandings of gender and sexuality, thereby allowing them to negotiate the role of women within the masculinist and heteronormative frame of the nation (especially because Nellie performed it dressed as a charro). In this study, I thus insist on the performative element of these embodied experiences to underscore the ambivalence and contingency of the emergence and dissemination of Mexican dance.

In this book I also engage Diana Taylor's theorization of performance. Taylor proposes performance not only as praxis or as an object of study but also as an epistemology, a way of understanding and being in the world. Her emphasis centers on the notion of knowledge: its production, transmission, reception, and circulation. For Taylor, performances "function as vital acts of transfer, transmitting social knowledge, memory, and a sense of identity."[70] Following Richard Schechner, Taylor claims that any event can be studied as a performance.[71] She prompts us to think about the ways "communal identity and memory," as the building blocks of individuals and communities, come to constitute "valid forms of knowledge." Thinking of performance not only as a methodology but also as an epistemology allows me to account for the plurality and multidimensionality of Mexican cultural production, particularly as it relates to regional and traditional dance.

I therefore build upon Taylor's and Guss's theorization of performance to engage these festive expressions as contested, contingent, and ambivalent sites that allow for a thorough interrogation not only of discursive and visual modes of representation but also of embodied knowledges and practices.[72] In repositioning the body at the center of the workings of lo mexicano, I show how the dancing body operates as a medium for/of contesting discourses of the nation. Bodily acts underscore the tensions with which cultural performances inscribe, negotiate, and reformulate Mexican nationalism. By moving the body from a fixed frame of reference onto slippery territory, cultural performances produce and simultaneously mobilize a radical possibility for the resignification of corporeal expressions. In focusing on embodied practices and the knowledge associated with these festive cultural performances, I grapple with the tensions enacted by racially and sexually marked bodies in contemporary Mexico.

As a historical and historicizing entity, the dancing body can gesture toward trajectories of the nation that have been negated, erased, and excluded in contemporary Mexican cultural production at home and abroad. I am interested in how moving bodies are required to constantly signify different social formations, such as gender, class, sexuality, and race, vis-à-vis lo mexicano. At the same time, the act of embodying these social formations opens the possibility of exceeding them or resignifying them. I see the body in movement as crucial for reflecting upon the tensions and contradictions of Mexican nationalism, from the continuous exclusion of Indigenous populations to the celebrations of Indigenous performances as symbols of the nation like the Yaqui Indians, from the disavowal of Blackness to the embrace of *jarocho* (a person of "mixed blood" from Veracruz) culture. The body, as I read it, operates as an archive but also as a means for archiving. The dance scholar Jane C. Desmond asserts that the movement prompted by the "historical materiality of the body" functions as a "historically particular register of meaning."[73] By focusing on how moving bodies rewrite the idea of the nation, I want to draw attention, on the one hand, to the frames of reference of different social formations of lo mexicano and, on the other, to the excess produced by the act of framing itself. Embodiments of Mexican nationalism depend on ethnoracial categories and their concomitant enactments of gender, sexuality, and class. Operating within the symbolic and material scaffolding of colonialism and modernity,[74] the dancing bodies I study, while performing an ideal of lo mexicano, may corporeally generate an excess that showcases the constructiveness of what these moving bodies are supposed to represent. Even though what I read as excess in the choreographed, embodied experience of lo mexicano may not necessarily lead to its resignification, it opens the possibility of imagining it otherwise.

Choreographing Mexico:
Kinesthetic Encounters and Dancing Histories

The Mexican regional and traditional dance that would come to be known as folklórico became a significant embodied means of grappling with Mexico's past, its ethnoracial diversity, and its heteronormative imperatives; of negotiating the incorporation of "living" Indigenous cultures of the present; and of attending to the gender and sexual performances of Mexican nationalism. By expanding our understanding of the aesthetic and material practices of lo mexicano—its conception, representation, and embodiment—Mexican dance operates as a site where an aesthetic sociality of the nation is enacted, registering other ways of feeling, being, and belonging. In *Dancing across Borders: Danzas y Bailes Mexicanos*, Olga Nájera-Ramírez, Norma Cantú, and Brenda Romero contend that dance practice and the narratives it generated in the Americas were important sites for the documentation and transmission of history and for the negotiation of social tensions during the colonial and postindependence periods, tracing the political, historical, and cultural developments of communities.[75] Mexican dance therefore opens up the possibility for a fruitful engagement with hegemonic constructions of lo mexicano and with the ways it is strategically produced and consumed.

Mexican regional and traditional dance, then, is a vital means of establishing shared values, experiencing culture, and making sense of reality. The dancing histories I explore in the following chapters—from an Indigenous reinterpretation of the Spanish Reconquista narrative through *La danza de los tastoanes* (chapter 1) and the multiple stages featuring Indigenous and traditional dancers at La Noche Mexicana (chapter 2) to Nellie Campobello's massive revolutionary choreography at the National Stadium (chapter 3) and the filmic renditions of Afro-Indigenous and traditional dances (chapter 4)—illuminate the critical role of moving bodies in the configuration and dissemination of structures of nationalism and the complex ways they shape and are shaped by corporeal practices. The kinesthetic encounters with multiple and often contradictory forms of Mexican nationalism bring to the fore the role that moving bodies play in setting in motion the ideological mechanisms that structure the nation. Dance not only allows individuals and communities to assert their bodies and their presence but also positions kinesthesia as a generative engagement with structures of power.

I understand kinesthesia as the body's awareness of its movement and position.[76] It is an ability to sense, literally, through various sensory organs, but I also take it to mean to *make* sense. Recognizing that we can register meaning from our awareness of movement and position invites us to consider how the body is implicated in meaning-making practices. Kinesthesia as a meaning-making paradigm, then, exemplifies an embodied understanding of the world. However, the ability to make sense out of movement and position necessarily implicates one's relation to the other. For example, Anna Pavlova's balleticized rendition of El jarabe tapatío kinesthetically enticed her massive popular audiences to corporeally recognize themselves as part of a modern yet Mexican sociality. In other words, kinesthesia is a way to relate to the other. The dance scholar Susan Foster theorizes this connection to the other via kinesthesia as a mechanism of empathy, that is, as an embodied operation to engage with the other.[77] What kind of interactions do we have with others through movement? How are we affected by other bodies in motion? To what extent did the one thousand girls performing El jarabe tapatío at the inauguration of the National Stadium kinesthetically summon Pavlova's choreography while inviting spectators to corporeally recognize themselves as modern Mexican citizens? Seeing others move has been proven to initiate a psychomotor reaction; similarly, imagining the other's movement triggers an embodied response. This exchange of ephemeral but material responses allows us to make sense, to draw out conclusions, and, as I contend in my theorization of "kinesthetic identification" in chapter 4, to imagine an alternative embodied mode of relating to the other.

Mobilizing kinesthesia as an analytic invites us to consider the relationship between bodily movement, aesthetics, and nationalism. I think of choreography as the intersection of corporeal motion, the sociopolitical, and the aesthetics.[78] I follow SanSan Kwan's theorization of choreography as "the conscious designing of bodily movement through space and time."[79] This definition calls for a relational understanding of the term, positing bodies as agents that are shaped by and that also shape contingent formulations of power. Furthermore, I draw from Andrew Hewitt's conception of choreography "not just as a way of thinking about social order" but also as "a way of thinking about the *relationship* of aesthetics to politics."[80] Both formulations center the "material of the human body and its relation to other human bodies" as essential to understanding the complex connection between the aesthetic and the political.[81] The performances and rehearsals of dancing histories in Mexico illuminate how corporeal practices are "structurally determined" and yet "improvised,"[82] thereby allowing for their resignification, failure, and experience otherwise even as they cite hegemonic modes of representation.

Throughout this book, I trace the choreographies of a festive Mexico and the cultural and historical valences at play that go beyond the notion of spectacle. I do not offer a historical overview of the development of Mexican dance.[83] Rather, I analyze key moments in the first half of the twentieth century when Mexican dance made it possible to articulate a national and collective culture and the power dynamics that formed it. The following chapters reflect on how the moving body materializes culture and the embodied subjectivities and corporeal histories that result from such a process. I seek to understand the configuration of a Mexican corporeality, which, as Melissa Blanco Borelli notes, "functions as a way to read the body along the social, cultural, and historical processes that shape it."[84] Mexican nationalism may appear time and again as a fixed referent and yet is constantly destabilized and rechoreographed by the dancing bodies that purport to represent it.

Although I center most of my discussion on the postrevolutionary period, it is important to remember that the Porfirian Belle Époque (1880–1910) vigorously cultivated an active dance scene, particularly in urban centers. As the Mexican dance historian Maya Ramos Smith has thoroughly documented, Mexican regional dances were part and parcel of Mexico's dance scene, together with a heterogeneous group of cultural manifestations such as zarzuelas, revues, theatrical dance, cancan, exotic/oriental dance, ballet, and modernist dance. In this sense, the *jarabe* (as an eclectic musical and dance genre) remained very popular with Mexican audiences, as it had been since colonial times.[85] Furthermore, the armed struggle of the Mexican Revolution drastically impacted artistic expression, particularly dance. The Mexican dance historian Alberto Dallal observes that the Revolution triggered the reevaluation of artistic performances, leading show business people to adopt the regional costumes and flamboyant outfits of *Tehuanas* (women from the Isthmus of Tehuantepec, Oaxaca), chinas poblanas, charros, and other popular costumes.[86] The changes caused by the armed conflict prefigured radical transformations in the social sphere, which also affected the cultural realm, including dance and other forms of spectacle and entertainment. The emergence of a nationalist dance, according to the Mexican dance scholar Margarita Tortajada, "cumplió su función política, participó en el proceso de cohesión nacional y México 'bailó' al conectar los cuerpos individuales con el cuerpo colectivo, dramatizando su relación" (fulfilled its political function, participated in the process of national cohesion, and Mexico "danced" connecting individual bodies to the collective body, dramatizing its relation).[87] Mexican citizens were moved by the choreographies of nationalism that offered them a form of identification with this staging of the popular, which was crucial for the creation of a people.[88]

In this book, I extend recent efforts to foreground the role that dance practices have played not only in the configuration of modern Latin American nations and the figuration of national imaginaries but also in the concomitant mobilization of cultural, political, and social engagement.[89] My work builds on this scholarship to explore the complex and contradictory ways Latin American and Mexican dance practices enable bodies to inhabit, embody, and reimagine national public spaces and discourses, while attending to the precariousness, fraught alliances, and shared complicities enacted by dancers on and off the stage. I join these efforts by focusing on movement, dance practices, and public manifestations of expressive culture to show how embodied cultural performances at once reproduce and resist normative renditions of lo mexicano. In so doing, I offer a more nuanced understanding of the way meaning is embodied and reformulated through bodies in motion.

Furthermore, by considering the transnational, transcontinental, and even colonial histories that inform Mexican dance practices, I engage with efforts by the dance scholars Victoria Fortuna and José Luis Reynoso to challenge the supposed "universality" of Western referents and the teleological centrality of European and US dance histories.[90] My work attends to the transnational flows and cultural exchanges that influenced and were influenced by the consolidation of Mexican dance, which until recently has been disdained in English-language scholarship.[91] At the core of my analysis is an attention to how embodied cultural performances and dance function as a meaningful public discourse about the social arrangements and landscapes that inform a shared sense of national belonging and civic life. Here, I draw from the critical work of the dance scholar Judith Hamera, who challenges us to rethink the relationship between bodies, histories, and urban spaces. Hamera asks that we consider dance, and performance more broadly, as a crucial "communication infrastructure" with the capacity to create "new shared aesthetic and social possibilities" and to negotiate identity, memory, and community making in a global city.[92] By considering dance as an archival site, a generative practice, and a form of sense-making, we treat movement as a world-making practice, that is, as an interpretative communal infrastructure.[93] In particular, I am interested in the mechanisms that reveal the cultural work of Mexican dance practices and the kinds of socialities they generate through and beyond any given festive performance, from Pavlova's rendition of El jarabe tapatío in bullrings and theaters and the Campobello sisters' reinterpretation of the dance to its appearance in Mexico's major cinematic hit *Allá en el Rancho Grande/Out on the Big Ranch* in 1936.

These various iterations of festive performances turned popular culture into a national choreography that had to be learned and performed. The Mexican people were asked to execute a social choreography that often intersected with their lived experiences, engaging various aspects of their existence, even if temporarily and fragmentarily. As Horacio Legrás observes, "This operation did not simply trade on objects, forms of affect, or patterns of behavior. It was also and fundamentally a transmutation of life-forms into political forms."[94] The national choreography of popular culture functioned as a common embodied language. The aesthetic and the political overlapped with the lived experience of the popular, at least with its ideation if not its performance. Legrás rightly notes that these instances "shared a modern ideology that saw the capacity for aesthetic representation as a precondition for figural or actual enfranchisement."[95] The critical potential of these festive performances lay in the possibility of a sense of a collective contemporaneity among its different players. The aesthetic as a potential site of coevalness, I argue, could only be summoned as long as it was rooted in bodily experience. I offer a reflection on the vital kinesthetic encounters that resulted from the tensions in the act of translation between aesthetics and lived experience, from operationalizing indigeneity and Blackness to conceiving the failures of popular representations and mobilizations as generative ways to produce alternative meanings.

Gestures, Embodiment, and Archives: A Reflection on Methodology

In this book, I grapple with the methodological implications of engaging lo mexicano and by extension Mexican dance as an embodied problematic rather than just as a question of representation. Again, previous analyses of Mexican nationalism have privileged discursive and visual practices. I would like to complicate these approaches by positing the body in motion as a site where the ideological imperatives of lo mexicano materialize and are simultaneously challenged (if only ephemerally). I am interested in exploring the lived consequences of embodying and mobilizing a sense of nationalism. By gesturing toward the possibilities of adopting a model that accounts for more than just resistance to the hegemonic construction of Mexican nationalism, I draw attention to the ways bodily practices enable modes of belonging that are at times complicit and/or resistant but that always cite a differentiated mode of lo mexicano.

Each of the following chapters attends to the ways bodies in motion activate or challenge scenarios of Mexican nationalism and its attendant representations. I read each work for movement—its structure, direction, and aesthetics—vis-à-vis its often neglected or at times exceptional position within a national archive, from extant footage of the celebrations of Mexican Independence in 1910 and periodicals and photographs of its subsequent celebration in 1921 after the Mexican Revolution to official or unpublished interviews, records, and newspapers articles of choreographers, dancers, and film directors. In so doing, I posit movement as a way to analyze the power, sense-making, and sociality of lo mexicano. Foregrounding movement, choreography, and embodiment enables me to consider historical, cultural, and material displays of power, while highlighting these displays' connection to race, ethnicity, class, gender, and sexuality. Instead of focusing on oppositional iterations of the nation, I approach performative instances of Mexican nationalism and expressive culture as key variables for understanding the fissures, excesses, and contractions of the embodiment of lo mexicano.

This book conceives the body as an archive and as a means for archiving. By codifying the contradictory displays of Mexican nationalism, the body in motion acts as a historical agent whose movements have the capacity to transform power dynamics, the archive, and itself. In effect, bodily actions carry a historicity that registers the power alignments that enable them. In her insightful analysis of queer gestures, the queer and cultural theorist Juana María Rodríguez contends that gestures operate "as a socially legible and highly codified form of kinetic communication, and as a cultural practice that is differentially manifested through particular forms of embodiment."[96] On the one hand, it is imperative to attend to the legibility of this cultural practice, that is, its discursive construction, but on the other, we must also consider the materiality of this locomotive phenomenon, that is, its embodied manifestation. Furthermore, Rodríguez insists on the indexing qualities of our corporeal movements: "Gestures reveal the inscription of social and cultural laws, transforming our individual movements into an archive of received social behaviors and norms that reveal how memory and feeling are enacted and transformed through bodily practices." Just as individuals are capable of producing these "affective and deeply political forms of corporeality," they are affected by the same power dynamics that such forms of corporeality expose.[97] Pointing toward the archiving potential of our bodies, gestures uncover the historicity linked to our movements, but, most important, they reveal how power dynamics condition and enable differentially profound affective and political forms of bodily expression. In this sense, gestures function as both a register of meaning and a means for negotiating various configurations of power.

By exposing power relations and our investments in them, gestures offer a nuanced understanding of how bodies signify such relations and can alter them. As the cultural theorist Carrie Noland claims, gestures, as "learned techniques of the body, are the means by which cultural conditioning is simultaneously embodied and put to test."[98] Gestures possess a formative and transformative quality that is fundamental to the body that performs them. On the one hand, gestures inscribe onto bodies a set of cultural practices that reveal the shared specificities of a given culture. On the other hand, gestures produce "kinesthetic sensations that remain in excess of what the gestures themselves might signify or accomplish within that culture."[99] To illustrate this point, I return to the example of El jarabe tapatío. The Russian ballerina Anna Pavlova "elevated" it from its popular origins to a modern, international stage, offering a balleticized rendition of it. Dancing en pointe, on her toes, Pavlova captured a complex interconnection between femininity, cosmopolitan dance, and Mexicanness when she first performed it in 1919. The Mexican dancers who performed El jarabe tapatío during La Noche Mexicana in 1921, which I address in chapter 2, danced it by similarly appealing to femininity and Mexicanness, while probably imitating Pavlova's balleticized version. And yet their kinesthetic experience allowed for an excess that differentiated their version of El jarabe tapatío from that of Pavlova's.[100] In this sense, I would like to reiterate the importance of the material and locomotive workings that bring to the fore the actual enactments of Mexican nationalism and the sensations that the body experiences upon performing them. These sensations are crucial for understanding how gestures signal a set of cultural practices and how they inscribe the body. This idea is the key to comprehending the potentialities of movement.[101] How did it feel for the Mexican dancers who performed El jarabe tapatío during La Noche Mexicana or for the one thousand schoolgirls at the National Stadium? What did it mean for these girls dressed as chinas not only to represent the nation but also to embody it?

When gestures are performed repeatedly, ambivalence and tensions arise from their contingent nature. The same gesture signifies different things in different contexts. Dancing El jarabe tapatío produced different meanings when performed en pointe by Pavlova on a stage and in Mexican huaraches by Nellie and Gloria Campobello, as I show in chapter 3. In new circumstances, the meaning produced by the same embodied gesture of nationalism puts in motion a different set of power dynamics. Accordingly, I think of embodiment as a process that allows me to engage the cultural practices enacted through bodily movement while addressing the kinesthetic experience conjured and "lived" at the individual level.[102] At this intersection lies the critical potential of embodied performative gestures. I engage Noland's model of analysis to draw attention to the contingent nature of bodily practices: "If performing gestures affords an opportunity to sense the discrepancy between what gestures *mean* (the meaning bestowed by cultural convention on them and therefore on the subjects performing them) and what gestures make us *feel* (the sensations we experience while performing them)—if, in other words, gesturing widens the gap between meaning and sensate being—*then gesturing can have the valence of critique.*"[103] The model is significant because we can no longer take at face value cultural embodied representations. This model of inquiry thus allows me to signal the slippages and the continuous threat of failure that embodying lo mexicano entails. Unlike the representations of Mexican nationalism crystallized through muralism or the novel of the Mexican Revolution, to name two recurrent examples, the performance of lo mexicano by and through bodies in motion always runs the risk of signifying—or rather gesturing, literally and metaphorically—something different. It is imperative not to take for granted the particularities of each individual body required to perform any given set of cultural practices. It is also crucial not to take for granted the ways the state required its citizens to perform a sense of lo mexicano through Mexican dance, distinctively and sometimes contradictorily embodied by the various actors and spectators I discuss throughout the following chapters.

Therefore, I use a queer methodology that gestures toward an assemblage of lo mexicano that does not presuppose a linear and teleological construction and a heteronormative rendering of the nation. Rather, this methodology privileges the contingent yet concrete ways bodies signify within specific contexts of nationalism. I seek to queer the study of Mexican nationalism by attending to embodied practices and knowledges and alternative historical formations (indigeneity, Blackness, nonheteropatriarchal constructions, and ephemeral archives) of the dominant historical narratives. Although queerness in my work does not necessarily index nonnormative desires and behavior, it informs the framing of my analysis of lived/material experience, felt/embodied knowledge, and the work of memory and imagination (collective or individual) in the various case studies in this book. Furthermore, and perhaps more important, queerness shapes how I account for other forms of evidence beyond the visual and the written text, and it influences my figuration of the archive and its concomitant hermeneutic and reading practices, as I discuss in the epilogue.

This book theorizes the ideation of lo mexicano as a queer assemblage. The dancing histories of Mexico reveal queer instances in which imagining the nation engenders conflicting yet at times redeeming embodiments of lo mexicano. In this work, I build on Jasbir Puar's discussion of queerness as an assemblage. She advances an approach that does not assume a legible construction of queerness and instead embraces the contingency of its configuration as the product of becoming. Rather than approaching queerness as a readily legible and material formation, "visibly, audibly, legibly, or tangibly evident," Puar proposes to think of queerness as a temporal, spatial, and corporeal contingent convergence, an assemblage that enables us to "attune to movements, intensities, emotions, energies, affectivities, and textures as they inhabit events, spatiality, and corporealities."[104] Understanding queerness as an assemblage allows me to queer the moving bodies that I study and their figurations in the archive. Queering lo mexicano does not just mean showing the fissures in its heteronormativity; it also means seeing it in terms outside identity politics, or beyond an identity paradigm. In other words, I think of lo mexicano not as what Mexican nationalism is and what it is not but as what it does or what it mobilizes. Because embodied performances are ephemeral, the archives of Mexican cultural production have failed to systematically register the contributions of a number of actors, from elite choreographers such as Nellie Campobello to Indigenous dancers such as the Yaqui Indians present at La Noche Mexicana. The imperative to trace exclusively visually, tangibly, and corporally legible resistant or alternative constructions of lo mexicano has long prevented the recognition of the contributions of moving bodies in public spaces and their attendant repercussions for the configuration of Mexican nationalism.[105]

By thinking of lo mexicano as a queer assemblage, I want to draw attention to the generative possibilities that arise when we privilege embodied cultural practices. My work therefore recognizes the "contingencies of belonging" that imagining and embodying a nation produce and mobilize. I acknowledge the challenges and dangers but also embrace the promises of this approach. As the case of cross-dressing in the performance of El jarabe tapatío by the Campobello sisters shows, reinforcing a coherent articulation of queer femininity was not the point. Though embodiments of queerness certainly evoke nonnormative subjectivities, these embodiments constantly inhabit contradictory positions. The Campobello sisters' position as women forced them at times to occupy contingent and complicit positions with respect to dominant articulations of Mexican heteropatriarchy. At the same time, however, I draw attention to two aspects that Puar astutely signals: the fictive and performative qualities of identification and the urgency of questioning the imperative of assuming that only "linear," "coherent," and "permanent" positions are capable of offering critiques.[106] Gestures of queer femininity are therefore relevant to critiques of heteropatriarchy.

Thinking of queer assemblages allows me to adopt a generative approach that does not ignore nondominant, nonpermanent, and not-easily-legible embodiments of lo mexicano. It allows me to recognize the workings of other contingent corporeal and cultural alignments that would otherwise be ignored and invisibilized in studies of Mexican nationalism or considered too complicit with hegemonic representations of the nation, such as folklórico dance.[107] These configurations of the nation, like the choreographies of Nellie Campobello, may advance a nationalistic normative agenda, but they allow for iterations of lo mexicano that performatively undo it, exceed it, and even deconstruct it. Ultimately, what is at stake is the exposition of lo mexicano as a construction that, like any other cultural form, needs to be continuously enacted to remain a constitutive frame of reference, as is the case with sex, gender, class, and race, to mention the most pervasive examples.

The cultural practices of postrevolutionary nationalism and their attendant symbolic, material, and embodied expressions acquired social legibility and thus meaning by recirculating preexisting narratives of and about Mexico.[108] Imagining, imaging, and eventually embodying lo mexicano required the circulation of narratives about the nation, its citizens, and its colonial, Afro-descendant, and Indigenous past. But it also required the creation or invention of a new vision of Mexico—a modern yet Indigenous nation. The queer and nationalist embodiments that I explore reveal the fantasies projected by intellectual and political elites onto the emergence of the "popular" as the idea of the nation. Although not all the fantasies were materialized, fantasy has played a role in the imagining of a festive Mexico and the tensions that the body signals as a point of convergence. Fantasy plays a crucial role in the configuration and transmission of embodied knowledge. But it also questions the limits of the real to allow for new imaginings of what the real can apprehend, disarticulating the norms that regulate our understanding of it. As Judith Butler contends, "to posit possibilities beyond the norm or, indeed, a different future for the norm itself, is part of the work of fantasy when we understand fantasy as taking the body as a point of departure for an articulation that is not constrained by the body as it is."[109] Butler repositions the body as that through which norms can be reconfigured and fantasy as the modality that can help us expand the limits of the real, what is present to the senses. The critical promise of fantasy resides in the possibility of questioning, expanding, or destabilizing our normative field of reality. Juana María Rodríguez, however, reminds us of the ways fantasy allows for other forms to occupy and expand the horizon of the possible. She rightly contends that "fantasy [. . .] functions not as an escape from the real-world materiality of living, breathing bodies, but as a way to conjure and inhabit an alternative world in which other forms of identification and social relations become imaginable."[110] Fantasy simultaneously repositions the body at the center of its workings and opens up the possibility of embodying that excess of the real or that elsewhere.

One of the primary questions I address in this study pertains to the methodological nature of our scholarly work within literary and cultural studies. The body requires an interdisciplinary approach that at times exceeds and at times reproduces the realm of representation. In analyzing lo mexicano as a queer assemblage, this study demands a careful consideration of the archive and the means of archiving. By focusing on the body, I carefully attend to the construction of archives and their attendant discourses. In so doing, I embrace a methodology that accounts both for the cultural practices I address in the following chapters and for my own positioning within the field of humanities. At stake is the legitimacy not only of objects of inquiry but also of the legibility of disciplinary practices. Here I draw from Diana Taylor's argument that hegemonic transmission of memory, identity, and knowledge systematically excludes and erases forms of transmission that are directly ingrained in our bodies. Thus, the notion of the archive cannot be taken for granted in this study.

Although history separates the source of knowledge (the archive) from the knower, history is still the product of a process or a "system of selection."[111] I build on Taylor's understanding of the archive to propose an analysis that reveals the ways I have produced my corpus. In so doing, I emphasize that the archive requires the repertoire in order to reproduce itself. By analyzing historical footage, photographs, periodicals, essays, voice recordings, and embodied practices vis-à-vis the active witnessing of and participation in live performances, I underscore how the archive of lo mexicano that I explore is already mediated by my own intervention.[112]

Archives are inherently embedded in genealogies of power, institutional or otherwise, that invite us to reflect upon the ethical responsibilities we face as scholars—particularly regarding Indigenous and Afro-descendant populations and gender and sexual minorities. The historian María Elena Martínez advocates a methodological approach that allows historical sources and performative acts—embodied knowledge transmission—to shed new light on the making and remaking of history and politics.[113] In fact, Martínez argues that imagination is part of historical writing. Simply stated, the study of history is "a process that entails the imagination and the use of the body and experiential knowledge as (re)sources." As she goes on to claim, "the privileging of writing by historians cannot entirely conceal the interpretative and imaginative dimensions of historical writing, the role that the experiential knowledge lodged in our bodies and minds plays in shaping how we understand and write about the past and the ways that the study of history in turn influences how we view the present."[114] In so doing, she highlights the significance of trans-, inter- and postdisciplinary dialogues that force us to expand our engagement with knowledge production and recognize that, as I contend, the archive always involves the repertoire.

As feminist and queer of color critiques have challenged us to do, we must continue to expand what constitutes evidence and "legitimate" modes of inquiry.[115] It is imperative, then, to continue to reflect on the ways our bodies and experiences shape our understanding of our objects of study and the personal stakes of our intellectual endeavors. Queering lo mexicano involves archiving as a political practice but also as a critical gesture. Furthermore, Gayatri Gopinath proposes, the queerness of the archive resides not just in the fact that "it acts as a record of queer desires, embodiments, and affiliations that connect different temporal moments" but also in its revaluation of "that which is seen as without value: the regional, the personal, the affective, the everyday."[116] By proposing Mexican nationalism as a queer assemblage, I position myself vis-à-vis the archive of lo mexicano I analyze. I have approached the study of performances of national identity, indeed dancing histories of Mexico, as a practitioner of folklórico dance for almost thirty years. This study benefited significantly not only from my academic training as a literary scholar but also from my experience and knowledge of a complex nationalistic performance art. My understanding of Mexican dance as a form of knowledge led me to reflect upon the significance and impact of movement as a system of signification.[117] What is the impact of my own performances of El jarabe tapatío upon my analysis of its discursive and visual representations? How is studying embodied expressions of the nation as conceptual categories different from experiencing them as performance practices at home and abroad? Ultimately, I see both the limits and the possibilities of this interdisciplinary scholarly endeavor that foregrounds the body as an object and as a subject of inquiry. My objective is not to argue that we need to move beyond literary analysis but rather to explore the connections among archives, disciplines, and bodies.

Performing a People, Imagining a Nation

Each chapter of this book traces the importance of embodied practices in the configuration of Mexico as a nation-state. Together they show how focusing on embodied performances of Mexican nationalism can produce alternative readings of the discourse of lo mexicano and the role that Mexican dance has played in its ideation and cultural practice. Chapter 1 analyzes the Porfirian centennial celebrations of Mexican Independence in 1910. First, however, it takes us back to an earlier moment elsewhere, June 1889, when the Aztec Palace, Mexico's pavilion at the Paris Universal Exposition, was officially inaugurated with a replica of a *teocalli*, a pyramidal temple. Mexico aimed to portray its glorious pre-European past as part of the larger history of civilization, and, in doing so, to rehearse a sense of an emerging cosmopolitan nation by inscribing the particularities of Mexico with a universal purpose.

Mexico's participation in the 1889 World's Fair in Paris illustrates the division and contradictions of Porfirio Díaz's regime, which lasted from 1876 to 1911. Chapter 1 explores how the centennial celebrations of Mexican Independence in 1910 were intimately intertwined with Mexico's Aztec Palace at the Paris Universal Exposition, with unforeseen consequences at the local level. Mexico's participation in the world's fair was a rehearsal that allowed the rewriting and reconceptualization of material culture but also, as I contend, a rehearsal that enabled a reassessment of embodied manifestations of indigeneity much prior to the postrevolutionary agenda with which such expressions are usually associated. The chapter examines how the massive *Desfile histórico* (historical parade) of the centenary celebrations materialized a notion of modern national history that would eventually cast indigeneity in Mexico not as an ideological and symbolic modern reference to the past but rather as an embodied cultural manifestation. In 1910, the Porfirian elites wanted to host a world's fair for the centennial festivities but decided on a pompous celebration of independence that followed similar scripts already rehearsed abroad. The festive performances of the centennial operated as ambivalent sites of cultural translations of a global narrative of cosmopolitanism, staging Mexico as an exotic yet modern nation. The centennial celebration of 1910, I argue, translated a sense of modernity within a local scenario, an act of cultural translation that had first been rehearsed abroad in 1889.

Chapter 2, "La Noche Mexicana and the Staging of a Festive Mexico," focuses on a massive fiesta celebration that took place in Mexico City's Chapultepec Park. "La Noche Mexicana," as it was called, re-created *ferias* (regional fairs) and featured both Indigenous and mestizo dances from all over the country, including the Sonoran Yaqui dancers and the *jaraneros* (jarana performers, here a term for dancers who performed an intricate couple dance with sophisticated footwork to very festive rhythms) from Yucatán. This multitudinous fair became a two-day spectacle described as "genuinely popular," where an evolving image of a festive Mexico was not only imagined but also staged. This chapter examines La Noche Mexicana and its impact during the festivities of the commemoration of Mexican Independence in 1921, the first celebration after the armed phase of the revolutionary war of 1910. I contend that La Noche Mexicana functioned as a means of performing and hence embodying the nation. Although it has long been argued that the figure of the mestizo embodies the modern Mexican national subject, scholars have not paid adequate attention to the meaning of embodied practices in the postrevolutionary context of modernization. Chapter 2 traces how the fiesta enacted an embodied sociality of the popular and the mestizo, while also considering how national and transnational processes formed the nation through the choreography of staged instances of Mexican nationalism. The rehearsal of an embodied sociality of the nation necessarily entailed the incorporation of the irreducible particularities of the diverse bodies that enacted it. Thinking of the nation as a fiction that is put into practice requires paying attention to the ephemeral but concrete gestures that bodily actions produce while performing a sense of Mexicanness, thereby showing complicities, failures, and even resistance to normative ideas of Mexican nationalism.

Chapter 3, "Nellie Campobello: The Choreographer of Dancing Histories in Mexico," centers on Campobello's dance trajectory. Known primarily as the author of *Cartucho* (1931), a novel of the Mexican Revolution, Campobello was also a dancer, an influential choreographer, and the director of Mexico's National School of Dance (1937–1983). Despite her foundational role in the emergence of a nationalistic, expressive culture in Mexico, there is a dearth of scholarly work in English that discusses the impact and legacy of how Campobello contributed to shaping Mexican dance. This chapter explores her role in the creation of a Mexican school of dance. I contend that while Campobello's dance career helped to institutionalize a hypermasculinized and mestizo nationalism, it also paradoxically helped to create spaces for female and queer embodiments of national subjects. This chapter traces how Campobello developed Mexican dance as a pedagogical practice through which the state formed its citizens and provided them with a means to read and consume Mexico's ethnic, sexual, and racial diversity. To examine this process, the chapter highlights Campobello's performance of El jarabe tapatío; her most famous mass choreography, *El ballet 30–30*; and her book *Ritmos indígenas de México* (Indigenous rhythms of Mexico, 1940). Throughout the chapter, I discuss Campobello's work and her impact on the emergence of Mexican dance as an embodied practice through which both the performers and the audience made sense of and took in nationalistic imaginaries of Mexico. I argue that Campobello's own body allowed for a kind of writing that continuously undid what she claimed to represent. The chapter concludes by turning to Campobello's own thoughts about her dance career and a reflection on why it was ignored for most of the twentieth century, like most of her writings. Ultimately, I address how dance allowed Campobello to rechoreograph the nation through her body and discuss the way we account for the ephemeral archive of dancing histories in Mexico.

Chapter 4, "Cinematic Renditions of a Dancing Mexico: *Folklórico* Dance in Mexican Film," focuses on the production of moving images of dancing bodies during the Golden Age of Mexican cinema in the 1930s and 1940s. From December 1930 to March 1932, the Russian film theorist and master Sergei Eisenstein resided and traveled extensively throughout Mexico, filming what would much later be released as *¡Que Viva México!* by Grigory Alexandrov and Nikita Orlov in 1979. Although unfinished due to a lack of funding and ideological differences, Eisenstein's film became not only a "mythical predecessor" but also a symbolic yardstick of Mexicanist filmography. Just as Eisenstein traveled throughout Mexico accompanied by intellectuals and artists such as Adolfo Best Maugard and Diego Rivera, so did his work, through stills, photographs, and footage, significantly impacting not only *which* "Mexico" was seen but, more important, *how* it was seen. This final chapter considers the emergence and subsequent recurring appearances of Mexican folklórico dance in films, including Eisenstein's *¡Que Viva México!* (1932), Fernando de Fuentes's *Allá en el Rancho Grande* (1936), and Raúl de Anda's *La reina del trópico* (1946), and argues that these representations fostered the creation, consumption, and circulation of bodies and images of a festive Mexico. I contend that a mestizo nation was simultaneously congealed and unsettled through the circulation of sound and images of moving bodies on the screen, in which the bodies that aim to materialize a sense of Mexicanness also enact its undoing. All three of these films incorporated iconic dance scenes that became emblems of Mexican nationalism. Eisenstein's inclusion of "La Sandunga" (the Oaxacan hymn of the matriarchal, Indigenous Tehuantepec region), de Fuentes's staging of "El jarabe tapatío" (Mexico's internationally renowned "hat dance"), and de Anda's incorporation of "La bamba" (Mexico's foremost dance and musical style of Afro-Indigenous roots) showcased Mexico's ethnoracial diversity. As ambivalent sites and sights of Mexico, these cultural performances on film in the postrevolutionary period enabled the formation and circulation of slippery kinesthetic identifications with contradictory renditions of a mestizo nation.

The epilogue, "Queering Mexico's Archive: Ephemerality, Movement, and Kinesthetic Imaginings," offers a reflection on the implications of approaching this project as both a scholar and a performer of Mexican folklórico dance in Mexico and the United States. I engage in performance ethnography in order to conceive of movement as a site of cultural memory, that is, as a means of registering and archiving meaning. I focus on my participation in the dance production of "Half and Halves: A Dance Exploration of the Punjabi-Mexican Communities of California," performed on April 10–11, 2015. I discuss the critical role of folklórico dancing communities in the United States and the stakes of engaging with or disregarding manifestations of popular culture within the Mexican diaspora. In this context, the epilogue grapples with the challenges but also with the generative questions and issues that arise from focusing on the ephemerality of any form of embodied sociality, such as folklórico dance, and other cultural manifestations that are too easily disregarded as noncritical and complicit with hegemonic formulations of nationalism. What does it mean to move across borders—disciplinary, aesthetic, material, communal, or otherwise? In closing, I discuss the urgency of considering embodied expressions as critical sites of knowledge and vital world-making practices. Approaching embodied manifestations and knowledge production, as well as the implications of their historical construction, requires expanding normative notions of what counts as evidence. Following the example of queer of color scholars, particularly José Esteban Muñoz, Juana María Rodríguez, and Ramón Rivera-Servera, I engage lived experiences as legitimate sites of evidence and consequently of knowledge production and circulation. By queering the Mexican archive, my work attends to the ephemera, the stories, and the embodied gestures that Mexicanness as an assemblage brings to the fore. The excess—what remains and lingers—highlights the importance of bodily practices for the configuration of Mexico as a nation-state but also, and perhaps more urgently, for Mexican American, Chicanx, and Latinx communities in the larger Mexican diaspora.

At its core, *Choreographing Mexico* complicates the discursive formulation of lo mexicano, while also addressing questions of knowledge production and circulation that focus on moving bodies and images in the early part of the twentieth century in Mexico (1910–1940). By taking an interdisciplinary methodological approach, I create an archive of ephemera that privileges the body and movement as sites of knowledge transmission. Ultimately, this work highlights the concrete ways dancing bodies produce meaning within specific contexts of Mexican nationalism at home and abroad.

CHAPTER 1

Rehearsals of a Cosmopolitan Modernity: The Porfirian Centennial Celebrations of Mexican Independence in 1910

On June 22, 1889, the Aztec Palace, Mexico's pavilion at the Paris Universal Exposition, was officially inaugurated. The facade of the palace and the external structure were meant to be a replica of a teocalli, a pyramidal temple. The front stairs leading to the entrance of the pavilion and the Toltec-like sculptures that served as columns, along with a series of representations of an Indigenous pantheon, revealed a genealogy of the so-called Aztecs, including deities and leaders of the Triple Alliance between Tenochtitlan, Texcoco, and Tlacopan.[1] With this display, Mexico aimed to present its glorious pre-European past as part of the broad history of civilization, and, in doing so, to rehearse its status as an emerging cosmopolitan nation. The pavilion, in other words, was intended to inscribe the particularities of Mexico with a universal purpose. Mexico's rehearsal of modernity, which took place right next to the Eiffel Tower, that new spectacle of modernization and technology, proved successful in attracting attention. The temple's architecture and design, however, were not consistently legible as part of Western cosmopolitanism.

When the Aztec Palace finally opened (it had originally been scheduled to open in March 1889), it contrasted dramatically with the other Latin American pavilions. The Argentinian palace, for instance, had been designed by the French architect Albert Ballu, whose architectural layout and style materialized an investment in industrialization, technology, and the French aesthetics against which the Mexican pavilion defined itself. Unsurprisingly, the reception of the Mexican pavilion was mixed. Among several competing descriptions of the Mexican pavilion and its inauguration, the chronicles of two major figures in the Hispanic world—Emilia Pardo Bazán, Spain's quintessential figure of naturalism, and José Martí, Latin America's modernist par excellence—best capture its contradictory reception. Pardo Bazán's chronicles were written for the American press and compiled in a volume titled *Al pie de la Torre Eiffel*. She was present at the inauguration of the Mexican pavilion, which she described as "a splendid building of Aztec architecture," at least to the extent that the Aztec style could be replicated based on the work of Mexican and English archeologists. For Pardo Bazán, however, unlike the rest of cosmopolitan buildings at the Universal Exposition, "el pabellón de Méjico no se exime de parecer una decoración de ópera—que tal es el defecto de estos *pastiches*, atendida la imposibilidad de darles en poco tiempo la armonía de líneas y de tono que sólo procura el transcurso de los años" (Mexico's pavilion cannot but seem like a mere set design for an opera. Such is the defect of these *pastiches*, which makes it impossible to give these buildings, in such a short span of time, the harmony of lines and tones that takes years to achieve).[2] According to Pardo Bazán, the effort was genuine, but it had failed. Her comparison of the Mexican pavilion to a mere opera set design reduced it to a pastiche that was at odds with the cosmopolitanism that the Paris Universal Exposition demanded and that the Eiffel Tower, after which she titled her chronicles, materialized. In addition to describing the Aztec Palace as a pastiche, Pardo Bazán insisted on Mexico's failed architectural design and misplaced diplomatic efforts. She went on to add: "En el desierto, y bajo un ramillete de árboles tropicales, no dudo que tendría este pabellón más simpática traza. La Exposición, con su industrialismo arquitectónico, prueba cumplidamente que una arquitectura es inseparable de un país" (In the desert, and under a cluster of tropical trees, I do not doubt this pavilion would have a better appearance. The Exposition, with its architectonic industrialism, proves definitively that an architectural style is inseparable from its country).[3] These comparative comments reveal her orientalizing and colonizing gaze. The exotic Mexican indigeneity she envisioned was better suited to an oasis in the middle of a desert, something that could have been displayed at the exposition by the countries that had been part of the declining Ottoman Empire, such as Egypt, Algiers, and Morocco. At the "Egyptian Street," for instance, crowds of Europeans consumed a display of their imagined version of the "Orient." Although Emilia Pardo Bazán made no mention of the French style decoration of the interior of the Mexican pavilion beyond lamenting not being able to try the *mezcal* on display, she made it clear that Mexico's Aztec Palace had failed to translate the "architectural industrialism" of the Universal Exposition. Mexico's display, in her account, was off the evolutionary path that the rest of the civilized nations were following, an "entertaining" spectacle but not an artistic one.

José Martí interpreted the Mexican Aztec Palace in an entirely different light. For Martí, the Mexican historian Antonio Peñafiel and the engineer Antonio de Anza had captured a sense of national history, agency, self-representation, and thus self-determination: "Como un cinto de dioses y de héroes está el templo de acero de México, con la escalinata solemne que lleva al portón . . . ¡Y ese templo de acero lo levantaron, al pié de la torre, dos mexicanos, como para que no les tocasen su historia, que es como la madre de un país, los que no la tocaran como hijos!" (Like a sash of gods and heroes stands Mexico's iron temple, with the solemn staircase leading to its main door. . . . This iron temple was erected, at the base of the tower, by two Mexicans, so that their history, the mother of a country, would not be touched by those who would not touch her as her sons!).[4] Rather than criticizing the Aztec Palace as a bizarre pastiche or associating it with the Orient, José Martí praised the connection between history, nation, and modernization. In his view, the iron temple was the natural expression of those who knew Mexico's history intimately. In fact, when compared to the rest of the Latin American pavilions, Mexico's was part of a hemispheric continuum of nations that, at the base of the Eiffel Tower, stood "elegantes y ligeros como un guerrero indio . . . ¡la miran, como los hijos al gigante!" (elegant and light as an Indian warrior . . . look[ing onto the tower], like children surveying a giant!)[5]

These competing descriptions reveal that Mexico's Aztec Palace represented simultaneously progress, technological advancement, and civilization (or at least a rehearsal of such ideals) and the non-Western, barbarous, exotic Other, which was evoked by the material and symbolic representation of the so-called Aztec Empire. And yet the Aztec Palace exemplified in many regards Mexico's own interpretation of progress and modernization and, perhaps most important, its inscription in the history of civilization. In other words, the Aztec Palace materialized Mexico's translation of a cosmopolitan modernity by staging Mexico's indigeneity. With the phrase *cosmopolitan modernity*, I refer to the world's fairs' facilitation of a shared experience of an "accelerated time and simultaneity." As Mauricio Tenorio-Trillo argues, the imperative for all nations to be "culturally and racially unique" while conforming to a grammar of cosmopolitanism became a "model" for modernity that at once demanded the "homogenization of all human characteristics and desires and recognized and appreciated the exotic and the bizarre,"[6] so long as the West policed such boundaries. While showcasing recognizable images of progress, democracy, industry, and technological innovations, the world's fairs allowed the nations to partake in a sense of shared universality that was predetermined by Western symbolic, material, and technological dictums.

Mexico's participation in the 1889 World's Fair in Paris illustrates the divisions and contradictions of Porfirio Díaz's regime, which lasted from 1876 to 1911. In this chapter, I show how the centennial celebrations of Mexican Independence in 1910 were intimately intertwined with Mexico's Aztec Palace at the Paris Universal Exposition, with unforeseen consequences at the local level. I argue that Mexico's participation in the world's fair was a rehearsal that allowed both the rewriting and reconceptualization of material culture and a reassessment of embodied manifestations of indigeneity that took place long before the postrevolutionary agenda with which such expressions are usually associated. I trace how the Mexican Aztec Palace materialized a notion of modern national history that would eventually repurpose the notion of indigeneity in Mexico—once an ideological and symbolic modern reference to the past, indigeneity became an embodied cultural manifestation. In 1910, seized by the desire to celebrate Mexico's centennial with a spectacle on the scale of a world's fair, the leaders of the Porfirian regime held a grandiose celebration of independence that followed the script they had rehearsed with the Mexican Aztec Palace. The festive performances of the centennial operated as ambivalent cultural translations of a global narrative of cosmopolitanism, staging Mexico as an exotic yet modern nation. By analyzing photographs, periodicals, and extant historical footage, I show how the centennial celebration of 1910 translated a sense of modernity within a local scenario, an act of cultural translation that had been rehearsed in Paris in 1889.

From Gods of Stone to *Crónicas vivas* (Living Chronicles): The Aztec Palace at the World's Fair in 1889

As a massive spectacle of modernity, the Paris Universal Exposition of 1889 celebrated more than the centennial of the French Revolution. It was the perfect opportunity to display on a global scale France's consolidation of material progress, technological advancements, and sense of nationhood. Like the other iterations of the world's fair since the first major international exhibition in England in 1851, the Paris

World's Fair of 1889 performatively staged progress and modernity as a universal truth. Universal exhibitions, after all, were sites where "culture—material or symbolic, local and foreign—was exhibited, performed, framed, and consumed as spectacle."[7] The massive stages and global exhibitions allowed attendees at major Western urban centers to consume the exotic Other, participating in the incipient experience of modern capitalism. These spectacles of modernity enabled the consumption of objects, products, and cultures while solidifying nationalism and the global dominance of the Western industrialized nations. The world's fairs were at once utopic scenarios and modern simulacra of what was to come—the ideals of progress, modernization, and cosmopolitanism to which all nations had to aspire.

For the Latin American nations, former colonies of the Iberian empires, the Paris Universal Exposition presented an unprecedented opportunity to participate in this spectacle of mass consumption, showcasing their emergent national industries and their wealth of natural resources and raw materials.[8] Paris became a global scenario in which to display the richness, untapped natural reserves, and cultural diversity of Latin American nations with the aim of attracting private investment from European nations and even promoting European migration to the Americas. The Latin American nations resorted to a variety of strategies to assert their cultural autonomy while abiding by European standards—cultural, material, and technological. To insert themselves into the international market, they mobilized their national cultures as a "resource": culture at the world's fairs was used to attain particular ends.[9]

Mexico's Aztec Palace symbolically and materially invested in the creation of a national culture as a means of participating in an increasingly globalized economy and in the spectacle of modernity that was displayed at the Paris World's Fair of 1889. This investment in museums, monuments, and the Paris World's Fair coincided with Mexico's own modernization and political consolidation at the end of the nineteenth century. The Paris Universal Exposition posited material culture as a marker of progress and modernity—that is, as a historical marker. At the same time, the international pavilions were a simulacrum, conveying a utopian longing for a world that was yet to come. The materials on display and the various modes of display at the Universal Exposition revealed the tensions between the physical and abstract symbolism of the objects that were meant to materialize a cosmopolitan nationalism to be consumed both at home and abroad.

In particular, the collected objects that Mexico showcased at the

World's Fair in 1889 revealed Mexico's bet that its "autochthonous" cultural heritage would be its ticket to modernity. The Mexican authorities in charge of the display had evidently made an effort to invest with a sense of "currency and relevance" objects that had served as historical referents. Objects like those displayed in Paris aimed to "trigger urban development" and attract market interest by "creating an aura of cultural distinction" and engendering new social meanings.[10] In this sense, we need to consider the tension between the physical and abstract meanings of the collected and displayed objects. These objects pointed toward an "economy of meaning" as an effect, rather than as an origin.[11] The cultural capital accrued by the material objects repurposed the meaning of the collected objects on display, inserting them into the global market and granting Mexico a sense of cultural difference. It also enabled Mexico to mobilize a sense of exoticism and otherness to appeal to foreign visitors and investors. The various narratives and material histories on display at the Paris Universal Exposition underscored the temporary, contradictory, and fragmented image of a cosmopolitan Mexico.

Nevertheless, as was the case for most Latin American nations and other former colonies, Mexico's greater challenge was to convincingly represent a nation that did not yet exist. In his pioneering study of Mexico's participation at the world's fairs, Mauricio Tenorio-Trillo notes that the Aztec Palace of 1889 was an "attempt to recapitulate and incorporate diverse interpretations of the domestic past; it was an experimental synthesis of Mexican perceptions of European commercial, industrial, and exotic appetite for the non-European; it was an effort to achieve the proper combination of particularism and universalism."[12] This attempt to represent Mexico as a cosmopolitan nation, even though it was no such thing yet, underlines the discursive and material tensions that the Aztec Palace conjured. By restaging the physical and abstract meanings of indigeneity abroad, the Aztec Palace mobilized a new economy of meaning for representations of indigeneity at home, grappling with Europe's demand for the exotic Other, Mexico's ambivalent investment in its past, and modernity's call to participate in a Western (i.e., European) sense of universality.

The architectural design of the Aztec Palace responded to the market as well as to the cosmopolitan demands of universalism and exoticism (see fig. 1.1).[13] For instance, the stairs symbolized an Indigenous set of experiences and behaviors deemed exotic and even barbarous by Europeans and other Latin Americans at the end of the nineteenth century, alluding to the human sacrifices that were associated with the so-called

Aztecs. The interior, however, responded to European architectural tastes and the logic of the market, showcasing collected objects in a quasi museum. Designed by Antonio Peñafiel, an archeologist and historian, and Antonio de Anza, an engineer, the Aztec Palace was divided into three main sections built in "the purest Aztec style." According to Peñafiel's description (*Explication de l'édifice*), "The building consists of a central portion which symbolizes with its principal attributes the Aztec religion, and two side pavillions, being a mythological representation appropriate to the purposes of the Exposition. . . . Between the side pavillions and the central portion six large figures have been placed; they represent the leading events in ancient Mexican history, the beginning and end of the nationality and autonomy of the Aztec tribes."[14] Overall, the building was 70 meters long by 30 meters wide, with a glass ceiling 14.4 meters high.[15]

The exterior of the Aztec Palace, the facade, prominently featured an eclectic series of Indigenous references. Antonio Peñafiel and the sculptor Jesús Contreras symbolically imbued these Indigenous figures with cosmopolitan and monumental characteristics. Located at the sides of the main entrance of the building, the Aztec Pantheon of kings included Itzcóatl, Nezahualcóyotl, Totoquihuatzin, Cacama, Cuitláhuac, and Cuauhtémoc. These figures of authority and heroism represented a genealogy

Figure 1.1. *Pavilion of Mexico, Paris Exposition, 1889.* LOT 6634, no. 149. The Library of Congress Digital Collections.

of Aztec domination and Mexico's "monarchies" of the Triple Alliance, which included Tenochtitlan, Texcoco, and Tlacopan. As Peñafiel explained in his description of the Aztec Palace, Itzcoatl was considered the "founder" of "Mexican nationality," Nezahualcoyotl the lauded "king poet," and Totoquihuatzin the expression of the power and hegemony of the Aztecs throughout Mesoamerica. The last three embodied the heroism of Tenochtitlan's defense against the Spaniards. Cacama became a martyr during the conquest, Cuitlahuac was the hero who expelled Cortés from Tenochtitlan, and Cuauhtémoc was the last Aztec *tlahtoani,* or lord, "the last defender of his country."¹⁶ The inclusion of these Indigenous heroic figures constituted Mexico's attempt to inscribe its Indigenous "monarchies" and "emperors" within the teleological historical understanding of Western civilization. Mexico too had been founded by extraordinary, epic, and noble people, as exemplified by their heroic fall.

The deities selected to represent aesthetically a Mexican Indigenous pantheon similarly accentuated the magnificence of Nahua mythology, positioning it vis-à-vis that of other ancient cultures, particularly the Greek culture. Centeotl, Tlaloc, Chalchiuhtlicue, Camaxtli, Xochiquetzal, and Yacatecuhtli embodied the deities of corn, rain, water, hunting, art, and commerce, respectively. Following Peñafiel's description of the facade, located on the right side, Centeotl, Tlaloc, and Chalchiuhtlicue represented the "protectors of Agriculture and of the fertility of the soil." They symbolically and materially encapsulated Mexico's agricultural richness and vast production. The other three located on the left side— Camaxtli, Xochiquetzal, and Yacatecuhtli—represented hunting, the arts, and commerce.¹⁷ Nevertheless, there were certain inconsistencies not only in their adscription to an Aztec pantheon but also in their symbolism. Xochiquetzal, for instance, was usually associated with sexual power and eroticism, and Camaxtli was also associated with fire and was not part of the Aztec pantheon. All the male and female figures, however, were sculpted with Grecian-like dress and physiognomy.¹⁸

The monumentalization and the stillness of Mexican indigeneity contrasted sharply with the provisional aspects of the building's construction. As the heroic and mythological figures outside the Aztec Palace illustrate, this conception of indigeneity based primarily on the legacy of the Triple Alliance (the so-called Aztec Empire) was still in flux, and yet it was monumentalized to present a solidified notion of Mexico's ancient past. Mexico capitalized on the demand for cosmopolitanism and on the acceptance of the exotic Other to showcase its uniqueness at the world's fair. At the same time, Mexico was grappling with the "reconstitution of its Indian past as an inherent component of Mexican nationhood" while attempting to reconcile its Spanish heritage and Indian present.[19] The Aztec Palace provisionally materialized a fragmented vision of Mexican indigeneity.

The pantheon of Indigenous *tlahtoanih* and deities summoned non-modern imaginaries of a pre-Hispanic, "exotic" past. Although rendered as sculptural motifs, the Indigenous statuary conjured a sense of agency through their attire, symbols, and corporeal gestures, particularly those embodied by the tlahtoanih. As seen in figure 1.1, their bodies and grand gestures presented them to the world's fair attendees as active leaders. Together with the Indigenous deities, they appeared as historical agents. The monumentality of the building also invited a kinesthetic engagement with the Indigenous statuary and architecture. In one sense, the Aztec architecture evoked the massive performances of a former imperial power and even violent spectacles of human sacrifice. The moving audiences then encountered different versions of indigeneity as they walked across the pavilion, climbed the stairs, or looked around inside. The Aztec Palace performed indigeneity and mestizo nationalism while participating in the choreography of modernity staged at the Universal Exposition.

To be clear, the construction of the pavilion was already a performative assemblage of sorts. Peñafiel and de Anza used European renditions of Mexican Indigenous architectural designs while aiming to include Parisian architectural modernity, or their imagined version thereof. For example, a concurrent exhibition titled "Habitations of Humanity" featured an "Aztec" dwelling built by Charles Garnier, the architect of the French Opera, who relied on the same sources the Mexicans had consulted: Désiré Charnay (*American Cities and Ruins*, 1863) and Eugène Viollet-le-Duc ("The Nahuas, The Toltecs," 1875). The presence of this Indigenous dwelling symbolically placed the Mexican pavilion outside modern architecture.[20] The Mexican pavilion's architecture was based on historical accounts that also served as translations for others. The Aztec Palace was therefore a translation of a translation; it was a triangulation of what it was supposed to be, Mexican *and* Indigenous.

As the staging of a modern national history, the Mexican pavilion positioned indigeneity in Mexico not as a symbol of the past but rather as a contemporary—if contingent—embodied cultural manifestation. I do not read the turn to Indigenous history as a failure or an abandonment of this history's original meaning.[21] Instead, Mexico's participation at the Paris Universal Exposition was a rehearsal, an *ensayo*, a performance trial or a work in progress. As a rehearsal, its physical, discursive, and symbolic staging set in motion a series of generative forces that led to a revision of material and embodied manifestations of indigeneity at home and abroad. Mauricio Tenorio-Trillo describes the Aztec Palace as an "overall essay on the modernity of the Mexican nation."[22] In Spanish, *ensayo*, essay or rehearsal, evokes not just an attempt but also the performative qualities of the idea of embodiment. Thus, this staging of Mexican indigeneity in Paris was an ensayo that mobilized in often contradictory ways the production and circulation of Indigenous imaginaries and their concomitant embodiments in Mexico.

Thinking of Mexico's participation at the Paris Universal Exposition as an ensayo requires us to be attuned to the often nonlinear trajectories, messy networks, and contradictory ideologies at play in its material, symbolic, and discursive execution. By recasting the contingent ways imaginaries and stagings of indigeneity functioned as ensayos, I show that they were sites in which Mexican indigeneity was produced relationally. These sites were particularly important because of the fraught and ambivalent ways the Mexican State has historically avowed and disavowed the presence and contributions of Indigenous communities. To be sure, the Aztec Palace was planned and built at a time when Mexican indigeneity was being reconceived as part of a glorious past, as the Porfirian regime's centennial festivities revealed. This reconception led to the co-optation of Indigenous bodies, labor, and cultures; in fact, they were displayed at the expositions in Atlanta in 1895, Nashville in 1896, Buffalo in 1901, and St. Louis in 1904 as part of Mexican villages or portrayals of the "Aztecs and their industries."[23] Nevertheless, positing the Aztec Palace as an ensayo invites us to attend to the ways it can signify an "excess or potentiality." Writing about the avant-garde, Sarah J. Townsend theorizes "the unfinished" as a "site of social conflicts, ideological contradictions, material limitations, and affective obstacles."[24] Similarly, Mexico's ensayo—the staging of the Aztec Palace in 1889—had complex and paradoxical effects on the conception of Indigenous histories and cultural contributions within and outside Mexico.

In my research on the Paris Universal Exposition, I came across a report that detailed a reevaluation and recognition of the dance of the tlahtoanih or *tastoanes* (lords) in Jalisco, a state that had yet to become a metonym for the nation. The ethnological study of the dance, the product of a series of reports requested from each state by the Porfirian government to assemble what would be highlighted at the Mexican pavilion in Paris, reveals the "ideological contradictions," "material limitations," and affective investments of writing about this particular manifestation of Indigenous embodied and expressive culture in Jalisco.[25] Written in 1889 by Alberto Santoscoy, a journalist, professor of history, archivist, and director of Jalisco's *Biblioteca Pública* (Public Library), the ethnological historical study (titled *La fiesta de los tastoanes. Estudio etnológico histórico*) encompassed a careful description and a historical analysis of "La fiesta de los tastoanes" (The feast of the tastoanes), a local festive celebration.[26] In its opening lines, Santoscoy indicated that the dance had been captured by "the rustic chisel of a potter" to be taken to Paris alongside a study explaining its origin and celebration, representing the only "Indigenous festivity" that was still preserved in the state of Jalisco.[27] In fact, he described this Indigenous celebration as a "crónica viva que conserva hechos precisos de nuestros anales, que guarda después de luengos siglos casi invívitas muchas de las costumbres de los antiguos y naturales dueños del país y que es imperecedero recuerdo de la unión de las dos razas que han dado procedencia al actual pueblo mexicano" (a living chronicle that preserves the crucial events of our history, that after long centuries has kept alive many of the customs of the ancient and natural lords of the country, and that serves as an everlasting reminder of the fusion of the two races that have given origin to the Mexican people of today).[28] Santoscoy recognized the historical significance of the celebration as a form of embodied history that kept alive the customs of the local Indigenous groups. The Indigenous dance functioned as a "living chronicle," registering the encounter between two peoples that had merged to form a nation. While acknowledging the presence and incorporation of "hideous" elements, he also designated it as a "monumento histórico" (a historical monument), given the significance of the occasion and its concomitant symbolism. This dance, like many Indigenous celebrations throughout Latin America, was a staging of historical events that impacted the local histories of Indigenous groups—"no es una simple danza, sino que se representa en ella una escena histórica" (it is not a simple dance; rather, it represents a historical scene), to use Santoscoy's words.[29]

More than a choreographed representation of a historical account (the violent encounter between the Spaniards and Indigenous groups from Guadalajara, one of the most important cities in Mexico then and now), La danza de los tastoanes was a rewriting of local Indigenous history. The performance of this dance introduced a significant change to an otherwise conventional storyline. The plot can be simply explained as the conflict between *moros y cristianos* (Moors and Christians), the fight between the Islamic Other (the Moors) and the Christians in the context of the *Reconquista* in Spain and its restaging after the conquest in Mexico. Typically, the Indigenous people were associated with the Moors, who had been defeated by the Spanish. The Spanish were favored by the Apostle Santiago, the patron saint of Spain, the Reconquista, and eventually the *conquista* in Mexico. In their restaging of this foundational scene, the local Indigenous people had the apostle Santiago sacrificed, "convirtiendo á los vencidos en vencedores y haciendo morir al que, según aquélla [la leyenda], sembraba la muerte entre los miembros de la misma raza" (turning the vanquished into the victors and bringing death to the one who, according to the legend, assisted the Spanish in killing the Indigenous people).[30] This particular performance of history constituted an Indigenous response to a deterministic view of history and the state's attempt to represent them. Locally, then, a notion of history and historical writing emerged that encompassed other modes of embodied knowledge and memory.

Santoscoy gestured toward the existence of unscripted knowledge, the *crónica viva*, or living chronicle, that was reactivated in the historical scenario enacted by La danza de los tastoanes. Through this scenario, the communities negotiated their relation to the past, present, and future. This instance of "history and/as performance" allowed embodied practices to, in Diana Taylor's words, "make the 'past' available as a political resource in the present."[31] In so doing, the tastoanes set in motion the reevaluation of historical knowledge as the product of a process of self-affirmation. Through their dancing, they staked their historical claim to their ancestral lands, reactualizing their sense of belonging and indeed the very notion of being Indigenous. Their moving bodies demanded a relational understanding of their living Indigenous history. Inadvertently, Santoscoy's study of La danza de los tastoanes revealed that the archive was the "product," not the "source," of historical inquiry, since it had to be classified as such. Consequently, he also revealed that Indigenous embodied practices have been, as Taylor has pointed out, "strategically positioned outside of history, rendered invalid as a form of cultural transmission, in short *made un-* and *anti*-historical by conquerors and colonialists who wanted to monopolize power."[32] Santoscoy commented that many, including himself, had disdained this Indigenous performance: "Esta fiesta que indiferentemente vemos pasar entre nosotros, burlándonos de élla, porque no comprendemos su significación, es todo un monumento histórico" (This festivity that takes place among us but which we are indifferent to, and even make fun of, because we do not understand its significance, is quite a historical monument).[33] Nevertheless, Indigenous moving bodies and embodied behavior had come to constitute one of the principal sources of knowledge for this particular community. The community, in fact, had organized itself around this festivity, as had many other communities across Latin America.

By resorting to the historical record, Santoscoy sought to render legible this embodied Indigenous form of cultural transmission, reinscribing it into history. After consulting colonial accounts and local historical records, Santoscoy was unable to determine whether the celebration referred to the battle of Tetlán or an attack against Guadalajara by Indigenous groups during the conquest of the region. He acknowledged that the tastoanes may have cited both, including the concomitant apparitions of the Apostle Santiago.[34] Once he had positioned this living chronicle in the realm of the historical, he speculated about how the Indigenous performance rewrote history itself. He went on to conjecture that

> la raza indígena, cuyos individuos, por una aberración que sólo se explica por el humillante estado en que se coloca al ser oprimido, celebraban festivamente su propio vencimiento por el Apóstol Santiago, con las ideas de la revolución de Independencia . . . y considerando la afrenta que se hacía en festejar la derrota y la muerte de sus antepasados, con levantado, pero injusto ánimo, tergiversó la leyenda . . . el desenlace de la representación de los *tastoanes*, de ese modo cambiado, vino á tener para los indígenas nobilísima significación: personificando en Santiago vencido, el poderío español quebrantado por la independencia patria, la fiesta de los *tastoanes* vendría á ser la celebración de la conquista de la autonomía mexicana.

> (the Indigenous race, whose individuals, due to an aberration that can only be explained by the humiliating state in which the oppressed are placed, celebrated festively its own collapse by the Apostle Santiago, with the ideas from the revolution of Independence . . . and considering the affront entailed by celebrating, with spirited but misplaced intent, the defeat and death of their ancestors, the legend was distorted . . . and the ending of the representation of the *tastoanes*, having been changed in this way, came to have for the Indigenous people a most noble significance: personifying in the defeated Santiago the destruction of Spanish power by the patriotic independence, the feast of the *tastoanes* would come to be the celebration of the conquest of Mexican autonomy).[35]

Santoscoy started by recognizing the deplorable and humiliating state in which Indigenous people, the oppressed, found themselves. But he then immediately ascribed a patriotic symbolism to their reinterpretation. He read into the "distorted" version of the events "the celebration of the conquest of Mexican autonomy," of its independence. The Apostle Santiago would therefore represent the destruction of the Spanish power, the literal embodiment of its defeat. And yet there is much more at play; after all, Santoscoy himself acknowledged this was just a "simple hypothesis."[36] One can only wonder whether there were multiple markers of indigeneity in this rendition of the dance—sartorial elements, linguistic signs, and kinesthetic referents—that escaped his limited understanding of the local forms of indigeneity that he had hitherto ignored. And despite the incipient forms of *indigenismo* (an assimilationist tendency to incorporate Indigenous expressions and motifs into national imaginaries),[37] he urgently warned his readers against "echar abajo ese monumento vivo de pasadas memorias" (demolishing that living monument of past memories), encouraged by a misguided "celo civilizador" (civilizing zeal) or led by their own ignorance.[38]

I read Santoscoy's study of this Indigenous performance as part of the competing trajectories, messy networks, and contradictory ideologies that the Aztec Palace generated at the local level. The Mexican pavilion, like many others displays in the following decade before and after the centennial celebrations of Mexican Independence, was an ensayo of a contingent historical materialization of a modern nation that had started to congeal the visual representation of an Indigenous Mexico. The Aztec Palace at the Paris Universal Exposition was not a simple failure, as Mexican government officials and many intellectuals of the time believed.[39] On the contrary, its staging led to a revaluation of the material and embodied culture of Indigenous groups in Mexico, as Santoscoy's study reveals, despite its paternalistic overtones.

The report, however, did not constitute a critical reflection on Porfirian indigenismo. Instead, it was part of the nonlinear recognition of the fraught incorporation and co-optation of Indigenous material and expressive culture. The acts of translation that the construction of the Aztec Palace demanded recall the original meaning of *translatio,* the literal moving of bodies, objects, and ideas. With these acts, the Mexican government staged the nation abroad before it did so at home. The objective was above all to create a national narrative that would place Mexico on the map as an equal to other Latin American nations, that is, as a country of primary sources with technological advancements. Aiming at a global narrative that was universal, recognizable, and acceptable, Mexico's participation in the Paris Universal Exposition led to other representations of that narrative that would soon be used to educate Mexicans at home in the nuances of cosmopolitan nationalism.[40]

In 1910, the Porfirian elites wanted to host a world's fair for the centennial celebrations of Mexico's independence from Spain, but they decided instead to stage a pompous celebration, attempting to follow scripts that had already been rehearsed abroad. The use of the Mexican Indigenous past and Mexico's investment in its national history were not necessarily at odds; rather, they were part of the same assemblage of Indigenous articulations that had been staged time and again abroad, as the Aztec Palace and La fiesta de los tastoanes of 1889 at home demonstrate, and as I explore in the next sections.

Translating a Cosmopolitan Modernity:
Las Fiestas del Centenario de 1910

The Centennial of 1910, commonly referred to as the *Centenario*, proved to be Mexico's best opportunity to showcase to European nations and the United States its economic and scientific developments, material progress, and strengthened civic culture—in other words, its modernity. The Centenario became a massive scenario for the spectacle of modernization, nationalism, and cosmopolitanism. In fact, the ideals of "order and progress" that marked the experience of modernity at the turn of the century, influenced by Auguste Comte's positivism, led Mexico to stage its own version of cosmopolitanism for the celebration of its independence from Spain. The colorful, exotic presentation did not undermine Mexico's cosmopolitanism; rather, it made the country unique, appealing to the generalized ideas that foreigners held of Mexico, which the Mexican government had reinforced at the various world's fairs.[41] This "desire for the world," as Mariano Siskind defines cosmopolitanism, sought to inscribe the cultural particularities of Mexico in "larger, transcultural networks of signification."[42] The Centenario, then, provided the Porfirian government with the ideal occasion to highlight its scientific, economic, and material advancements, promote a sense of nationalism, solidify its commitment to state formation, and, in so doing, partake of the experience of modernity and cosmopolitanism.

Although the Centenario did not reach the status of a universal exhibition, as some members of the Porfirian elite such as Antonio A. de Medina y Ormaechea had envisioned,[43] it attracted a significant number of foreign visitors, diplomatic missions, official delegates, dignitaries, and special envoys. Twenty-eight nations were represented at the centennial; six of them (France, Spain, the United States, Italy, Japan, and Germany) sent special diplomatic missions.[44] The Centenario also brought to Mexico City a large number of people from different parts of the country as well as members of the Mexican diaspora in the United States.[45] The centennial celebrations were part of a global trend in Western Europe, the United States, and Latin America in which political groups in power made an orchestrated effort to cultivate a shared political culture and historical memory through words and images[46] and through bodies in movement that reshaped public spaces and national narratives. Officials in Mexico, inspired by the centennials of United States Independence in 1876, of the French Revolution in 1889, and of other Latin American nations such as Argentina, seized this opportunity to portray their country as a liberal and modern nation.

The desire to have Mexico participate in the global choreography of "order and progress" led the Porfirian government to stage a series of massive festivities for the occasion, to inaugurate a multiplicity of monuments and social institutions, and to host numerous academic and scientific congresses in September of 1910.[47] The planning of the Centenario officially started in April 1907, when Porfirio Díaz created a ten-member National Centennial Commission led by Guillermo Landa y Escandón, the mayor of Mexico City.[48] The organizers established several committees to coordinate events in Mexico City and throughout the nation, raise funds, and attract private capital as well as foreign governments, investors, and the press. The Centenario was the perfect occasion to improve Mexico's image as a modern nation abroad and promote a national civic culture at home. Genaro García, the official chronicler of the festivities, congressman, and director of the National Museum of History, Archeology, and Ethnology, worked with a group of historians to document the vital presence of foreign delegations in the festivities, particularly through the inauguration of monuments, including monuments to Alexander von Humboldt (inaugurated by Germany), Louis Pasteur (by France), and George Washington (by the United States).[49]

A significant number of the events during the Centenario revolved around the construction of public projects and major academic and scientific congresses. The public projects included a modern mental hospital (Manicomio General La Castañeda); new buildings for the Ministry of Defense and the Ministry of Foreign Affairs; elementary and secondary schools, a school for the deaf and blind, teacher-training schools for men and women (Escuela Normal de Maestros and Escuela Normal de Maestras), and the National University; public parks; and hydraulic works dealing with drainage, particularly the extension of the Gran Canal del Desagüe; as well as the foundation for the National Penitentiary in San Jerónimo Atlixco; the renovation of the National Museum of Archeology, History, and Ethnology; the realization of a wide range of exhibitions on topics including popular hygiene, Japanese, Spanish, and Mexican products, art, and industry; and the celebration of national and international congresses such as the National Medical Congress, the National Congress of Elementary Education, the first National Congress of Students, and the International Congress of Americanists and Indianists, which was attended by Franz Boaz, who would remain in Mexico to direct the government-funded International School of Anthropology.[50]

Mexico City had been radically transformed in the years prior to the Centenario. In fact, the use of public space became a battleground in the configuration of (creole) nationalism during the Porfiriato. The Díaz regime was therefore characterized by two distinct fronts: the francophile progressives and the nationalist mythologizers.[51] The Porfirian elites' efforts to attract foreign recognition and capital led them to imitate French architecture and urban planning, particularly Baron Georges-Eugène Haussmann's remaking of the Champs-Elysées. Barbara A. Tenenbaum notes that there was also a push for the "reevaluation of the Aztecs," especially in the construction of the statue of Cuauhtémoc in 1887, which inaugurated a "neoindigenist style."[52] The erection of the monument of Cuauhtémoc materially and symbolically gestured to the Aztec imperial legacy to promote the centralization of the state and the consolidation of Díaz's power. This rendition of Indigenous history foreshadowed the monumentalization of indigeneity staged during the Paris Universal Exposition with the Aztec Palace, which also featured the figure of Cuauhtémoc.

Furthermore, the transformation of the urban space reflected the construction of an ideal city that materialized its investment in modernization, science, and economic progress. To reshape the urban landscape, the Porfirian government had to displace and resegregate Indian communities, workers, and internal migrants. But the urban transformation of Mexico City had less to do with displacements and social reforms than with the geographical expansion of the city. As Mauricio Tenorio-Trillo observes, the "ideal city . . . was conceived as a conquest not only over tradition, chaos and backwardness but also over nature," and so the city's expansion was a "frontier expansion."[53] Even though the Zócalo remained the center of power, the Paseo de la Reforma became the backbone of the idealized modern city. It connected the former center of power with modern, elegant, and wealthy *colonias* (neighborhoods) such as Condesa, Cuauhtémoc, Juárez, and Roma as well as with the Castle of Chapultepec, the residence of the president of Mexico. These neighborhoods had electricity, wide streets and avenues, gardens, and other amenities.

There were, however, a few celebrations during the Centenario that centered on public displays of nationalism, particularly the inauguration of the monument to Mexican Independence, El Ángel de la Independencia, and the monument to Benito Juárez, El Hemiciclo a Juárez. These monuments were part of an array of national symbols on the Paseo de la Reforma and Juárez Avenue, respectively. The monument of independence and Benito Juárez represented the materialization of Mexico's modern history, from its claim to sovereignty to the establishment of a liberal state. The French-trained architect Antonio Rivas Mercado designed the "Winged Victory" sculpture that monumentalized Mexico's sovereignty, independence, and modernity.[54] The Juárez monument, in the Alameda, was designed by the French-trained sculptor Guillermo Cárdenas. For the historian Michael J. Gonzales, the erection of a pure white marble sculpture of Juárez monumentalized the "transformation of an Indian into the acculturated Mexican who symbolises modernity, secularism and liberalism."[55] Benito Juárez certainly represented modernizing liberal ideals (the reforms for which his government had relentlessly fought), the secularization of the state, and the consolidation of the republic after the fall of the French-imposed emperor Maximilano de Habsburgo. Both monuments symbolically, discursively, and materially linked the Díaz regime to a national history of liberation, modernization, and republicanism.

Together with the commemoration of massive displays of nationalism, the erection of these patriotic monuments redefined the public space of Mexico City in 1910. The major streets and avenues that served as festive stages for the centennial functioned as monumental scenarios for the transformation of the city and the performance of history. By reactivating and making visible what was already there, the monumental scenarios of the centennial not only framed the unfolding social drama of a Mexican cosmopolitan modernity but also operated as "meaning-making paradigms that structure[d] social environments, behaviors, and potential outcomes," to draw on Diana Taylor's conceptualization of scenarios.[56] Two events clarify how Mexico City transformed itself into a monumental scenario for the rewriting of history and the structuring of a new mestizo, nationalist civic culture. The first event was the arrival of Miguel Hidalgo y Costilla's baptismal font in the city, accompanied by his granddaughter Guadalupe Hidalgo y Costilla and thirty thousand children. The second was the official return of José María Morelos y Pavón's uniform by the Spanish representative, the Marquis de Polavieja, who also bestowed upon Porfirio Díaz the honorific Order of Carlos III.[57] Hidalgo and Morelos, as the founding fathers of the Mexican nation, allowed the Díaz regime to establish a direct, material link to a genealogy of independence heroes. Although the presence of the granddaughter of Hidalgo emphasized the conflation of Díaz with the nation's liberator, it was Morelos's uniform, which received the treatment of a state funeral, that enabled the regime to exalt Morelos as the epitome of mestizaje and to reconcile with Spain. The official chronicler, Genaro García, praised Morelos as a mestizo national hero: "Morelos es la figura legendaria por excelencia y, además, es el mestizo que simboliza la fundición de las dos razas . . . que producen una nueva rama con todas las grandezas de aquéllas. Morelos es, por esto, representante genuino de la nacionalidad mexicana" (Morelos is the legendary figure par excellence, and he is also the mestizo who symbolizes the fusion of two races . . . who produces a new branch with all the greatness of the other two. Morelos is, for this reason, a genuine representative of a Mexican nationality).[58] By honoring Hidalgo and Morelos, the centennial planners sought to establish a connection among state formation, civic culture, and liberal and secular leaders and policies.[59] The baptismal font and the uniform, two material objects, set in motion a mestizo nationalist discourse that framed the Díaz regime as the natural heir in a lineage of patriotic heroes. These massive performances staged and strategically activated scenarios of Mexican national history and mestizaje.

The parading of history and the performance of the past in the monumental urban scenario of Mexico City in 1910 did more than establish a liberal version of the country's history. The Porfirian cultural and political elite invested substantially in the development of a national historical narrative that was intended to solidify Mexico's position among modern nations. As part of this effort, the past was symbolically and materially manipulated to conform to the requirements of Mexican nationalism, which had been already rehearsed and displayed at the Paris Universal Exposition. The Porfirian elites mobilized the past as a mechanism to shape national subjectivities and imaginaries during the centennial celebrations of 1910. The emergence of Mexico as a modern nation, therefore, set in motion a series of discursive tactics that emphasized the performance of the nation as a whole. The commemorations of Independence in Mexico in 1910 and 1921 were two related yet dissimilar instances in which discourses about memory and history operated as sites for the legitimization of state power.[60] A significant shift occurred between the Porfirian regime and the postrevolutionary government: whereas the former held an evolutionary understanding of history, the latter embraced cultural relativism, as I discuss in chapter 2. The Porfirian regime resorted to history to forge a sense of Mexican nationalism and to impose a teleological understanding of the historical progress of the nation. In the Porfirian regime's hands, history was wielded as an "instrument of power." According to the historian Annick Lempérière, the past "suministra el material para forjar el patriotismo de los ciudadanos, alimentar el orgullo nacional, cultivar el espíritu de sacrificio y esfuerzo por la patria y generar la conciencia de que la época presente es el feliz desenlace de una evolución histórica" (provides the material to forge a sense of patriotism among citizens, to foster national pride, to cultivate a spirit of sacrifice and effort on behalf of the country, and to make people conscious of the fact that the present is the best outcome of historical evolution).[61] The configuration and eventual imposition of a "historical consciousness" that rendered Mexico a modern nation, governed by the ideals of order, progress, and evolution systematically ignored the presence and contributions of the Indigenous and peasant populations in vast areas of the country. The performance of the past became a means of connecting the local with the national and of establishing connections, both imagined and material, among various national and international actors.

The festivities of 1910 had a pedagogical cast, as did the festivities of 1921. Citizens were formed via the enactment of a nationalistic cultural identity based on a progressive, liberal, and teleological understanding of history. While the emphasis was on educating Mexico's increasingly diverse population, the Centenario was designed to translate a sense of cosmopolitanism and modernity for Mexican nationals and foreigners alike. As a creative process imbricated in the cultural, geopolitical, socioeconomic, and even epistemological spheres, the translation of cosmopolitan modernity at home led the Porfirian elites to consider the contradictions, misunderstandings, and misrepresentations of a country that was considered exotic and incompletely modern abroad.[62] Mexico's grandiose entrance into modernity, then, was a fraught enterprise.

In this sense, Mexico's cosmopolitan facade did not imply a stable conception of modernity. The city had been remodeled to stage an ideal representation of Mexico, particularly along the Paseo de la Reforma, which featured both a historical route that highlighted Mexico's road to independence, from the statues of Columbus and Cuauhtémoc to the recently inaugurated Ángel de la Independencia, and the Haussmann-inspired Paseo that showcased Mexico's modern amenities and cosmopolitan architecture. The material renovations were intended to benefit the upper and middle classes and the foreign nationals residing in Mexico's multiple international neighborhoods. This urban, idealized Mexico was a sanitized version that reflected Mexico's order, progress, and technological development.[63] And yet the staging of a modern and cosmopolitan Mexico turned the country into a battlefield. Mexican cosmopolitan modernity became a spectacle not just because its staging demanded theatricality but also because competing images of a modern Mexico mediated and conditioned social relations.[64] As I discuss in the next section, the multitude of bodies in movement introduced even more complexity into the image of a modern Mexico. The social relations that were choreographed by the Centenario make it possible to observe how embodied practices generated other social possibilities, instantiating forms of resistance, complicity, and intervention that translated a sense of modernity and cosmopolitanism in Mexico in 1910.

Performing a Nation: *El Desfile Histórico de 1910*

Although the government's emphasis in the festivities of 1910 was on proving to foreigners and to Mexico's middle and upper classes that Mexico was modern, numerous cultural performances allowed people from different classes and ethnoracial groups to witness the staging of a so-called cosmopolitan nation. On the one hand, the centennial celebrations organized by the Porfirian regime in September 1910 literally paraded before an admiring world a rapidly modernizing nation that was at once cosmopolitan and exotic. On the other hand, by privileging the public display of his idea of a modern Mexico, Díaz gave the Mexican people "their first public lesson of visual culture."[65] The Porfirian state apparatus promoted a vision of a cosmopolitan and yet Indigenous nation. This vision was not just displayed, it was also performed.

El Desfile Histórico (the Historical Parade), held on September 15, was a crucial celebration that set in motion the liberal vision of the Díaz regime. Because it mobilized the body politic of the Mexican nation, its spectators witnessed bodies in movement that both claimed and disavowed a contingent embodied sociality. The Desfile enabled the circulation of contending forms of nationalism. The corporeal motions of the thousands of attendees and hundreds of participants during the Desfile negotiated nationalism in complex and contradictory ways. The dance scholar SanSan Kwan invites us to consider how "structures of nationalism are determined and negotiated through the moving body."[66] Kwan proposes to understand community identity as the dynamic interplay between moving bodies, history, and space, reconfiguring urban space as the product and process of the intersection between social, material, and corporeal alignments.[67] By rethinking how bodies in motion signify through space and time, we can better understand the plural and complex ways embodied practices materialize a sense of nationalism. In reframing bodily motion as an integral part of community identity and the contested but persistent idea of nationalism (i.e., lo mexicano), I shed light on the concrete and symbolic ways moving bodies choreograph meaning across contradictions.

The Desfile Histórico enacted three significant historical moments, staging the official version of Mexican history advanced by the Porfirian cultural and intellectual elites: the encounter between Moctezuma and Hernán Cortés; the Spanish commemoration of the Conquest of Mexico, El Paseo del Pendón; and the triumphant entrance of El Ejército Trigarante (The Army of the Three Guarantees) in Mexico City. Guillermo de Landa y Escandón and José Casarín choreographed the reenactment of a historically "accurate" and "authentic" vision of Mexican history. Genaro García notes that the Desfile required the most "laborious preparation" of all the festivities during the Centenario.[68] This monumental staging of Mexican history proved an enormous success. Although the official chronicle estimates that between 50,000 and 70,000 people witnessed the parade, other estimates posit 100,000 or even 200,000 people.[69] The performance of the past enacted by the Desfile not only reconfigured the urban space but also reformulated the interactions of the thousands of participants and attendees with Mexico's official history and the contingent embodied sociality conjured through this massive mobilization.

The conquest, the colonial epoch, and independence were therefore privileged in the first public lesson in the visual culture of Mexico's official past.[70] The first scene staged the meeting between Moctezuma II and Cortés, featured one thousand individuals representing mostly Aztec and Tlaxcaltecan Indians and the Spanish conquistadors, including Cortés and Doña Marina or Malintzin (the translator known as Malinche). Warriors; priests; principal lords from Texcoco, Ixtapalapa,

Coyoacán, and Tlacopan; nobles; noble Indigenous women; and servants accompanied Moctezuma and his court. They were immediately followed by Cortés and Malintzin, together with the Spanish cavalry, infantry, harquebusiers, crossbowmen, captains, Catholic friars, servants, and, of course, Tlaxcaltecan Indian warriors.[71] The parade went from Plaza de la Reforma via Juárez and San Francisco Avenues toward the Zócalo, where the participants staged the historic meeting between Moctezuma and Cortés.

The second historical scene represented the colonial ceremony commemorating the Spanish Conquest, El Paseo del Pendón, which normally took place every August 13.[72] Approximately eight hundred participants wore the colonial attire of various ranks, featuring the Viceroy, colonial judges from the *Audiencias* (Spanish courts), important members of the *Ayuntamiento* (town hall), royal advisors, religious authorities, senior officials, members of the army, and Indigenous officers.[73] The parade's route for this scene left from the temple of San Hipólito and proceeded toward San Diego Street and then from San Francisco Avenue toward the Zócalo. The Spanish men wore powdered wigs and eighteenth-century formal attire, marching with all pomp and circumstance to the Zócalo, where a stage had been set up with royal banners to mark the Spanish territory and authority.[74]

The third historical scene staged was the victorious entrance of the Ejército Trigarante (Army of the Three Guarantees) in Mexico City, headed by Agustín de Iturbide. The insurgent army featured other prominent commanders such as Vicente Guerrero, Guadalupe Victoria, Manuel Mier y Terán, and Anastacio Bustamante.[75] The procession followed the same route as the first, from Plaza de la Reforma toward the Zócalo. Following the Ejército Trigarante and the regiments that accompanied it, allegorical floats sent by various states (including Sinaloa, Tabasco, Veracruz, Michoacán, Hidalgo, and Colima) commemorated representative battles and scenes of the War of Independence.[76]

The Desfile started promptly at 10:00 a.m. The pictures that accompanied the *Crónica Oficial* and newspaper articles from the time show thousands of civilians from all classes and ethnic backgrounds packing avenues and wide spaces like the Alameda and overcrowding the narrow streets of the colonial part of the downtown area surrounding the Zócalo, the destination of the Desfile Histórico. Genaro García observed that "el gentío sobrepasó toda previsión, pues se desbordaba en las aceras de las calles y avenidas; llenaba enteramente la Plaza de la Constitución; se apiñaba en los balcones, aparadores, tribunas, puertas y zaguanes, y no dejaba ventana, azotea ó torre que no invadiese para admirar el espectáculo que iba á tener lugar" (the massive crowd exceeded all expectations, as it overflowed the sidewalks of streets and avenues; packed the Plaza de la Constitución; and gathered on balconies, store windows, grandstands, doors, and hallways, sparing no window, terrace or tower from which to admire the spectacle that was about to take place).[77] The city center turned into a vital monumental scenario that resignified not only the public space of Mexico City but also the scenes witnessed by thousands of spectators. This was a material and symbolic rehearsal of a Mexico that was yet to come.

The numerous pictures and chronicles from the event emphasized the contrast, excitement, and crowds. In one of the most elaborate chronicles of the Desfile, published by the popular newspaper *El Imparcial*, the author, waiting with the other journalists in front of the National Palace at the Zócalo, commented that people were "invading" the space in front of the National Palace to such an extent that by 10:30 a.m. there was no room left for the parade, despite the efforts to clear a path for the various contingents. He lamented that the event that was designed especially for the people could not be enjoyed because of the crowds that thronged the streets: "pero fué la muchedumbre, inquieta muchedumbre, que, ávida de presenciar el soberbio espectáculo, se aglomeró como un mar inquieto . . . lo que impidió . . . nada menos el que ella misma gozara del desfile" (the massive, restless crowd, eager to witness the magnificent spectacle, crammed together like a restless sea . . . which, ultimately, prevented it from enjoying the parade).[78] As shown in figure 1.2 (an image of the float with Hidalgo's bust, part of the third historical scene), at one point the Desfile and the crowds merged into one. Balconies, windows, terraces, and sidewalks overflowed with thousands of attendees, yet the enthusiastic chaos did not deter people from trying to catch a glimpse of the monumental parade.

The descriptions of the thousands of people overcrowding the streets contrast with those of the historical scenes. Figure 1.3 illustrates several contingents of the parade, emphasizing the first scene, representing the meeting of Moctezuma II and Cortés.[79] The first image on the left page includes the procession of the Catholic friars, followed by a group of Spanish conquistadors, symbolizing the union between the Spanish Crown and the Catholic Church and the dual conquista that took place. Below that image, a group of Indigenous men carry their insignias and shields, wearing their customary attire with the corresponding headpieces and sandals. The third image shows a group of Spanish drummers in front

Figure 1.2. "El Desfile Histórico," *La Semana Ilustrada*, September 23, 1910. Courtesy of the Biblioteca Miguel Lerdo de Tejada de la Secretaría de Hacienda y Crédito Público.

of a group of Indigenous women and men, and the fourth image shows a group of mounted Spanish soldiers. The caption states simply that these images portray the "Indians and Spaniards" during the Desfile Histórico. The right page is divided into halves. In the top half, we see the beginning of the procession, as the caption reads. Although many people were waiting for the parade, this was not the crowd that would later gather at the Zócalo or the Alameda. People were able to move around, and one can discern a line of officers on each side of the street, making sure there was enough room for the parade to pass by. The bottom half of the page features three photographs of Indigenous men wearing sandals and headpieces and carrying shields or a ceremonial staff, followed by other Indigenous men dressed similarly. What is most interesting about these images is not that they prominently feature three Indigenous men but that the latter are described by the caption as follows: "Diversos tipos indígenas.—Por su fisonomía y por lo propio de sus vestiduras, estos hombres daban una fuerte impresión de realidad" (Various Indigenous types.—Due to their physiognomy and the appropriateness of their dress, these men gave a very strong impression of reality).[80] These three Indigenous men come across as somber, austere, and stoic in the pictures. In this sense,

Figure 1.3. "El Gran Desfile Histórico," *La Semana Ilustrada*, September 23, 1910. Courtesy of the Biblioteca Miguel Lerdo de Tejada de la Secretaría de Hacienda y Crédito Público.

they certainly give the impression of that imagined "reality" with which non-Indigenous Mexicans associated Indigenous groups.

In his efforts to portray an authentic representation of these foundational scenes of Mexico's history, José Casarín sent agents to the states of Tlaxcala, Chiapas, Oaxaca, Morelos, and San Luis Potosí and even to the National Penitentiary to recruit Indigenous people to participate in the parade. For instance, the Tlaxcaltecan contingent of Indigenous men had been sent by the governor of Tlaxcala, Próspero Cahuantzi, upon request. Casarín also requested twenty beautiful Indigenous women from the governor of San Luis Potosí, Manuel Sánchez Rivero, as well as 250 Indigenous men. The state of Morelos was also supposed to send 250 Indigenous men, but the men refused to participate because they were afraid they would be sent to war.[81] This response from Indigenous groups in Morelos captures how certain Indigenous communities strategically resisted the state's interpellation to perform indigeneity to fit cosmopolitan narratives and national discourses.[82] Similarly, the organizers recruited Spaniards or Spanish-looking Mexicans to portray the *gachupines* (people born in Spain, which became a derogatory term for Spaniards during the fight for independence) during the parade. This insistence on supposed historical accuracy demanded an active reformulation of embodied performances of indigeneity and colonial fantasies. Certainly, Indigenous people from different geographical locations belonged to different ethnic groups. And yet Casarín choreographed their embodied experience of indigeneity to perform the nation en masse. One of the chronicles notes that 2,800 people participated in the Desfile, including students, professionals, and numerous people from all social classes.[83]

Whether they came from Indigenous communities in other states, the penitentiary, or surrounding urban areas, Indigenous people caused as much anxiety and ambivalence as they elicited admiration. The Porfirian government had certainly taken the necessary steps to deal with their physical presence in the city. In fact, some officials suggested that Indigenous people trade their cotton pants for "regular" pants and their sandals for shoes so that they could mix with the rest of the popular classes in Mexico City, symbolically whitening their presence. This suggestion was ignored. Paradoxically, the festivities depended on the invisible labor performed by urban Indigenous communities and hundreds of other workers and servants. The number of Indigenous people living not far from the Zócalo and the neighboring communities had recently been growing because of the forced displacements, as their lands were taken away from them and privatized.[84] The reality was that the Porfirian bourgeoisie and foreign visitors shared the public space during the festivities with both Indigenous people and peasants, as well as with visitors who had arrived from other states, thanks to the reduced prices of train tickets.[85]

In many ways, then, the Desfile paraded a crystallizing notion of lo mexicano, performing an official version of history and choreographing a fraught sense of civic culture. The Desfile was not just a "visual nationalistic lecture" [86] but also a performative and kinesthetic lesson that called Mexican nationals to corporeally recognize themselves in a monumentalized patriotic history and foreigners to partake of the exotic cosmopolitanism that Mexico offered. It is significant that the literacy rate in Mexico overall had increased only from 14.4 percent to 19.7 percent between 1895 and 1910; in Mexico City, the literacy rate was estimated to be only 45 percent. The process of educating the peasant and Indigenous populations and inculcating a national identity via public education remained in many regards unfinished, if not a failure.[87] Despite the continuing need for public education, many of the events, like the Garden Party in Chapultepec Park, were exclusive, designed entirely for the upper classes and foreign dignitaries.[88] With the exception of public events, such as the inauguration of the Ángel de la Independencia and the Juárez monument, access was restricted. And yet the fact that some events were public, with some of them becoming spectacles for the masses, reveals that the shaping of a mestizo nation required grappling with indigeneity not only discursively and visually but also corporeally.

This indigeneity was symbolically and physically embodied, which is to say that Indigenous bodies operated as a site for the expression and representation of beliefs and values. For non-Indigenous Mexicans and foreign visitors, the physical presence of hundreds of Indigenous people marching through the streets of Mexico City provoked ambivalent responses. Above all, there was a sense of nostalgia for the glorious Indigenous past of the so-called Aztec Empire. As one of the chronicles notes, "El grupo de Moctezuma era aún más brillante: despertaba en la imaginación el recuerdo de aquella corte de los emperadores mexicanos, soberbia por las riquezas naturales empleadas en sus ornatos y también por la fiereza de sus guerreros" (Moctezuma's group was even more brilliant: it awakened in the imagination the memory of that court of Mexican emperors, a pride for the natural wealth used in their ornaments and also for the fierceness of their warriors).[89] The performance of the past summoned vivid images of the splendor of the Aztec civilization. In doing so, it appealed to the imagination of and affective investments in a sense of exoticness that was expected as part of the experience of modernity in a country like Mexico. Genero García similarly notes that Moctezuma's entourage was "notable por la brillantez y riqueza de sus trajes, armas, distintivos é insignias. . . . El conjunto resultaba original y, además, noble, por lo que arrancaba, á su paso, ruidosos aplausos" (notable because of the brilliance and richness of its garments, arms, emblems, and insignias. . . . The group came across as original, and also noble, which is why it elicited an enthusiastic ovation as it passed by).[90] Overall, the material objects signaling a glorious Indigenous past—the garments, the insignias, the golden palanquin, and the décor—conjured a sense of distinctiveness. This exotic distinctiveness was produced by the corporeal motions of real Indigenous people.

Moctezuma's entourage and palanquin became one of the best-received and best-documented contingents of the Desfile Histórico. Figure 1.4. illustrates how Moctezuma II traveled throughout the city as if he were a contemporary, encountering thousands of spectators before his official meeting with Cortés in the Zócalo. Interestingly, the caption of figure 1.4 symbolically suggests such a historical continuity: "Moctezuma II, Emperador de los aztecas, paseó por las principales avenidas metropolitanas

Figure 1.4. "Moctezuma II," *La Semana Ilustrada*, September 23, 1910. Courtesy of the Biblioteca Miguel Lerdo de Tejada de la Secretaría de Hacienda y Crédito Público.

la mañana del 15 de Septiembre de 1910" (Moctezuma II, Emperor of the Aztecs, passed through the main metropolitan avenues the morning of September 15, 1910). The image portrays this festive encounter. To the left and right of the entourage are several men from different socio-economic backgrounds and ages (as shown by their attire and especially their hats), admiring the Indigenous men carrying Moctezuma II or smiling straight at the camera. The Indigenous men carrying Moctezuma II look more composed and serious, and most of them look straight at the camera. Unlike Moctezuma II, who is wearing sandals and an ornate headpiece with an eagle, the Indigenous men who carry him on a golden palanquin are barefoot and wear simple headpieces with two or three feathers. All of them wear their long hair down and are dressed in loincloths and long capes. One can only wonder how these Indigenous men felt about embodying the glorious Aztec past while being reminded of the bodily excess of their presence. Although they may well have come from different localities and belonged to different ethnic groups, they were reduced to a normative understanding of indigeneity and consigned to the pre-Hispanic era of the so-called Aztecs. Their choreographed embodied experience at once erased and mythologized their Indigenous singularity.[91] Their actions and symbols were intended by the festivities' organizers to conjure a long-gone past, and yet through the very performance of that past and their moving bodies, the Indigenous participants reaffirmed their own contemporaneity. Figure 1.4, then, captures the embodied responses by spectators and parade participants to scenarios of nationalism and technological innovation, particularly those of the Indigenous people who performed the nation.

Whereas the Porfirian liberals wanted to celebrate Indigenous elements pertaining to the past, they sought to restrain and even deny the Indigenous people's physical and cultural presence, for instance by limiting their movement throughout the city. Some scholars, noting this contradiction, characterize the presence of Indigenous people during the Desfile Histórico as simply the result of the Centennial planners' obsession with authenticity and historical accuracy. But the Indigenous people and the spectators of the Desfile Histórico were more than "living mannequins" or historical props.[92] Through their bodily movements, they enacted an alternative form of collectivity that allowed them to rehearse a sense of community identity that materialized during the revolutionary and postrevolutionary periods. Their coming and moving together allowed the emergence of what SanSan Kwan has termed "affinities in motion," which are "alternative forms of collectivity, always implicated in formations of power, sometimes resistive, always temporary."[93] Produced by bodies in movement at particular spatiotemporal instances, the contingent community formations generated via affinities in motion make it possible to consider formulations of indigeneity during Mexico's festivities that went beyond the exploitation of Indigenous people as living historical props for authenticity and accuracy. Although Indigenous participation was framed within a liberal understanding of history and social stratification (that Indigenous populations needed to be modernized to become productive citizens and workers), the physical presence of thousands of Indigenous people and peasants and their responses and resistance to choreographies of nationalism and modernity enacted an alternative embodied sociality.

Even though it is impossible to know for certain what affective investments were held by Indigenous people, peasants, workers, and the popular classes, because most of the archival material privileges the voices and experiences of foreigners and members of the Porfirian elites, we can consider the ephemeral residue of what remains, the traces left by those who are otherwise ignored. In this act of "queering the archive," we can trace the movement, affects, and embodiments of individuals who are no longer here. As the queer theorist José Esteban Muñoz contends, we must grapple with "an evidence that has been queered in relation to the laws of what counts as proof."[94] In other words, Muñoz challenges us to go beyond normative understandings of evidence to recognize other forms of knowledge and communication. This reconception of evidence makes it possible to analyze how embodied cultural performances were experienced in a particular time and space.[95] In this book, this methodological move is less about replicating embodied practices than about creatively approximating gestural materials from extant ephemera to recognize how meaning is produced through bodies in motion and to expand our understanding of these rehearsals of Mexican nationalism.

Unlike most of the available archival materials, which summon movement through static objects such as chronicles, official programs, and historical photographs, the extant historical footage of the festivities (particularly the Desfile Histórico) enables me to consider the actual movement of the multitudinous crowd that witnessed, experienced, and participated in the centennial celebrations. Thanks to the restoration of the historical footage by the Filmoteca Nacional (the Universidad Nacional Autónoma de México's National Film Library), I was able to consult footage attributed to the film studios of the Hermanos Alva (Alva Brothers) and Salvador Toscano.[96] The footage shows people standing or running to follow the parade and their embodied responses to the various processions and the presence of cameras. Many of the people moving in the back of the sidewalks belonged to the lower classes, as indicated by their clothing: shawls, braids, hats, and sandals, to mention a few recognizable items.[97] In the extant footage, we can see Indigenous women wearing their traditional *rebozos*, accompanied by other women and sometimes children, as well as men belonging to the popular classes, leaving ephemeral traces of their bodily comportment. Unlike most of the bourgeoisie and the middle and upper classes, Indigenous people, workers, and other members of the lower classes did not sit in the grandstands, stand on balconies or at windows, or occupy the front rows with parasols or elegant hats to shade their faces from the sun. Such costumes and accessories, together with the space their wearers occupied, marked the spectators' class and social status. Indigenous people, peasants, and lower-class workers struggled to get a glimpse of the different processions;

Figure 1.5. "Desfile Histórico," still from *Desfile Histórico 1910 de Salvador Toscano.*
Courtesy of Filmoteca UNAM, Dirección General de Actividades Cinematográficas.

they ran from one place to the other, bringing their children with them, and at times even jumped.

In figure 1.5, an image taken from the historical footage from Salvador Toscano's work, there is still an emphasis on the conglomeration of people and the monumentality of the Desfile. Nevertheless, a different kind of collectivity is set in motion. The camera is positioned at a higher angle and remains stationary. The image shows part of Moctezuma's large entourage. Unlike the official chronicles that try to relegate Indigenous presence to a nostalgic past, here we can observe the tensions of the official discourse via its embodiment and performance. The footage shows a rehearsal of a different kind of collectivity. Figure 1.5 captures bodies in movement as well as gestures and other corporeal motions, even though a number of people are standing still to watch the procession. In addition to the two long rows of Indigenous people marching in the middle of the street and the hundreds of spectators standing on each side, a group of women on the left side of the image wear long skirts and traditional shawls. These Indigenous or peasant women are moving down the street following the procession while interacting with each other and the rest of the audience: some are walking behind the standing crowds; others are carrying their children; some are stepping back from the crowds; and a couple of younger women are jumping. Some men follow, running, jumping, and going along with the procession. As the parade moves along, a visual tension emerges between what is being represented—the magnificence of an Indigenous past and its monumental staging—and the affinities in motion that highlight the ambivalence at play: between members of the Porfirian middle and upper classes who are corporeally engaging with the Indigenous people in the Desfile through applause, smiles, hand motions, and other embodied gestures, and the bodies of the Indigenous people, peasants, and workers who are also physically present at the parade. All these people witness the Desfile, occupy the same space, clap together, and share a festive experience, rehearsing a contingent embodied sociality.

The ephemeral traces of the Desfile Histórico captured in the moving pictures of the extant footage can only gesture toward the kind of alternative collectivity produced by moving bodies. Whereas these affinities in motion may not necessarily signal alternative formulations of power, they point to the contradictory and complex ways bodies in movement operate within regimes of control and the affective investments generated in such experiences. These ephemeral traces in the official archive are significant because they invite us to consider different ways the nation in 1910 was rehearsed, felt, and collectively experienced even before the Mexican Revolution, which began just two months later in November 1910, and the advent of the cultural postrevolutionary agenda of the 1920s and 1930s.

The Indigenous Bodies of Mexican Nationalism

At the inauguration of the 17th Congress of Americanists during the Centenario, Justo Sierra, considered the most prominent intellectual figure of the Porfiriato, spoke to national and international delegates, including Franz Boas and Edward Seler, regarding Mexico's Indigenous presence. He remarked, "Todo ese mundo pre-cortesiano cuyos archivos monumentales venís á estudiar aquí, es nuestro, es nuestro pasado, nos lo hemos incorporado como un preámbulo que cimenta y explica nuestra verdadera historia nacional, la que data de la unión de conquistados y conquistadores para fundar un pueblo mestizo que . . . está adquiriendo el derecho de ser grande" (All of that pre-Cortesian world, whose monumental archives you have come to study here, is ours, is our past; we have incorporated it as a preamble that explains and lays the foundations of our true national history, which dates back to the union between the conquered and the conquerors to found a mestizo people that . . . is acquiring the right to be great).[98] Sierra's remarks reveal the ambivalence and contradictory position of the Porfirian liberal elites. On the one hand, they positioned Indigenous people as inferior, degenerated, and underdeveloped, explaining their racial inferiority via pseudoscientific and positivist discourses. On the other hand, they shared a belief that Indigenous people could be redeemed via education.[99] There was, however, an increasing focus on mestizos, who could become not only productive citizens and workers but also the legitimate inheritors of a world to come, a mestizo world whose monumental past congress attendees studied as part of Mexico's true national history, as Sierra's words illustrate. The Indigenous bodies of Mexican nationalism therefore had to be transformed into productive mestizo citizens.

The material transformation of Mexico City and the scripts rehearsed for the Centenario required the Porfirian elites to grapple with the physical and symbolic presence of Indigenous people. The Porfirian indigenismo exemplified by Justo Sierra and José Casarín and by the author of the chronicle of La danza de los tastoanes, Alberto Santoscoy, resorted to different strategies to deal with the physical presence of Indigenous Mexicans, not just their representations. The promotion of a Porfirian mestizaje required members of the intellectual, cultural, economic, and political elites to attend to the increasing mobilization of Indigenous bodies in rural and urban areas. Although the Porfirian indigenismo did not seek to integrate Indigenous voices per se, it was forced to grapple with the undeniable presence of Indigenous bodies, which had yet to become productive citizens.

For Carlos Monsiváis, the festivities of the Centenario were ultimately "un paréntesis, una ensoñación programada" (a parenthesis, a planned fantasy).[100] As I have discussed throughout this chapter, the centennial festivities and Mexico's participation in the Universal Exposition reveal more than just a fictional or fantastical account of the Porfiriato.[101] These festive instances are critical windows onto the power dynamics that structure competing social and cultural relations. The expressive cultures I have analyzed in this chapter, from La danza de los tastoanes to the Desfile Histórico, illustrate how the Porfirian regime engaged with Indigenous difference, not just discursively and visually but also corporeally and kinesthetically.

With the fall of the Porfirian regime a year after the centennial celebrations in 1911, the notion of a modern, cosmopolitan Mexico collapsed. So too did the dreams of scientific and economic progress and the consolidation of a mestizo nation.[102] The Revolution of 1910 would last a decade, preventing any other major attempts to instantiate a sense of a cosmopolitan modernity. And yet the revolutionary movement allowed for the rehearsal of other kinds of affinities in motion. The alternative collectivities brought about by the armed struggle enabled Mexican citizens from all social classes and ethnoracial groups to experience a sense of community identity that in many ways had been anticipated by the centennial celebrations. A contingent, shared sense of community, always embedded in power structures, had enabled the participants and spectators of the Centenario to imagine and perhaps witness a different kind of future together, an embodied sociality that would have to wait until 1921 to crystallize again.

CHAPTER 2

La Noche Mexicana and the Staging of
a Festive Mexico

On September 6, 1921, *El Universal*, one of Mexico's most widely circulated newspapers of the time, published an article titled "La Noche
Mexicana en el Bosque de Chapultepec" (Mexican Night at Chapultepec
Park), offering a plan for staging a massive fiesta celebration to take place
during the last week of September. The event was expected to attract at
least thirty thousand people. Bourgeois women and the civic associations they represented, such as the Red and White Crosses, were to play
an important role, staffing the multiple stands that would be scattered
throughout the park to sell flowers, confetti, and other festive goods. The
article went on to explain: "Existe el propósito, para que nada falte a lo
típico de esta fiesta, de que las damas encargadas de los puestos vayan
ataviadas no sólo del clásico traje de china poblana, sino también del de
tehuana, ranchera, norteñas, mestizas . . . y todos aquellos objetos de arte
típicamente nacionales" (So that no traditional element in this festivity is
left out, it is intended that the ladies in charge of the stands wear not only
the classic china poblana costume, but also that of the Tehuana, ranchera,
norteña, mestiza . . . and all other typically national, artistic objects).[1] The
organizers were relying on the bourgeois women to embody the great
diversity of Mexico, which at this moment was not reduced to the iconic
figures of the china poblana and the charro; it also included *norteñas,
mestizas, rancheras*, and of course Tehuanas.[2] And to further emphasize
the popular and regional character of the celebration, the article mentioned that "En los puestos habrá vendimias, entre otras cosas, de agua
fresca, la que estará depositada en las clásicas ollas tapatías y será servida
en jícaras bellamente decoradas por los indios de Pátzcuaro. No faltarán
los puestos de platillos mexicanos, como de asados de pollo, enchiladas,
tamales, atole y buñuelos" (Among the things for sale in the stands, there
will be agua fresca, which will be stored in classic Tapatío pots [i.e.,

from Guadalajara] and will be served in bowls beautifully decorated by the Indians from Pátzcuaro. Typical Mexican dishes will not be missing, such as chicken stews, enchiladas, tamales, atole [hot maize drink], and buñuelos [fritters]).[3] The food and objects, together with the bourgeois women wearing traditional attire, had to represent the country's regional variations, classes, and ethnoracial groups, a mosaic of Mexicos, a celebration of a country that was both imagined and performed. The spectacle of popular and regional symbols implied a narrative that recognized these symbols as typically Mexican, acknowledging the contributions and skills of the Indigenous people from Pátzcuaro alongside those of the Red and White Crosses and the bourgeois women who represented them.

The morning of September 28, 1921, *El Demócrata: Diario independiente de la mañana* announced on the front page in bold red letters: "La 'Noche Mexicana' congregó en Chapultepec ayer, a muy cerca de quinientas mil personas" (The "Mexican Night" Brought Together in Chapultepec Yesterday Close to Five Hundred Thousand People). The subtitle emphasized the success of the evening: "Esta Noche Será Memorable Siempre que se Recuerde Algún Gigantesco Regocijo Genuinamente Popular" (This Night will be memorable whenever such a massive rejoicing genuinely popular is remembered).[4] The article included an image of two *trajineras*, the typical decorated boats from Xochimilco, with people dressed as charros and chinas singing and paddling as well as members of the bourgeoisie in Mexico's iconic Chapultepec Park. In addition to enthusiastically summarizing the events, the author of the piece underscored the coming together of different classes. The "calm" bourgeoisie and the people, el pueblo, converged en masse in a scene described as one taken from the *Arabian Nights* or from the royal gardens of Versailles, although it was still profoundly "Mexican." The article's references, both cosmopolitan and popular, gestured toward the need to describe Mexico with imagery that used the cultural grammar and vocabulary of the arrival of modern times. In so doing, the newspaper article invited readers to literally imagine a festive nation, that is, to construct a visual and abstract idea of a Mexico that celebrated the diverse groups that made it modern and popular by resorting to national visual designs and figurative foreign references. Everyone, according to the article, was meant to see themselves reflected in this emerging iteration of a postrevolutionary festive Mexico. Even the lighting, signaling the presence of modern technology, contributed to the effect: it was a "genuinely popular" spectacle where the image of a modern Mexico was not only imagined but also staged.

La Noche Mexicana took place in Chapultepec during the centennial of the consummation of Mexican Independence in 1921. It re-created regional ferias featuring both Indigenous and mestizo performers from all over the country, including the Yaqui dancers from Sonora and the jaraneros from Yucatán, in addition to the traditional chinas poblanas and charros and the increasingly popular Tehuanas representative of Oaxaca. Although the figure of the mestizo has come to embody the modern Mexican national subject, the meaning of embodiment in the postrevolutionary context of modernization has yet to be carefully examined, as I discussed in the introduction.[5] Analyzing historical photographs, pamphlets, and periodicals, I show how the fiesta enacted an embodied sociality of the popular and the mestizo, while also considering how national and transnational processes operated in the formation of the nation through the choreography of staged instances of Mexican nationalism. These nationalistic and popular renditions of the nation attempted to represent Mexico as cosmopolitan.[6] In this chapter, I probe the way the imagery of a festive Mexico emerged corporeally, gesturing toward the importance of movement for the configuration of a shared national cultural background. La Noche Mexicana's re-creation of a regional feria and Indigenous and mestizo dances functioned as a state pedagogical practice; that is, it was a rehearsal of a nationalistic embodied sociality of lo mexicano that came to configure processes of citizen formation and national belonging in postrevolutionary Mexico.

La Noche Mexicana is a unique scenario in which to examine the tensions that arose from the staging of a cosmopolitan yet locally diverse nation. The embodiment of a nationalistic aesthetics exposes the continuities, discontinuities, and contradictions of the postrevolutionary cultural agenda. This staging created an exportable image of the nation to be consumed by national and international audiences, while simultaneously inviting Mexicans to self-identify with the cosmopolitan trends of the epoch. The self-exoticization of Mexico allowed intellectual and cultural postrevolutionary elites to participate in the construction of an already cosmopolitan national identity, as discussed in the previous chapter. By resorting to an orientalist and modernist grammar that was already cosmopolitan, postrevolutionary thinkers could jump from the local and national scales to the international. This elevation of the national via the cosmopolitan, incorporating Asian, European, and North American tropes, highlights the contradictions involved in staging a nationalistic modern aesthetics. These cosmopolitan discursive and visual representations contrasted with the real bodies and objects from different parts of Mexico that gathered in the fiesta's public space.

By examining the staging of La Noche Mexicana as a paradigmatic event, I explore the cultural exchanges that took place within Mexico while considering the ways the configuration of lo mexicano responded to complex transnational phenomena. I treat lo mexicano as a scenario, with symbolic, material, and physical dimensions, that produced an imagined and embodied rendering of the nation.[7] By focusing on the staging and the embodied performance of a national identity, I argue that the shifting and ambivalent scenario of lo mexicano helped crystallize a popular idea of the nation. In what follows, I show how La Noche Mexicana was created by intellectual and cultural elites, even as the gathering of individuals to embody a modern nation performatively undid and at times even exceeded the state-sponsored project of nationalism. La Noche Mexicana was ultimately a rehearsal of what became a cosmopolitan sense of lo mexicano that at once reinforced and disavowed the fiction of a national unity.

1921: The Centennial Celebrations and the Staging of a Popular Nation

The celebrations of the consummation of the Mexican Independence in 1921 were preceded by the last centenary celebrations of the Porfirian regime in 1910, as discussed in chapter 1. The centennial celebrations of 1921 both shared the Porfirian principles and departed from them in substantial ways. The postrevolutionary government and intellectuals wanted to present Mexico as a modern nation, cosmopolitan and technologically advanced, yet with a unique Indigenous presence. In this sense, the postrevolutionary government resorted to some of the mechanisms used by the Porfirian regime, particularly those related to festive productions and public displays of the ideal vision of the nation. Nevertheless, the postrevolutionary celebrations differed from the Porfirian festivities in the vision of the nation they sought to represent and in their emphasis on the historical events that had helped to create a modern and diverse Mexico. The contributions of Mexico's Indigenous groups could no longer be displaced to an ancient past; after all, Indigenous people were increasingly present in urban centers, especially Mexico City, after the armed phase of the Mexican Revolution. Education, then, became crucial for the dissemination and imposition of an evolutionary understanding of history. The pedagogical drive that had marked the festivities of 1910 also played a role in 1921: citizen formation was inculcated via the enactment of a nationalistic cultural identity based on a progressive and teleological understanding of history.[8]

The postrevolutionary government continued the Porfirian lesson on visual culture and took it a step further by teaching Mexican citizens to perform this vision, that is, to embody it. While the postrevolutionary cultural and intellectual elites did not radically transform the evolutionary and cosmopolitan approach of the Porfirian regime, they embraced a form of cultural relativism that allowed them to incorporate the rural and Indigenous populations that had migrated to Mexico City. This cultural relativism acknowledged the coexistence of Indigenous populations without transcending the evolutionist imperative of progress and modernization, as exemplified by Manuel Gamio's *Forjando patria*. As the planning of the centennial celebrations began, the intellectual, political, and cultural elites became concerned with promoting a sense of scientific progress that accounted for modernity but that attempted to reach out to the populations the Porfirian regime had largely ignored, the Indigenous, rural, and popular classes that had been radically mobilized by the Revolution and could no longer be disregarded.

As a result, numerous events were planned to engage these large sectors of the population: from bullfights, circuses, dances, and parades to baseball games, popular arts exhibitions, health-care promotion activities, and even constructions of *escuelas del centenario* (centennial schools) to endorse public education.[9] The government also launched numerous initiatives to promote health care and patriotism: flag days, pledges of allegiance, free car tours at Chapultepec Park, and even a Declaration of the Rights of Children.[10] The Spanish and German societies, among others, organized their own commemorations. In fact, even though the rhetoric of the festivities was patriotic in character, the postrevolutionary government was also invested in attracting foreign interest, and it succeeded in enticing twenty-two nations from Latin America, Europe, and Asia to participate in the centennial.

The postrevolutionary government also relied on civic organizations, newspapers, and a newly formed committee to reach out to the vast numbers of Mexicans who had been affected by the Revolution of 1910. The turmoil of the armed phase of the Revolution caused massive numbers of bodies to be in constant movement, and migration from rural to urban spaces increased during the postrevolutionary period.[11]

Unlike the Porfirian government, the postrevolutionary government lacked the resources and infrastructure it needed; in fact, this was the first time the federal government had celebrated Mexican Independence in such a scale after the Revolution of 1910. The emphasis was actually on the centennial of the consummation of Mexican Independence, September 27.[12] Álvaro Obregón needed to distance and differentiate his government and festivities from the Porfirian celebrations. But it lacked the resources. Obregón's government then had to impose a tax—*el impuesto del centenario*—that thousands of city dwellers paid. Key cabinet members of Obregón's government, such as Alberto Pani, Plutarco Elías Calles, and Adolfo de la Huerta, who had briefly been president of Mexico in 1920, were part of the planning commission.[13] A series of newspaper articles published in *El Universal*, *El Demócrata*, and *Excélsior*—some of the main sponsors of the centennial celebrations—reveals the extent to which the committee in charge of the festivities relied on public and private organizations to carry out the activities of the centenary. *Excélsior*, *El Demócrata*, and *El Universal*, Mexico's three principal newspapers, took clear ideological and political positions: they were conservative, populist, and moderately conservative, respectively.[14] With the literacy rate in México City around 50 percent, these newspapers were crucial for disseminating information regarding the festivities; they also influenced the public opinion and political rhetoric of the time.

The newspaper articles of the period documented and emphasized the popular character of the festivities in the months prior to the celebrations. On May 15, 1921, a short article in *El Universal* confirmed the "popular character" of the centennial celebrations and extended an invitation to various associations to actively participate. The article announced the names of the individuals who were part of the organizing committee: Emiliano López Figueroa, president; Juan de Dios Bojórquez, vice-president; Carlos Argüelles, treasurer; Martín Luis Guzmán, secretary. Although the president of the committee, Emiliano López Figueroa, acknowledged the celebration of some events that were not open to the general public, the program itself was essentially of a "popular character" and was designed to celebrate the consummation of the independence movement. Most of the festivities would be unprecedented in that they were to be organized for all social classes, without any restrictions; they were to take place from September 15 to September 27.[15] Another article featured in *El Universal* on June 2 reiterated the accessibility of the festivities, broadly described the major proposed activities, and drew attention to a couple of key elements. First, a variety of activities hitherto designed mostly for the upper classes were organized for all classes in order to mobilize a sense of "Mexicanness" among the participants and hence a sense of belonging. Second, the centenary would stage Mexican products, cultural or otherwise, for foreign audiences, including an exhibition of "popular art" (although showcasing products was not the celebration's main focus).[16] Sharing the language of progress characteristic of the Porfirian regime, the article's focus shifted from industrial products to the inclusion of local artistic and cultural products made by el pueblo. The description of the Exposición de Arte Popular discursively elevated the goods and the "artistic objects" "fabricated" by el pueblo to cultural objects worthy of being displayed.[17] Functioning as yet another public lesson in visual culture by the government, the Exposición de Arte Popular aimed to identify the diversity of Mexico's local artistic production and include it alongside the industrial goods produced in the country. But what rendered these artistic products legible as "Mexican"?

The configuration of a Mexican visual aesthetics played an essential role in producing a sense of national belonging. As Rick López astutely argues, focusing on the creation of a national aesthetics reveals "how art has served not just as a medium of conquest, resistance, and *mestizaje* but also of nation formation, accommodation, and solidarity."[18] On the one hand, artisan products were marketed to an international audience, and many of the key players, especially the intellectuals, already belonged to transnational networks in the cultural, economic, and political spheres.[19] On the other hand, the consolidation of a popular nationalistic cultural movement intensified the exchange between the intellectual and cultural elites, the transnational markets, and the "local experience."[20] The nationalistic postrevolutionary project responded to local and transnational developments that simultaneously advanced and altered the configuration of a popular aesthetics and the concomitant interpellation of a national public.

The formation and dissemination of a national aesthetics constituted a major pedagogical enterprise. The centenary festivities were designed to celebrate Mexican Independence, but at the same time the staging of lo mexicano required the education of el pueblo. Accordingly, the postrevolutionary government launched an aggressive campaign to teach Mexican citizens how to partake in the incipient sense of national belonging. The article "El pueblo tendrá acceso" revealed the critical role played by education in the formation of a nationalistic culture. It highlighted the impact of education in promoting the "artistic environment" that already existed within the nation and that had not been properly fostered before, mentioning the work of José Vasconcelos in the Ministry of Education as paramount for this cultural task.[21] The pedagogical dimension of the postrevolutionary project was crucial for the emergence and configuration of a national aesthetics, foregrounding the intersection between the arts and education. Here lies the fundamental difference between the Porfirian and the postrevolutionary nationalistic projects: whereas the former featured the discursive and visual construction of lo mexicano, the latter involved the formation of a popular national public through a pedagogical praxis centered on an embodied experience: the coming together of bodies.

In the postrevolutionary project, the festive character of the celebrations was conflated with the notion of the popular, an aspect that Vasconcelos eventually promoted through public education and the development of cultural projects, including massive and numerous public performances, such as the inauguration of the National Stadium. The insistence on the broad accessibility of the centennial festivities thus underlined the celebrations' dual nature, both festive and educational:

> Por primera vez en México, el pueblo tendrá acceso a espectáculos que siempre habían sido dedicados a las clases privilegiadas; esta disposición que es muy acertada, tendrá por objeto además de un carácter festivo, el de educación, ya que muchos de esos espectáculos consistirán en conciertos, funciones teatrales, representaciones de ópera, juegos florales, sin olvidar los torneos de viriles deportes que seguramente serán el ejemplo para que se instituyan en nuestro país agrupaciones que procuren el desarrollo de nuestro [sic] cultura física.

> (For the first time in Mexico, the people will have access to the spectacles that had always been destined for the privileged classes; this arrangement, which is a very good one, will have not only a festive objective but an educational one, since many of those spectacles will consist of concerts, theatrical functions, opera performances, floral games, as well as tournaments of virile sports that certainly serve as an example for instituting in our country associations that foster the development of our physical culture.)[22]

These public performances were meant to shape national bodies into citizens—and into a national audience, given the importance of cultural performances. The events were spectacles of citizen formation. The public performances were to be festive, given the celebratory character of the events, yet they were also to educate the public, particularly those who had never had access to such spectacles. If "virile sports" attempted to promote and develop a "physical culture," the cultural productions formed Mexican citizens through the embodied performance of a nationalistic cultural identity.

Encouraged by the state-sponsored organizing committee of the centenary, private and civic institutions actively contributed to the formation of this identity, organizing their own events that, as in the case of *El Universal*'s "India Bonita" pageant (see fig. 2.1), literally shaped the embodiment of a gendered nationalistic aesthetics.[23] The parades, beauty contests, massive performances, exhibitions, and other such festivities were aimed at reconfiguring the notion of the popular and the Indigenous to make them suitable for inclusion in the national image. The performance of these bodies in public places therefore revealed a complex picture that articulated female and Indigenous embodiments of lo mexicano.

It is at this juncture that the body becomes paramount for grasping

Figure 2.1. María Bibiana Uribe, "La India Bonita," *El Universal*, September 1921. Photo Courtesy of Biblioteca Miguel Lerdo de Tejada de la Secretaría de Hacienda y Crédito Público.

the contingency of lo mexicano, especially as illustrated in the case of La Noche Mexicana. The focus shifted from representing a cosmopolitan vision of Mexico primarily for foreigners and the elites to staging a popular and therefore more diverse image of Mexico for the people as well. Even though the postrevolutionary vision of Mexico was still the product of the intellectual and cultural elites, influenced by the cultural currents of the moment (as it had been in the Porfirian regime), the incorporation of the popular into the imagery of the nation ultimately led to the staging of ambivalent and at times conflicting scenarios of Mexico.

The staging of lo mexicano thus organized a process whose meaning was always incomplete, transitory, polyphonic, and ambivalent. The moving bodies of the festive productions from the centenary celebrations contrasted with the more conventional image of lo mexicano, understood as static, hyper-masculine, and mestizo. Thinking of lo mexicano as a scenario, as both a metaphor and a mechanism, allows us to attend to its symbolic and material cultural construction, which is embedded in larger historical processes. By focusing on the notion of a scenario as a site where these processes are enacted, I draw attention to the material and symbolic power of the staging of national narratives, popular or otherwise.[24] The affective and symbolic power of lo mexicano congealed through its continuous rehearsal, through repetitive stagings. The significance of lo mexicano as the enactment of the popular derives from such historically ritualized operations. Diana Taylor insists that the physical place where representations take place and the actions represented or scenes metonymically complement each other.[25] She contends that scenarios function as "meaning-making paradigms that structure social environments, behaviors, and potential outcomes . . . [making] visible, yet again, what is already there."[26] I want to highlight the signifying function of scenarios and their ability to make visible what already exists in a given spatiotemporal frame, functioning as a structuring mechanism that predates any particular staging. Along with the physical and symbolic construction of any scenario, the spectators/actors partake in the elaboration of narratives of what is represented in any given place. By foregrounding the role of bodies in motion in public spaces, I attend to the ways the popular emerges corporeally, highlighting both the performativity and the physicality of a shared embodied cultural background. Forming and informing a national public—educating the spectators and actors of Mexican nationalism—and operating as a mechanism and a metaphor, the scenario of La Noche Mexicana allows us to think about the material, corporeal, and discursive ways lo mexicano was presented and represented in 1921.

Summoning La Noche Mexicana: Visual and Discursive Scenarios of a Festive Mexico

La Noche Mexicana is a useful site in which to examine scenarios—discursive, material, symbolic—and their concomitant choreographies of Mexican nationalism, the emergence of competing nationalistic narratives, and the consolidation of a national public. Contrary to the advertising discussed at the beginning of the chapter, La Noche Mexicana was originally intended to emulate a European garden party to showcase Mexico's technological modernity, including its electric lighting and paved roads. In 1910, the Porfirian Garden Party that took place during the centennial festivities showcased a spectacle of fireworks and lighting with a battle of boats.[27] It was a visually spectacular event. The mythical theme of an allegorical battle of floats combined the preference of the Díaz regime for European tropes along with the staging of modernity through a show of lights. La Noche Mexicana, however, would be not a garden party but a feria, a popular, multitudinous fair. The state's sponsorship of La Noche Mexicana was crucial for the cultural integration of the nation. La Noche Mexicana and the Exposición de Arte Popular were completely sponsored by the postrevolutionary regime, placing contemporary Indigenous and popular culture at the center of the nationalistic enterprise.[28]

This radical shift, from the privileging of European aesthetics by the Porfirian regime to the acknowledgment and inclusion of Indigenous and popular cultural production, marked the development of a national aesthetic discourse. As Rick López has noted, both La Noche Mexicana and the Exposición de Arte Popular "celebrated folkloric expressions [that] conflated campesinos and Indians, and though some of the arts they drew upon had urban roots and grew out of mestizo or even Spanish practices, they generalized the forms they celebrated as coming from 'rural Indians.'"[29] These "folkloric expressions," however, required the intellectual and cultural elites to select, process, and disseminate them to national and international audiences.[30] On the one hand, this process recognized an "Indigenous essence" as the raw material from which to elaborate a national aesthetic language; in so doing, it emphasized the need for an artistic and intellectual intervention in order to bring it up to Europeanized aesthetic standards. On the other hand, for a national public to emerge, the cultural and intellectual elites had to "indigenize" European cultural forms to make them legible to the public.

While I share López's view that the emergence of an aesthetic language, specifically a "visual aesthetics," was one of the major consequences of the state-sponsored intellectual and cultural interventions, I want to draw attention to the impact that public cultural performances and particularly La Noche Mexicana had on the emergence of a corporeal national culture and to the way this staging of the nation made it difficult to produce a unified rendering of the nation. La Noche Mexicana produced an embodied idea of the nation that drew from cultural practices of the international scene while treating Mexico's resources as raw materials in a gesture of self-exoticization and self-aestheticization. At the same time, the staging of this particular Mexican scenario was performatively complicated and at times undone by the embodied performances and gestures of the bodies that cited the idea of a festive Mexico. This staging was the result of an assemblage of what eventually became a cosmopolitan sense of Mexicanness that mobilized and simultaneously unsettled the fiction of a national unity.[31] The nationalistic corporeal expressions attributed to lo mexicano speak of an embodied form of sociality that highlights how bodies signify on their own in addition to or despite being asked to represent something else. In this sense, the staging and therefore the shifting and ambivalent scenarios of lo mexicano that La Noche Mexicana ultimately represented juxtaposed the elitist representations of the nation with the concrete yet ephemeral actions of various national bodies.

Before discussing the impact of the embodied sociality choreographed by La Noche Mexicana, it is important to consider the pedagogical motivations and the discursive and visual components of the postrevolutionary cultural project. After all, the staging of La Noche Mexicana occurred discursively through promotional materials and advertisements prior to the event. The proliferation of visual and discursive representations of lo mexicano during the centennial festivities reflected the need to disseminate national icons and ideals among the general public. The postrevolutionary thinkers needed to legitimate the regime and unify the nation while rendering consumable and therefore teachable a Mexican cultural identity. The cultural and political debates of the time centered similarly on the ideal of a bond between a national aesthetics and education. The aesthetic dimension of lo mexicano was intimately linked to patriotism and education.

The pedagogical impulse that characterized the formation of a cultural identity resonated differently corporeally than it did discursively and visually, particularly as staged at La Noche Mexicana. The periodicals and photographic archives reveal a complex picture of the physical and symbolic bringing together of bodies to represent the nation, a gathering that at times disrupted and exceeded the state-sponsored project of nation building that circulated through the promotional materials of the event. La Noche Mexicana brought together a popular public on two consecutive nights in Chapultepec, Mexico, in late September 1921.[32] Starting in mid-September, local newspapers such as *El Demócrata* and *El Universal* advertised the programs of the numerous activities that were taking place daily during the centennial celebrations. The day before the festival of La Noche Mexicana, Sunday, September 25, *El Universal* published a note stating that the entrance to the event would be entirely free, given the great public interest in the celebration, ensuring access to all citizens without the need for a ticket or an invitation.[33] The committee had originally intended to charge five pesos, but they had soon run out of tickets. As the note claimed, 160,000 people had expressed interest in attending; 15,000 tickets had already been printed and distributed, potentially leaving out 145,000 people. This short note also confirmed the title of the event, "Noche Mexicana," and the activities, such as regional songs and dances, a cavalcade, and carnival activities typical of a feria in addition to fireworks and a lighting show.[34] The significance of this celebration of Mexican nationalism was cemented by the expected attendance of President Álvaro Obregón.

Adolfo Best Maugard, a cosmopolitan artist, had been hired in August 1921 to stage a spectacle of modern nationalism. Best Maugard had long been part of the national scene. He had previously worked with Manuel Gamio and Franz Boas in 1911, illustrating the pre-Hispanic objects they had found while excavating in Teotihuacán.[35] Later in the decade, after a stay in Europe during the armed phase of the Revolution, he had designed the scenography for *Fantasía mexicana*, Anna Pavlova's famous performance that included the interpretation of El jarabe tapatío, first in Mexico in 1919 and later in New York in 1920.[36] *Fantasía mexicana* staged the story of a group of women selling flowers who fell in love with a group of charros in Xochimilco. It featured nine popular Mexican sones, with El jarabe tapatío as the climax; Pavlova danced it en pointe dressed as a china poblana with Alexandre Volinine as a charro.[37] In his design of a traditional Uruapan gourd as the scenography and backdrop for this "avant-garde" performance, Best Maugard was inspired by cosmopolitan modernism, romantic primitivism, and postrevolutionary nationalism; indeed, as Rick López claims, he created "nothing less than a new aesthetic vocabulary of *mexicanidad*."[38] The mixture of aesthetic, material, and corporeal languages that *Fantasía mexicana* put on stage brought to the fore the tensions and collisions between modernity and tradition, which Pavlova's body literally mobilized as she danced to the tunes of a Mexican popular song. Her moving body symbolized modern beauty and corporeal discipline, enhanced sonically and visually by Mexican traditional art. Best Maugard therefore played a foundational role not only in consolidating a discursive and visual language of lo mexicano but also in producing lo mexicano's performance and embodiment. To accomplish this, he championed an Indigenous aesthetics as representative of the nation. This Mexican cosmopolitan artist aestheticized certain elements of Indigenous artistic productions and literally put them on stage.[39]

On Monday, September 26, 1921, *El Universal*, together with *Excélsior, El Demócrata,* and other major newspapers, published the entire program of La Noche Mexicana, with activities starting at 7:30 p.m.[40] It emphasized various moments throughout the night that captured different aspects of the cultural nationalism at play in this staging of lo mexicano. The program began with an allusion to Reforma, Mexico City's principal avenue and the gem of the Porfirian celebrations, as the epitome of a country in transition, with carriages and vehicles, symbols of a modern urban metropolis. Yet as soon as the people arrived at the entrance and crossed the spectacular arch that symbolically and materially demarcated a festive space, they would enter a different world, a fiesta of an "essentially Mexicanist" character. The multiplicity of temporal and spatial coordinates and the description of activities reinforced the idea of a confluence of various Mexicos in one location: the Chapultepec Forest. Whereas the Spanish name refers to a forest (*bosque*), the Nahuatl name emphasizes the geographic description of the hilly place (*tepetl*); the literal translation is the "mount of grasshoppers." The place itself was referred to as a scenario. This use of the term recalls Taylor's definition of scenario, which denotes a physical space and the behaviors, actions, and discourses that coconstitute it. The Chapultepec Forest, with the legendary *ahuehuetes*, commonly known as the "Moctezuma" cypress, immediately evoked the long pre-Hispanic and colonial history of the place and the more recent history of the US invasion, the French occupation, and the Porfirian regime. Cosmopolitan but pointedly local, the Chapultepec Forest epitomized the massiveness and sophistication of the celebrations: the physical space, the stages, the lighting, the performances, and the national public.

The scenario that La Noche Mexicana staged conjured different publics. The appearance of a national public depended upon the summoning

Figure 2.2. Entrance to Chapultepec Park, designed by Adolfo Best Maugard. IISUE/ AHUNAM/Fondo Martín Luis Guzmán Franco/Sección: Historia de la Revolución Mexicana/Caja: 167/E18-00925.

of a sociality that enabled "contingent adscriptions" to an idea of Mexico. Michael Warner contends that a public conjures a "stranger sociality," a mode of belonging that actualizes the discourse that produces it.[41] In the case of the print media and promotional materials, such as the publication of the program that encouraged people to participate in the centenary celebrations, the aim was to foster a sense of national belonging, thereby creating not equal citizens (there was a distinction between bourgeois women and "Indians") but rather a national public. It is because of this sense of openness and impersonality characteristic of the notion of publicness, as Warner proposes it, that the term *public* is more useful than *citizenry* for describing the interpellation of a national sociality in 1921. In his assessment of Benedict Anderson's foundational book *Imagined Communities*, the Mexican cultural critic Claudio Lomnitz rejects the presupposition that nationalism creates a single imagined community, because it differentiates "full citizens" from partial or "weak" citizens such as women, children, and Indigenous groups. Instead, he proposes a redefinition of nation as a community in which a "full citizen" can act as a "potential broker" between the state and other "part citizens."[42]

Both Lomnitz and Warner insist on the potential of being a participant in the national community.

Despite the differentiated access to an imagined community, the organizers of La Noche Mexicana conjured a popular embodied sociality that could not be reduced to total or partial citizenship. This fostering of a national public implied that participation was potentially open to anyone, even if not equally so. Crucial to the success of this national mode of belonging was the discourse of a nationalistic aesthetics and the investment in and insistence on the popular character of the festivities. In order to conjure a national public, references to lo mexicano needed to be continuously emphasized. The aesthetic language that described a national public thus enabled the world it aimed to represent. The popular character of Mexican nationalism similarly responded to the need to create a tradition that would appeal to the masses, and yet it also needed to address the aesthetic demands of a cosmopolitan, modern postrevolutionary Mexico. This appeal to the masses had significant symbolic and ideological repercussions for future enactments of lo mexicano. As Roger Bartra has claimed, the creation of a people, el pueblo, was shaped by the emergence of a spectacle of a national culture that would allow el pueblo to see itself reproduced in its staging.[43] However, the staging of the popular needed to be able to offer a form of identification with the audience that went beyond symbolic and metaphorical language: what was needed was embodiment. This staging of the popular had to produce an embodied sociality that required the participation of different sectors of the Mexican population: from Indigenous communities, peasants, and urban workers to the bourgeoisie and the (international) political and economic elites.

La Noche Mexicana in the Chapultepec Forest, then, conjured differing experiences of Mexico. The regional music and dances and the jamaica in general evoked the mythical and exotic Mexicos represented on three stages. The modernist scenography of the stages, as captured in figures 2.2, 2.3, and 2.6, contrasted with the performers who were summoned to signify the nation and with the bourgeois women invited to staff the booths showcasing Mexican goods and an array of Mexican traditional costumes. Most events took place between 8:30 p.m. and 10:00 p.m., when a series of shows was performed on the main stage around the lake, announced by fireworks, from dances and songs to the eruption of a replica of the volcano Popocatepetl followed by the playing of the national anthem and the lighting of the forest. This celebration of an assemblage of Mexicos staked a claim to modernity and as an amalgam of traditions carefully selected by Best Maugard. Mexico was tied to modernity via its technological advancements and spectacles, and yet it remained distinctly regional. Best Maugard's works emphasized this contrast through the various stages and pavilions whose modernist sceneries he created and through the performance of regional dances, particularly those by chinas and Tehuanas. Paying particular attention to the "Mexican elements" that composed the different national arts, the program published in *El Universal* underscored that the musicians, performers, and dancers were "exclusively Mexican."

Not unlike the program for the rest of the centennial festivities, the program for La Noche Mexicana invited the readers into a choreography of a festive Mexico. It provided a spatial, temporal, and kinesthetic orientation for the massive congregation of a national public. Smaller stages were placed strategically throughout the forest; figure 2.3, for instance, shows dancers from the state of Yucatán. This festive geography performatively summoned a variety of Mexicos. It was the fireworks, however, that marked the temporal choreography of the events, drawing attendees to the main stage to witness the major events of the evening, including the performance of dancers dressed as Tehuanas, chinas, and

Figure 2.3. Dancers from Yucatán. IISUE/AHUNAM/Fondo Martín Luis Guzmán Franco/Sección: Historia de la Revolución Mexicana/Caja: 167/E18-00924.

charros, with María Cristina Pereda as the prima ballerina. The official program brochure, which was illustrated by Best Maugard, emphasized the spatial, temporal, and kinesthetic orientation of La Noche Mexicana, as it included a map of Chapultepec with all of the stages and routes of circulation, a schedule with all the evening's activities, and a detailed explanation of the purpose and major components of the celebration.

The official program brochure provides an excellent example of the ways the aesthetics, pedagogy, and embodiment of lo mexicano created contested, incomplete, and fractured fields of collective action and belonging. Best Maugard deployed a modern aesthetic language in the program's assemblage of Mexico. This language illustrates the ambivalence in the process by which the so-called "exclusively Mexican elements" were translated from visual and discursive referents in the program to corporeal citations on stage. La Noche Mexicana is described as follows in the official program brochure:

La Noche Mexicana es una glorificación del arte nacional de México. . . . Los artistas desconocidos, los que traman en silencio la urdimbre inicial del arte mexicano, cuyas manifestaciones más refinadás [sic] y más áltás [sic] aun están por venir, inspiraron los motivos fundamentales, en esta fiesta de multiple [sic] significación. Porque es un canto al arte nacional autóctono; porque es un resumen de toda suerte de manifestaciones artísticas populares; y porque en ella el pueblo de México se mirará a sí mismo, como en un espejo prodigioso, con una fisonomía que hasta ahora él mismo casi desconoce.

(The Mexican Night is a glorification of the national art of Mexico. . . . The obscure artists, the ones who quietly lay the groundwork of Mexican art, whose most refined and elevated manifestations have yet to come, inspired the basic motifs of this multifaceted fiesta. Because it is a hymn to the autochthonous national art; because it is a synthesis of all kinds of popular artistic expressions; and because in it the people of Mexico will see in themselves, as if looking in a marvelous mirror, a physiognomy that until now had been virtually unknown to them.)[44]

The emergence of a national ideal of lo mexicano responded to cosmopolitan exchanges and cultural currents of the time. Yet it also responded to the materialization of its imagining within the nation. The program simultaneously recognized and denied the artistic qualities of Mexico's art. It glorified national artistic production and elevated it to the realm of the aesthetic while acknowledging that its most refined manifestations had "yet to come," suggesting that the current Mexican artworks were raw materials to be processed, not yet art in their own right. At the same time, it pointed toward the exemplary character of the artistic manifestations staged in La Noche Mexicana that were to serve as a "marvelous mirror" to define a pueblo, or to conjure it, because it was unknown to itself. In this sense, the program addressed the pedagogical component of the festivities; the emphasis shifted from what was represented to what was also performatively done.

The representation of the Tehuana is significant here, because its presence increasingly signaled Mexico's complex investment in the visually Indigenous yet racially contentious gendered construction of Mexican nationalism (see fig. 2.4). The women from Tehuantepec would eventually be immortalized by the Russian Sergei Eisenstein's film *¡Que viva México!*, Diego Rivera's paintings, and Frida Kahlo's attire. At La Noche Mexicana, the figure of the Tehuana was exalted with a dance number accompanied by an orchestra of 350 musicians. Its ubiquitous presence in the descriptions and pictures of the events reveals how Mexican women in particular embodied the nation. Best Maugard's Tehuana is probably one of the most intriguing illustrations that appeared in the

Figure 2.4. "Tehuanas," scenery designed by Adolfo Best Maugard. IISUE/AHUNAM/ Fondo Martín Luis Guzmán Franco/Sección: Historia de la Revolución Mexicana/ Caja: 167/E18-01018.

official program brochure. Unlike the figures of the china and the charro, who were to become the epitome of a Mexican traditional couple in popular expressions and official discourses, the Tehuana was featured on her own. She captured the aura of strong Indigenous women in this era of modernization:

> El prodigio de nuestra tierra caliente se ha concretado en una flor prodigiosa: la tehuana . . . ; toda esa cálida y apasionada fecundidad de la tierra caliente fueron precisas para crear a la mujer de Tehuantepec. . . . Si hay en alguna parte de México resurrecciones instintivas de la equilibrada gracia helénica, es en Tehuantepec. Cuando miramos, amodorrados por la furia solar, el paso de una tehuana con el busto firme y recto, los brazos ondulantes y un largo y lánguido vaivén de las anchas faldas agitadas por el viento, se nos figura asistir, como en sueño, a una evocación de la Grecia artística y heróica. Hay, pues, en redor de esta mujer una amplia y humana palpitación de clasicismo. Y por ella y para ella, la vida se llena en aquella región de una fuerte, de una clara, de una melódica serenidad, que se refleja en la música, apasionada, graciosa y lánguida; en la proporcionada lentitud de los movimientos; y hasta en el majestuoso balanceo de los árboles, cargados de siglos.

> (The wonder that is our *tierra caliente* (hot land) has been materialized in a wondrous flower: the *Tehuana* . . . ; all of the heat and passionate fecundity of the *tierra caliente* was necessary to create the woman of Tehuantepec. . . . If anywhere in Mexico there are native expressions of Hellenistic grace and poise, it is in Tehuantepec. When we admire, dazed by the solar fury, the gait of a *Tehuana* with her firm and straight bust, her undulating arms, and the long and languid swinging of her wide skirts rustled by the wind, it is as if we are witnessing, as in a dream, an evocation of the artistic and heroic Greece. Enveloping this woman is an expansive, human palpitation of classicism. And because of her and for her, life in that region becomes infused with a strong, clear, and melodic serenity, which is reflected in the passionate, gracious, and languid music; in the measured slowness of the movements; and even in the magnificent swaying of the trees, laden as they are with centuries.)[45]

This discursive description of the Tehuana emphasizes a new set of corporeal, spatial, and temporal registers. The serenity of the regional music, the languidity evoked by the movements, and the swaying of the centenary trees conjure an image of a land displaced in time. At the same time, her body is conflated with nature, as if one were an extension of the other. The text is clear that the Tehuana is the product of nature: "all of the heat and passionate fecundity of the *tierra caliente* (hot land) was necessary to create the woman of Tehuantepec." It is notable, however, that she is described and illustrated in motion. The "measured slowness" of her bodily movements is mirrored by the languid swaying of the lush landscape that surrounds her and the music characteristic of the region. Despite the classical references that gesture toward another temporality and spatiality, her movement vocabulary, her gait reminds us of her animate presence, of her strong but gracious poise.

Evoking a primitive paradise of sensuality, Best Maugard's depiction of a Tehuana looks not like a Mexican Indigenous woman but like a South Asian Indian woman. Even though his staging of Tehuanas attempted to capture the same displacement in time and space illustrated by the picture, each Mexican woman who dressed as a Tehuana on and off stage during La Noche Mexicana invoked a much more complex iteration of Mexican Indigenous femininity through the particularities of her body. One can only wonder how tall, skinny, or brown each dancer, bourgeois lady, or Indigenous woman was. Yet each of their corporeal alignments cited differentially a sense of lo mexicano. Moreover, in figure 2.5, the embodied aesthetics of the woman's pose and bodily gestures cite the orientalist formulations characteristic of dance modernisms. After all, Best Maugard was influenced by the aesthetics of modernist primitivism and the dance modernisms choreographed by Serge Diaghilev's Ballets Russes. The dance historian Mitchell Snow documents the restaging of Russian folk arts and the stylistic influence that the Ballets Russes had on Mexican and other Latin American artists, including Diego Rivera, Roberto Montenegro, Adolfo Best Maugard, and even Carlos Mérida. For Snow, the penchant for decorative painting and incorporation of folkloric elements can be connected directly to the aesthetics of the Ballets Russes and the Spanish painter Hermen Anglada, one of the most influential painters of the Belle Époque in Paris, a friend and avid supporter of Diaghilev and his dance company, and an influential reference for Best Maugard and Montenegro, among others.[46] The body language of the Tehuana, then, discursively, visually, and kinesthetically cited the aesthetic sensibility of dance modernisms.[47]

The figure of the Tehuana illustrated by Best Maugard undoubtedly conjured and materialized a plethora of imaginings of the nation. The discursive description of the Tehuana vis-à-vis its visual rendition draws

Figure 2.5. "La tehuana," *Noche Mexicana en los Lagos de Chapultepec.* Designed by Adolfo Best Maugard. Biblioteca Nacional de México. Fondo Reservado.

attention to the figure's emergence as a provisional assemblage of competing aesthetic and corporeal referents. In the image, Best Maugard clearly borrows from other aesthetic currents of the time, such as art nouveau, primitivism, and orientalism. The Mexican art historian Karen Cordero explains how this painting of a Tehuana responded to Best Maugard's attempt to "refine" the popular for the upper classes. In fact, it belonged to a series of paintings that Best Maugard did while living in the United States. Mixing European and orientalist elements with Mexican motifs, he deliberately infused these paintings of a distinct "Mexican character" with clear elements of art nouveau. According to Cordero's description of the image, the planimetric, simple composition, the medium point, and the dress of the Tehuana itself originate in Mexican popular art; however, one can immediately see the artistic influence of art nouveau and Japonism, and even that of Henri Matisse, in the figure of the Tehuana dancer and the fireworks and black sky that serve as a background for the painting.[48] Visually speaking, a mixture of artistic trends is at play;

a mixture can also be recognized in the pictures of the scenography designed by Best Maugard. As noted previously, the scenography of the various stages, particularly the main one in the middle of the lake, and the arches that adorned the entrance to the park showcased the stylization of a new visual conception of Mexico.[49] Inspired by Mexican nature, the designs Best Maugard put on display during La Noche Mexicana mirrored the background in the Tehuana painting.

Best Maugard offered an aestheticized image of Mexico that was not reduced to a visual iteration. The bourgeois women dressed as Tehuanas at the various booths selling Mexican goods did not necessarily embody the Tehuanas depicted and described in the official program brochure with orientalist, Greek, and art nouveau references. The gender dynamics suggested by these images and the imaginings they inspired contrasted sharply with the modernizing efforts of the epoch. The "chicas modernas," or modern girls, exemplified by the flappers from New York who performed at the Teatro Iris in the middle of the centenary celebrations, are a case in point.[50] With short hair, strapless short dresses, high heels, and nylons, the New York dancers offered a new vision of modern femininity. Whereas the Tehuanas were portrayed in a mystical land, the chicas modernas were meant to capture the experience of the city. In an insightful study, the historian Ageeth Sluis shows how the modernization of Mexico City, marked by its urbanization after the Revolution, can be related to changing ideas about gender and the place of women in society. The modernization of the city resulted in the increasing visibility of women's bodies. The cityscape was to contain, rule, and mold the female bodies that were in turn to represent the city. Marked by transnational influences, such as flappers and other international iterations of "la chica moderna" such as the Tiller Girl troupes and chorus line dancers, the emergence of female deco-bodies that resembled the New Woman (racialized, productive, and a normative mother and wife) fostered the gendered view of the urban city. Put simply, according to Sluis, women were rendered "spectacles," and the "spectacle driving [the] new culture industries taught women to perform modern identities through makeup, clothes, posture, mannerisms, and attitude."[51] The contrast with the regional Mexican embodiments of femininity present at La Noche Mexicana could not have been greater.

In many ways, however, the Tehuanas and the chicas modernas from New York City embodied culturally specific responses to the experience of modernity. Their choreographies of femininity responded to the fears, desires, and illusions projected onto their bodies in motion.

Their corporeal referents and movement vocabulary conjured a sense of modernity and cosmopolitanism, reorienting spectators' sensibilities toward an avant-garde aesthetics of modern European and US dance.[52] Each figure, then, embodied and choreographed the idea of the modern. Dancing bodies mediated national boundaries and negotiated questions about race, gender, and sexuality. In Europe and the United States, the "disavowed and sublimated unease with modernity was projected onto others." This process of othering created what the dance scholar Ramsay Burt has termed "alien bodies," "the Others of modernity in terms of race and gender."[53] Nevertheless, Mexico ambiguously encompassed the worlds of both the modern and the exotic Other. Unlike the Tehuanas, whose pose and corporeal movements gestured toward the Orient through distinctly Mexican markers, the chorus line of "chicas modernas" exemplified with precision and uniformity the rationalizing and alienating process of capitalist modernity reminiscent of the Tiller Girls, characterized as a form of "Taylorist" dancing.[54] But in the context of Mexico, their bodies and movement represented more than the logic of mass production. The chicas modernas also embodied freedom, strength, health, and the occupation of public spaces until then reserved for men.

The mass media circulated images of a changing, modernizing nation so assiduously that they became the object of a craze in the 1920s. In this period, the emphasis on the national and the cosmopolitan went hand in hand. As Pérez Montfort observes, in popular theater and the media (the press, radio, and film) displays of what was rendered as typically Mexican became as fashionable as other forms of urban entertainment such as flappers and the Mexican *bataclán* (the Mexican adaptation of the Parisian variety spectacle).[55] This phenomenon was not confined to Mexico City. Throughout the country, even in remote areas, Mexican denizens received a visual education via the dissemination of mass-produced nationalist artifacts.[56] But a visual education was not the only one they received. Mexicans soon experienced the first iteration of what would become a common embodied practice of Mexican nationalism: the festive celebration of "Noches Mexicanas."

Conjuring Other Mexicos: Festive Choreographies at La Noche Mexicana

The day had finally arrived. But, unexpectedly, the long-awaited event had to be postponed due to torrential rain in the country's capital, which lasted until the following day.[57] The massive event would continue to be free, according to the official program printed in newspapers, with no restriction beyond the physical capacity of the Chapultepec Forest. Due to its success, La Noche Mexicana was repeated two nights in a row, Tuesday, September 27, and Wednesday, September 28, 1921. In this section, I analyze the visual and discursive descriptions of two other accounts of the events. In addition to El Demócrata's celebratory report with which I opened the chapter, El Universal published two consecutive articles following each of the celebrations. The first, by Manuel Palavicini, highlights the combination of activities to which I have alluded: the electrical illumination, the masses, and the physical presence of people from different parts of the country. In his article, Palavicini captured the experience of La Noche Mexicana as the moving image of a changing nation. Palavicini's interaction with a large number of people and the massive lighting of the city's most important park, Chapultepec, heightened his sense of a modern Mexico. Yet he set the scene to take the readers back to a familiar, almost quotidian scenario. He described the stands like those found at any regional fair, decorated with what would be designated from then on as Mexican motifs: "Los puestos de refrescos y 'confetti' están adornados con pinturas de colores brillantes, que son estilizaciones de los dibujos típicos, tan populares en todas nuestras tiendas baratas, y que hasta ahora no se habían sabido aprovechar como motivos decorativos" (The drink and confetti stands are decorated with bright colored paintings, which are stylizations of the typical drawings that are commonly found in all our cheap local stores and which until now hadn't been thought of and used as decorative motifs).[58] In this way, Palavicini discursively elevated the otherwise popular designs and decorations to a national aesthetics. These images and drawings regularly found at cheap, local stores were now part of the repertoire of national iconography.

It was not only popular visual imagery that was mobilized. The most dynamic mobilization that took place was that of thousands of people. La Noche Mexicana rallied an unprecedented number of people intrigued by the celebration of a popular fiesta. During this fiesta, bodies that had not been previously deemed representative of the nation were placed on stages to perform Mexico. Certainly, the celebration included the figures of the chinas and even Tehuanas, who were increasingly popular as icons of Mexican nationalism. They occupied the center stage in the middle of the lake built for this occasion and were featured in the closing numbers of the celebration. As the official program printed in newspapers indicated, Best Maugard had planned dances for the Tehuanas, chinas, and charros, with María Cristina Pereda as the prima ballerina performing with an all-Mexican cast. But their performances were not what the articles highlighted. It was the jaraneros from the southern state of Yucatán and the Yaqui Indians from the northern state of Sonora that captivated the masses and reporters. As noted in several articles from the various iterations of La Noche Mexicana, and Manuel Palavicini's in particular, the scenes of dancing Yucatecos and Yaquis was so mesmerizing that they literally took the center stage in the pictures and descriptions of the event. Palavicini attempted to capture how the staging of an assemblage of Mexicos from the southern and northern borders of the nation enthralled the massive audiences:

> En las cruces de las calzadas se habían instalado pequeños escenarios, en los que se hizo un derroche de color y de buen gusto, para simbolizar en cada uno, con motivos gráficos, los bailes nacionales, que se ejecutaban por nativos de diversas partes del país. Los yucatecos, con la música lenta y lasciva de las costas, que lleva quejas mezcladas con notas distintas que interrumpen el sentido general de la música. En cambio, los indios "yaquis" sin más acompañamiento que el de sus pasos y los curiosos instrumentos que esgrimen incansables, se retorcían inverosímilmente, mientras brillaban con destellos de bronce, sus rostros cincelados y sudorosos. Muchos minutos repitiendo el mismo movimiento, para cambiar después a uno muy similar y que da impresión de una estabilidad muy grande de carácter. Se comprende fácilmente que deben tener algo de faquires de la India, que permanecen tanto tiempo en una misma posición sin moverse; éstos bailan con su monotonía que cansa y que lastima. Debe ser un pueblo de leyendas tristes como su música y cansadas como sus bailes, que con un sonsonete unísono y un movimiento igual, de cadencia no variada, impresionan profundamente.

> (In the intersections of the streets, small stages had been set up, in which a feast of color and good taste were displayed to represent in each one, with pictorial motifs, national dances, which were performed by members of groups from different parts of the country. The people from Yucatán, with the slow and lascivious music from the coast, which carries laments mixed with different notes that disrupt the general sense of the music. Instead, the Yaqui Indians, without much accompaniment other than that of their steps and their curious instruments that they wielded tirelessly, twisted in such an

unlikely way while their faces, chiseled and sweaty, shone with bronze sparkles. Repeating the same movement for several minutes, only to change to another very similar one that gives the impression of great firmness of character. It is easy to see how they might have in them something of the faquirs from India, who remain for a long time in the same position without moving; these Yaqui Indians dance with a monotony that tires and hurts. They must be a people with legends as sad as their music and as tiring as their dances; tapping in unison and moving continuously to an unchanging rhythm, they make a profound impression.)[59]

This assemblage of Mexicos juxtaposed groups and regions from the two opposite sides of the country, different scenarios of a festive nation in movement. The Yaqui Indians from the border state of Sonora captivated Palavicini. He chose to describe the representatives from opposite ends of the country and from the areas the farthest from the city of Mexico. For the Yucatecos, however, Palavicini focused not on the dance movements but on the sonic imaginaries of this tropical region, evoking its paradisiacal, slow, and lascivious rhythms, which contrasted sharply with the ambience of the massive crowd in Chapultepec Park. It was not as common in this period to portray Yucatán as an exotic, distant, and tropical coastal region, given the primacy of the ports of Veracruz and Acapulco and the relatively scarce commercial and tourist activities there. Yucatán, according to the cultural critic Maricruz Castro Ricalde, eventually came to be associated with the Mayans, not with the tropics.[60] The language Palavicini used for the dancers, then, reminds us that the understanding of the diversity of Mexico was still being negotiated.

Immediately after describing the Yucatecos, Manuel Palavicini described the sonic, visual, and kinesthetic imaginary of the Yaqui Indians. This time, Palavicini took the reader from the monotony of dancers' steps and the precarious instrumentation they featured to their distinctive stoic facial expressions. Describing them as sculptured, monument-like figures, the critic struggled to capture the repetitive, monotonous movement of the Yaqui Indians. In fact, he grappled with the description of the almost imperceptible changes of dance steps to the point that he compared the dancers to faqirs from India, known, as he went on to say, for holding the same position without moving. The allusion to Indian imagery evokes the increasingly common perception of Black and brown bodies as the epitome of the exotic Other; references to them were considered a sign of modernism.[61] Unlike the slow-moving Yucatán dancers, the Yaqui

Indians seemed to give the impression of dancing without movement, and yet their monotonous, repetitive, and untiring performance profoundly impacted Palavicini.

What did it mean to relate to others through the literal and metaphorical movement of bodies? Although it was a perceived absence of movement that enthralled Palavicini, the way he related to these moving bodies was influenced by his witnessing and imagining of their movement. That is, he related to the Yaqui Indians not only sonically, as he did with Yucatecos, but also *kinesthetically*. The dance scholar Susan Leigh Foster challenges us to think of kinesthesia, the awareness of one's body's motion and position, as a mechanism for relating to others that is always framed within a specific sociohistorical context. What she calls "kinesthetic empathy" involves a process whereby "one experience[s] muscularly as well as psychically the dynamics of what [is] being witnessed."[62] Palavicini's description reveals how he responded kinesthetically to the movement of the Yaqui dancers, that is, how he imagined it and therefore experienced it as an embodied interaction with and through the Indigenous Other.

Palavicini discursively distanced himself from the Yaqui Indians by associating them with the faqirs of India and then with a distant, desolate, and tired people. Yet his kinesthetic experience of their dances and music left a profound impression on him, bringing him closer to them and enacting a different kind of embodied sociality. Palavicini's descriptions illustrate how an emerging indigenista narrative at once celebrated and denied the contributions of Indigenous cultures, as the intellectual and artistic work of Manuel Gamio, Adolfo Best Maugard, and eventually José Vasconcelos (to name but a few) demonstrates.[63] In fact, the passage analyzed previously offers a glimpse of the slippery vocabulary that was to become standard for naming the Indigenous. Rather than resorting to what we now consider clichés of the Indigenous Other (the monotony, the endurance, and the suffering), Palavicini attempted to grasp what he was corporeally experiencing through and with the moving bodies of the Yaqui *pascola* (ritualistic Indigenous dance) dancers. The ambivalence of the indigenista discourse often subordinated Indigenous populations to the state in the name of civilization. At the same time, "indigenismo" played a crucial role in promoting a sense of contemporaneity and coexistence between Indians and non-Indians, "the core of the mestizo nation," as Estelle Tarica reminds us.[64] The Yaqui dancers described by Palavicini and captured in figure 2.6 reveal an awareness of a shared time and space: a contingent spatial, temporal, and corporeal convergence of an assemblage of Mexicos.[65]

Whether or not Palavicini ended up denying the coevalness of the Yaqui, as many indigenista narratives of the time did, he captured kinesthetically the different kinds of affects and attachments fostered by an embodied interaction with these other Mexicos. This was not a minor feat. The fact that Indigenous people were *present* and not just *represented* forced Palavicini and the audience in general to grapple with an embodied convergence with the Indigenous Other. Furthermore, this interaction revealed that the language later deployed to describe racial and ethnic difference was still crystallizing. Palavicini's word choice signaled the inadequacy of language to capture such a kinesthetic encounter between different Mexicos and the failure of language to describe Mexico's diversity. The act of naming indigeneity, of rendering it discursively legible, was performatively undone by the visual imagery captured in the pictures of the "Indigenous" bodies these articles claimed to represent. A stable notion of indigeneity could not yet be taken for granted.[66]

The dancing nation staged at La Noche Mexicana brought together an unusual group of people, an incipient national audience before an understanding of Mexican citizenry had congealed. The written and visual accounts that survive from the several iterations of the event illustrate the role played by women and Indigenous people in the consolidation of a nationalistic sense of embodied expression. The descriptions I have found offer a vivid glimpse of what it may have been like to walk across the Chapultepec Park, experiencing different corporeal conjurings of other Mexicos. *El Universal Ilustrado* published on Thursday, September 29, 1921, a short article titled "La 'Noche Mexicana' en el Bosque de Chapultepec" ("Mexican Night" at Chapultepec Park), which featured six pictures complementing the descriptions offered by Palavicini elsewhere. This article also included a note that *El Universal Ilustrado* was the only newspaper that had photographers for this event, at least for its first iteration. This is not a minor detail, considering the scale and significance of the event.

Framed and decorated with drawings that alluded to Indigenous designs and graphic symbols resembling Adolfo Best Maugard's drawing method, the pictures of *El Universal Ilustrado* captured the scene of a manufactured assemblage of lo mexicano. This visual grammar also pointed to the Indigenous difference that ultimately constituted a Mexican visual iconography. Interestingly, the two largest pictures were not those of the chinas, Tehuanas, or even the Yucatecos jaraneros, as in the other articles, but rather of the Yaqui Indians dancing surrounded by hundreds of people and the main stage in the middle of the lake. These

Figure 2.6. "La Noche Mexicana en el Bosque de Chapultepec," *El Universal Ilustrado*, September 29, 1921. Photo Courtesy of Biblioteca Miguel Lerdo de Tejada de la Secretaría de Hacienda y Crédito Público.

large photographs were surrounded by more conventional frames, as if the readers were looking at two framed pictures at a museum.

The article featured in *El Universal Ilustrado* also focused on the massiveness of the celebration, from the thousands of lightbulbs illuminating Chapultepec Park to the thousands of people witnessing the events. Overall, the six pictures the article included visually emphasize the various performances that the public witnessed. Three of the four displayed on the left side of the page showcase the performers on the main stage, while the other focuses on a smaller stage with a group of women dressed as chinas sitting in front of a table. The first picture on the left side showcases a china and charro couple with Yucatecos in the background, on what was the main stage in the middle of the lake, as indicated by the decorations and the caption. They are dancing "El 'jarabe' auténtico," as the legend states; this identification is confirmed by the charro hat on the floor; the dance is what would become known as El jarabe tapatío, or Mexican hat dance. Although the photograph is in black and white, one can still make out the elaborate costumes. The second picture shows five Yucatecos dancing. This evidence corroborates the assertion that they had their own stage and also performed on the main stage. The dancers wore the traditional gala dresses, or "ternos yucatecos," typical of the *vaquerías* (festive celebrations in Yucatán), and the men even wore the traditional "alpargatas," sandal-like footwear from the peninsula. The photographs stand in dramatic contrast to Palavicini's description of the dances performed by the Yucatecos. The costumes indicate that they were likely dancing *jaranas*, traditional mestizo dances from Yucatán. This is why the Yucatán performers were also called *jaraneros*. Maricruz Castro Ricalde has noted that the article mentions the "gracia exquisita de su raza" (the exquisite grace of their race), as if to suggest that they belonged to Mayan Indigenous groups. Furthermore, the complex rhythms and footwork of the jarana yucateca would certainly have contrasted with the tropical lasciviousness that Palavicini described.[67] The description of the dances, therefore, reveals that the Yucatecos performed not pre-Hispanic Mayan dances but rather jaranas, which emphasized the visual and discursive contrast of such representations of the peninsula.

The last picture on this first page, with women dressed as chinas on a different stage, allowed the readers to take a closer look at the festive decorations that Adolfo Best Maugard designed for the occasion. The stage itself featured as a background one of Best Maugard's designs, illuminated with lightbulbs all the way around its contours. The composition on the background displayed a vase decorated with basic patterns and two birds on each side, a design characteristic of the visual grammar embraced and disseminated by Best Maugard. Considered together with the pre-Hispanic, Indigenous-like drawings to the left and right corners of the pictures, these elements exhibited a mosaic of Mexico. The two main photographs that appeared on the right side focused on what were probably the most popular and well-attended stages of La Noche Mexicana. The one on the top half of the page featured the main stage in the middle of the lake from a considerable distance, emphasizing its magnitude and the massive number of people in attendance. Many of the attendees' faces are lost in the darkness of the picture, which accentuates the lighting of the main stage, a sight that must have been impressive for the time. The second picture displays the stage where the Yaqui Indians performed.

These two pictures are divided into two parts: the stages and the public. The second picture, the largest picture of the six, highlights the Yaqui pascola dancers, most of whom are dressed in white attire. The photograph visually portrays the contrast between the moving Yaqui male dancers and the standing spectators, represented mainly but not exclusively by members of the bourgeoisie. The pascola dancers wear white pants and headpieces. Likely moving in circles or lines as was traditionally done in pascola dances, the *pascoleros* at the front of the lines look down while playing their *sonajas* (rattles). They are moving in the same direction, as if in a procession. On the opposite side, we see the audience members, facing the stage. Many of them are men, wearing suits and hats typical of the period. As in other pictures, some of them wear charro hats. There are also a few women and children. The picture reveals how the movement, as monotonous as Palavicini found it, captivated the audience members, who look straight ahead in the picture. The short article described the pascola as an "encanto agreste" (wild charm), suggesting an animalistic kind of nature that is very much in line with the wilderness of Mexico City's urban forest, el Bosque de Chapultepec. The visual description therefore contrasts with the discursive renderings of the Indigenous performance, such as Palavicini's.

While the audience in the photograph might seem at first glance to be homogenous, it was not. Numerous people from the so-called "popular" classes were also part of the massive crowd that overfilled the Bosque de Chapultepec. This significant detail is corroborated by the text of the piece. In fact, the anonymous author of the article in *El Universal Ilustrado* lamented the agglomeration of people and the disorderly interaction and misbehavior of some of the attendees, a testament that it was open and free to everyone: "¡Lástima que la aglomeración de personas, el desorden inherente a toda fiesta donde la entrada es libre y donde se cuelan elementos imbéciles, haya deslucido esta 'Noche Mexicana,' digna de recordación!" (What a shame that the agglomeration of people, the inherent disorder of every fiesta where admission is free and where imbecile elements get in, had spoiled this "Noche Mexicana," so worthy of remembrance).[68] Without the descriptions of the events by the anonymous author, the pictures would reveal an orderly celebration, undoubtedly crowded but without the kind of unruly behavior the descriptions suggest. Not surprisingly, then, the two largest pictures showcased the multitudes present during the event. These images of well-attended performances at various stages gave the impression of an orderly assembly, as if the attendees had assigned places. Yet the author insisted that the "absurd agglomeration" took away from the festivities to the point of spoiling an otherwise memorable occasion: a massive re-creation of an authentic manifestation of lo mexicano.

The same author in *El Universal Ilustrado* confirmed the celebration of a second edition of La Noche Mexicana, wishing it were not as crowded and full of the "disorderly elements" typical of popular fiestas as the massive event of the night before. For the author of this piece, the celebration of La Noche Mexicana brought to the fore the "alma de la República, dispersa y casi olvidada por los intelectuales exóticos y por el pueblo" (soul of the Republic, dispersed and almost forgotten by exotic intellectuals and by the people).[69] Whereas the Porfirian centennial celebrations had been orchestrated by the intellectual elite, the author, in line with postrevolutionary thinking, derided as "exotic" intellectuals those who were otherwise known as "científicos" (scientists).[70] And yet he also condescendingly criticized el pueblo for their behavior and for their disdain of nationalistic manifestations. The people, in this author's view, contradicted and even undermined the efforts to mount an authentic popular celebration. Nevertheless, this event ultimately synthesized a nationalistic effort to recognize and reframe these artistic and embodied expressions of the centennial festivities as such, "[un] generoso esfuerzo de difusión nacionalista, bello ademán de mexicanismo" (a generous effort of nationalist dissemination, a beautiful gesture of Mexicanness).[71] Despite the fear of and fascination with the masses by the organizers, Mexico proved itself capable of offering a spectacle comparable to those of European cities. To do so, it exoticized itself, treating its resources as raw materials and exploiting the grammar of the international scene, including modernist and orientalist tropes. This local yet cosmopolitan choreography of nationalism exemplifies the multiple ways the staging of lo mexicano was made to produce meaning.

Embodying the Nation

In the preceding sections, I have shown how we can conceive of the visual, discursive, and corporeal renditions of lo mexicano as instances of a contingent nationalistic sense of belonging. The staging of La Noche Mexicana enabled the consolidation of what would later be imposed as a national tradition of lo mexicano, yet the bodies that were intended to represent an idea of the nation performatively conjured other Mexicos. As I have shown, La Noche Mexicana enacted an embodied sociality. The literal coming together of bodies during this event meant that their particularities could not be entirely dissolved or reduced, thereby complicating the transmission of a national culture. Juana María Rodríguez reminds us that bodily acts help us imagine and foster a shared corporeal background, citing material and ephemeral alignments, which

Figure 2.7. "La Noche Mexicana." IISUE/AHUNAM/Fondo Martín Luis Guzmán Franco/Sección: Historia de la Revolución Mexicana/Caja: 167/E18-00651.

ultimately define our embodied sociality. According to Rodríguez, the "particularities of our embodied selves, our age, contours, color, and corporeal histories, have the ability to transform the meaning of words and gestures."[72] The bodies congregated in La Noche Mexicana ultimately suggest a more complex history of lo mexicano, at times redeeming and at times oppressive.

While the vision and aesthetic language might have been the product of an intellectual and cultural elite, the bodily acts and encounters of the thousands of people congregated at La Noche Mexicana, particularly of the people who were not from Mexico City, continuously reminded both the elites and el pueblo of the fractures, excesses, and failures of this idea of lo mexicano. The picture shown in figure 2.7, part of the collection of the Fondo Martín Luis Guzmán Franco at the Archivo Histórico de la UNAM, probably never circulated. And yet it condenses the tensions and contradictions of the incipient postrevolutionary nationalistic project. The barefooted girl captured in this photograph contrasts starkly with the dressed-up members of the bourgeoisie who surround her and the stagings of the nation in the other images. Standing next to a policeman and a bourgeois man, she is a reminder that La Noche Mexicana conjured a popular public that was policed and differentiated symbolically, corporeally, and materially. Her small body dressed in simple clothing differs significantly from those of the young ladies wearing Tehuana or china poblana costumes at the various events organized for the celebrations, the chicas modernas (flappers) whose images circulated in newspapers and magazines, and the bourgeois women in the picture. Her presence and bodily actions—we see her extending an arm, probably selling confetti—performatively undid and exceeded what La Noche Mexicana, conceived as "popular," attempted to represent, to contain. The picture, in fact, renders visible the different intensities and complex sociocultural dynamics at play during La Noche Mexicana.

The thousands of bodies in movement during the celebration produced an enticing affective space whose historical and social dimension cannot be separated from the body and whose ephemerality makes it challenging to register. The shared experience of the attendees likely provoked an acute sensorial event. Thousands of bodies moving back and forth for hours produced a festive space that operated as an incipient embodied sociality of lo mexicano, a shared corporeal background generated through the collective experience of the centennial celebrations, directly and indirectly.[73] One often disregarded yet readily available way to access the ephemeral traces of the embodied sociality that enacted the centennial celebrations, particularly La Noche Mexicana, is through print media. Specifically, to understand how this lived experience was reframed after its time and place of articulation, one needs to retrace how it produced and circulated a particular imaginary of a festive Mexico. On October 13, 1921, *El Universal Ilustrado* published as an editorial device a letter, "Ecos del Centenario" (Echoes from the Centenary), in the section titled "La semana en consonantes por Zas" (The Week in Consonants by Zas).[74] Allegedly composed by an Indian named Juan Pitasio Bielas, copied by Zas, and addressed to Cuca, Juan's wife, the letter recounted the events that Juan witnessed during the centennial celebrations of 1921 (see fig. 2.8). It was accompanied by drawings depicting three scenes from the festivities that framed the two columns of writing capturing the voice of the Indian Juan. The writing stood in dramatic contrast to the three drawings representing the bourgeois character depicted at the top and the bottom of the letter.

By highlighting the tension between the visual and discursive registers, the letter offers competing "echoes" of the centenary, indeed a cacophony. One immediately notices that the drawings illustrate a *catrín* (bourgeois male) as the main spectator of the various events. The figure

Figure 2.8. "Ecos del Centenario," *El Universal Ilustrado,* October 13, 1921. Courtesy of the Biblioteca Miguel Lerdo de Tejada de la Secretaría de Hacienda y Crédito Público.

of the catrín had come to embody the upper classes, summoning the rigidity, cosmopolitanism, and cultural imaginary of a Porfirian Mexico. His attire, gendered corporeal language, and movement choreographed his social status, engendering a sense of modernity while he strolled through the city as a Mexican flâneur. Dressed as a typical catrín in a frock, the figure in the illustration is actively intervening in the parade that is depicted. This parade was one of the major events during the centenary celebrations. Among various moments of Mexican history, such as the arrival of the Spaniards in Tenochtitlan, the parade featured *El Universal's* float with María Bibiana Uribe, the recently proclaimed winner of the India Bonita pageant. The float, as seen in the sketch, presented the monumental figure of Cuauhtémoc at the front of the vessel, with María Bibiana Uribe in the back, crowned atop the pyramid with the "Aztec Calendar" behind her and the emblem of the newspaper, an eagle with open wings and a globe, on top of her. Six other Indigenous women were part of the float, which was decorated with typical Mexican plants, such as magueys and cacti. The illustration in the newspaper offered a much simpler rendition of the float. The vessel, pulled by a group of oxen, featured only the monument of the "Aztec" warrior and the figure of "La India Bonita" atop the pile of rocks, including the emblem of *El Universal*. The most striking aspect of the illustration is the presence of the big, barefoot, sweaty figure of el catrín, holding his shoes over the heads of the oxen. The distressed pose of the monumental bourgeois man suggests an eminent clash with the float, or rather with the Indigenous figures. Not only is he leaning as if walking toward the float, heading west, but his facial expressions and shoes also threaten to smash the small Indigenous figures heading eastward toward him, rendering them vulnerable to destruction. Is this the imminent fate of the Indigenous people, caught in the path of the cosmopolitan, civilized bourgeois man? One can only wonder. The two scenes portrayed at the bottom of the page, however, suggest a completely different picture, marked by the total absence of Indigenous people. The one on the left captures what seems to be the same bourgeois man contemplating from afar the main stage of La Noche Mexicana and the fireworks. Leaning back on his cane, the contemplative catrín admires from a distance what was described by commentators of the events as one of the highlights of the festivities: the pyrotechnics. Letters and scrolls dominate the last scene. The catrín places into a big envelope a series of written documents, though it is not clear what they contain.

The uncertainty of the images paradoxically mirrors the discursive tension found in the body of the letter purportedly composed by the Indian Juan Pitasio Bielas. The writing offers a textual performance aimed at capturing the linguistic expressions of an Indigenous man who went to Mexico City and experienced the festivities. Addressed to Cuca, the letter reveals that the "indio ilustradito" (the little erudite Indian) Juan, as he describes himself, is the catrín depicted in the drawings. His report to Cuca focuses on precisely the activities captured in the illustrations: he went to the parade to see the India Bonita and La Noche Mexicana, and he sent Cuca the newspapers with descriptions of the events. The visual and discursive tension of this account underscores something that I have addressed in this chapter and will continue to explore in the chapters that follow: the public cultural performances bring to the forefront the complex interplay between the representation of the nation, of lo mexicano, and its embodiment. The images and the language used to represent the nation during the festivities of the centenary are performatively undone by the embodied presence of the people they aim to represent. The bodies undermine the representation of lo mexicano, of el pueblo, gesturing toward an excess that fails to be contained by nationalist iconography.

As I have shown, the cultural performances witnessed by Juan Pitasio Bielas demonstrate the ways state-sponsored cultural projects attempted to shape the nation, yet they were always exceeded and contested through the bodily actions of Mexican citizens. In effect, the letter offers a textual and cultural performance of its own. It pretends to capture the orality associated with the Indigenous, rural population of Mexico. The writing showcases the elisions, pronunciation, and vocabulary associated with el pueblo, or rather with its linguistic performance as imagined by the editors of a news magazine. The letter opens with a reference to a regional product, "lo ques la cajeta de Celaya" (that which is the caramel spread from Celaya).[75] From the beginning, the letter is clearly a cultural textual performance in terms not only of content but also of form. The "cajeta" (caramel spread or Mexican dulce de leche) was probably one of the regional products showcased at the various expositions and events, maybe even at La Noche Mexicana, as a so-called "authentic" Mexican product, as was the register of Spanish that described it and the rest of the events: "lo ques" versus "lo que es" (that which is); "enviten" versus "inviten" (invite us); "Nochi" versus "Noche" (night). Even more important is the third line of the letter: "no ha habido fiesta en donde no me enviten" (there has not been a party where I was not invited). Juan, the narrating voice, emphasizes the accessibility of the festivities, which were, of course, designed for all social classes. The imagining of el pueblo, however, is complicated by what follows: he is unable to attend a party because, as the reader finds out later in the letter, his frock coat, his "levita," was dirtied by the masses, the "hervidero," at La Noche Mexicana. Is the bourgeois attire of the Indian Juan mocking, praising, or simply imagining a different vision of el pueblo? For whom and why? Is it an attempt to elevate el pueblo to the international scene, paradoxically reducing it to a sort of neocolonial and cosmopolitan mimicry? The sartorial elements and comportment required by organizers reveal the cosmopolitan fantasies and the differentiated access to these allegedly open events.[76]

The letter calls attention to the role of the press in the centenary celebrations. The newspapers not only informed Mexicans about the festivities but also discursively formed an ideal of a national citizenry. In this sense, the media helped to create a national public. Cuca was not present at the festivities, which signals the differentiated access to them, but Juan sent her the newspapers along with his letter to make her a part of the celebrations, while revealing that he was one of the thousands of people who traveled to partake in the festivities: "En los periódicos / que te enviao / van tiatros, toros, / desfile y carros" (In the newspapers I have sent you, there are theaters, bulls, the parade, and floats). The nationalistic cultural performances formed Mexico's citizens. In so doing, they also created a Mexican public, as did the newspapers that aimed to establish national readerships. This letter written by an "indio ilustradito" shows how these processes of formation were related. The rehearsal of the nation performed at the centennial celebrations was captured, disseminated, and restaged by the national press. Juan directs the reader's attention to two of the most massive public displays of the nation: the parade and La Noche Mexicana. He recounts his experiences attending the events as follows:

¡Y de los carros, uno! ¡es la sangre que grita!
Tú bien sabes, mi Cuca, que nací en Panzacola;
soy indio ilustradito como tú y esta sola
ilusión me condujo a ver la India Bonita . . .
No te enceles, Cuca,
no te enceles, hija,
¡si al cabo tú eres
mi india bonita!
No grité, ni nada,
me estorbaba todo:
cubeta, los guantes,
el paragua, el choclo . . .
¡Malaigan las prendas
que la moda trajo:
ansí ni es uno indio
ni civilizado! . . .
No quiero, por más que quiero,
recordar el hervidero de la Nochi Mexicana,
pues por culpa de esa broza mandé planchar mi alevosa
y no juí a casa de Juana.
Y repitieron la Nochi
Mexicana con derrochi de todavía más ecsesos . . .
No juí por tonto o por vivo y por este otro motivo:
que costaba cinco pesos.
Después el desfile, los charros, clarines . . .
¡y yo en las tribunas! ¡y aquellos botines

mi apretaban todo lo que no imagines!
¡con decir que quise verlo en calcetines!

(And out of all the floats, one! It's the blood that calls!
You know well, my Cuca, that I was born in Panzacola;
I'm a little erudite Indian like you and this mere
illusion brought me to see the India Bonita . . .
Don't be jealous, Cuca,
don't be jealous, daughter,
after all you are
my India Bonita!
I didn't yell or anything,
everything bothered me:
hat, the gloves,
the umbrella, the brogue shoe . . .
Goddamn the garments
that fashion brought about:
they make you neither Indian
nor civilized! . . .
I don't want to remember, though I'm trying,
the teeming mass of people at the Noche Mexicana,
because of that riffraff I had my cloak ironed
and I didn't go to Juana's house.
And they repeated the Noche Mexicana
with a tremendous display of even more excesses . . .
I didn't go cause I'm stupid or smart and for this other reason:
it cost five pesos.
After the parade, the charros, bugles . . .
and me in the grandstands! And those boots
were so unbearably tight, you can't imagine!
to think that it made me want to see it in my stocking feet!)[77]

In these descriptions, Juan makes a number of contradictory statements. He positions himself as an "indio ilustradito," like Cuca, but compares himself and his wife to "la India Bonita." Juan and Cuca share the same "blood" as la India Bonita and hence the same Indigenous heritage. In a rhetorical maneuver, Juan reduces the parade to a single float, that of María Bibiana Uribe. The praise of her Indigenous beauty already captured in her title, "la India Bonita," gestures toward a shared understanding of an embodied sense of a racialized and gendered national aesthetics. Juan's reaction to María Bibiana's Indigenous beauty, which he compares to that of his wife ("tú eres mi india bonita" [you are my India Bonita]) underlines the racial and gender tensions associated with a sense of national pride: the Indian woman is the embodiment of the nation.[78]

In a way, Juan experiences a sense of national Indigenous belonging, yet his body performatively reveals the provisional, transitory, and fragmented nature of the emerging Mexican nationalism. He complains that

> [le] estorbaba todo:
> cubeta, los guantes,
> el paragua, el choclo . . .
> ¡Malaigan las prendas
> que la moda trajo:
> ansí ni es uno indio
> ni civilizado!"

> (everything bothered [him]:
> hat, the gloves,
> the umbrella, the brogue shoe . . .
> Goddamn the garments
> that fashion brought about:
> they make you neither Indian
> nor civilized!)

His attire, which represents a cosmopolitan aesthetics, visually and discursively contrasts with that of la India Bonita and the legendary figure of Cuauhtémoc in the first illustration. The sense of indigeneity that is visually represented, however, is discursively complicated once the reader realizes that the catrín is the Indian Juan. The simultaneous presence of multiple signifiers of Mexican indigeneity (the ancient glory of the "Aztec" civilization and the contemporaneous manifestation embodied by la India Bonita) collides with the popular and also cosmopolitan sense of national belonging represented by the "indio ilustradito." In fact, the cosmopolitan iteration of Juan calls attention to the conflicting and contradictory implications of embodying a cosmopolitan sense of the nation. Juan's fashionable attire constrains him and renders him neither "Indian" nor "civilized." The two iterations of the nation are not coeval; in fact, Juan implies they are oppositional. The parade, the nation on a stage ("el desfile, los charros, clarines" [the parade, the charros, bugles]), allow the people to witness the nation and in so doing to become a public "en las tribunas" (in the grandstands). Yet the experience of participating in the cultural performance of lo mexicano as a cosmopolitan, modern Indian triggers an embodied reaction that emphasizes the tension at stake: "¡y aquellos botines / mi apretaban todo lo que no imagines! / ¡con decir que quise verlo en calcetines!" (and those boots / were so unbearably tight, you can't imagine! / to think that it made me want to see it in my stocking feet!). What seems to threaten to destroy the Indigenous figures of the float, as depicted in the illustration, symbolizes the failure and excess of the staging of lo mexicano. Juan's rejection of shoes ultimately captures the ambivalence, complexity, and indeed the failure of an Indigenous man's performance as a member of the cosmopolitan bourgeoisie, rehearsing the modernizing project of the nation.

I have ended this chapter with an analysis of a textual and visual representation of el pueblo to emphasize the importance of focusing on bodies when we ask how the nation is experienced through cultural performances. Even though the visual and textual registers capture the complexities of the ever-changing field of lo mexicano, I want to draw attention to the ambivalence of the experience of the nation and its concomitant iterations at the level of the body. Juan is a discursive invention, but an invention that pays very close attention to embodiment. Here it is useful to note that Rodríguez theorizes sex and dances as embodied modalities that are "understood within defined frames of legibility and recognition that emerge from accumulated lived experience, but also from the worlds of media, storytelling, and the fantasies these vicarious forms inspire."[79] As the drawings and the letter remind us, the staging of the nation was conceived mainly as a dichotomous confrontation between the Indian and the civilized man, between the great Indigenous past and a modern cosmopolitan future. Nevertheless, perhaps paradoxically rendered throughout the letter, the visual and the textual may not necessarily circulate the same fractured, provisional, and incomplete project of the nation that the bodily actions reveal. The Indigenous man wearing a frock coat embodies a clash between differing temporal and cultural frames. Although the newspaper operated as a stage, one that was not equally accessible for el pueblo, it still exemplified the power that mass communication would gain. Newspapers, as I have shown, framed the experience of the centennial events, particularly La Noche Mexicana. The articles and images they published and circulated set the stage for the nation by imagining it and then discursively performing it.

In this chapter, I have used La Noche Mexicana to analyze the frames that made lo mexicano legible and recognizable while exploring the elements that exceeded it. The rehearsal of an embodied sociality of a national identity entailed the incorporation of the irreducible particularities of bodies. In this sense, events such as the massive celebration of La Noche Mexicana functioned as rehearsals and hence embodiments of the nation. Thinking of the nation as a fiction that is put into practice means paying attention to the ephemeral but concrete gestures that bodily actions produced while performing lo mexicano, thereby showing complicities, fractures, failures, and even resistances to normative ideas of Mexican nationalism.

In the next chapter, I discuss how Nellie Campobello's dance career interpellated and choreographed a national audience. Campobello's body allowed for a kind of performative writing that continuously undid what she claimed to represent, a national narrative of a heteronormative and mestizo nation. By privileging the body, I acknowledge that lo mexicano is an idea that is always changing, incomplete, and becoming. The consolidation of a corporeal expressive culture came later; its rehearsal began in late September 1921 during the Noche Mexicana.

CHAPTER 3

Nellie Campobello: The Choreographer of Dancing Histories in Mexico

In October 1921, less than a month after the tremendous success of La Noche Mexicana, the Teatro Arbeu featured the Ballet del Centenario (Ballet of the centenary), showcasing the same performances that had been acclaimed at the centennial festivities in Chapultepec. Against Adolfo Best Maugard's exquisite backdrop of a Mexican modernist fantasy (see figure 2.4), the popular dances once again attracted crowds of spectators. Writing for *El Universal Ilustrado*, Jerónimo Coignard (Francisco Zamora) shared with his readers his reflections on the emergence of a Mexican ballet. He captured the ambivalence with which the Mexican public had received El jarabe tapatío during La Noche Mexicana and now once again at the Teatro Arbeu, where Pavlova had danced two years earlier, in 1919: "Porque el público metropolitano, aun haciendo un gesto 'snob' de incredulidad cuando se le dice que aquello es 'ballet,' se rinde a la seducción del baile, popular como ninguno entre nosotros, y olvida por un momento que los bailarines no se sostienen en la punta de los pies, que no visten a la rusa" (Because the metropolitan public, even with a 'snob' gesture of incredulity when they are told that that is 'ballet,' surrenders to the seductiveness of the dance, popular as none other among us, and forgets for a moment that the dancers do not stand en pointe, and do not dress as Russians). He concluded "que aquello es cosa nuestra, estilizada, 'elegantizada', refinada todo lo posible, para que pueda exhibirse, decorosamente, en el escenario en que se balanceó, admirablemente, por cierto, la señora Pawlova" (that that is our thing, stylized, 'elegantized,' refined to the utmost, so that it can be shown, decorously, on the same stage where, by the way, Ms. Pavlova herself swayed admirably).[1] The dance education of the Mexican public continued, attempting to reconcile vernacular expressions such as El jarabe tapatío with the European dance tradition of the ballet. After all, Pavlova had set a new standard for the "balletization" of Mexican dance during her first visit in 1919 (see fig. 3.1). Mexican audiences had already been exposed to ballet, and, perhaps in the spirit of the centennial celebrations, they allowed themselves to be seduced once again by a popular dance that was theirs, stylized, "refined," and not en pointe, but theirs. Mexican dances were now staged and consumed at theaters, performed "decorously" as part of the repertoire of a Mexican cosmopolitan entertainment.

Eleven years after Pavlova's first visit, in 1930, Nellie and Gloria Campobello performed El jarabe tapatío again. The Campobello sisters, or the Campbells, as they were then known, had just returned from Cuba. The sisters had successfully debuted in 1927 in Mexico City with the dance company of the Texan Miss Lettie H. Carroll. Miss Carroll's dance school, the only "serious" one in the city, offered an annual recital that showcased the girls' skills and performed at national celebrations, fund-raising events, clubs, and modeling agencies.[2] The Campobello sisters' success abroad and their recent return to Mexico not only confirmed their dance attributes and expertise but also highlighted the repertoire that dominated the current dance scene both at home and abroad. An

Figure 3.1. Anna Pavlova. Joseph Rous Paget-Fredericks Dance Collection, BANC PIC 1964.023:347–POR. Bancroft Library, University of California, Berkeley.

article published in early May 1930 in one of the most circulated cultural weekly journals of the era, *Revista de Revistas*, praised their accomplishments overseas as well as their dance repertoire: "Nelly y Gloria Campbell, gentil pareja de bailarinas artistas . . . cuya gracia, un poco griega y otro poco azteca, llena por completo un escenario cuando estas nerviosas y extrañas muchachas se proponen desarrollar un programa matizado con cadencias y ritmos evocadores de las danzas antiguas y con danzas nuestras, llenas de color y de vida" (Nelly and Gloria Campbell, a charming pair of dance artists . . . whose grace, a bit Greek and also a bit Aztec, fills the stage completely when these nervous and strange girls set out to present a nuanced program with cadences and rhythms evoking ancient dances and with our own dances, full of color and life).[3] In the title of the piece, "Artistas nuestros que triunfan en el extranjero" (Local Artists Who Triumph Abroad), one can already note a celebratory tone as well as an insistence on referring to the dancers as local artists, not foreign but ours, "nuestros." Mexico too had artists, and their triumph combined the classic beauty and aesthetics of the Greeks with those of the Aztecs. The talent of two Mexican women, two "nervous and strange girls," gave life to ancient rhythms and, perhaps more important, to Mexico's own dances, "full of color and life." The article made clear references to the vocabulary and aesthetics of the modernist movement, thereby inserting the Campobello sisters into the circuit that dominated the international dance scene.

The performance of El jarabe tapatío by the Campobello sisters had a different purpose and impact than Pavlova's did. It did not "elevate" Mexican dance to the world-class manifestation of Pavlova's ballet, but rather reiterated what Pavlova had already accomplished. The Campobellos had already included El jarabe tapatío in their repertoire abroad alongside other popular Mexican dances. Pavlova's interpretation of the dance in 1919 had contributed to its image as a "national" or "Mexican" dance. When the Campobellos performed it, it exemplified the use of local, regional, and traditional dances as a means of interpreting a Mexican national identity. In fact, the Campobellos' performance gained much of its significance from its perceived contrast to Pavlova's balleticized interpretation, because the sisters were seen as "reclaiming" El jarabe tapatío for Mexican dancers while maintaining a high level of artistic quality. The cultural critic Carlos del Río succinctly stated in 1930, "El primer espectáculo de danza mexicana de alta calidad estética que en México me han ofrecido lo debo a Nellie y a Gloria Campobello" (The first spectacle of Mexican dance of high aesthetic quality that I have been offered in Mexico was thanks to Nellie and Gloria Campobello).[4] Their performance not only confirmed the aesthetic value of Mexican dance but also reclaimed El jarabe tapatío for the national imaginary. The Campobello sisters performed the iconic Mexican couple, dressed as el charro (a Mexican cowboy wearing traditional attire) and la china poblana (Mexican traditional festive attire), and were celebrated by their public as symbols of the national. In fact, del Río highlighted that the Campobello sisters did not dance in traditional ballet shoes but rather in Mexican huaraches, confirming the dance's status as a national symbol. This simple yet critical observation points to the movement vocabulary deployed by the Campobello sisters: they did not dance en pointe but most likely on their heels and soles.

These two related events—Pavlova's rendition of El jarabe tapatío and the Campobellos' performance of the same dance—reveal the importance of Mexican dance for the construction of a national identity, as well as the role of women in the configuration of lo mexicano. I am interested in the importance of Mexican dance as a cultural field that evinces the fissures and tensions that were present from the very beginning in the creation of a mestizo postrevolutionary cultural nationalism. Mexican regional dances, which would eventually lead to the creation of folklórico dance, became a significant embodied means both of telling Mexico's past and of negotiating the incorporation of "living" Indigenous cultures of the present. Throughout this book, I mobilize the term folklórico in Spanish to recognize its particularities as an established dance practice and discipline in Mexico and the global Mexican diaspora.[5] Folklórico dance organized and systematized the kinesthetic formation of Mexican national subjects, that is, the formation of national subjects through movement and through their awareness of movement, as discussed in the introduction. In this capacity, folklórico dance became a contested site for controlling and normalizing national bodies and establishing a mestizo aesthetics of movement. The dance trajectory of the Campobello sisters, Nellie Campobello in particular, is crucial to understanding the nationalization of a Mexican dance aesthetic.

Nellie Campobello played a critical role in the emergence of a Mexican school of dance. Primarily known today as a novelist of the Mexican Revolution, she was also a dancer and an influential choreographer. Her dance career contributed, simultaneously and paradoxically, to the institutionalization of lo mexicano as hypermasculinized and mestizo and to the creation of spaces for female and at times queer embodiments of national subjects. With *embodiment*, I refer to the ways bodies represent and materialize an idea of the nation symbolically, materially, and physically. Nellie's choreographic rendering of Mexico opened up a space for the circulation of female bodies and voices within the nation; however, I place the figure of Nellie Campobello and her role in the emergence and institutionalization of Mexican dance within a process of incomplete signification, resulting from the ambivalent, provisional, and fragmentary cultural boundaries of Mexican nationalism. In this sense, the case of Nellie Campobello is paramount. Not only was she a pioneer of Mexican letters, the first self-taught woman to write about the Mexican Revolution, but she was also a pioneer in the creation of dance as a nationalist discipline in postrevolutionary Mexico. Interestingly, and perhaps not surprisingly, her career began in both fields around the same time and peaked around the same time as well, particularly during the 1930s and 1940s.[6] Campobello choreographed and advanced a national mestizo dance logic that relied on an *indigenista* approach to movement. By layering authenticity claims grounded in indigeneity onto the movement vocabulary, kinesthetic qualities, and dance aesthetics she deployed, Campobello negotiated the tensions and contradictions of her project of fostering technical excellence, engaging with modernist aesthetics and aspirations, and grappling with her predilection for ballet vis-à-vis the consolidation of modern dance in Mexico.[7] Her unique position as a dancer, writer, choreographer, and, finally, director of the National School of Dance led Campobello to consolidate the nationalization of Mexican dance. Throughout this chapter, I discuss the work of Nellie Campobello and her impact on the development of Mexican dance as a pedagogical practice through which the State formed its citizens and provided them with a means to read and consume images and ideas of the nation—its embodied imaginaries.

Performing the Nation: "Shaping Society through Dance"

The Porfirian regime actively promoted and celebrated a nationalistic ritualized behavior. "Performance education" became a key signature of the government's efforts to disseminate and dramatize its ideology and power. In the second half of the nineteenth century, the Porfirian government placed a great deal of emphasis on the active education of the people. The government invested in the creation of a "symbolic territory," according to the dance historian Roxana Guadalupe Ramos Villalobos, whereby architecture, sculpture, festivities, theater, music, and dance became an influential way to "summon, persuade, appeal to the sentiments and conscience" of the Mexican people.[8] Material culture and performance arts interpellated citizens into a nationalistic imaginary.

Perhaps the best example to illustrate the systematic dissemination of such ritualized public behavior is the work of Justo Sierra. As the Minister of Education, Sierra actively promoted a "performative" education of children in schools. In 1902, he officially established the *fiestas escolares* (school festivities) to celebrate the end of an academic year. The dance historian Alberto Dallal contends that Sierra systematized the organization and pedagogical preparation of both teachers and students to plan the presentation of songs, declamation of poetry, theater, and dance. The performances included at least one or two months of rehearsals, which honed the staging skills of the teachers and the artistic talents of the pupils, who were the citizens of the present but the artists of the future.[9] In short, the fiestas escolares sought to educate and form citizens to be spectators of the performance of spectacles, which would eventually include the performance of the nation, particularly through dance.

During this period, popular dance, music, and festivals, along with performances of high culture such as ballet and opera, acquired a particular prominence. Traveling artists visited Mexico City and offered their shows to the consolidating middle and upper classes. As a result, so-called popular manifestations soon began a process of transformation. Mexican expressive forms of popular culture needed to be transculturated with those imported from abroad.[10] Local expressions of dance, song, and music incorporated and adapted the repertoire of foreign ballets and operas to "Mexicanize" them. Moreover, the performance of power became the trademark of the Porfirian regime itself. As Dallal notes, "Díaz hizo que su propia imagen resultara elemento fundamental en el proceso 'civilizador' de su gobierno; él mismo se volvió un espectáculo junto con desfiles, fiestas cívicas, celebraciones y festividades escolares, faranduleras y dancísticas" (Díaz made it so that his own image would become a fundamental element in the 'civilizing' process of his government; he himself became a spectacle together with the parades, civic commemorations, and school, social, and dance celebrations and festivities).[11] The Porfirian performance of power and Sierra's incorporation of children into this national enterprise reveal the significance of schools in the configuration of a national public.[12]

The performance of Mexican regional and traditional dances allows us to expand our understanding of the aesthetic and material practices of lo mexicano—its conception and representation—and its embodiment.

Dance played a crucial role in the formation of lo mexicano and the parallel configuration of a national public. As an artistic expression, however, it needed to be regulated to make sure it conformed to the aesthetics of postrevolutionary Mexico.[13] To underscore its national foundations, the local took on a new precedence vis-à-vis the bourgeois, cosmopolitan dance practices that were popular in the first two decades of the twentieth century. Michelle Clayton points out that dance operated as a mechanism to negotiate cultural, political, and historical differences between the Western, modern world and its "Others," ethnic, historical, sexual, or otherwise. Clayton claims that in the early 1900s, dance's vital role was "to provide a bodily image—and simultaneously, a somatic experience—of other cultures, often as part of variety shows that had much in common with world's fairs or amusement parks."[14] Similarly, Mexican dance functioned as a mode of representing the diversity not of Western "Others" but of Mexico's own culture, history, and racialized sexual and gender roles during the establishment of *misiones culturales* (cultural missions) in the era of José Vasconcelos. The consolidation of folklórico dance on the national and international scenes, in fact, can be traced back to the cultural and political agenda of Vasconcelos. As in the case of popular arts and crafts, folklórico dance was produced for both a local and an international audience, and it was the result of a series of negotiations between popular and elite sectors.

José Vasconcelos pioneered the reform of the educational system. He was named the president of the National University of Mexico in 1920 by Victoriano Huerta and in 1921 was made the director of the Ministry of Education (Secretaría de Educación Pública [SEP]) by Álvaro Obregón. Students and young women encouraged by Vasconcelos reached out to remote places, where they launched misiones, built schools, and actively promoted the arts.[15] The creation of misiones culturales throughout the country in 1923 was intimately intertwined with the promotion of dance. In her classic study of Mexican dance, *Danza y poder*, Margarita Tortajada Quiroz claims that the misiones "estaban inspiradas en los misioneros de la Colonia que habían logrado la hazaña de llegar a todo el país, aprendiendo las lenguas indígenas y enseñando la cultura y religión occidentales. Los nuevos misioneros eran laicos y debían apren-der las artes, artesanías y creencias indígenas para después llevarlas a las ciudades" (were inspired by the missionaries of the Colony who had carried out the great deed of reaching the whole country, learning Indigenous languages, and teaching Western culture and religion. The new missionaries were secular and had to learn Indigenous arts, crafts, and beliefs to later take them back to the cities).[16] The *misioneros* (missionaries) thus approached "local knowledges" as raw materials that were to be processed and transported from the rural communities to the Western, modern arena of the nation.[17]

Dance, then, became a crucial mechanism for disseminating an ideology of collective national belonging, thereby instilling a sense of Mexican identity. By literally and symbolically bringing together Indigenous and peasant communities, dance and other expressive cultural practices, such as theater, enacted the national project that Vasconcelos had envisioned. As regional and local dances became part of the curriculum in rural areas, the misioneros began to record and learn these dances in order to teach them later in the nation's capital and other urban areas. In doing so, they created, as Mary Louise Pratt points out, an urban public for "rural artistic forms," reorienting local artistic expressions toward the national realm.[18] Dancing enabled processes of subject formation in both rural and urban areas. The misiones culturales became vital for the production, transmission, and circulation of an embodied nationalist cultural capital.

Dance promoted a display of lo mexicano for a national audience, while simultaneously functioning as a marker of cultural specificity. The performance arts, such as dance and theater, were essential to Vasconcelos's program, particularly the misiones culturales. Whereas only a limited number of people could travel to Mexico City to see the murals, performative arts involved a large number of participants and spectators, including people with no formal education, literacy, or even knowledge of Spanish.[19] Inspired by the policies of Russia's Anatoly Lunacharsky, the dissemination of performative arts through the misiones culturales and the subsequent programs developed in Mexico City highlight the role of schools in this endeavor and the state's attitude toward the ethnoracial diversity of Mexico. The state's approach to Indigenous people revolved around embodied practices. Rick López points out that "as public schools in the 1930s tried to improve Indians by teaching them Indigenous dances from the far corners of Mexico [. . .], they pressured those same students to abandon their local traditions, including not only such imposed 'traditions' as poor hygiene but also their native language and folk religious practices."[20] Indigenous embodied practices had to be selected, sanitized, and reorganized to fit an "ethnicized" idea of the nation.

Unlike the Porfirian political program (discussed in chapter 1), the Indigenous in postrevolutionary Mexico did not belong to an ancient past; therefore, the state created mechanisms to engage with the contemporary presence of Indigenous bodies and their attendant cultural practices.

Margarita Tortajada Quiroz asserts that dance served as a means to record, and I would add to interpret, embodied and expressive practices and to disseminate them throughout the nation for over a decade. In fact, between 1926 and 1938 the Dirección de Misiones Culturales (Office of Cultural Missions) distributed materials that included information regarding local dances, costumes, musical scores, choreographies, illustrations, and descriptions. These materials assisted misioneros throughout the country in celebrating artistic festivals where local communities presented their own dances and other artistic expressions.[21] The work of the misiones brought to the fore the intimate connection of dance to the formation and interpellation of Mexican citizens.

There were other embodied platforms that intersected with the national to socially interpellate Mexican citizens during this period, including physical education and national sports. As with performances of military power, the consolidation and dissemination of physical education and sports at schools and official events, particularly during the celebration of the centenaries in 1910 and 1921 (as discussed in the previous chapters) became part and parcel of the choreography of nationalism. These embodied pedagogies responded to and participated in efforts to mediate the experience of modernity, especially urban modernity. Ramsay Burt observes that such forms of body culture, from modern dance to mass gymnastics, affected the ways individuals grappled with their interaction with the masses and the mechanization and bureaucratization of work and leisure, thereby shaping modern subjectivity.[22] Body culture also reasserted the national in embodied terms; that is, "the body represented a politicised image of the nation."[23] The dance historian Claudia Carbajal Segura contends that monumental choreographies and mass spectacles such as the inauguration of the National Stadium helped to consolidate and reproduce aesthetic and ideological imaginaries in Mexico, especially during the 1920s and 1930s.[24] Cultural and physical displays of nationalism, military parades, and mass gymnastics, among other spectacles, invited Mexican individuals to corporeally recognize themselves as part of the nation. In so doing, such choreographies of nationalism enabled bodies in movement to shape the social space they inhabited.

The presence of women in public spaces had not diminished after the end of the Revolution. Even though the Revolution did not drastically change women's roles, it gave women opportunities to renegotiate their place within the emergent modern Mexican nation-state.[25] Modernizing currents and transnational processes further complicated the role of women in the postrevolutionary period. Through the often-contradictory dynamics of urbanization and industrialization, the public presence and active participation of women in public life led many to ask questions about how they were enacting their citizenship. Jocelyn Olcott contends that women sought to accrue and claim their rights as citizens primarily through "status (e.g., sex, property, or literacy), activities (e.g., labor, military service, or community activism), or affiliation (with a party, union, or official organization)," but these rights were continuously disputed in the aftermath of the Revolution.[26] Women simultaneously challenged masculinized structures and reinforced them. On the one hand, the active political participation of women destabilized the patriarchal configuration of exclusively male civil engagement, and dance in particular allowed women to create physical and political spaces of their own.[27] On the other, female cultural producers also reinforced masculinized national ideas. It is precisely at the center of such gendered entanglements that Nellie and her sister Gloria Campobello emerged. The dancing career of the Campobellos began in the 1920s in the middle of a cultural revolution led by José Vasconcelos, in an era when the roles of women at times challenged and at times reinforced a unified, masculinized construction of the nation.

The Dancing History of Nellie Campobello

The Campobello sisters contributed to the configuration of state-sponsored Mexican nationalism, and their dance practice embodied its performance. By actively continuing the cultural work that the misioneros had started, they underscored the role of dance in schools and other popular venues and its relationship to the formation of Mexican citizens.[28] Nellie and Gloria Campobello had started their dancing career in the 1920s after seeing a 1925 performance by Anna Pavlova, the icon of international dance who first visited Mexico in 1919. Gloria and Nellie Campobello began taking classes with the Costa sisters, Amelia and Linda, who had arrived in Mexico in 1904 as part of Aldo Barilli's Compañía de Baile de Pantomima. They continued with Carmen Galé and afterward with Stanislava Moll Patapovich and Carol Adamchevsky, two Polish dancers who had been trained in Warsaw and Saint Petersburg, respectively. Although Mexico did not have a proper dance school at the time, the Campobellos began dancing with the Texan Miss Lettie H. Carroll, whose dance school was regarded as the only formal dance academy in Mexico City, showcasing the dance skills of affluent children in its annual recital.[29]

The Campobellos joined the company and debuted with "Carroll's Girls" in March 1927. They were part of four numbers; Nellie interpreted three masculine roles, including a young man in "Una fantasía oriental" (An Oriental fantasy), a sailor, and the god Pan in a duo with Gloria in "Una fantasía bucólica" (A bucolic fantasy).[30]

I will now let Nellie herself explain how the sisters became involved in the world of dance. The following excerpt comes from a 1972 interview secretly recorded by Patricia Aulestia, dancer and founder of Ecuador's National Ballet (1967–1970) and the eventual founder of Mexico's National Center for the Research and Documentation of Dance, Centro Nacional de Documentación, Información e Investigación de la Danza José Limón (CENIDI).

> NC: Andábamos con niñas millonarias, nosotras no éramos ningunas pelagatos pero no teníamos millones como ellas. Le puedo mencionar nombres, tengo toda la documentación. Entonces las norteamericanas siempre humillan al mexicano. Y cuando la señorita Carroll nos arregló, que no era maestra, sino que ella dijo: "Voy a meter a estas niñas a que hagan una prueba . . . que si al público de México . . . o lo que sea" Yo en mi Historia de la Danza, que casi tengo terminada, la pongo a ella en un lugar prominente. Pero esto ya fue posterior a Pavlova. Entonces le dije yo a Gloria: "¡Vamos a bailar como bailan, vamos a bañar a estas gringas!" Y debutamos, éramos doce muchachas jovencitas, y casi escuela, de doce, once años teníamos. Y las mejores eran las niñas Campbell, que éramos nosotras. Porque yo llevaba al apellido de mi padrastro, Campbell. En el Larousse está que Campbell es Campobello, sólo que ellos le quitaron las dos oes. La historia de los Campbell comienza con Giselle de Campobelo, que fue el que fundó esa dinastía allí, una de los Campbell, somos grandes ¿no? . . . Yo no soy Campbell, mi hermana Campbell. Las niñas Campbell, que por cierto dijo la señorita: "Son mexicanas", fueron las que nos llevábamos todo, y además las que bailábamos y teníamos gusto por el arte. Entonces yo solamente lo hice para demostrar a los mexicanos que podíamos darles en la mera . . . a las gringas. Y que nosotros lo hacíamos mejor. Yo inventé un . . . fíjese, siendo chica, era así, inventé . . . yo tengo tipo de boxeador, siempre he sido muy atlética sin ser gorda. Y salí vestida de boxeador; a hacer de boxeador y que peleaba, y boxeaba y que esto . . . mire ¡fue la ovación!

(We would hang out with millionaire girls; we were not nobodies, but we did not have millions like they did. I can mention to you their names; I have all the documentation. Then the Americans would always humiliate the Mexicans. And when Miss Carroll made the arrangements, and she was not a teacher, but she said: "I'm going to include these girls so that they can be tested. . . . So that the Mexican public . . . or whatever." In my *History of Dance*, which is almost finished, I give her [Miss Carroll] a prominent place. But this was after Pavlova. Then I told Gloria: "Let's go dance like they dance; let's go show these *gringas* [Americans] what we're made of!" And we debuted; we were twelve young girls—quite a bunch—and were eleven or twelve years old. The Campbell girls were the best, and that was us. Because I had my stepfather's last name, Campbell. In the *Larousse* [Encyclopedic Dictionary] it is stated that Campbell is Campobello; it is just that they got rid of the last two o's. The history of the Campbell starts with Giselle Campbelo, who founded that dynasty there, one of the Campbells; we're important, aren't we? . . . I'm not a Campbell; my sister is a Campbell. The Campbell girls, who by the way said Miss [Carroll] "are Mexicans," were the ones that received all the attention, and the ones who danced and had a taste for art. Then I just did it to show that the Mexicans could wallop these girls . . . the *gringas*. And that we did it better. I invented a . . . listen, being a girl, I was like that, I invented. . . . I have the physique of a boxer; I've always been very athletic but not fat. And I came out dressed as a boxer; I played a boxer that would fight and would box and this. . . . Look, it was an ovation!) [31]

In this fragment, Nellie offered her own version of how and why she and Gloria got involved in dance. She alluded to her vast knowledge of the field, referencing briefly the history of dance she claimed to be writing at the time. And she did not shy away from positioning herself and Gloria as talented young Mexican girls vis-à-vis the gringas, despite or perhaps thanks to their last name, Campbell. She recognized the importance of debuting with Miss Carroll and, even if in passing, mentioned Pavlova's performance as an inspiration. Nellie also emphasized her versatility and ability to perform masculine roles and the creative interventions her muscular, athletic body allowed her to carry out.

The excerpt also highlights the ephemeral materiality of a little-known recording of one of the few extant interviews of Nellie Campobello. Even though I was able to piece together Nellie's dance career via official documents, newspaper articles, scholarly works, and Nellie's own writing, I cite her assessment of her legacy as a dancer and choreographer in this secretly recorded interview to illustrate her strategic creation of her own mythology. On January 4, 1972, Patricia Aulestia hid under her poncho a recording device, *una grabadora*, and taped what appears to be perhaps the only existing recording of Nellie's voice. Nellie's voice and the rest of the sounds and other utterances are impossible to completely textualize, and yet they can be heard, or rather sensed, in line with José Esteban Muñoz's notion of ephemera as an alternate modality in which to index traces of lived experience.[32] Nellie's disappeared archive—all of her work that was not published or recorded or was eventually lost—is a site where unrealized possibilities persist as eminent potentialities, which might come to fruition when we hear her voice that moves us when we evoke her movements.[33] Following a queer generative approach to relating to archives and producing evidence, I believe that Campobello's voice gives the researcher the restorative power to *access* and *assess* her legacy as one of Mexico's most important cultural producers before her forced disappearance in 1985 and her mysterious death in 1986, as I discuss at the end of the chapter.

This fragment, then, reveals Nellie's creation of a myth about herself, her origins, and her genealogy, which she managed to keep a mystery for her entire life. (In 1965, the literary critic Emmanuel Carballo published what may be the only formal interview that Nellie Campobello ever gave in which she revealed information about her origins, apart from the prologue of the edited volume with her writings published in 1960, *Mis libros* [My books].) She claimed variously to have been born with the Mexican Revolution, to bear Comanche blood, and, as revealed in this interview, to be part of the Campbell dynasty, only to disavow it by clarifying that only Gloria was a Campbell. Although she suggested that she was a young girl, part of the group of eleven- and twelve-year-olds who debuted with Miss Carroll, Nellie Campobello was born María Francisca Luna in Villa Ocampo, Durango, in 1900.[34] Her sister Gloria was born Soledad Luna in Parral, Chihuahua, in 1911.[35] Thus, Nellie Campobello was a twenty-seven-year-old woman when she debuted with the Carroll Girls, and her sister was sixteen. Nellie relied on her self-created myth not just to protect herself from scrutiny but also to claim authenticity and authority in her knowledge and abilities. After all, dance demanded years of training, ideally since childhood. Nellie was also able to manipulate her own family history to conceal sensitive information, including the identity of her and Gloria's protector when they moved to Mexico City from Chihuahua in 1921, and to position herself as a legitimate, self-taught cultural producer, asserting her skills as a writer, dancer, and choreographer.

Despite their success in 1927 with "the Carroll Girls," who would become a sensation in the coming years, the Campobello sisters soon left the world of dance, only to reappear again in 1929 in Cuba. The Campobellos had traveled to Havana, Cuba, where they debuted at the Teatro Martí as part of a Mexican show with the Orquesta Mexicana de Charros de Mondragón in July 1929. They were part of a Mexican spectacle, interpreting dances from Yucatán, other popular dances, and Mexican jarabes, including El jarabe tapatío (see fig. 3.2). The Charros de Mondragón were en route to participate in the official program of the Mexican government at the expositions in Seville and Barcelona.[36] The Campobellos stayed behind. It was not until January 1930 that they began dancing again, at the Teatro Campoamor together with Adria Delhort as part of the program before film screenings. In late January, they started performing at the Château Madrid, where Nellie and Gloria, hired by Fausto Campuzano, presented "los bailes típicos de su bello país . . .

Figure 3.2. "Las hermanas Campobello," *Diario de la Marina* (Havana, Cuba), January 26, 1930. Ministerio de Cultura y Deporte. Subdirección General de Cooperación Bibliotecaria.

las danzas clásicas y los 'ballets' modernos con sorprendente habilidad" (the typical dances of their beautiful country . . . classical dances and the modern 'ballets,' with surprising skill).[37]

Upon their return from Cuba, the Campobello sisters joined the Ministry of Education (SEP), invited by Carlos Trejo y Lerdo de Tejada, the subsecretary of public education who had seen them perform in Cuba, where he was the ambassador. Their sudden return to Mexico launched them as pioneers of a school of Mexican dance. As Nellie Campobello stated, the SEP "nos ofreció [un puesto] para danzar en las escuelas y en las colonias pobres, así como para contribuir con nuestra danza en actos oficiales o políticos, y crear espectáculos escolares en los estadios" (offered us a position to dance in schools and in poor neighborhoods, and also to collaborate with our dance in official or political celebrations and to stage school productions in stadiums).[38] The Campobellos became instructors of *bailes mexicanos* (Mexican dances); they also performed dances they had studied during their "cultural" trips in order to create new steps and new plots.[39] After their return from Cuba, the Campobellos, along with other dance teachers from the SEP, joined the efforts to promote dance as a national endeavor and create the first institutions dedicated to the study and promotion of dance, starting with the Escuela de Plástica Dinámica (School of Dynamic Plastic Arts), which I discuss in the next section. In this work, the Campobellos followed the lead of the misioneros. They too engaged local embodied practices and knowledges as resources to be taken from their rural Indigenous and peasant communities and restaged for urban audiences. Indigenous embodied practices had to be transculturated to materialize the idea of the nation.

International processes that can be related to the dance career of the Campobellos, especially Nellie, resulted in the consolidation of dance as a field through which the notions of gender, race, and sexuality associated with lo mexicano were negotiated. The emerging national body had to be shaped and educated. According to the Mexican dance scholar Sophie Bidault, the body of the female dancer actualized the experience of the performance of the nation: "además de injertar autenticidad y espiritualidad en la danza mexicana, la bailarina de los años treinta debía dar cuerpo a una experiencia comunitaria, propiciar la integración de todos los estratos sociales y cumplir con los objetivos populistas de los gobiernos nacionales" (besides injecting authenticity and spirituality to Mexican dance, the female dancer of the 1920s had to embody a communal experience, foster the integration of all social strata, and fulfill the populist objectives of the national governments).[40] Performing the nation required a specific kind of gender performance. As mentioned in the previous chapter, the figure of the flapper, or chica moderna, dominated the urban scene, functioning as a marker of modernity and cosmopolitanism. But the image of the flapper stood in direct contrast to revolutionary values.

Nellie Campobello entered the public scenario performing the masculinized gender ideal of a nation. In her attitude and behavior, she promoted the figure of a combative cultural revolutionary. The press often portrayed her as virile, combative, and committed, and she reinforced this image. Furthermore, Nellie displayed many of the characteristics associated with revolutionary manliness; she was frank, brusque, and a kind of "modern Eva," well liked among the intellectual and cultural elites, with a "revolutionary spirit."[41] Nellie, however, seems to have considered herself more than a "modern Eva." In the interview with Emmanuel Carballo, Nellie attributed to her clothing aspects of her character. Her description operates as an allegory of her personality: "Soy muy exigente con mi ropa. Si alguien la toca, si se cae al suelo, no me la pongo. Antes de usarla, debe estar intacta. En casa, uso cierta ropa de tipo un tanto varonil: camisa de leñador y pantalón que recordaría a un soldado de Gengis Kan" (I am very strict with my outfits. If someone touches them, if they fall to the ground, I won't wear them. Before using them, they must be intact. At home, I wear a certain kind of clothing that is somewhat manly: a lumberjack shirt and pants that would remind you of one of Genghis Khan's soldiers). She went on to describe her footwear: "En vez de zapatos, llevo sandalias un poco más grandes que el pie, para que me quepan las medias de lana. Me gusta escribir con esa ropa. . . . (En ocho días acabo un par de zapatos. Piso como bestia.)" (Instead of shoes, I wear sandals a bit bigger than my feet so that they fit with my wool socks. I like writing in those clothes. . . . [Within eight days I go through a pair of shoes. I stomp like a beast.]).[42] In the interview, Campobello masculinized her attire and her personality. She rejected conventional markers of femininity and insisted on identifying with masculinized traits, physical markers, and material objects, such as the lumberjack jacket, pants, and footwear.[43] She also claimed certain animalistic characteristics, like her stomping. Her gestures and bodily comportment conveyed a sense of autonomy, strength, and independence that matched her commanding and at times authoritative personality. In the interview, she even compared herself directly to Genghis Khan, with whom she claimed to have conversed from time to time and whom she admired. Yet Nellie also emphasized something that she would insist on the rest of her life: a sense of purity, of being untouched, "intact" like her clothing. She always asked to be addressed as "Señorita Campobello" (Miss Campobello). How, then, did the Campobellos come to embody a gendered idea of the nation?

One of their first public performances documented after their return from Cuba was El jarabe tapatío, which has since come to represent the most recognizable dance connoting lo mexicano. El jarabe tapatío had previously consolidated its status as a national dance during the inauguration of the National Stadium in 1924, when five hundred couples performed it (as I discuss in the introduction; see fig. I.2).[44] Pavlova's interpretation of it in 1919 also contributed to its image as a "national" or Mexican dance. But the Campobellos' performance, as mentioned earlier, contrasted significantly with Pavlova's. This time two women claimed El jarabe tapatío for Mexican dancers, displaying a level of artistry equal to the two foreign dancers. In his description of the performance of the Campobello sisters, the cultural critic Carlos del Río enthusiastically stated that

> una poderosa, inteligente intuición . . . hizo que Nellie y Gloria Campobello descubrieran lo que en verdad es el jarabe, y lo bailaron sin miedo, apasionadamente. No las detuvo la falta de bailarín. Nellie, a la que ayudan su antecedente de existencia montaraz, su gusto por la aventura, su silueta, es el hombre admirable que cerca, persigue, vence a la mujer, la domina en una final alegría. (No lo bailan en zapatillas sino en huaraches).

> (a powerful, intelligent intuition . . . made Nellie and Gloria discover the truth about the jarabe, and they danced it without fear, passionately. The lack of a male dancer didn't stop them. Aided by her early experience of rustic life, by her taste for adventure, and by her silhouette, Nellie is the admirable man who pursues, besieges, and defeats the woman and who dominates her in a final joy. (They dance it not in ballet shoes but rather in huaraches).[45]

This performance of El jarabe tapatío at once reinforced and contested heteronormative formulations of gender roles, as seen in figure 3.3. Nellie, described by del Río as an "hombre admirable" (admirable man), encloses, persecutes, and defeats the woman. The imperative to keep a heteronormative gender binary led del Río to read Nellie as the "man" who "dominates" the woman at the end of the dance. The "final joy" noted by del Río marks the festive tone of the nationalistic framework that positions the Campobellos' rendition of the dance as superior to Pavlova's.

However, del Río's description also captures two subtle yet significant differences in the Campobellos' interpretation. The authenticity of their rendition of this iconic Mexican dance relied on distinct changes in choreography and movement vocabulary. The dance historian Mitchell Snow has documented, following the description by Frances Toor of El jarabe tapatío in *Mexican Folkways*, that it was Carlos Trejo y Lerdo de Tejada who asked the dancers to turn the jarabe into a "rite of court-ship."[46] Whereas originally the dancers faced each other, Nellie as the charro pursued the china, Gloria, until she surrendered or, in the words of del Río, until Nellie "dominates her in a final joy." This courtship dance corporeally cited revolutionary tropes of masculine daring and

Figure 3.3. Nellie and Gloria Campobello dancing El jarabe tapatio. Courtesy of Archivo Histórico de la Escuela Nacional de Danza de Nellie y Gloria Campobello. Fondo Nellie Campobello.

force, embodied by Nellie's silhouette and her experience of a "rustic life" in northern Mexico, thereby choreographing the regional into the national. In fact, this choreographic change was adopted as standard.[47] Del Río's description also refers, almost in passing, to the Campobellos' movement vocabulary and aesthetics with the mention of sandals. The use of huaraches implied more than just a change in dance footwear. It indicated technical and aesthetic hierarchies in the movement vocabulary that was representative of Mexican dance: dancing with the heels and soles rather than en pointe. The Campobellos likely combined the music adaptation, movement vocabulary, and choreographic elements from Pavlova's rendition with the technical and expressive modernist aesthetics that they had embraced in Cuba. But through their performance of the jarabe, they undoubtedly tried to distance themselves from other renditions and dance traditions to assert their legitimacy as authentic Mexican dancers.

The performance of the Campobellos, then, allows for a different reading of the heteronormative construction of Mexican nationalism. In performing the iconic Mexican couple, el charro and la china poblana, the sisters performed what might be called a queer or queering gesture, and yet they were still celebrated by the public as the symbols of the national—of lo mexicano. In this sense, the Campobellos' performance offered a "spectacle" of Mexican dance despite the lack of a male dancer, a role that Nellie seems to have easily occupied. The public appearances of the Campobello sisters performing traditional dances revealed the tangled gender politics of the masculinized mestizo cultural sphere at the time. But my attribution of a queer subversive quality to the figure of Nellie Campobello needs interrogation; such subversion should not be uncritically celebrated or taken for granted. To what extent did the Campobello sisters, particularly Nellie, actively disavow a heteronormative role for women within the state, and to what extent did they foster heteronormativity? Licia Fiol-Matta argues that Chilean poet Gabriela Mistral "created a public discourse that supported a conservative role for women within the state, but her private life deviated significantly from the state prescription."[48] I read Nellie in an analogous way. Although Nellie Campobello's private life did not substantially challenge conservative notions about the role of women, her dancing body, which embodied lo mexicano, was read by male commentators as the body of a man. This reading gestured toward slippery modes of dominant and disidentificatory forms of spectatorship. This tension is why Nellie is crucial to understanding the importance of Mexican dance for the process of nation building. The fact that women played a central role in the emergence of dance as a cultural field produced a queering of the otherwise heteronormative Mexican nationalism and deepened the fractures and tensions that were present from the very beginning of the postrevolutionary cultural national projects.

The Campobellos, then, actively continued the cultural work that the misioneros had started. The work of the misiones exemplified the importance of dance in schools and public spaces for forming and interpellating Mexican subjects.[49] By the 1930s, the Mexican State regarded dance as essential for the education of its citizens.[50] The cultural politics during this period fostered the reworking of women's roles within the nation-state as performers, spectators, consumers, workers, students, and political actors.[51] The imperative to perform the nation led to the occupation of public spaces by otherwise marginalized subjects, including women, peasants, workers, children, and at times Indigenous people, alongside the bearers of masculinized forms of civic engagement, particularly soldiers, state bureaucrats, and members of the elite. Vasconcelos had been the one to envision such extraordinary public displays of nationalism. As demonstrated by the celebrations planned for the inauguration of the Estadio Nacional (National Stadium) in 1924, with the massive choreography of El jarabe tapatío performed by one thousand schoolgirls, public dance choreographies revealed the state's investment in an embodied pedagogy of Mexican nationalism.[52] In the 1930s, similarly massive choreographies—especially mass ballets—dominated the dance scene, illustrating the complex intersection between the state, Mexican dance, and gender roles.

The Campobellos choreographed a number of public dance performances and massive ballets, including *Barricada*, *Clarín*, *Simiente*, and the *Ballet 30–30*. Choreographed by one of the Campobello sisters with music by Francisco Domínguez, these "symbolic ballets" exalted the revolutionary fight and the concomitant changes brought about by the Mexican Revolution, promoted the role of education, and called on audience members to become productive citizens and to corporeally recognize themselves in embodied performances of nationalism.[53] Mass ballets and similar public performances enabled the state to literally rehearse and embody collective understandings of citizen formation and national belonging, in which the women played a key role.[54] The ballets gave the state the ability to choreograph a vision of union between the people, the nation, and the state, thereby enacting "a cohesive and disciplined social body" and dramatizing it via a combination of folklórico dance, theater, mime, musicals, film, and acrobatics.[55] These massive spectacles choreographed a sense of mestizo nationalism. They served to mobilize the people while enabling dance practitioners, particularly women, to create and inhabit spaces of their own. The Campobellos choreographed several *ballets masivos*, massive ballets, but they also created numerous folklórico numbers based on their continuous trips and public performances throughout the country and the research undertaken while traveling, including jaranas yucatecas, *jarabes michoacanos*, and *bailes itsmeños* (dances from Yucatán, Michoacán, and the Isthmus, respectively). The emergence of Mexican folklórico dance was practically simultaneous with its institutionalization, as it relied on the state for funding. The institutionalization of dance as a national project thus came about with the creation of the Escuela Nacional de Danza (END), the National School of Dance, as I elaborate later in the chapter. But the development and establishment of Mexican dance as a national project was first rehearsed through the public and massive displays of bodies in movement, dancing the history of Mexico.

El Ballet 30-30: Mexico's Revolutionary History in Movement

Dance became a contested terrain that mobilized women to perform the nation, even as they negotiated aesthetically, symbolically, and physically competing discourses about femininity, women's bodies, and gender roles. The effects of the public presence of women and their political participation, however, were ambiguous. Despite challenging the exclusivity of a public, male civic engagement, women activists and cultural producers also perpetuated masculinized national ideas and public participation. Furthermore, transnational phenomena such as "flapperism" affected the image of women, particularly in urban areas, because their presence elicited anxieties about the influence of the United States and Europe that triggered the control and policing of female bodies.[56] In this context, Nellie came to embody a nationalistic alternative to foreign influences, foregrounding the centrality of the female body in the cultural and political project of nation building. Nellie Campobello's choreographies thus had a pedagogical impact on the public performances of dance, particularly balletized renditions of Mexican regional dances. By participating in these transformative displays of female nationalism, thousands of young women and girls rehearsed a social order that placed women at the center.

Mexican dance summoned women in particular to perform the nation, and the Campobellos joined the call to dance. One of their major public performances after their return from Cuba was the massive choreography of *El ballet simbólico 30–30* (The Symbolic Ballet 30–30). The title is a reference to 30–30 rifles, a popular assault weapon during the Mexican Revolution, particularly among Francisco "Pancho" Villa's famous cavalry, La División del Norte. When recounting how this mass ballet came about, Nellie Campobello could not think of a better way to commemorate the Mexican Revolution than with the famous "Marcha de Zacatecas" (March of Zacatecas), a patriotic military march from the northern state of Zacatecas that had become a musical metonym for the call to arms of the Revolution of 1910. With this reference, Nellie emphasized her regional allegiances; after all, she was a Villa sympathizer in a time when he was widely regarded not as a national hero but as a bandit. Nellie beautifully commemorated his and his soldiers' fight in her acclaimed novel *Cartucho*, published the same year, 1931.[57] Perhaps most important, however, she recast women during the revolution as those who incited the people to arms. In the ballet, Nellie herself embodied the torch that ignited the Revolution.

The ballet was divided into three key moments: "Revolución" (Revolution), "Siembra" (Sowing), and "Liberación" (Liberation). It was choreographed by Nellie and Gloria Campobello and Ángel Salas, with music by Francisco Domínguez, under the artistic direction of Carlos González.[58] In the first part, a red virgin (Nellie), with a torch in her hands, ignited the revolution by awakening women, freeing them, and arming them to fight with 30–30s, leading the uprising. In the second part, women helped men to rebuild the nation by cultivating the fields. In the third part, the symbolic union between peasants, workers, and soldiers led the people, el pueblo, to its own liberation.

In the 1972 interview recorded by Patricia Aulestia, Nellie discussed the creation of the *30–30*, as the symbolic ballet is commonly known. Although the choreography changed over the years, the *30–30* kept its basic three-part structure. Nellie described the various parts in the interview as follows:

Patricia Aulestia (PA): ¿Cuando comienza usted . . .? o sea, sigue con el *30–30* a comenzar a hacer danza creativa, coreografía, eso es lo que me interesa.

Nellie Campobello (NC): En 1931 nos preguntó Carlos González: "¿Qué tienen hecho para festejar la Revolución". Entonces yo me paré y dije: "Pues yo tengo hecha una cosa que se llama *30–30* y

con la Marcha Zacatecas" (la tararea) Y empecé a bailar, como una
Marsellesa . . . no, la Marsellesa no, como una mexicana del norte,
porque allá en el norte somos bravas, nosotros les pegamos a los
hombres.

PA: Sí.

AK: ¿Usted es de Durango?

NC: Yo soy de la sierra de Durango, de donde son los más temibles
batallistas. Mire, pregunte usted allí en dónde se formó el general Villa,
Urbina, todos. . . .

NC: El ballet del *30–30* es el pueblo que duerme y luego la antorcha
que viene, con una mujer en rojo—que era yo—con los cabellos de
fuera y descalza. Auténticamente descalza, no como las bailarinas
modernas que se ponen a dar sus vueltecitas esas, furris, que no pueden
hacer en baile clásico. Se ponen una taloneras aquí, yo con el pie . . . tú
lo viste como bailaba yo, con el pie. . . .

PA: Bueno, pero aquí hablando de . . .

NC: Y luego vino la siembra . . . momento . . . llegó el triunfo de
la Revolución, luego vino la siembra, es el argumento. Y luego vino la
Escuela Rural.

PA: Ah, qué bien.

NC: Todo fruncido, y no hice . . . yo nada más hice el momento de
la Revolución. Luego hicieron la siembra, que la puso mi hermanita
Gloria, muy bella (tararea una melodía) y después de aquella . . .
¡pám-pám-pám! una cosa yo hacía así . . . no sabe usted como soy yo
moviéndome . . .

PA: ¿Me podría usted decir cuáles . . .

NC: Todavía me muevo.

(Patricia Aulestia: When do you start? . . . I mean, you begin with the
30–30 to continue to develop creative dance, choreography, and that's
what interests me.

Nellie Campobello: In 1931, Carlos González asked us: "What have
you prepared to celebrate the Revolution?" Then I stood up and said:
"Well, I have created a thing that is called *30–30* with the 'Marcha de
Zacatecas' [she sings it]." And I started to dance, as a Marseillaise. . . .
No . . . as a Marseillaise no; as a Mexican woman from the north,
because there, in the north, we are brave; we hit men.

PA: Yes.

AK: Are you from Durango?

NC: I'm from the mountains of Durango, from where the most fearsome warriors are. Look, ask around there where General Villa, Urbina, and all the others were bred. . . .

NC: The ballet *30–30* is [about] the people that sleep and then a torch comes, with a woman in red—it was me—with her hair loose and barefoot. Authentically barefoot, unlike modern dancers who just do their little pirouettes, very paltry, that they can't do in classical dance. They wear their ballet heels here, but I do it with my foot. . . . You saw how I danced, with my feet.

PA: Well, talking about . . .

NC: And then came the sowing. . . . Wait . . . the triumph of the Revolution took place, then came the sowing, that is the plot. And then the rural school came.

PA: Ah, very well.

NC: All very snooty, I did not do it. . . . I just did the moment of the Revolution. Then they did the sowing, that was choreographed by my sister Gloria, very beautiful [she sings the melody] and then that . . . ¡pam-pam-pam! A thing I did like that. . . . You have no idea how I am moving. . . .

PA: Can you please tell me which ones . . .?

NC: I still move.)[59]

In this account, Nellie assumed her role as a cultural producer, choreographer, and dance scholar. Dance allowed Campobello to write and perform the nation through her body, to choreograph it. In so doing, she reminded the audience that movement operates as a mode of signification that is always situated within a historical and social dimension that cannot be separated from the body.

In this excerpt and throughout the interview, Nellie Campobello strategically cited foreign, national, and regional references to position herself, her choreographic work, and her aesthetic and political alliances. First, she alluded to the natural spontaneity with which she produced her dance projects, gesturing to her innate creative abilities. When Carlos González asked about an artistic number to commemorate the Revolution of 1910, Nellie, as she recounted, immediately got up and started dancing to the melody of the "Marcha de Zacatecas."[60] Although she first described herself as a Marseillaise, she soon corrected herself to identify as a woman from the north of Mexico, aligning herself with the region's brave women and men, including Villa. With this identification, she asserted her political and aesthetic alignments through her suggested movement vocabulary and her embodiment of the distinct gendered attributes associated with northern Mexican revolutionaries. As with the case of her performance of El jarabe tapatío, this kinesthetic operation allowed Nellie to cite corporeal tropes of masculine daring and force while choreographically integrating the regional into the national. By 1972, music and dances from the north of Mexico, particularly *corridos* (Mexican ballads), were intimately connected to the Mexican Revolution. In summoning the Mexican Revolution through the "Marcha de Zacatecas," Nellie activated a distinct nationalist movement vocabulary and aesthetics, by then a staple of public commemorations of the revolutionary struggle.

Even more telling is her recollection of the choreography of the *30–30*, because it revealed her aesthetic investments and technical preferences regarding the staging of Mexican dance and its attendant movement vocabulary. In the interview, Nellie described the first part of the *30–30* that she choreographed: "Revolución." As mentioned earlier, this section represented the start of the uprising, led not by men but by women, with Nellie as the initiator of the armed movement. Nellie, dressed as a red virgin, danced throughout the stadium, barefoot and with her hair loose, displaying her dance skills and criticizing modern dancers, particularly those who had come from abroad and lacked a material and symbolic connection to the land, *la tierra*.[61] The *30–30* required a telluric connection to the dance and place of the performance, and Nellie insisted on this connection through her movements, embodiment, and technical and aesthetic references. Her emphasis on dancing barefoot positioned her as an authentic and legitimate Mexican dancer, while allowing her to disdain the technique of modern dancers who, according to Nellie, could not even manage to execute proper pirouettes. Her references to movement vocabulary and dance aesthetic preferences reveal the technical and aesthetic hierarchies she relied on to stage Mexican dance. These kinesthetic references show how Nellie used her dance technique as a set of "communicative and interpretative conventions shared by performers and audiences," to borrow Judith Hamera's definition of dance technique, that is, as a mechanism to produce, consume, and render intelligible dancing bodies within a particular community.[62] It is not surprising, then, that Nellie practically dismissed the rest of the ballet, apart from the section choreographed by her sister Gloria. This section, "Siembra," focused on women's work to rebuild the nation by sowing and cultivating the fields, followed by the arrival of rural schools, representing the state.[63] Here

Nellie sang the melody choreographed by Gloria, suggesting its aesthetic beauty through her embodied reenactment, only to disrupt it with an abrupt interjection: ¡pam-pam-pam! She interrupted her narration to shift the focus to her moving body. Once again, at age seventy-two, Nellie corporeally aligned herself with a gendered embodiment of her revolutionary choreography, asserting her strength, command of the performance scenario, and ability to move. Her recollection mobilized her to reclaim her authority and position as a willful performing subject: *Todavía me muevo* (I still move).

I have cited Nellie's own description of the *30–30* instead of an official account to emphasize the kinesthetic remembrance and embodied memory of her reenactment. Her recounting of the events is significant because it allows the listener or reader to connect affectively to the embodied remembering. When we reconstruct Nellie's story in our imaginations, we grapple with the ways bodies—racialized, gendered, and classed—set meaning in motion. Nellie wanted to make sure people knew she could still move, and she asked her interlocutor to imagine her movements and the embodied particularities of her choreographies of nationalism. In the recording, we can hear Nellie singing the "Marcha de Zacatecas," often described as Mexico's second national anthem. Her singing invites her interviewer to dance along just as she did. Nellie's voice, singing, and dancing called her interviewer then and us now to respond corporeally to her ephemeral traces.[64]

In centering her experience as a woman who is a cultural producer, Nellie also elucidated the complex gender dynamics at play and the specific coordinates from which she acted and conjured such nationalistic imaginaries. Although men also participated in this massive choreography, women had a central role, especially Nellie, as the symbolic initiator of the Mexican Revolution. This was no minor feat. Women had indeed participated in the armed phase of the Revolution, but their contributions were ignored in the official rhetoric, which emphasized the poor men who exhibited their manly prowess alongside such famous heroes as Álvaro Obregón, Emiliano Zapata, and Francisco Villa. The "Symbolic Ballet 30–30," as one of the massive celebrations held in 1931, enabled women to occupy the public sphere and reclaim their active role in the transformation of the country's history before, during, and after the Revolution.

It is impossible to overstate the tremendous impact the *30–30* had on future generations of dancers in Mexico and on the role of massive ballets in public venues. The *30–30* showcased the power of bodies in movement and the ability of dance to form citizens on a monumental scale. As a

mural in movement, the *30–30* revealed how the official postrevolutionary discourse could be literally embodied, not just represented, and it
implied that artists and the Mexican people needed to play an active
role in the transformation of the nation. When it premiered in 1931,
"La marcha de Zacatecas" emphasized the regional and nationalistic
character of the choreography. In 1935, during the presidency of Lázaro
Cárdenas, it was replaced with "L'Internationale," a composition from
the French Revolution that would later become the official song of the
Communist Party of the Soviet Union.[65] Accordingly, the third part of
the *30–30* included the choreographic formation of a communist hammer
and sickle, leading some to describe this massive dance as a "proletarian
ballet."[66] For the dance historian Claudia Carbajal Segura, the *30–30*
positioned Cárdenas's government and policies as the "pinnacle" of
the revolutionary struggle and transformation, associating them with
a "socialist" agenda that sought to integrate a "harmonic" society by
mobilizing its main agents: the peasants, the urban workers, the soldiers,
and the women.[67]

Periodicals of the time captured the collective and communist symbolism of the choreography of the *30–30*, its massiveness, and, of course,
the movement of the dancing women in contrast to the static men from
the state government and the armed forces, including the sitting president
Lázaro Cárdenas. *El Universal*, *El Nacional*, and *Excélsior* published several pictures from the new celebration of the "Día del Soldado" (Soldiers
Day), put together by the Secretaría de Educación Pública and organized
by the Departamento de Bellas Artes at the National Stadium. The various articles and images showcased how the massive choreography of
the *30–30* set ideologies of the time in motion. On April 38, 1935, *El
Nacional* displayed four rows of pictures from the celebration, a total
of fourteen images (fig. 3.4). The first row of three pictures features the
president Cárdenas and his wife, Amalia S. de Cárdenas, witnessing the
massive ballet, surrounded by members of the Mexican armed forces and
the federal government, including the Secretary of War and Marine Forces
Pablo Quiroga and the Secretary of State Juan de Dios Bojórquez. The
second and third row highlight the choreography of the *30–30* next to
groups of soldiers and police members. The horizontal display of these
seven images places the formation of dance and military subjects at the
same physical and symbolic level. The hundreds of dancers from local elementary and middle schools shared the center stage with men in uniform.
Such displays of soldiers' force were part and parcel of choreographies
of nationalism in Mexico and across the globe, particularly during the

centennial festivities in Mexico and as part of the rise of totalitarian and fascist regimes in Europe. Similarly, the emergence of dance modernist aesthetics and related forms of body culture, displayed on occasions such as the dance festival during the 1936 Berlin Olympic Games, served to propagate political ideologies and state propaganda.[68]

These powerful images allude to the kinesthetic formation of Mexican subjects, not only in terms of their own awareness of their movements and (social) position, but also in terms of how their movements and position were imagined. The images clearly reveal the active role of women during the celebrations. The first two pictures of the second row show a group of seated young soldiers who are attentively witnessing the massive choreography performed by the women in the second picture, shown dancing in two rows, holding flags with one hand and extending

Figure 3.4. "Gráficas de la Conmemoración del Día del Soldado," *El Nacional*, April 23, 1935. Courtesy of Biblioteca Miguel Lerdo de Tejada de la Secretaría de Hacienda y Crédito Público.

their skirts with the other. The next three pictures highlight the second and third part of the *30–30*: "Siembra" and "Liberación." We first see a group of dancers, women and men, performing Gloria's choreography: they are planting the fields to rebuild the nation after the Revolution. The last picture, the first of the third row, captures the hammer and sickle and the crowded stadium as "L'Internationale" plays. In the celebrations, women were called upon to take action. Andrew Hewitt proposes to conceive of staged and everyday movement as a "social choreography," that is, as a "medium for rehearsing a social order in the realm of the aesthetic."[69] The rehearsal of alternative spaces and roles for women in front of the president and the armed forces—the patriarchal symbols of the state—enabled women to creatively experience forms of femininity that did not involve the constant policing of their bodies. It was during the presidency of Lázaro Cárdenas that women mobilized en masse to fight for their rights, particularly their right to vote. Even though they ultimately failed, the rehearsal of their movements in the realm of the aesthetic and the political enabled them to set in motion an ideology that recognized them as equals, just as the images of the performance of the *30–30* symbolically did.

Thinking about how ideology was embodied and mobilized on a

Figure 3.5. Nellie Campobello performing the *30-30*. Courtesy of Archivo Histórico de la Escuela Nacional de Danza de Nellie y Gloria Campobello. Fondo Nellie Campobello.

massive stage at the National Stadium challenges us to consider how women's movements allowed them to disrupt normative gender roles and spaces. The physical and material symbolism of the *30–30* mobilized a kinesthetic identification that positioned women as the leaders of social action. Evelia Beristáin, a student at the Escuela de Danza, recalls the impact of witnessing Nellie Campobello symbolically lead the uprising: "nunca se me va a olvidar la imagen de Nellie Campobello, con aquella antorcha, vestida toda de rojo, corriendo por todo el Estadio antiguo, levantando al pueblo" (I will never forget the image of Nellie Campobello, with that torch, dressed all in red, running through the old stadium, stirring up the people).[70] As illustrated in figure 3.5, Nellie's performance became an opportunity for thousands of women to physically and symbolically rehearse a transformation of Mexican female subjectivity; to be active agents of change; to refuse to comply with normative gender roles. The dance scholar José Reynoso notes that the *30–30* led to the reconfiguration of Mexican female subjectivity, as "it produced a legitimized way for women to proactively be and impact the world, not just as decorative additions but also as fierce leaders" in the creation of a modern postrevolutionary Mexico.[71] In this context, dancing enabled women to position themselves as national assets. In so doing, they mobilized a "relational infrastructure" that enacted "templates for sociality" for performers and audiences alike; that is, their performance of the *30–30* activated corporeal encounters that revealed "flows of power and pleasure" that rendered their bodies in motion legible as sociopolitical agents.[72] As willful performing subjects, the Campobellos, like Evelia and the rest of the dancers, kinesthetically experienced a sense of freedom, strength, and agency, and they corporeally invited the audience members, including the president himself, to recognize these qualities in them. Nellie herself evoked this experience in the interview: "Empecé a bailar . . . como una mexicana del norte. Porque allá en el norte somos bravas; nosotros les pegamos a los hombres" (I started to dance . . . as a Mexican woman from the north, because there, in the north, we are brave; we hit the men).[73]

Nellie played a crucial role in promoting dance as a means of solidifying a national body politic. Her artistic work enhanced an otherwise reductive understanding of "popular" art by exposing the masses to regional dances and fostering an emerging sense of a shared Mexican corporeal background through lived experience and a shared musical soundscape. The *30–30* would continue to be performed as a complete production until 1946 and in fragments until 1960, when it was performed for the last time in Mexico's Palace of Fine Arts.[74] Nellie's most important legacy, however, is not her choreographies, but the foundational role she played in the institutionalization of dance as a practice and a field of knowledge production.

La Escuela Nacional de Danza and *Ritmos indigenas de México*: The Formation of National Subjects through Movement

In the 1930s, competing emergent dance traditions revealed the political trajectory of state ideology in Mexico. As a pioneer of Mexican dance, Nellie Campobello, along with her sister Gloria, came to be known for her massive choreographies in stadiums and other public venues during the presidency of Lázaro Cárdenas (1934–1940) and for the role she played in the institutionalization of a dance practice. Nellie Campobello was appointed the director of the Escuela Nacional de Danza in 1937, only five years after its founding in 1932. Despite difficulties and tensions with other choreographers, state bureaucrats, and artists such as Rodolfo Usigli and Celestino Gorostiza, Nellie continued as its director until 1983. The Escuela Nacional de Danza represented the consolidation of "danza académica," or academic dance, in Mexico. Guided by nationalist aims, the Escuela Nacional de Danza conceived dance not just as a praxis but also as a site for producing and transmitting knowledge. In other words, dance was conceived as a pedagogical project. From its inception, Mexican danza académica therefore endeavored to systematize a pedagogy of movement as a political project. To highlight the importance of movement for the formation of Mexican subjects, I turn to Nellie's work with the Escuela Nacional de Danza during its foundation in the 1930s and to the book she produced in 1940 with her sister Gloria, *Ritmos indígenas de México* (Indigenous rhythms of Mexico), the first systematic attempt to propose a genealogy of movement in Mexico.

The establishment of the Escuela Nacional de Danza made dance a fundamental part of the postrevolutionary cultural project. The first attempts to consolidate the project of Mexican academic dance were made by the Escuela de Plástica Dinámica, created by the Russian Hipólito Zybin. His work proved essential in the development of a systematic curriculum that was intended to bring dance up to the national standards for painting and music and the international standards for ballet and modern dance. The Mexican dance historian Roxana Guadalupe Ramos Villalobos, tracing the emergence and curriculum development of the Escuela Nacional de Danza, contends that Zybin, who had been trained in the Russian school of ballet, aimed to establish a comprehensive dance education.[75] Zybin sought to form *actores completos* (complete actors) who were able to express any cultural manifestation through their bodies. Accordingly, he defined *plástica dinámica* (dynamic plastic art) as the intersection of various cultural activities: theatrical dance, plastic arts, and poetry. He claimed that such a fusion of expressive art would generate new "fenómenos psíquicos-físicos en los individuos y en las masas" (psychic and physical phenomena among individuals and the masses).[76] In addition to actores completos who would create a national ballet based on the folkloric study of Mexican dances, however, the Mexican government needed teachers.

Although it operated for only ten months, the Escuela de Plástica Dinámica paved the way for the creation of the Escuela de Danza. By the 1930s, the Mexican government had realized the significance of dance compared to other spheres of national culture, particularly music and muralism. As Margarita Tortajada has shown, the establishment of a state-sponsored school of dance meant recuperating autochthonous dances throughout the country, essentially continuing the work of the misiones culturales and muralists, which had proved the effectiveness of their organizational, theoretical, and artistic cultural work.[77] Furthermore, the main objective of a professional dance academy would be to create a form of Mexican dance with a curricular program that provided the technical and conceptual foundations for dancers to command their bodies and experiment with the production of artistic embodied expressions based on traditional popular dances.[78]

In 1932, a state-sponsored school of dance was inaugurated. Carlos Mérida, its first director, underscored the importance of systematizing the production and transmission of dance knowledge, thereby revealing his vision for the recently created dance academy. Mérida emphasized the connection between dance's form and its content, or ideology. In his writings, he insisted on the necessity of the development of a "systematic, modern, and effective education" for the transmission of culture and the artistic traditions of Mexico.[79] Moreover, he emphatically contended that approaching dance in an "empiric" and "cursory" way would not meet the real needs of the country. Instead, he insisted that form and technique must reflect the ideological expression demanded of this art form.[80] Mérida ultimately fought for the recognition of dance as one of the most important modalities of artistic expression, hence the urgency of systematizing its teaching in an institution with the proper scientific foundations. Although he acknowledged the significance of studying

Mexico's Indigenous and popular dances, Mérida emphasized the need to create a dance tradition parallel to Russia's, which he regarded as the most sophisticated expression of this popular art. As he stated, part of the innovation of the Russian school of dance was to mobilize Russia's folkloric elements as "plastic elements" and not as nationalistic markers, which was how Mexican choreographers and dance practitioners engaged Mexican folkloric rhythms.[81] This last point is where Mérida departed from the Campobellos' vision, which was significant, considering that Nellie was in charge of teaching Mexican dances at the time. Nellie was a strong advocate of nationalism; Mérida, in contrast, opposed an "empiricist" version thereof:

> Si nosotros llevamos nuestra idea de investigación por los campos del folklore y de las danzas aborígenes, deberemos cuidar de que éstas sean elementos para realizaciones de carácter ideológico en forma de ritmos plásticos, pero nunca con tendencias a afianzar un espíritu de nacionalismo o con el propósito de ofrecer regalo al turista: bastante tiene éste con todas las chinas poblanas que desfilan por los escenarios de nuestros teatros.

> (If we apply our idea of research to the fields of folklore and aboriginal dances, we must be sure that these become elements for ideological expressions in the form of plastic rhythms but never with the tendency to reaffirm a spirit of nationalism or with the purpose of offering a gift to the tourist, as she already has enough with all the chinas poblanas parading on our theater stages.)[82]

In the formation of Mexican dance instructors and dancers, Mérida championed the prioritization of dance technique and an active research agenda that involved documenting dance practices throughout the country. Yet, as the quotation illustrates, it was imperative that such research regard corporeal and rhythmic expressions of Indigenous cultures, the "aboriginal dances," as the plastic elements and rhythms that would serve as the foundation for all dancistic expressions beyond essentialist renditions, thereby avoiding nationalistic overtones. Influenced by modernist aesthetics and aspirations, Mérida viewed Indigenous forms as the foundation of the movement vocabulary that would be used to create modern dance expressions.

Modern forms of body culture were part of this nationalist endeavor to create a Mexican school of dance. In addition to classical ballet, taught by Zybin, and Mexican regional dances, taught by Nellie Campobello, the curriculum included Dalcroze eurythmics; "Greek" dance or "Ducanism"; modern theatrical dance, including tap and acrobatics; and foreign popular dances from Russia, Spain, and Portugal.[83] It was during this period that Martha Graham visited the school in 1932 and the Ballets Russes de Monte Carlo directed by Wassily de Basil performed at the inauguration of the Palacio de Bellas Artes in 1934, both paramount representatives of modern dance aesthetics and technique.[84] Even more important, however, was the school's effort to document Indigenous and popular expressive culture. During Mérida's tenure, a plan was launched to research and record Indigenous and mestizo dances throughout the country in 1933. The Plan de investigación coreográfica de las más características danzas del país (The choreographic research plan of the most characteristic dances of the country) sought to register the most iconic dances as part of the school's mission to create a systematic record of choreographies, organize Indigenous and popular expressions, and develop original plastic and rhythmic kinesthetic expressions and movement vocabulary for the formation of dancers and dance teachers.[85] The dances documented included *jaranas yucatecas, chilenas, sones huastecos,* and *danza de los viejitos, danza del venado,* and *matachines,* to mention a few prominent examples. In 1934, the school had its first student recital, with dances choreographed by the Campobello sisters including *Cinco pasos de danza, Bailes itsmeños, Danza de los Malinches,* and *La virgen y las fieras.*[86] Ultimately, Mérida's emphasis on the technique, form, and aesthetics of the dances contrasted with the nationalistic tendencies of the government, particularly during the Cárdenas presidency.

In 1935, Francisco Domínguez became the second director of the recently formed Escuela de Danza. He played a critical role during the cultural missions as an ethnomusicologist. In addition to forming dance instructors, the Escuela de Danza was tasked with the preservation, reconstruction, and creation of Mexican popular and traditional dances based on the cultural materials amassed by the misiones culturales. In fact, the Campobellos served as resident experts on the subject. The ultimate objective was the creation of a Mexican ballet. In order to develop a national and popular repertoire, the school either invited local dancers or relied heavily on the research conducted by the misioneros.[87] During this period, 1932–1937, the Escuela de Danza consolidated these activities as the pillars of Mexican dance.

But Domínguez was unable to secure the necessary funding to continue with the preservation of Mexican dance and the creation of a Mexican ballet. In January 1937, Nellie Campobello became the third director of what was then called the Escuela Nacional de Danza. Nellie continued to advance the pedagogical mission of the school, but she also promoted its professionalization, emphasizing dance technique and theatrical/stage practice and increasing the number of performances and activities with the Department of Fine Arts.[88] Nellie fought to change public opinion regarding dance, which was not considered a proper career for women. In fact, Nellie wanted the school to be exclusively for women, since there were only seventeen men, seven of whom attended regularly, versus 350 women.[89] Classic technique would help elevate the status of dance (and of the dancers) from a form of spectacle and entertainment to an expression of art. Two years later, in 1939, after a series of internal conflicts with various representatives from the Department of Fine Arts, Nellie was finally able to get the National School of Dance recognized as professional, authorized to grant official degrees to its students as professors of dance.[90]

Guided by nationalist principles, the Escuela Nacional de Danza conceived dance not just as praxis for training professional dancers but also as a site for the production and transmission of knowledge. Dance, in other words, was seen as a pedagogical and epistemological realm. Here it is important to think of dance not just as a product, the performance seen by an audience, but also as a process. This approach draws attention to the various factors that configure dance praxis as an "economy of representation" with a specific history, one that is inserted in a matrix of values and power where meanings are negotiated. The dance scholar Jane Desmond suggests thinking of kinesthesia as a "historically particular register of meaning,"[91] which means reflecting on the multiple ways our bodies are made to signify and to archive meaning. The kinesthetic renderings of power relations (e.g., class, race, gender, and sexuality) highlight critical processes of signification. The importance of the study of dance lies at the core of this network of power. As Desmond goes on to say, "Whether as practice or product, dance is an act of presentation and representation that literally embodies the political, the historical, and the epistemological conditions of its possibility."[92] This perspective brings to the fore the tensions between a hegemonic representational framework, such as Mexican state-sponsored nationalism, and individual and collective kinesthetic engagements with it, such as those of Mérida and the Campobellos.

As a presentation and representation of Mexican nationalism, the Escuela Nacional de Danza became a contested terrain for the configuration of this nationalism. The Campobello sisters embarked on the consolidation of a *danza mexicana*, a Mexican dance, that remained in constant tension with modernizing currents, particularly as represented by the work of Anna Sokolow and Waldeen—two American dancers who moved to Mexico in 1939 and were pioneers in the establishment of modern dance.[93] The Campobellos' rejection of foreign and modern ("non-Mexican") dance practices is exemplified by the publication in 1940 of their book *Ritmos indígenas de México* (Indigenous rhythms of Mexico). This work offered a catalog of the kinesis or movement of lo mexicano. It was signed by both sisters, although evidence exists that it was Nellie who wrote it, with drawings by their brother Mauro Rafael Moya.[94]

In *Ritmos indígenas de México* (1940), Nellie and Gloria Campobello proposed what can be thought of as a kinesthetic ontology of lo mexicano. Through this undertaking, the Campobellos established Indigenous rhythms and dances as the primary materials informing their dance practice. As they stated in the prologue, "el principal objeto de este libro es señalar los ritmos indígenas mexicanos como el material básico de las danzas que nos son propias: ofrecemos aquí las líneas elementales, el principio y raíz de nuestras futuras disciplinas coreográficas" (The main objective of this book is to point out Mexican Indigenous rhythms as the essential material for our own dances: we offer here the basic foundations, the beginning and root of our future choreographic disciplines).[95] In an effort to define Mexican dance, they systematically observed and examined Indigenous embodied practices—the daily practices performed with and through Indigenous bodies. Their project aimed to recognize Indigenous dance practices as a form of knowledge and to systematize its transmission. One of the most striking aspects of their book is the initial emphasis not on the elaborate movements that might characterize ritualistic dances but on everyday forms of bodily expression: "Hemos tomado en cuenta como primer material para este trabajo la expresión propia de los indios, el ritmo que imprime a su cuerpo el andar, su porte, sus ademanes, y, en general, todos sus movimientos, incluso los que pueden deducirse o componerse partiendo de muchas danzas antiguas y ya casi perdidas" (We have taken as the main subject matter for this work the very own expression of the Indigenous people, the rhythm they instill in their bodies when walking, their demeanor, their gestures, and in general, all of their movements, including those that can be traced back to many ancient and now nearly extinct dances).[96] It was in everyday movements that they claimed to find traces of the corporeal rhythms that defined an "authentic" expressive embodied culture in Mexico. And it was through the careful observation and analysis of Indigenous embodied expressions and quotidian choreographies that the Campobellos were able to create their dances. They developed a theory based on Indigenous rhythms and the kinesthetic understanding and enactment of their embodied expressions. Although similar endeavors had been undertaken elsewhere, such as the dance notation system developed by Rudolph von Laban in 1928 in Germany and the *Ballet Alphabet: A Primer for Laymen* by Lincoln Kirstein, published in 1939 in the United States, Mexican dancers and choreographers did not adopt these systems immediately, and it is very unlikely that the Campobellos were familiar with them.[97] In any event, *Ritmos indígenas de México* was the first methodical effort by dance practitioners and choreographers to index and systematize the knowledge pertaining to Indigenous movement vocabulary and choreographies in Mexico.

The Campobello sisters discursively and kinesthetically constructed a category aimed at defending "authentic" Mexican cultural and embodied practices against a wave of "de-Mexicanization" of traditional values.[98] In her discussion of Nellie, the dance scholar Sophie Bidault argues that in resorting to Indigenous embodied practices, the Campobellos' aim was less to recover and preserve the traditions of the past than to counteract the advances of modern forms of dance expression.[99] They decried the incorporation of foreign styles and false representations made by those who, according to them, did not know the "authentic" Mexican rhythmic expressions. In the book, the Campobellos asserted that "vestidas de tehuanas o mestizas, o simplemente de indias, andan por ahí muchas bailarinas norteamericanas o rusas que al interpretar lo exterior de los bailes nuestros no consiguen apartarse un instante de lo que es esencial en los bailes suyos" (dressed as Tehuanas or mestizas, or simply as Indians, there are many American and Russian dancers, who, in trying to embody the exterior of our dances, are unable to distance themselves even for an instant from what seems essentially theirs).[100] The policing of "authentic" dance expressions encompassed not only dance practices, but also practitioners. It was not only foreign-born dancers who failed to properly perform Mexican rhythms; Mexican-born dancers also engaged in inauthentic interpretations of Mexican dance practices.[101] This drawing of boundaries was a rejection of modern aesthetics and yet also part of the modernist tendency to identify with or claim the exotic/Indigenous Other.

As a pioneer of Mexican dance, Nellie Campobello, together with Gloria, played an important role in the systematization of knowledge of Mexican dance. Despite these problematic interventions, the Campobellos elevated to an intellectual realm that which had been considered "popular" and "subaltern."[102] Moreover, they gave national topics and themes a new aesthetic status. Nellie and Gloria envisioned these practices as the "pillars" of Mexico's "choreographic expression," whose "richness and development will be secured through the enthusiasm and the vigilance of these technical dancers [*danzarinas técnicas*], who undoubtedly will use this material."[103] In a manifesto, they not only proposed such manifestations as "pure and original" and hence foundational for Mexican dance practice but also established the *danzarinas técnicas*, the technical dancers, as the ones responsible for their dissemination, development, and even use, emphasizing the disciplinary nature of dance as well as its pedagogical and epistemological impact (see fig. 3.6).

Despite its nationalistic and normative understandings of women's bodies and voices, Nellie Campobello's work continually undid that which it claimed to represent. Although a thorough discussion of her literary legacy is beyond the scope of this chapter, I would like to point out some of the ways Nellie resorted to literature and indigenismo in her quest for independence, not unlike other literary figures such as Rosario

Figure 3.6. Nellie Campobello and her students. Photo Courtesy of Archivo Histórico de la Escuela Nacional de Danza de Nellie y Gloria Campobello. Fondo Nellie Campobello.

Castellanos. In an astute analysis, Estelle Tarica contends that Castellanos strategically mobilized indigenismo and a regional affiliation to Chiapas both to claim an "independence—intellectual, aesthetic, female" and to write herself into a national narrative.[104] These particular spheres of independence—intellectual, aesthetic, female—also characterized Nellie's search for autonomy: she made similar claims about her *norteño* (northern) origins and connections to local Indigenous groups such as the Rarámuri. Writing, just as much as dancing, enabled Nellie to carve out a space of her own within the national cultural boundaries that conditioned her autonomy. Nevertheless, this quest for autonomy came at a price. Her dance and written practice, like Castellanos's, resulted in the denial of coevalness of Indigenous people, which points toward the interconnection between individual transformation and the writing of the nation.[105]

This ambivalence was particularly reflected in the discourses of indigeneity that Nellie drew on in her work. Like many indigenista thinkers of her time, Diego Rivera for instance, Nellie simultaneously recognized and denied the contributions of Indigenous people as the primary markers of nationalism. To craft a voice of their own, the Campobello sisters combined the language of dance with the cultural tropes of indigenismo. What was more important and radical was their reinscription of the body into the writing of the nation. In the prologue of *Ritmos indígenas*, the Campobello sisters wrote: "Refiriéndonos concretamente a México, podría decirse que los indios hablan más claramente con el cuerpo que con la lengua. La costumbre de ser en todo silenciosos y parcos contribuye en ellos a que hallen en el movimiento el verdadero vehículo de su expresión, y esto aun en el caso de aquellas tribus que por un hondo sentimiento de orgullo hablan poco" (Referring concretely to Mexico, it could be said that the Indians speak more clearly with their bodies than with their language. The custom of being silent and laconic in everything contributes to their finding in movement the true vehicle of their expression . . .).[106] Certainly such a description reveals the Campobellos' exoticizing language and colonizing tropes. Yet it simultaneously posits bodily movement as a language of signification. It is thus important to emphasize that the Campobellos advanced the emergence of an indigenista discipline through the repositioning of the body: the body produces language and meaning; the body signifies. *Ritmos indígenas*, then, clearly evinces the entanglements between the indigenista cultural politics of the period and an embodied understanding of indigeneity in Mexico.

Through their careful examination and detailed description of

Indigenous bodies and their movements, the Campobellos offered a systematic analysis of an Indigenous corporeal culture. The Mexican dance scholar Margarita Tortajada has also noted that the Campobellos comprehended and addressed the historical and social dimension of the body and its writing through movement, which is always already part of a structure or system of signification.[107] The signifying function of movement reveals the intricate ways culture is inscribed and experienced through the body. The Campobellos wrote:

> si alguien quiere conocerlos, entrever lo que hay en ellos de profundamente humano . . . debe acercarse a verlos caminar, a ver cómo mueven su cuerpo en el reposo o en el trabajo, y, sobre todo, a verlos bailar, o mejor dicho, a verlos en sus bailes. Desde el punto de vista de la danza todo esto tiene la misma trascendencia que, en otros órdenes, tendría oírlos hablar y verlos vivir. De este modo consigue penetrar el origen de su plástica, se comprueba el tipo y calidad de sus movimientos actuales y posibles o, en una palabra, de su ritmo, en reposo y en actividad.

> (To know them, and to ascertain what is profoundly human in them . . . one must get up close and see them walk, see how they move their body in stillness or in their work, and above all, see them dance, or better yet, see them in their dances. From the point of view of dance, this is just as important as hearing them speak and seeing them live would be in other spheres. In this way, one is able to penetrate the origin of their art and behold the type and quality of their actual and possible movements, or rather, their rhythm, in stillness and in activity.)[108]

The Campobellos made a case for focusing on kinesis—on movement—as a system of signification. In fact, they claimed that as a system of knowledge, communication, and signification, dance and therefore movement were as important as the verbal or visual regimes—as important as hearing Indigenous people talk and seeing them live and act. Their understanding of kinesis was so thorough that they even addressed movement in stillness; one gets information from observing someone resting as much as from someone walking.[109] Nevertheless, the Campobellos emphasized the importance of dancing or, better yet, seeing Indigenous people in their dances: "verlos en sus bailes." "Seeing them in their dances" implies paying attention not only to movement but also to the context in which the movement is reproduced because any specific setting would impact the "type and quality of the actual and possible movements."

The Campobellos were acutely sensitive to the production and reproduction of movement. In what can be defined as a form of "performance ethnography," they gestured toward the unbreakable bond between knowledge and knower and the necessity of both for knowledge transmission to take place.[110] Dance emphasizes that certain kinds of knowledge

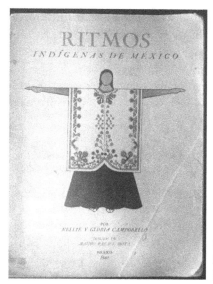

Figure 3.7. *Ritmos indígenas de México* (1940). Photos courtesy of the author. Private collection.

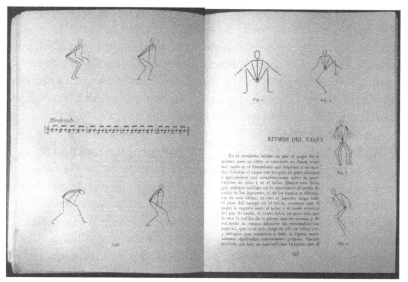

can only be transmitted through bodies, the principal characteristic of what Diana Taylor names the repertoire: embodied expressions of knowledge. This is one of the key insights of the Campobellos' work: although they were complicit with indigenista cultural politics, they understood the significance of embodied cultural expression.

With *Ritmos indígenas de México*, the Campobellos made the first systematic attempt to trace a genealogy of movement in Mexico. In effect, they proposed a genealogy of what Carrie Noland calls "gestural performatives," that is, the "coded and carefully policed movements that constitute an embodiment, a kinetic, corporeal support, for cultural (discursive) meanings."[111] The choreographic study documents and analyzes rhythms from the Yaqui, Maya, Tarahumara Indigenous groups and from the states of Oaxaca, Michoacán, Jalisco, and Estado de México. To illustrate, I quote at length one of their descriptions of the movements of the Yaqui Indians:

Camina el yaqui con los pies un poco abiertos y apoyándose casi completamente sobre la parte exterior de ellos y en el talón . . . análogo en la apariencia al modo de andar de los japoneses. . . . Movimientos precisos, tensión nerviosa, ademanes bruscos como de animal siempre alerta, parecen ser la actitud y el dinamismo a que al yaqui da vida constantemente, hasta cuando se hunde en la mayor quietud. . . . Se comprende por todo lo anterior que en las danzas que el yaqui ejecuta, los quiebros del cuerpo, bruscos y rápidos, semejan relámpagos o líneas en zig-zag, y que estos giros profundos alternen con grandes pausas en que toda la tensión y el alma del danzarín parecen quedarse estáticas y en acecho. El contraste, que no estriba en diferencias de vitalidad, pues tanta vida expresa aquí la quietud como el movimiento, hace de estos giros de danza algo increíble. Y ello se debe también a que no necesita el yaqui ejecutar saltos ni adoptar figuras teatrales aparatosas para dar la sensación de que está bailando grandiosamente.

(The Yaqui Indian walks with her feet slightly open, supporting herself almost completely on the exterior part of her feet and on the heels . . . much like the stroll of the Japanese. . . . Precise movements, nervous tension, abrupt motions like those of an animal always on the alert— these seem to be the attitude and dynamism which the Yaqui Indian constantly gives life to, even when she is submerged in stillness. . . . It follows, from all of the above, that in the dances that the Yaqui Indian performs, the brusque and sudden contortions of the body look like lightning flashes or zigzag lines, and that these pronounced contortions alternate with long pauses during which all the tension and soul of the dancers seem to remain static and in waiting. The contrast—which does not stem from differences in vitality, since here there is as much life expressed in stillness as in movement—makes these turns of dance something incredible. And that is also because the Yaqui Indian does not need to perform jumps nor adopt elaborate theatrical figures to give the impression that she is dancing magnificently.)[112]

The detailed description the Campobellos provided highlights competing discourses in the performance of Indigenous movements. At the beginning, they drew a comparison between the walk of the Yaqui Indians and that of the Japanese by stressing the distribution of their body weight either at the heels or at the heels and the external part of the feet. Focusing on kinesis allowed the Campobellos to establish a comparison between two unrelated cultures: one of them greatly admired in Mexico and the other still struggling for recognition. At the same time, the Campobellos used this comparison to establish their expertise in dance, making an ambivalent appeal to modernist aesthetics. The description of the walk, however, does not stop there. The balancing of these movements must be read by a spectator. The Campobellos were aware that these gestures had a valance that constituted one of the "plastic expressions" characteristic of the Yaqui Indians. The gestural references to modernist aesthetics act as a rhetorical maneuver to denote their dance expertise and to legitimate their work. In this way, the Campobellos invited and even anticipated comparative gestural and performance studies across national contexts.[113]

Dance technique, as a "relational infrastructure," also led the Campobellos to ascribe to the Yaqui dancers a muted theatricality that frames the authenticity of their performance. The movements of the Yaqui Indians are compared not just to those of the Japanese but also to those of an animal that is always alert, "even when she is submerged in stillness." What is interesting about this comparison is the emphasis on the kinesis of stillness. To appreciate motion in the seeming absence of movement reveals an understanding that the body is in continuous motion as a living entity. Moreover, describing not just festive instances but also everyday motions stresses a continuum of movement that signifies according to the occasion, sharing a kinesthetic and corporeal background. In fact, it is only when they described the everyday movements of the Yaqui Indians that the Campobellos moved on to discuss their dances. They pointed toward the continuum between movement and stillness, between the "sudden turns of the body" and the "long pauses," "for as much life expresses here stillness as movement." The sociocultural valance of these two instances of motion resides in the fact that "the Yaqui Indian does not need to perform jumps nor adopt elaborated theatrical figures to give the impression that she is dancing magnificently." Figure 3.7 captures some of the qualities of movement, gestures, bodily comportment, and corporeal intensions and expressions of Yaqui dances. Designed by Mauro Rafael Moya, the illustrations reveal some of the intricacies of the notation system and descriptions proposed by the Campobellos.[114] Certainly, for the Campobellos, the movements of the Yaqui Indians constituted an embodiment charged with cultural meanings.

Ritmos indígenas therefore represents one of the first systematic efforts to propose a genealogy of cultural meanings through the movements of the body, underscoring that the body is both a signifier and a signified, that it creates cultural meaning and is simultaneously created by it. Certainly, their work contained biased and exoticizing depictions of Indigenous people. It perpetuated the indigenista narratives that still circulate today, effectively erasing indigeneity while seeming to recognize it. Yet I want to emphasize the importance of their work for the use of a language of movement and the establishment of a discipline that even today informs the way we engage with, recognize, or deny Indigenous forms of cultural expression.

Nellie's Mexican Dance

I conclude this chapter by turning to Nellie's thoughts about her dance career. In 1960, Nellie published a compilation of her written work, titled *Mis libros* (My books). In the poem "Estadios" (Stadiums) dedicated to the motherland, "la patria," Nellie wrote:

En todos los estadios
donde para ti he danzado,
he ido sumisa a prosternarme ante tu imagen,
y entre luceros y nardos, tú patria,
forjada con devoción,
me hiciste estatua en silencio,
estatua en paso de danza,
que humilde toca tu suelo,
suelo en que estoy engarzada

(In all the stadiums
where I have danced for you,
I have been submissive in prostrating myself before your image,
and among bright stars and spikenards, you, homeland,
forged with devotion,
made me a silent statue,
a statue in a dance step,
that humbly touches your soil,
soil in which I find myself stuck).[115]

Nellie, referring to the nation, acknowledged that she was part of the postrevolutionary cultural enterprise (see fig. 3.8). Yet she felt betrayed and silenced. In the prologue, she also revealed the ambivalence she felt when performing the nation and for the nation: "Aunque yo me preguntaba: ¿Por qué andamos aquí? ¿Por qué tengo que danzar en estos estadios enormes, en este suelo ardoroso que remueve la tierra, que sofoca mi aliento? . . . Era la patria; ella lo quería así. Los hombres que tenían la ley ordenaban que fuéramos por todos los estadios, que respiráramos la tierra y la cal" (Even though I asked myself: Why are we here? Why do I have to dance in these enormous stadiums, in this ardent soil that stirs the dirt, that suffocates my breath? . . . It was the motherland; she wanted it this way. The men who had the law ordered that we go to all stadiums, that we breathe the dirt and the lime).[116] Nellie was clearly aware of the gender and power dynamics of her era. Men were the law.

Like her writings for most of the twentieth century, Nellie's dance career was in many ways ignored because of her strong personality and her overt and unquestioning nationalism. Yet her own body allowed for a kind of writing that continuously undid what she claimed to represent, the prevalent national narrative of a heteronormative and mestizo nation.[117] Mexican regional and traditional dance, folklórico, made the past and the ethnic diversity of the country tangible. Performances of lo mexicano were staged to create citizens and foster a sense of nationalism; they operated as embodied pedagogical practices. Through her dance and her body, Nellie drew from two distinct yet intersecting modes of participation: her danza mexicana interpellated Mexicans via corporeal tropes of lo mexicano, while she embodied ritualized movements that gestured toward the ideological and material ways in which nation building and cultural nationalism took place.

In 1983, Nellie Campobello was seen for the last time at the Escuela Nacional de Danza, where she was the director from 1937 to 1983. Nellie

Figure 3.8. Nellie Campobello as a Tehuana. Courtesy of Archivo Histórico de la Escuela Nacional de Danza de Nellie y Gloria Campobello. Fondo Nellie Campobello.

had already stopped going to the school regularly in 1982, and María Cristina Belmont had taken over her responsibilities. She was last seen in 1985 and then disappeared. She was kidnapped by María Cristina Belmont and Claudio Fuentes, who were supposed to be her caretakers. In her last public appearance, she was seen with Belmont and Fuentes's lawyer, Enrique Fuentes León, at the court, where it was determined that she had not been involuntarily deprived of her freedom, as the Instituto Nacional de Bellas Artes y Literatura (INBAL), the National Institute of Fine Arts and Literature, had accused. Nellie's physical health and overall well-being had visibly deteriorated. After Nellie failed to make a public appearance for an event in her honor at the Palace of Fine Arts (to which only Claudio Fuentes showed up), her grave was found in the state of Hidalgo in 1998. The Human Rights Commission of Mexico City launched an investigation. In 1999, her remains were taken back to her native Durango, in Villa Ocampo.[118]

By positing movement as a site of embodied cultural memory, that is, as a means to register meaning and archive it, I attend to the implications of researching the legacy of Campobello's dance career as a dancer and literary scholar myself. Ultimately, I have attempted to address how we are connected to the ephemeral and missing archive of a disappeared body and silenced voice while recognizing my own personal, intellectual, and affective investments. Throughout her life, Nellie acted as a cultural producer, choreographer, and dance scholar. Dance allowed Nellie to rechoreograph the nation through her body. In so doing, she pointed toward the complex ways movement operates as a mode of signification, and, more important, toward the ways nation-making involves a historical and social dimension that cannot be separated from the body. In the final chapter of this book, I discuss how these choreographies of Mexican folklórico dance moved from stadiums and other public venues to the silver screen during the Golden Age era of Mexican cinema in the 1930s and 1940s. By considering how iconic films from the era incorporated dance scenes as part of their visual narratives, I analyze the contradictory renditions of Mexican nationalism through moving bodies on screen.

CHAPTER 4

Cinematic Renditions of a Dancing Mexico: *Folklórico* Dance in Mexican Film

On June 11, 1931, *El Ilustrado*, Mexico's popular weekly, published the first of a series of articles describing the ongoing work in Mexico of the Russian avant-garde director Sergei Mikhailovich Eisenstein, who was then filming in Tetlapayac, Hidalgo. Penned by A.F.B. (Adolfo Fernández Bustamante),[1] the article, "Einsenstein [*sic*], el magnífico" (Eisenstein, the magnificent), revealed that the Russian film master was working on a series of short episodes that would present "typical and strong aspects" of the Mexican Republic without featuring film stars. Instead, Eisenstein would feature as the main actors the masses and local, "autochthonous," and "vernacular" types such as Indigenous people and peons in a film that would likely be titled "¡Viva México!"[2] Most notably, the article publicized nine pictures, the first to be published of the various scenes, montages, and film work of Eisenstein and his crew, who had been in Mexico since December 1930. The pictures, spread over two pages, included five images of Zapotec Indigenous women from Tehuantepec, or Tehuanas; one image of a man reclining in a hammock; two of a bullfighter, or *torero*; and one of an affluent young lady in a carriage (see fig. 4.1). Interestingly, only one of the images featured Eisenstein, filming a group of Tehuanas along with one of his crew members, Edward Tissé. The article identified David Liceaga as the torero in the pictures, leaving without names the various Indigenous women wearing elaborate Tehuana attires who occupy more than half of the pictures selected. At the center of the page spread, however, the contrast between a Zapotec young girl and an elderly Indigenous woman holding a golden necklace highlights the leading role of Indigenous women in Eisenstein's filmic iconography. The Indigenous bodies on photographs and stills from the work in progress portrayed a racialized cartography of southern, western, and central Mexico.

In the article, Fernández Bustamante (A.F.B.) emphasized the significance of a visual language that would differ strikingly from the dominant visual idiom of Hollywood, which often failed to capture the complexity of the Mexican experience. What the critic advocated was less a fictional rendition of Mexico's people and places than an aestheticized rendition of Mexico's reality. An implicit argument in these articles revolved around the documentary quality of cinema as a medium for indexing actual bodies and places vis-à-vis their representations.[3] The new local filmic language needed to clearly differentiate itself from the language that had already been established by Hollywood, particularly during the 1920s. In the 1920s, over 78 percent of all the films to which Mexican audiences had access were American films.[4] And yet, as the film historian Laura Isabel Serna notes, this foreign film culture was not simply imposed; Mexican audiences invested in film consumption as part of their experience of modernity and cosmopolitanism, and certainly as a means of exploring a sense of national belonging.[5]

Although Eisenstein's film remained unfinished—Eisenstein neither edited it nor saw it completed—until the 1979 reconstruction by Grigorii Alexandrov, the circulation of stills and images from the film and the

Figure 4.1. "Eisenstein, el magnífico," *El Ilustrado*, June 11, 1931. Courtesy of Biblioteca Miguel Lerdo de Tejada de la Secretaría de Hacienda y Crédito Público.

mere presence of the Russian master in Mexico left an indelible mark on Mexican cinema. The Mexico rehearsed by Eisenstein was an Indigenous, revolutionary Mexico. In fact, the last shot of the film illustrated the contradictions and tensions of Mexican modernity: Eisenstein's revolutionary modernity was embodied by a mestizo, Indigenous-looking child, the son of a *soldadera* (woman soldier), whose story we will never know.

The child appears in the "Epilogue," the last episode of Eisenstein's film and the film's best-known and perhaps most circulated fragment.[6] It opens with a sequence dominated by a landscape of rural Mexico, Indigenous peasant women covered with rebozos, and the sight of the Popocatepetl and Itztacihuatl volcanoes in the background. Then the camera takes the viewer to a festive setting. The music immediately introduces the sound of El jarabe tapatío. Its now familiar melody, a continuous sonic and kinesthetic referent throughout this book, contrasts with the sounds of a modern Mexico, the railroads, highways, or harbors that Eisenstein would have liked to cinematically capture.[7] And yet the cinematic bodies summon a different temporality. The opening sequence of the "Epilogue" emphasizes the embodied continuation of nonmodern times, with spatial references that evoke an Indigenous peasant existence: open, monumental, natural surroundings. The following sequence abruptly shifts the viewers' attention to a group of festive rumba dancers. Their movements and bodies conjure a nondiegetic frame of reference from beyond Mexico: their pelvic movements, flexed bodies, and shoulder motions gesture toward Afro-Caribbean kinesthetic imaginaries with the dancing of Cuban *guaguancó*. A Mexican viewer, listening to the chords from El jarabe tapatío, would notice the lack of choreographic synchronicity. There is no recognizable Mexican zapateado in this sequence. Instead, the corporeal imagery and the movement of the dancers emphasize the sensual and eroticized renditions of Afro-Caribbean rhythms that showcase Mexicans' festive interactions with an image of an immobilizing death. As the voice-over announces: "Death comes along dancing!"[8]

The sequence in which *rumberas* (women rumba dancers) and men with masks dance Cuban guaguancó to the tune of "El jarabe tapatío" kinesthetically capture the fissures and tensions of a mestizo aesthetics and a Mexican modernity. Whereas the sonic imaginaries evoked by the traditional jarabe reinforce a sense of belonging and relatedness that is distinctively "Mexican," the moving bodies of the rumberas and the masked men dancing invite a sense of Afro-diasporic intimacy and interconnection. In so doing, they cinematically prefigure the connection of Afro-diasporic imaginaries to modernity and to a tropicalized Black-ness that still dominates cultural and artistic flows in the Americas, particularly between Mexico and Cuba.[9]

The symbolic gesture of including a sequence with rumba dancers dancing to El jarabe tapatío in the "Epilogue," which was supposed to capture a modernizing Mexico, anticipated by a decade the narrative that portrayed the changing Mexico as simultaneously modern, urban, and tropical. The dancing gestures and motions cited a sense of Blackness and modernity that was already part of the Mexican imaginary and that would eventually be associated with a tropicality that was displaced to the Caribbean, and yet somehow was distinctly Mexican. This cinematic sequence illustrates how Mexicans sonically and corporeally created a sense of belonging and relatedness to one another that became an integral part of Mexican modernity. It also marks a trajectory that takes viewers from an Indigenous Mexico to a mestizo and even Afro-mestizo nation.

Analyses of the Golden Age era of cinema in Mexico have illustrated how a Mexican national identity came to be represented in film, with lasting effects.[10] Iconic dances that produced an image of a festive Mexico became a key component of many films of the era, and yet these dances, which reveal tensions and conflicts in Mexico's modernization, have not yet been thoroughly studied. By focusing on the moving bodies in these dance scenes, this chapter highlights the role that movement and dance played in the imagining of lo mexicano while shedding light on the ways these images circulated across audiences and were consumed. The shift from a dominantly narrative depiction of Mexico to a more visual and kinesthetic register captured the complex and often contradictory ways Mexican audiences imagined others. Cinema, as a new visual medium, also proved crucial in interpellating a national audience at home and abroad, not just in the United States but also throughout Latin America.[11] The traditional and regional dances in these films ultimately choreo-graphed a sense of nationalism, acting as a form of choreo-politics.

In this chapter, I focus on moving images of bodies in motion, perform-ing what would become iconic folklórico dances in Mexico and abroad. By examining films, stills, and periodicals from the years prior to and during the Golden Age era of Mexican cinema in the 1930s and 1940s, I argue that dancing bodies on the screen performatively undid the ho-mogeneity of the postrevolutionary nation-building project. The dancing scenes of Mexican traditional and regional dances in Sergei Eisenstein's *¡Que viva México!* (1932), Fernando de Fuentes's *Allá en el Rancho Grande* (1936), and Raúl de Anda's *La reina del trópico* (1946) revealed the contradictory nature of the imaginaries the modernizing film industry produced: they were at times complicit with and at times resistant to the state-sponsored project of nationalism. Together, these films capture the trajectory from a visually Indigenous Mexico to the consolidation of nationalistic mestizo imagery and the triangulation of Afro-mestizo expressions via the Caribbean. The performances of "Sandunga" (the Oaxacan hymn of the matriarchal, Indigenous Tehuantepec region) in Eisenstein's film, El jarabe tapatío (Mexico's internationally renowned "hat dance") in de Fuentes's film, and La bamba (Mexico's foremost dance and music with Afro-mestizo roots) in de Anda's film set in motion contrasting visual narratives that enacted ambivalent and slippery kinesthetic identifications with Mexico's ethnoracial diversity and the imposition of mestizo imaginaries. These festive dances not only helped to codify lo mexicano by ascribing particular cultural values to moving bodies and their performances but also expanded the idea of Mexico kinesthetically, choreographing modernity in rich, varying, and contradictory ways. The sound and images of dancing bodies on the screen, therefore, reveal how Mexican spectators imagined the movements of "the Other" and, more important, how Mexican spectators at home and abroad were called to kinesthetically identify with the movements of these dancing bodies, that is, to corporeally recognize themselves in their bodies in motion. The result was a performative, embodied engagement with the films' moving images of Mexico.

Moving Images of a Changing Mexico, Eisenstein, and the Making of Cinematic Indigeneity

Sergei Eisenstein's arrival in Mexico coincided with the consolidation of cinema's role as one of the primary aesthetic, social, and epistemological modes in which to create a national fiction and capture the experience of modernity.[12] The rise of mass media was one of a series of changes that occurred in the aftermath of the Mexican Revolution; others included mass migrations to urban centers and the introduction of new technologies, leading to an accelerated process of industrialization and modernization. The film scholar Andrea Noble contends that the mass migration to urban centers in the increasing modernizing and industrializing postrevolutionary Mexico led citizens to reconfigure their "geographical, cultural and moral co-ordinates," a process that was intimately connected to the shifting sensory perception portrayed in mass media. The presence of mass media, together with institutionalized and state-sponsored official events, commemorations, rituals, monuments, and public arts (particularly muralism and, I would add, dance), played a crucial role in the process of national "imagining."[13] By the mid-1930s, radio, cinema, and print media such as magazines, newspapers, and comics had become intertwined with the everyday experiences of regular people. This technological revolution brought with it a re-education of the senses and sensory perception.[14] Cinema not only contributed to the visual education of the masses but also helped make the senses more central to grapple with the experience of modernity, particularly as it engaged with the audience's affective regime.[15] The modern and the new shocked audiences into a different mode of being, belonging, and relating to a rapidly changing environment.

Film affects people, then, on an epistemological level. Film accelerates a paradigmatic shift in how one apprehends the world: from the textual to the visual and, in the case of Mexico and Latin America, which had high rates of illiteracy in first part of the twentieth century, to the experience of the modern through the visual. As Juan Sebastián Ospina León contends, film technology and its concomitant culture (particularly through melodrama) were able to "register and make sense of [modern] change."[16] They rendered legible the experience of the modern, including the consolidation of new forms of sociability, the reconfiguration of private and public spaces, and the rapid industrialization and modernization of urban centers. Dance, sports, and physical culture similarly responded to and participated in a rapidly changing experience of modernity. New movement vocabularies and physical exercises such as calisthenics and rhythmic gymnastics emerged as a reaction to modern life and the incorporation of technology.[17] As was evident at the inauguration of the National Stadium, discussed in the introduction, Mexico responded with its own choreographies of modernity, which included massive displays of gymnastics, physical exercises, and Mexican traditional dances. The experience of modernity was in this sense registered at the level of the body. If the experience of the modern was an experience of the senses, it is crucial to understand how regimes of embodiment were implemented and imposed. Dance practice registered, made legible, and allowed people to negotiate the tensions of modernity in postrevolutionary Mexico.

The emergence of muralist painting as the dominant medium through which Mexico was visually depicted also consolidated a new semiotic system that posited the gaze as the primary means of apprehending and therefore creating a Mexican reality.[18] The body became a generative site and sight that mediated the experience of this dynamic shift: from the narrative realm to the visual one and, as I contend in this book, to the kinesthetic. The body also facilitated the conjuring and coexistence of multiple temporalities, and particularly the framing of the Indigenous and at times Black Other as located in the past. It was not just the implementation of new technologies that enabled the layering of temporalities but also the ability to capture, produce, and reproduce the body's movement. The incorporation of visual technologies, such as photography and film, and of mass media, such as radio and print culture, generated complicities and exclusions that unified and homogenized the visual representations of the nation.

If muralism had taught the Mexican public how to consume visual imaginaries of the nation and established a mestizo aesthetics as the dominant visual language for the representation of the nation, cinema consolidated the imaginary of lo mexicano. After all, Mexican cinema helped to make sense of the experience of the modern in textual, visual, sonic, and kinesthetic terms. Films were projected across the country, and the circulation of cinematic images through stills, magazines, postcards, and even calendars expanded their reach and impact.[19] Eisenstein's visit, then, did more than engage the new technology of cinema with the native and autochthonous Other. He also helped to consolidate Mexico's engagement with its local Indigenous communities, legitimizing the state-sanctioned cultural practices. Eisenstein, as Noble contends, portrayed Indigenous Mexico differently than did the state-sponsored cultural producers and Mexican intellectuals of the time, but, more important, his unfinished film elevated Mexican visual imagery, and indeed the whole of Mexico, to an international realm "worthy of contemplation."[20]

Eisenstein's cinematic work figured and reconfigured the cinematographic image of Mexico, of lo mexicano. It reinscribed an aesthetics and framing of Mexico's diverse ethnoracial landscape that extended the impact of Mexico's muralism. With the advent of the film industry came new mechanisms for production and distribution, and soon the industry became one of the primary means of the mass dissemination of cultural products. In the process, Eisenstein's film became the obligatory point of reference for visual depictions of Mexico's landscape and ethnoracial diversity.[21] This was one of the major effects of Eisenstein's presence in Mexico: the making of ¡Que viva México! changed the conception of the Indigenous. Once portrayed folklorically as an ancient and long-gone people, as at the Paris Universal Exposition discussed in chapter 1, they came to be seen as a continuous presence and a means of entering the avant-garde. This technological and aesthetic shift did not do away with the first conception; rather, the folkloric image of Indigenous people produced by the camera was avant-garde in its conception, as I discuss in the next section.[22]

Although Eisenstein's film never reached the big screen during his lifetime, *¡Que viva México!* circulated in Mexico and the United States via articles, pictures, stills, reports, private screenings of rushes of the immense amount of footage recorded (close to 200,000 feet of film), and even an actual market release of part of his footage from Mexico as *Thunder Over Mexico*.[23] What set Eisenstein's art apart from other work is that he sought a "collective expression" that would capture the "transcendental collective meaning" of each of its manifestations. In so doing, Eisenstein allowed Mexicans to contemplate themselves anew, recognizing, according to his special assistant, guide, and adviser Agustín Aragón Leiva, "how great and profound is our tradition, our life, our beauty."[24] Through the use of new technologies and new cinematic forms, Eisenstein consolidated a cinematic visual language in and about Mexico and placed it immediately in a transnational arena, where up to this point Mexico had been represented almost exclusively by Mexican muralism.

While certainly the Russian master had his own series of aesthetic and theoretical investments, his work did not take place in a vacuum. Eisenstein's work not only depended on Upton and Mary Craig Sinclair's funding but also was carefully monitored by the Mexican government via the appointment of none other than Adolfo Best Maugard, whose job was to ensure that there would be no scenes that would offend the "dignity of the Mexicans."[25] Adolfo Best Maugard accompanied Eisenstein's crew for ninety-four paid days, including trips to Tehuantepec, Colima, Yucatán, and the Hacienda Tetlapayac, Hidalgo, until he was replaced by Bolívar Sierra.[26] Upon his arrival, Eisenstein and his crew actively interacted with the Mexican cultural and intellectual elites, particularly the Mexican muralists, such as Diego Rivera, José Clemente Orozco, David Alfaro Siqueiros, Jean Charlot, and Roberto Montenegro. This constant exchange with Mexican artists and intellectuals led to an artistic cross-pollination. For instance, Rivera invited Eisenstein to visit the *Casa Azul* (Blue House), where he met Frida Kahlo.[27] Likewise, Eisenstein and Rivera visited together the murals at the National Palace and the Palace of Cortes in the city of Cuernavaca. According to Inga Karetnikova, "Eisenstein liked this gradual unraveling of Rivera's visual narrative from one historical episode to the next. His own montage usually shattered the continuity of narration; Eisenstein strove to establish the 'sign' of an event."[28] In this sense, Eisenstein's work was more closely related to that of José Clemente Orozco, who was also known for his emphasis on the "symbolic image" rather than the story per se.[29] Eisenstein's aesthetic and theoretical work, then, mediated and was mediated by his engagement with Mexican muralist aesthetics and other state-sponsored projects, which influenced the creation and representation of an Eisensteinian Mexican subject, or *typage*, and landscape.

Eisenstein's unfinished rehearsal of a moving avant-garde aesthetics both complemented and transcended what had been accomplished by the Mexican muralists. His aesthetic praxis and theorization as seen in his avant-garde cinema and in his theoretical writings, particularly with regard to the montage and ideogram, revealed aesthetic sensibilities similar to those expressed by Mexico's muralists and intellectuals of the time.[30] Mexican muralism and Eisenstein's avant-garde cinema deployed similar strategies to grapple with the "experience of the shock of modernization (the famous shock of the new)."[31] This urge to mediate the increasing shock with the new and the modern and to create artistic alternatives to Western capitalist modernities led Eisenstein to explore the Orient, not unlike the rest of the European left intellectuals and artists in the 1920s.[32] According to the Russian cultural studies critic Masha Salazkina, just as the Mexican muralists had sought to mediate different temporalities and a plethora of contradictory experiences, Eisenstein gravitated toward a kind of "utopianism," one that became "linked to new formulations of temporalities as mediated through the body on the screen."[33] In the same way that the Indigenous body appeared as noncontemporaneous, displaced onto a "pre-Hispanic" temporality under the discourse of mestizaje, the body in Eisenstein's work "mediat[ed] between the individual and the collective historical experience"[34] as part of an alternative (and revolutionary?) temporal register.

The body became a key site in which to negotiate not just different temporalities but also the varying processes through which divergent and at times contradictory ideas of the modern materialized. During his stay in Mexico, Eisenstein explored and personally experienced the contradiction of inhabiting spaces and temporalities that seemed irreconcilable, which he captured in his drawings, writings, and unfinished film *¡Que viva México!*[35] In fact, the mise-en-scène of his aesthetic and theoretical preoccupations guided the shooting of the "Prologue," the sequence that opens *¡Que viva México!* In this first sequence, we see images of pyramids and Indigenous deities such as Quetzalcoatl and Tlaloc, similar to the sequence in Eisenstein's film *October* (1927) that portrays images of the divine.[36] In the second sequence, however, Eisenstein's film rehearses his notion of an intellectual montage, juxtaposing Indigenous people with stones and representations of Mayan deities.[37] The 1979 reconstruction of the unfinished film made by Grigorii Alexandrov and Nikita Orlov includes the reading of the manuscript written by Eisenstein for each of the sections, or novellas, as he called them, that divided the film: "Prologue," "Sandunga," "Fiesta," "Maguey," "Soldadera," and "Epilogue." The voice-over reading the passages in Russian for the "Prologue" emphasizes the copresence of multiple temporalities: "Time in the prologue is eternity. It might be today. It might as well be twenty years ago. Might be a thousand."[38] The first shots of human beings that appear on the screen correspond directly to the textual description of the permanence of time: "For the dwellers of Yucatan, land of ruins and huge pyramids, have still conserved, in feature and forms, the character of their ancestors, the great race of the ancient Mayas. Stones—Gods—Men—."[39] There is a visual and discursive conceptual tension at play in the cinematographic montage in this scene between stones, gods, and men. The image of figure 4.2 captures the visual continuum between the stillness of stone deities and the motionless but animate human figures; the relationship between

Figure 4.2. "Prólogo," *¡Que viva México!* (1932). Screen capture from film.

those two is simultaneously rendered through a visual and discursive sense of immutability. The divine figures and the human bodies of Mayan descendants gesture toward the kind of conceptual "product" (subject or ideogram) that such a contraposition generates.

This generative approach invites the viewers to witness the presence of an ancient, almost timeless past in the eternity of the present. By contrasting two "representables," men and stone gods, Eisenstein cinematically stages his notion of the ideogram.[40] For Eisenstein, this montage fractures the limits of a concrete reality, of what is "representable," and pushes the viewer to engage with the images at the intellectual level. However, juxtaposing the images of the Mayan people with their stone deities visually enhances what the voice-over describes: "The people bear resemblance to the stone images, for those images represent the faces of their ancestors."[41] More than a fracture with a concrete, representable reality, the opening sequences of the "Prologue" invite the viewer to establish a connection between the past and the present, revealing a sense of animism present in these initial sequences.

In the "Prologue," there is clearly a visual and discursive continuity between the past and the present. The images of an immutable past and the motionless but animate human figures capture the stillness of an eternal time. Interchanging close-ups and long medium shots at a very slow pace exacerbates the immutability of the pyramids and the petrified gods, visually and discursively connecting them to the living Indigenous Mayans whose bodies continue to actualize the presence of the past and simultaneously engage with the choreography of modernity. Masha Salazkina argues that "the ruins are presented as structures of permanence, a permanence then further emphasized by the resemblance between the stone carvings and the figures of the Indians whose bodies, and more specifically faces, become the sites for displaying the continuity of time. This is a realm where history cannot exist because there is no change; no history but rather a permanent prehistory hovering over the present."[42] Even though I agree with Salazkina's reading of the Indigenous bodies and pyramids as literal displays of the continuity of time, there is another epistemological operation at play here. Eisenstein insists on the multiplicity of temporalities, not just the continuation of an old temporality. The Russian director was actually fascinated by the simultaneity of spatiotemporal referents found in Mexico: "Eisenstein was amazed that in Mexico the sequence of epochs was presented not 'vertically (in years and centuries), but horizontally, as the geographic coexistence of the most diverse stages of culture.'"[43] One could certainly assume that time has not passed or that history cannot exist due to lack of change, as Salazkina indicates, but it is also possible that such a time can coexist with another sociohistorical reality. More than a continuation of a singular temporal frame, the various sequences introduced in the "Prologue" suggest the contemporaneity of multiple temporalities.

Just as the Mexican Pavilion or teocalli in Paris discussed in chapter 1 functioned as a cosmopolitan scenario in which Indigenous architecture could be staged as Mexico's platform for engaging with modernity, the temporal disjunction captured in this sequence through cinematographic montages, somber aural cues, and off-synch movement reveals the tensions and dynamism at play in this scene, which do not portray indigeneity as exclusively past-oriented. The sculptures displayed in 1889 Paris responded to the plasticity ascribed to indigeneity to signal Mexico's uniqueness and grandiose past, and yet they were used to stake a claim to modernity and its concomitant aesthetics, particularly the aesthetics associated with the cultural revolution of the 1920s and 1930s.[44] The opening shots of the "Prologue" initially have a similar function. The scenes of Indigenous deities from the National Museum of Anthropology and ceremonial centers, such as Teotihuacán or Chichén Itzá, capture the monumentality of an ancient past to be contemplated, accentuated by the exoticizing and solemn nondiegetic music. And yet their juxtaposition with Indigenous bodies, faces, and landscapes through experimental uses of the camera and filming techniques indexes an indigeneity that is cinematically rendered as monumentally modern. While the style evokes the social realism characteristic of Eisenstein's silent films, such as *Battleship Potemkin* (1926) and *October* (1927),[45] the camera angle introduces a pictorial element that oscillates between the quasi-phrenological rendition of Indigenous faces via extreme close-ups and poetic portraits of indigeneity that appear experimental and experiential. The formal aesthetic of the film emphasizes the temporal tension between sound and off-synch movement captured by a static camera, from palm leaves slowly moved by the wind like the hair of the Indigenous people to almost imperceptible facial and bodily gestures. The multiple temporalities—the contrast between the Indigenous monuments and architecture embedded in the past and the Indigenous bodies and the animated landscape (the tropical flora and fauna and natural phenomena like the sun rays and wind)—call into question the view of indigeneity as ontologically trapped in the past.

Eisenstein's experimental filming techniques capture an experiential and sensorial impression of Mexico. Before his trip to Mexico, Eisenstein had been exploring the rendering of Otherness and its relation to the "primitive" through his theorization of the montage as a mode of perception in order to elicit a more "primal, less conscious response in the spectator."[46] Linking Otherness to the idea of "layered representation," he placed the primitive, a form of consciousness and source of renewal, at the center of revolutionary art. As Laura Podalsky insightfully observes, Mexico became a site of "release" and "renovation" where "logical thought became subsumed to feeling." Influenced by contemporary discourses of anthropology, Eisenstein set out to discover the "mechanisms of early thinking which would allow unmediated link between the emotional states of artist and spectator."[47] Mexico certainly represented that space where the modern and the primitive coexisted. Moreover, we ought not to forget that Mesoamerican monumental architecture was performative, designed as a sacred stage for embodiment, movement, and action. Its aesthetic, ritualistic, and material framework treated movement as fundamental to Indigenous spiritual and political life.[48] As stages for performances of power, the Indigenous architecture that was cinematically captured served as a reminder of the dynamism that continued to animate Indigenous life and as a scenario for the choreographies of Indigenous cosmovisions. At once folkloric/confined to the past and avant-garde, Indigenous cultural expressions advanced narratives that helped Eisenstein reframe Mexico's past, present, and future through modern technologies, techniques, and aesthetics.

The "Prologue" has also been considered Eisenstein's cinematic tribute to the Mexican muralist David Alfaro Siqueiros in conceptual terms, if not aesthetic ones. Between 1923 and 1924, Siqueiros painted *Entierro de un obrero* (Burial of the sacrificed worker), which depicted the burial of a communist worker but was left incomplete for political reasons. By comparing the mural with the scene of the burial in the "Prologue," the viewer can draw parallels to the theme and, perhaps more important, to the camera work that privileges vertical and horizontal frames, with medium close-ups and extreme close-ups of the faces of the Indigenous people. I concur with Salazkina when she contends that it is the juxtaposition of Siqueiros's mural and Eisenstein's sequence of the burial that gives meaning to the history of the film, "not merely as an ethnographic documentary and a record of ancient traditions and rituals still alive in contemporary Mexico, but as a historical and dialectical engagement with the material, in particular through the coexistence of temporal moments that fascinated Eisenstein in Mexico, the co-presence of an authentic past and a revolutionary present."[49] This interactive engagement illustrates the creative process at play during the shooting of the film. Eisenstein's encounter with muralism also influenced the work of Siqueiros himself, who went on to write an essay that drew on the theoretical principles of the montage to analyze Mexican muralist production.[50]

Beyond the impact that Eisenstein may have had on the development of the Mexican muralist movement and vice versa, my aim here is to highlight the dynamic dialogue between these artists and the consolidation of a semiotic field through which a Mexican visual aesthetics was configured. To be sure, the postrevolutionary visual aesthetics had already been established in the decade before, as I discussed in the previous chapters. After all, the Mexican muralists I have mentioned were already recognized as masters at home and abroad. Nevertheless, the encounter with the Russian film director signaled the emergence of a cinematic and visual language that would legitimate precisely the aesthetics of mestizaje embraced by Mexican muralism as visually Indigenous. Yet this aesthetics failed to encompass, and indeed erased, the real ethnic diversity of Mexico, including the presence of Afro-descendants and Asians, to mention two prominent examples. Eisenstein's encounter with Mexico thus reconfigured the mechanisms of conceiving and representing lo mexicano through moving images.

Eisenstein's "Sandunga": Indigeneity in Motion

Dance and music quickly became intimately associated with Eisenstein's rendition of authentic Mexican imaginaries. Local traditional songs and dances, which continued to be present in the quotidian experience of the Indigenous and peasant communities portrayed in Eisenstein's cinematic project, enhanced the aesthetic language that his film attempted to capture and re-create. Manuel Castro Padilla reportedly was going to work on the synchronization of Mexican music, including traditional religious songs such as "El Alabado" (The praised one), to capture the simple, deeply rooted customs of Mexican Indigenous people.[51] And yet little attention has been paid to these performative aesthetic elements of filmmaking in an era prior to the introduction of sound, which in Mexico would arrive with the release of *Santa* (Moreno) a year later in 1932. Whereas others have discussed the visual language and representation of indigeneity in Eisenstein's project in Mexico, here I would like to focus on the bodies in movement that set these entangled representations of Mexican nationalism in motion.

What best captures the complexity and intricacy of Eisenstein's aesthetics is the filming of the moving bodies of Indigenous women, which is the subject of the first episode, or novella, in ¡*Que viva México!* Upon his arrival, Eisenstein traveled to the Tehuantepec region in Oaxaca in early 1931, accompanied by his assistant and censor Adolfo Best Maugard, who served as his interpreter and mediator with the local communities. For thirty-four consecutive days, he filmed his first novella, "Sandunga," which centers on two major elements: the tropical landscape of Tehuantepec, capturing visually and discursively the slow passage of time, and the celebration of a traditional wedding within a Zapotec matriarchal community of Tehuanas, the largest Indigenous group in the Isthmus of Tehuantepec. "Sandunga" tells the story of Concepción's marriage, including its arrangement, preparations, and celebration. It is significant that Eisenstein filmed local Indigenous and peasant community members, according to Best Maugard's report to the Ministry of Education.[52] They rechoreographed a traditional song, "Sandunga," which has become a traditional hymn for the region and, paradoxically, a popular wedding song despite narrating the loss and mourning of a mother. "Sandunga" frames the soundscape of this novella, advancing the story of Concepción aurally and kinesthetically.

Unlike the motionless positions of Indigenous people in the "Prologue," this first novella captures the tensions between the supposed stillness of life and the active movement of the Indigenous women of the Tehuantepec region. Although we will never know how Eisenstein would have filmed "Soldadera," the part of the film portraying the women soldiers of the Mexican Revolution, "Sandunga" features women of all ages with special attention to the young Concepción, whose story is depicted in this novella.[53] Here movement is gendered and, of course, racialized through the cinematic framing of Indigenous spaces, activities, and landscapes. In contrast to the depictions that became staples in the representation of Mexican women in film, from their racialized portrayal as "white-as-Indigenous" women (to use the analytic proposed by Mónica García Blizzard) to submissive characters with limited agency who are constrained to the private sphere,[54] "Sandunga" captured Indigenous women from Tehuantepec as community members in charge of their actions and even futures, with agency over their deeds. Although men appear in the novella, it is the women who dominate the screen. The gendered and ethnic distinction between the public and private spheres cannot contain the literal and symbolic mobility of Indigenous women. At stake is the representation of an otherwise utopian world centered on the experience of Indigenous women, a matriarchal society that is still alive in the Tehuantepec region, now internationally known for its *muxes*, or what is called Mexico's third gender.[55]

Analyses of the film often dismiss or take for granted the kinesthetic and dance scenes of the Tehuanas, and yet it is in these moments that critical ruptures and contradictions in what has come to be considered a hegemonic representation of a gendered ethnic diversity in Mexican film are set in motion.[56] The exploration of Tehuantepec women vis-à-vis nature in the filming of "Sandunga" mobilized a gendered visualization of "the primitive." For Podalsky, this operation depicted Tehuantepec as the "womb of the revolution," hence the name "Concepción," or conception. It is not surprising that Eisenstein conceived of the "female body as a trope for the nation," because he understood the "stages of civilization" as gendered, positing women as sources of "regeneration."[57] The dancing bodies, however, conjure other temporalities that fracture what would otherwise be read as hegemonic representations of the nation. As discussed in chapter 2, Tehuantepec had already acquired the mythical quality of time immemorial and the association with an Indigenous noncontemporaneous time.

One aspect worth noting has to do with the person who exerted the most influence on Eisenstein's portrayal of the Tehuanas and the Tehuantepec region. It is true that Eisenstein established a close relation with Diego Rivera and that he had already read descriptions of Mexico by locals and foreigners, such as Anita Brenner's *Idols behind Altars* and a couple of numbers of Frances Toor's journal *Mexican Folkways*, paying particular attention to women's independence and the Indigenous matriarchal society.[58] Nevertheless, it was Adolfo Best Maugard who introduced Eisenstein's crew to the area and who served as their interlocutor, not only linguistically (he was the only one who spoke Spanish) but also culturally, connecting them with locals and contextualizing and explaining the latter's cultural practices, traditions, and ideology.[59] In his report of their thirty-four-day stay in Tehuantepec, Best Maugard recounted that they first had to gain the trust of the local community. For instance, he mentioned that the locals were paid and consulted in the filming of this novella.[60] Some Indigenous men, however, thought the cameras would allow the crew members to see through women's clothing, while others simply were resistant to participating.[61] Furthermore, Best Maugard already had his own ideas and renditions of the region. As the images elaborated by Best Maugard and the description of the Tehuana in the official program brochure of "La Noche Mexicana" discussed in chapter 2 illustrate, the region of Tehuantepec and the figure of the Tehuana summoned a sensuous, paradisiacal time that fostered a state-sponsored mestizo aesthetics. This often-ignored fact erases the complex and ambivalent relationship of Best Maugard with the representation of the women of Tehuantepec. Similarly, the dancing of "Sandunga," which provides the nondiegetic music for most of the episode, confirms these images as part of the tropical, slow-paced, and mythical space of the isthmus. And yet the continuous movement and dancing also call attention to the collective practices of these Indigenous communities, who were and still are very much alive, reenacting and reinventing the practices they have preserved for generations.

Even though "Sandunga" displaces Indigenous people to a lost-in-time paradise, the cinematic form that Eisenstein used in the filming of the Tehuantepec novella functions as an ethnodocumentary. Joanne Hershfield proposes that we think of Eisenstein's film as "ethnography staged as fiction film,"[62] whereas Masha Salazkina contends that like an ethnodocumentary, "Sandunga" captures "a more accurate historical reading of the women who were filmed for that novella as opposed to the representation of the abstract mythological Tehuanas."[63] I argue similarly that the documentary-like quality of the film indexes the tension between representations of Indigenous communities and Indigenous people's embodied practices. The ethnodocumentary quality of the sequences of the Tehuantepec region helps us trace the daily activities at the market in this matriarchal society and the festivities, rites, and activities that take place around the planning and celebration of a wedding. As Best Maugard's report indicates, the celebration of these festivities was specifically re-created for the purposes of filming them.[64] Nevertheless, it is crucial to recognize that the community itself did celebrate such an important rite of passage.

The movement and dancing of "Sandunga" posit Indigenous female corporeality as a lived presence, directly challenging the recognizable tropes of indigenismo that seek to confine it. Their moving bodies signify indigeneity differently and enact history. The Zapotec descendants on screen therefore summon and cite their ancestors through their embodied practices, contesting a static sense of indigeneity. The filmic representation of Indigenous women in "Sandunga" contain indexical traces of the corporeal histories of the Indigenous communities visited by Eisenstein and their crew members. Their actions on screen can be read as an embodied statement responding to specific modes of colonizing corporeal histories that render Indigenous bodies as non-contemporaneous, innocent, and primitive. This reading of Indigenous corporeality is similar to the critical dance studies scholar Melissa Blanco Borelli's reading of *mulata* bodies as "an active corporeality—a lived body with experiences in the material world—rather than as a static product of national discourses represented through visual art, literature, music, and religious iconography."[65] Even though it deals with filmic bodies, *¡Que viva México!* functions as a visual document, indeed as an ethnodocumentary, that records the embodied experience of Indigenous women. Their bodies in movement in the novella "Sandunga" conjure a corporeally situated Indigenous historicity.

The bodies of Indigenous women in "Sandunga" animate alternative markers of indigeneity that point to other Indigenous subjectivities. By contesting colonial tropes of passive indigeneity through their moving and dancing, the Tehuanas in "Sandunga" assert their sentient bodies as vehicles for affirmation, self-expression, and even pleasure. These moving women are full of life and coexist with elements of coloniality, such as the material (and spiritual) presence of the church, and modern ones, such as the presence of cameras. Their dresses, which have come to be a cosmopolitan staple representing Mexican indigeneity and nationalism, also materialize the historical specificity of their cultural expression. In his thorough description of the intricate differences in Tehuana dresses, the renowned Mexican painter, illustrator, and ethnologist Miguel Covarrubias explains that the black velvet or satin dresses featured geometrical designs or elaborate floral patterns resembling those of the Manila shawls. In addition to their silk and printed English cotton, Tehuana women took pride in their gold necklaces, as the novella clearly illustrates, made with English, American, Guatemalan, and Mexican gold coins from the Porfirian-era construction of the train that tied the port of Salina Cruz, Oaxaca, to Coatzacoalcos, Veracruz.[66] The sequences of the market scene, for instance, are intertwined with close-ups of the growing gold necklace, highlighting its historic specificity and symbolic importance and materializing the labor and agency of women in its creation. Instead of rendering the body a "locus of utopia," then,[67] Eisenstein paradoxically captures the complex and contradictory ways Zapotec women inhabit a historically specific corporeality. Whereas there is a push to render them as mere aesthetic ornaments of a premodern utopia, the camera indexes the cotemporaneity and agency with which Indigenous bodies materialize culture and engage with a rapidly modernizing, albeit still colonial, world.

In "Sandunga," dance is a fundamental act for the creation and regeneration of a community, a site of negotiation of gender and ethnic practices, and an instance where embodied cultural memory is transmitted.

There are two dance sequences in this novella: one that focuses on the courtship between Concepción and her fiancé, Abundio, and another at the end of the wedding performed exclusively by women. The first dance scene transitions the narrative from the marketplace to a festive dance space. The market scene ends with Concepción selling bananas and other goods and then with a close-up of the gold necklace she has been creating as her dowry (which is featured in the series of pictures in figure 4.1). The next image is a close-up of Abundio, described by the voice-over as "Concepción's object of affection." This comment, which is the first time the spectator sees a close-up of Abundio in the novella, establishes a direct visual and discursive link between the necklace and Abundio. The next shot features both Concepción and Abundio, chatting, flirting, and smiling as the nondiegetic music of "Sandunga" begins.

In this first dance scene, we observe the gendered differentiation of the dance space; women sit across the dance floor of an *enramada* (arbor), which the men cross to invite them to dance. The women are smiling and talking among themselves, looking at the men who soon will be approaching them and letting themselves be looked at. The film positions the camera at a distance and invites the spectator to participate in the dance. At the same time, it reminds us of our role as observers and witnesses, since the camera is placed behind palm tree leaves, as if we were too in the enramada. Then the camera cuts to a medium shot of Abundio beckoning Concepción to dance. As the dance gains momentum, the camera alternates between a medium long shot and medium shots of the dancers and close-ups of Concepción and Abundio. The nondiegetic music of "Sandunga" seems almost too fast for the tempo with which it is usually associated. Unlike most contemporary iterations performed at traditional *velas* (festivities held in honor of local patron saints), the Indigenous men and women dance to the sound of "Sandunga" while embracing, as if it were a relaxed waltz. In fact, the slow-paced rhythm of "Sandunga" and other local sones invites dancers to waltz to it, but with a twist (see fig 4.3). The man places his right hand just above the waist of the woman (and at times even on her shoulder blade), slightly extending his left hand to his partner. The woman rests her left hand on the man's right shoulder and extends her right hand, placing it gently on her partner's palm. The embrace is not necessarily close, which allows women to determine the kind of intimacy they want to establish while dancing.

This dance sequence enables the spectator to attend to the particular styling of the dancers. In effect, the dancing operates as a gendered

Figure 4.3. "Sandunga," *¡Que viva México!* (1932). Screen capture from film.

trial-and-error session where the bond with a prospective partner is temporarily enacted. In the synopsis of the script of the film sent by Eisenstein directly to the editors of *Experimental Cinema*, he noted that the "dance hall is the only place where a youth and a girl may meet."[68] Through dancing, the couples hold each other in an act of mutual belonging, as suggested by the close embrace between Concepción and Abundio and other Indigenous couples. Over the course of the scene, some couples move together in circles or semicircles around the dance floor; some go forward and others backward. Some, such as Concepción and Abundio, remain in the same space for the most part, whereas others go around the dance floor, perhaps suggesting less intimacy with their dance partners. The alternating shots also allow us to see the two basic steps performed by the local couples, showcasing the movement vocabulary characteristic of the region. The first is a simple shift of the body weight from side to side, a swaying back and forth; the man typically starts with the left foot, shifting his weight to the left leg so that the right foot is free to take a step and shift the body's weight back to the right leg. The partner mirrors this motion, swaying her body back and forth as well. The leading partner may start with a forward basic step, but as seen in this sequence, some of them move sideways instead of forward, and some even travel backward. Their partners mirror them, shifting their weight back and forth and maintaining the rhythm with the music. The second basic step follows the same principle but is executed in groupings of three. The man starts with his left foot and the woman with the right one, with the man usually stepping forward, though they can also move sideways or backward. Both partners sway slightly on their feet. They separate their feet, shifting their body weight, and close them on two to then step again, separating their feet on three and shifting their body weight so that the other leg is free to start the next grouping of three. This movement has become a staple of the dance repertoire of the region. It is gentle and delicate, without accentuating the hip. The arm movement varies, but it tends to be constrained, simply allowing the body to move as it shifts its weight back and forth. Instead of constant circular motions aiming to elevate the dancers' bodies, as in ballroom waltz, the Tehuantepec dancers execute the basic steps while stepping firmly on the ground as they dance barefoot (particularly the women) or with simple sandals. The cinematic rendition of Tehuantepec's movement vocabulary therefore served to register and codify Indigenous gender norms, social dynamics, and cultural expectations.

Throughout this dance sequence, it is the body that sets cultural meaning in motion. Perhaps it is not a coincidence that the voice-over remains silent during the entire sequence. In addition to capturing the bodily movements of a dancing community, the camera brings us closer to their faces, particularly those of Concepción and Abundio and another young Indigenous couple. Whereas the men and Concepción smile often, displaying their pleasure and joy, the other Indigenous girl does not. On the contrary, she gazes back at the camera as if to signal that it is invading her personal and intimate space. Her direct gaze is a reminder that she can gaze back at those filming her. This gesture of alienation illustrates how Indigenous people, especially the women whose lives and activities the novella captures, responded to and engaged with the modern technologies of still and motion cameras. The filming techniques and close-ups might have framed Indigenous women as exotic and primitive. But their corporeal responses to visual technologies asserted that, as Natasha Varner puts it, "Indigenous experience remained multifaceted and included varying degrees of engagement with—and departure from—efforts to police ever-narrowing parameters of 'authentic' Indigeneity."[69] These moments when we as spectators see them staring directly back at the camera, at times coyly and at other times defiantly, index the non-verbal and corporeal language that Indigenous women deployed in these instances of self-affirmation and self-fashioning.

The communal dance also establishes a material and symbolic space in which to initiate the rite of passage of marriage. In this sequence, there are several close-ups of characters that seem not to be part of the dance, such as small children and even a small goat next to a pile of coconuts. But the presence of small children, the goat, and the coconuts foreshadows what comes next: the marriage and the creation of a family in this tropical landscape. After all, throughout the novella, Eisenstein resorted to the use of montage and the voice-over to suggest the various life cycles at play. It all starts with a man sitting down on a hammock whose silhouette fades into the shape of the necklace Concepción arduously works to craft (an image that is also captured in figure 4.1). The voice-over discursively frames the hard work of Concepción in the marketplace and all her actions before and after the dance sequence of "Sandunga": "May your necklace bring you happiness." The necklace, like the elaborate dresses the Tehuana women wear to the dance, acts as a material marker of the historical specificity that the still and motion cameras capture: the women's bodies and apparel link them to the land they occupy.

The second sequence that alludes to "Sandunga" as a non-diegetic soundscape comes toward the end of the novella, and it highlights the grandiosity of the Tehuanas and the landscape they inhabit. This sequence evokes a harmonious and sensuous feeling that animates the landscape, plants, and animals. It takes place right after the wedding and consummation of the marriage (suggested by the removal of the necklace from Concepción's neck) but immediately before the last shot of Concepción, Abundio, and their child on a hammock, which symbolically closes the life cycle in the tropics while beginning it again with the creation of new life. This time around, however, the sequence features a group of approximately nine young Indigenous women dressed in their full Tehuana attire in a medium long shot. Though the young Tehuanas' gait resembles the three-beat basic step described above, as if they were almost dancing, the camera focuses on visually and symbolically capturing the styling and intricacies with which each Tehuana fashions herself and the tropical landscape that produces her. In fact, in the aforementioned synopsis published in *Experimental Cinema*, Eisenstein titles this last section "The Sandunga" and describes it by mentioning the rhythm of a cycle that directly alludes to the song: "The Sandunga that always sings in the air whenever happiness comes—either in dreams or in reality. While throughout the tropical forest under the peaceful fragrance of the palm-trees life pursues its habitual daily course."[70] This is a sentient and animate space. The arm movement of the young Tehuanas, swinging their skirts to the left and to the right along with the swaying of their bodies as they take steps forward and backward, captures this feeling through the traditional light skirt work typical of this dance. The slow movements of their skirts also resemble the movement of the sea as the waves slowly come and go. Here the close-ups from a low angle echo to a degree Best Maugard's description of their gait, discussed in chapter 2: "the gait of a *Tehuana* with her bust firm and straight, undulating arms, and a long and languid swinging of the wide skirts rustled by the wind." One can only speculate about the extent to which the sequence was his idea after all.

The Indigenous bodies, then, operate as both a sight, part of a native landscape and utopian space onto which Indigenous people are dis/placed, and a site where the subject/landscape dyad that Eisenstein's work advances is contested and destabilized. The allegorical mode of representation frames Indigenous bodies in a tropical paradise where there is a communal relation between humans, animals, and landscape, as the opening sequences of the novella exemplify. And yet the indexical quality of the images and footage captures the historical specificity and even the agency of bodies in constant movement. While Masha Salazkina has also noted this filmic tension between an allegorical mode of representation and the historical specificity of images that portray Indigenous embodied expressions as part of recognizable tropes of Mexican postrevolutionary aesthetics,[71] she concludes that the focal point of scenes in "Sandunga" is the ornate dresses and decorations, the "center of the spectacle [that] act as a narrative force," not the female bodies themselves.[72] Nevertheless, the constant movement of Indigenous women should not be ignored. It is through their movement, especially dancing, that a notion of indigeneity is contested and expanded.

The tropical landscape, with palm trees and lush greenery, frames the corporeal statements of the Tehuanas in "Sandunga." As Natasha Varner notes, Eisenstein's cinematic vocabulary came to serve as a paradigm for the "fetishization" of Indigenous faces. His still and moving images posited that "Indigenous beauty had value beyond the folkloric bounty seen in material culture and that there was pleasure to be found in the images of the Indigenous body that was stylized and fragmented by close-ups."[73] Nevertheless, there is an ongoing tension between the narrative and visual languages that render Indigenous people noncontemporaneous and the dancing, reactions, and documentary-like shooting that make their bodies contemporaneous and active producers of their own filmic space. And while it can be argued that the women's dance objectifies their bodies once again, it foregrounds a sense of agency that they display kinesthetically throughout this novella.

The main events of the novella revolve around the market, the popular dance, and the wedding, foregrounding instances where gendered and racialized cultural norms are negotiated. The cinematic apparatus, which determines which bodies and landscapes the spectator can see, conditions the embodied stories and histories of the Indigenous subjects on the silver screen. It creates a temporal framework that invites the spectator to project indigeneity onto a distant utopian space, and yet the dancing and moving bodies enable a different kind of engagement with this filmic scenario that goes beyond the utopian. The indexical quality of the image enables the spectator to witness the ways Indigenous bodies assert their agency, experience pleasure, and materialize other imaginaries. The body thus becomes a site that registers contested knowledge of indigeneity, capturing and circulating an embodied cultural memory that need not be reduced to utopian, noncontemporaneous spatiotemporal coordinates. Instead, the moving camera invites the spectator to witness and at times even participate in the kinesthetic experience of a living, dynamic, and thriving Indigenous culture, effectively rechoreographing "Sandunga."

El jarabe tapatío, *Allá en el Rancho Grande*, and the Contradictory Performances of a Modern Mexico

Filmed a couple of years after Eisenstein's stay in Mexico and the ensuing controversy over the unfinished production of *¡Que viva México!*, *Allá en el Rancho Grande* (*Out on the Big Ranch*, 1936) shared a number of elements with its predecessor: an emphasis on the visual over the narrative in Mexican film productions, the predominance of landscapes and recognizable Mexican features (such as magueys), and a romanticized portrayal of the countryside, Indigenous and peasant communities, and these communities' customs and ritualistic practices.[74] When *Allá en el Rancho Grande* became a hit in 1936, its success came in great part because it drew on established cinematic, musical, and, I contend, kinesthetic traditions: the singing Hollywood Western, the *ranchera* ballad (re-mediating the way it was portrayed not just on the radio but in cinema), and, more important for my analysis, Mexico's *teatro de revistas* (revue theater) characters, narrative framework, and musical elements.[75]

It also constituted a rejection of the negative portrayal of Mexican nationals in Hollywood cinema and a clear embrace of a conservative, highly stylized, and depoliticized rendition of a prerevolutionary Mexico, which contrasted drastically with the socialist reforms and active social agenda of the Lázaro Cárdenas government.[76] In so doing, it represented a radical refusal of exclusively urban and US-influenced culture and imaginaries, foregrounding a more local and yet transnational representation of Latin America that had not been produced by the United States.[77]

Set in 1922 but evocative of a prerevolutionary time, Fernando de Fuentes's *Allá en el Rancho Grande* depicts an idealized rural Mexico in a musicalized melodramatic comedy, with a paternalistic and conservative take on the good hacienda owner and the "derecho de pernada" (droit du seigneur) subtheme, already a well-known storyline of the time, considering its Spanish and Argentinian renditions.[78] De Fuentes's previous trilogy, *El prisionero 13* (*Prisoner 13*, 1933), *El compadre Mendoza* (*Godfather Mendoza*, 1934), and *¡Vámonos con Pancho Villa!* (*Let's Go with Pancho Villa*, 1935), presented critical takes on the Mexican Revolution and its multiple factions: a critique of the cruel militarism of the Victoriano Huerta presidency in the first film; the "apolitical, opportunistic class" that supported the Revolution as long as it did not threaten their economic interests during the Venustriano Carranza government in the second; and the "cataclysm" and lack of a clear social or political agenda of Francisco Villa in the last one.[79]

Although Fernando de Fuentes directed *Allá en el Rancho Grande*, it was Gabriel Figueroa who played a prominent role as a cinematographer with his work for this film, which was his first major production in Mexico. In fact, Figueroa won an award at the Venice Film Festival for the cinematography in *Allá en el Rancho Grande*; the first of a series of prizes at Venice, Cannes, and Berlin Film Festivals, many of which were for his collaborations with Emilio Fernández. *Allá en el Rancho Grande* was the cinematic production that inaugurated the Golden Age of Mexican cinema. In this film, the aesthetic and thematic concerns that would characterize Figueroa's work became evident. Throughout the film, prominent Eisensteinian shots fix the camera at lower angles to frame the people in the scene and juxtapose them with a large open space that seems to consume them. The Mexican landscape becomes the protagonist of the sequences. Although Figueroa never worked with Sergei Eisenstein directly in Mexico, his work was significantly influenced by Eisenstein's "composition of open spaces" and by German expressionist cinema.[80]

Figueroa's work as director of photography in the most iconic films of the era engaged with two primary pictorial traditions: landscape and portraiture, from colonial and natural landscapes, particularly the Mexican skies, to the faces of anonymous extras and Mexican stars, including María Félix, Dolores del Río, and Pedro Armendáriz. Partaking of the modern visual aesthetics of the time, "produced by technical images and sounds,"[81] Figueroa's cinematographic work contributed to the consolidation of visual literacy and modernity through the technical reproduction and massive circulation of moving images. In a sense, Figueroa was responding to technical innovations and the emergence of a modern visual language centered on subjects and spaces.[82] It is important, however, to acknowledge the impact of the Mexican Revolution on the emergence of the regime of visuality as the dominant sensorium of power in the first decades of the century. Considerably better documented than World War I and the Russian Revolution, the Mexican Revolution was characterized by the dramatic mobilization of anonymous masses that literally and figuratively swept the nation. Photography (and to some extent footage from the time) did more than index the otherwise "unscripted" reality; it also began to organize something that was not yet present, serving as "the sensory representation of an overarching reality that could not itself be made the subject of representation."[83] The Revolution forced the expansion of the dominant visual regime as a means of grappling with the abrupt appearance of the masses in public places and their dynamic armed mobilization across the nation to capture the visual movement between the city and the countryside. By focusing on landscapes and faces/*rostros*, Figueroa foregrounded the fusion between subject and landscape in Mexican cinema. This identification, characteristic of Mexican cinema, solidified the primacy of the image in Mexican narratives.[84] If Eisenstein's work elevated Mexico to the international arena and rendered it worthy of contemplation, as the muralists had done, Figueroa's photography congealed, à la Eisenstein, the kind of subject-landscape dyad to be contemplated. The subject and the landscape together made visible the importance of cinema in the creation of a national fiction and the interpellation of a national audience. This visual operation symbolically crystalized the identification of Mexican audiences with the places, people, and embodied practices that they saw represented on screen.

Figueroa's portrayal of Mexican landscapes played a starring role in Mexican cinematic production, which elevated him to the point that he was considered Mexico's "fourth muralist." His cinematic landscapes operated as dynamic sites where an epistemological shift occurred—a generative space that produced and was produced by its viewers. In a sense, all landscapes mediate our relations with the space with which we interact. On the one hand, a landscape naturalizes the mechanism through which it is configured via images, symbols, and the like. On the other, it conjures up its own viewers, conditioning their relationship with their surroundings.[85] Figueroa deployed the technology of the camera to configure the national landscape that had been anticipated by the muralists and Eisenstein, naturalizing and framing the space captured in his moving images.[86]

The landscapes that would become iconic were fabricated in conjunction with the subject/rostro that came to index lo mexicano. The beauty of the landscape, then, was always already positioned vis-à-vis the subjects on the screens. This subject-landscape dyad naturalizes the fabrication of a visual language mediated by the camera. Through a series of juxtapositions of subjects and landscapes, Figueroa presented a mestizo Mexican fiction in a unified visual regime. Carlos Monsiváis contends that Figueroa deployed a unifying optic that became his major contribution to the Mexican film industry. Even if it was impossible to apprehend lo mexicano, there was a clear nationalist conviction in his cinematographic work. And due to this nationalist conviction, as Monsiváis suggests, "el México inventado se torna, estéticamente, en el México real" (the invented Mexico becomes, aesthetically, the real Mexico).[87] Figueroa's photography mediated the viewers' relation to their own environment, expanding, transforming, and even creating aesthetically a reworked version of Mexico's reality.

The symbolism and imaginaries summoned by the silver screen also revamped the role of the gaze. Carlos Fuentes, in his analysis of the legacy of Figueroa's work, goes on to argue that "de esa fabricación, de ese artificio, somos a fin capaces de ver la verdadera realidad, es decir: la realidad creada" (out of that invention, out of that artifice, we are able to finally see the true reality; that is: the constructed reality).[88] For Fuentes, Figueroa's photography not only gave an identity to millions of people who had remained in the "facial anonymity" of the masses throughout centuries but also, perhaps more important, changed Mexico's own identity.[89] In consolidating the subject-landscape dyad, Figueroa conjured its viewing public, calling on Mexicans to recognize themselves on the silver screen. What Figueroa ultimately accomplished was to turn the gaze on the spectators themselves. Cinema captured more than the emergence of a people in postrevolutionary Mexico; it captured the process by which Mexicans acquired a face/rostro within a national landscape, cinematically rendering their slow emergence from anonymity.

The revolutionaries had claimed the public sphere for their cause, but the institutionalization of the Revolution of 1910 paradoxically reclaimed it for the bourgeoisie and the elites. During the postrevolutionary period, however, the reappearance of the masses in the public sphere was not simply an embodied or discursive process but an emergence that was negotiated in the visual realm. The cinematic appearance of the pueblo simultaneously produced and reproduced a sense of national belonging in which the kinesthetic played a significant role. In this sense, Eisenstein's depiction of Mexico and Figueroa's faces and landscapes drastically impacted the visual representation of lo mexicano, enhancing and consolidating the state-sponsored aesthetic project of postrevolutionary Mexico. They offered back to the spectators a vision with which Mexican citizens identified themselves at home and abroad: utopian, nostalgic, and domesticated, particularly during a period of substantial internal and external migration. However, and perhaps most important, cinema required the spectators to make an interactive investment in order to develop an intimate connection. By rendering the spectators part of the landscape (an idealized vision, certainly, but one that resonated with thousands), the moving images of the silver screen reconfigured the audience's relationship to a narrative of the nation. The work started by Eisenstein and continued by Figueroa and the rest of the acclaimed film directors of the Golden Age era invited the audience members to become complicit with and participants in this representation of Mexico. This also meant complicity with and participation in the major exclusions perpetuated by Mexican cinema and the erasure of the complex ethnoracial differences that existed throughout the country.

It is crucial, then, to consider the often contradictory and at times ambivalent representations that the moving images of the silver screen conjure. One of the major impacts of *Allá en el Rancho Grande* derived from its reworking of established genres, such as the revista genre, the musicalized and nostalgic representations of a long-gone past, cowboy singing films, and melodrama. In the specific case of Mexican cultural and cinematic production, *Allá en el Rancho Grande* also incorporated regional markers, including a folkloric and highly stereotypical depiction of rural life; a decidedly artificial Mexican Spanish; well-known artists such as Tito Guízar, who was already known in the United States; two musical trios; and, most relevant to this chapter, the performance of El jarabe tapatío. In the cinematic renditions, these otherwise folkloric representations of Mexico, some of which were active elements of the contemporary performance scene, not only carried their original meanings but also reframed these meanings, their circulation, and their consumption.

One of the major characteristics of this era of increased migration, rapid industrialization, and social reforms was the turn to nostalgia as a way to create a sense of community and national belonging. This transformation was significantly accelerated by the impact of radio and live broadcasting and the emergence of sound cinema, particularly melodramatic and musicalized genres. Song and music, as primary components of films in the era, bridged communities across the nation and even in the transnational arena. The transposition into new contexts of artistic production, particularly music, led to the resignification and deterritorialization of cultural imaginaries and consequently to the development of an "aural identity," as Marvin D'Lugo has termed it.[90] Insisting on the ways listening triggers processes of community formation and recognition of shared cultural practices at home and abroad, D'Lugo argues for the importance of music for the production of social memory, cultural bonds, and ultimately a mode of transnational identity formation beyond the state, enhanced by sound technologies.[91] Music enabled the creation of imagined aural communities, deterritorializing the musical memory to expand and foster an aural mode of relating. Technology significantly expanded the reach and circulation of music, reworking listening practices, embodied memory, and the social significance of an "aural identification."

Music, reproduced and remediated via sound technologies of the time such as radio, the phonograph, and cinema, facilitated the creation of an aural transnational identification, a pan-Latin American aural identity. This aural form of identification fostered the emergence of shared meaning-making cultural practices, operating as a community-building mechanism. Nevertheless, I call attention to the concomitant process of *kinesthetic* identification, enhanced particularly via the incorporation of dance scenes of regional and traditional songs. In the case of the Mexican *comedia ranchera Allá en el Rancho Grande*, there is a drastic difference between the kind of international market and community it interpellated via its aural identification with distinct Mexican sounds and the community it called up kinesthetically via its regional dances. The dance scene of El jarabe tapatío materialized a localized kinesthetic identification that paradoxically fomented a cultural bond that was primarily regional, unlike the sonic identifications it encouraged or the aural identity it promoted. By 1936, El jarabe tapatío had become a national staple of the public school curriculum, cultural festivals, official ceremonies, and popular performances.[92] Because folklórico dance was already part of a shared kinesthetic background for Mexican audience members, most of whom were spectators of folklórico dance or even former performers, it triggered a kinesthetic response.

Music and dance have certainly served as complex and contradictory cultural markers of Latinidad in film production in and about Latin America. By resorting to Latin American rhythms as signs and sites of irreducible difference, cinematic narratives have operated as ambivalent and slippery cultural spaces where these rhythms constitute imaginary foundations and demarcations. The result is that they produce a sense of national belonging, but they also flatten out Latin American cultural variations. Rhythms have also served to mark differences of class, gender, race, sexuality, and ethnicity in order to render a sense of the Latina/o/x and Latin American experience in cinema. In this capacity, they function as "ambivalent signs of nationness."[93] The film scholar Ana M. López astutely observes that if "at one level—that of supranational/colonialist appropriation—rhythm can be used to collapse the very differences it embodies, at another level—individual, subnational, contestational—rhythm has also served to posit spaces for rewriting and resisting the homogeneity of the generalizing force of nationness."[94] Rhythms operate as a "signifying" form that invokes and elides the production of a sense of national belonging, thereby imagining and sustaining a community.[95] By turning body movements into signifying bodily attitudes, indeed embodied statements, rhythms enable the production of differentiated spaces that may collapse difference or may constitute a site in which to resignify and resist homogeneity.

Rhythms, then, allow for the creation and circulation of culturally differentiated imagined communities. If, as López points out, Latin American nations have been continuously sung and danced,[96] it is important to examine how embodied statements contributed to and defied representations of lo mexicano in films. In this sense, although *Allá en el Rancho Grande* idealized the past, an analysis of the first cinematic sequence of El jarabe tapatío reveals that the dance scene served as a site and sight of the symbolic and cultural work of musicians and dancers and as a visual testimony of the faces/rostros that the technology of the moving image made legible. The dancing and the rhythms set in motion by the performance of El jarabe tapatío led to the creation of differentiated cultural bonds and a new imagined community, one that remained localized kinesthetically even as others were more transnational sonically.

The inclusion of a cinematic sequence focused exclusively on El jarabe tapatío played a pivotal role in the portrayal of a festive Mexico. It high-lighted the folkloric rendition of the film and its reliance on stereotyped, highly legible markers of local culture, particularly of lo mexicano. And yet it also revealed the significance of Mexican regional dances for the representation of an imagined nation. The dance scene, which precedes the cockfight in the middle of the film, mobilized the use of cultural markers around a nostalgic portrayal of Mexico for audiences at home and abroad, particularly among migrant groups within Mexico and the Mexican diaspora in the United States.[97] It juxtaposed rapid urbaniza-tion, modernization, and the attendant class and racial anxieties that characterized them with the seemingly homogenous and pacific times before the Mexican Revolution, even though the action is supposedly set in 1922 at first and then in 1935. On the one hand, the film tackled the political and social anxieties that surrounded the election of Lázaro Cárdenas and his socialist agenda, particularly in terms of land reform; on the other, the film directed the viewers' attention to idealized rural visions of a country that no longer existed and from which some had

Figura 4.4. "El jarabe tapatío." *Allá en el Rancho Grande* (1936). Screen capture from film.

been displaced. These juxtapositions are played out visually, sonically, and kinesthetically during the dancing scene (see fig. 4.4).

As soon as the dance begins, the viewers see a medium long shot of the dancers. In the film, Olga Falcón and Emilio Fernández interpret El jarabe tapatío. The body positions of the dancers are rather flexed throughout the dance, with the man pursuing the woman as she resists his advances until the end; it is, after all, a dance of courtship. The woman is clearly wearing the famous china poblanas: a sequined dress with a representation of Mexico's national emblem of the eagle and the serpent, the traditional rebozo across her chest and back, and two long braids. The man does not wear a full charro outfit; he lacks the jacket. But he does have charro pants, a black charro shirt with its corresponding charro tie, and a traditional sarape, a poncho that he uses to engage with his dancing partner. As soon as the music starts, so does their zapateado, the percussive footwork characteristic of Mexican folklórico dance and part of Mexico's popular dance repertoire, over a wooden platform. The zapateado produces a rhythmic stomping with the tapping of the feet, alternating between fully flat and the heel or the toe, depending on the region and style. The trios Murciélago and Tariácuris, who had just had their sing-off, played the music for El jarabe tapatío.[98] This interpretation of El jarabe tapatío is not a balleticized version like Anna Pavlova's but rather one that was probably representative of the time, a time when the Campobellos sisters were touring the country dancing El jarabe tapatío alongside other cultural producers, popular performers, and even schoolchildren, as discussed in the previous chapters. The opening dance scene, then, immediately called its spectators to recognize a familiar visual, sonic, and kinesthetic repertoire.

Whereas non-Mexican audiences abroad may focus simply on the festive rhythm of the string instruments alongside the enhanced percussion of the zapateado by the dancers (i.e., making an aural identification), the three-step sequence characteristic of popular Mexican percussive dancing allows Mexican audiences to kinesthetically identify with one of the staples of the Mexican dance repertoire, even if they have never danced it themselves.[99] The visual, sonic, and rhythmic identification with the zapateado is enabled by a material and embodied kinesthetic identification with a cultural practice that summons and fosters an intimate bond of sociability, that is, an embodied sociality that is culturally and historically situated. Throughout the performance, the stomps, the shuffles, the slides, the pauses, and the strikes corporeally conjure different parts of Mexico and thus communicate kinesthetically with Mexican viewers. Together with the aural referents of El jarabe tapatío, a bricolage of Mexican tunes and sones, the various dance steps enact a "cultural poetics," what cultural theorist José Limón terms the "acts of cultural interpretation focused on aesthetically salient, culturally imbedded textualities and enactments."[100] In this sense, the performance of El jarabe tapatío embodies an aesthetically salient and culturally embedded form of Mexican cultural poetics.

It is up to the audience members to decode the intricate aural and kinesthetic textualities of the performance of El jarabe tapatío. Divided into three sections, the dance scene invites audience members to recognize themselves in the dancers. The first section opens with the traditional zapateado performed by Olga Falcón and Emilio Fernández. The second section is characterized by a traditional musical arrangement in triple meter.[101] Even though this is not a sung version of El jarabe tapatío, this section is known as the *son del atole* (*son* refers to traditional Mexican stringed-music and *atole* to a hot maize drink). This second section is performed with the corresponding dance step of *borrachos* (drunken ones), which consists of a three-part step stomping to the side with the right or left foot, stepping with the opposite one behind the stomping foot to then stomp again with the first foot while changing the body weight and direction. In this section, the man pretends to be drunk while the woman swings from side to side, shifting her body weight, in another three-part step that resembles the borrachos but involves stepping and placing the opposite foot in front of the stomping one. However, only the initial stanza is sung; the rest is whistled. In the next musical section, the use of the sarape showcases the ultimate motive of the dance: to seduce and entrap the woman. In this musical section of the dance, the audience observes the dancers flirting with the sarape, pursuing each other and exchanging it. In the next musical section, the dancers continue to court each other with the sarape, particularly the man, who tries to capture the woman. There is a first plane here. The protagonists of the film are in the background, and the musicians are on the side. The rest of the audience, which is quite diverse, is audibly present through cheers and whistles. At times, the camera places us close to the dancers; we do not always see their footwork, but we can hear it throughout the entire sequence. The only extreme close-up we have of the dancers' feet comes when they dance with the sombrero. Olga Falcón dances on the brim of the hat, jumping on top of it with both feet while shifting her body weight. Emilio Fernández only steps on the brim of the hat with one of his feet as he too jumps around the hat following the woman. The woman dances on top of the hat as he kicks in every other step. Here, the patterned footwork showcases the skills of both dancers and consequently the complex kinesthetic textualities that are culturally embedded in the dance.

Then comes the festive final section: the "Diana," a traditional tune played to mark a celebratory finale. This famous musical arrangement at the end of El jarabe tapatío is captured in a medium long shot; the dancers face the camera but look elsewhere, toward the public. At times during the dance, the camera situates the viewers as if they too were spectators sitting with the rest of the pueblo. At the end of the dance, the camera turns to a Mexican man dressed in a charro outfit who utters a famous Mexican cheer. Everyone else joins him, and immediately afterward, a white man, Peter the gringo, is unable to utter anything other than "Whoopee!" as he takes his cigar by the wrong end. This short scene indexes the gringo's lack of the cultural background that the others share and also gestures toward Hollywood's inability to render an "authentic" representation of Mexican or Latin American traditions. Then the camera turns to the middle of the ring, placing the viewer behind a line of charros as if to make the viewer part of the audience. We now become spectators of the cockfight. Rather than performing a balleticized rendition of El jarabe, the dancers showcase the elaborate and patterned footwork and the intricate yet recognizable steps of the popular dance. Aside from one extreme close-up of the zapateado, the camera remains primarily in three positions: in a medium, full, or medium long shot. In this sense, it does not rechoreograph the dance. On the contrary, it invites the viewers to become spectators of this dance, as if we were present in the cockfighting ring. From these primary positions, we see the entire bodies of the dancers and their footwork. Overall, the performance of El jarabe tapatío serves as the ultimate example of the enactment of a Mexican cultural poetics that required both the audience members within the scene and the viewers of this major cinematic hit to decode and interpret the prevalent aural and kinesthetic textualities of lo mexicano.

The film also asks the viewers to interpret the diversity of the audience in the cinematic representation of a cross-class scenario. After all, the *palenque*, or fighting ring, frames and helps to choreograph an imagined sociality of lo mexicano within and outside the film. In an insightful question in their classic study of Mexican cinema, the cultural critics Carlos Monsiváis and Carlos Bonfil wondered whether the palenque was in fact the cradle of lo mexicano: "¿El palenque cuna de la mexicanidad?"[102] It is through distinct camera shots that the film invites the viewers to identify with the various audience members in this iconic Mexican scenario. The diversity of Mexican social and cultural backgrounds present at the cockfight portrays the Mexican people as anonymous or at best stereotyped, and yet it also allows viewers to recognize themselves in the facial and sartorial representations of the audience members. It is before the singing battle and during the dance scene that the viewers encounter Eisensteinian typages of Mexicans, particularly through shot/reverse shots that disrupt Hollywood's 180-degree rule, oscillating between continuity editing and monstration.[103] Two sequences capture this cinematic operation. The first is a series of close-ups that indexes the faces/rostros and types of the Mexican people in attendance, which the viewers have not really seen until this point. Their attire and distinctive hats trace a cartography of various places of the Mexican Republic and their class status, particularly in the first six shots, where the audience witnesses an array of mostly men from various backgrounds. The first man to make a bet sports a *cuera tamaulipeca* (a distinct embroidered leather jacket from the northern state of Tamaulipas) with its corresponding scarf tied around his neck; the second wears a full, albeit less luxurious and elaborate, charro outfit and a velvet charro hat. The next wears a *caporal* shirt (a kind of adorned and embroidered shirt associated with foremen in central and western Mexico) and a traditional wide-brimmed hat, the *sombrero de ala ancha*. The next to bet is the only woman, with a traditional rebozo, long braids, earrings, and a ribbon on her head, accompanied by a boy with a wide-brimmed palm hat to her left and another spectator to her right. The next shot features three men from distinct socioeconomic backgrounds sitting in the front row, one wearing a simple wide-brimmed palm hat, another a velvet charro hat, and the third an embroidered and elaborate palm hat, surrounded by other men with charro and caporal shirts, charro outfits, and even one man sporting a northern plaid shirt and a corresponding northern style hat. The last shot before returning to the leading characters is of an American man, a gringo, who is visibly fatter than his Mexican counterparts. He wears glasses, a Texan-style hat (*tejana*), and a dress jacket and shirt (a stereotypical portrayal, to be sure), and he is surrounded by a man dressed in a charro outfit with an elaborate hat and another man wearing a regular jacket, black shirt, and a wide-brimmed palm hat. The display of a variety of men, clearly marked as Mexican, sporting distinct shapes and sizes of mustaches or none at all, and the occasional woman in the audience brings out of "facial anonymity" the otherwise ignored Mexican people at home and abroad.

In addition to sonically and kinesthetically experiencing a Mexican imagined sociality via the performance of El jarabe tapatío, the viewers visually encounter ethnoracial and class diversity among the audience members via a series of close-ups and shot/reverse shots of other spectators. The second sequence whose cinematic operation and camera work invite viewers to kinesthetically, sonically, and visually identify with the jarabe takes place after the first musical section of El jarabe. Here the camera moves from the dancers to the protagonist, José Francisco (Tito Guízar), who is completely seduced by the performance of the dance, holding the cock while the blade is put on for the fight. After a close-up of the blade, we see a medium shot of the other two men preparing the rival cock; a medium shot of the *hacendado* (landowner) (René Cardona), who is enjoying the performance and sports a luxurious and elaborate charro outfit; a medium long shot of the dancers; a medium shot of the musicians playing El jarabe; and finally, with the camera moving back to the dancers, a medium long shot as they again perform the musical section with which the song started. The camera then traces another series of close-ups of a set of Mexican rostros. There is only one close-up of a woman, wearing traditional attire that differs little from that of the female dancer on stage, a choice that reflects the predominantly male-centered space of the palenque.[104] The other subjects of the close-ups are five men wearing various traditional costumes and their corresponding hats. All except the drunk spectator at the end are absorbed and static while they enjoy the performance of a well-known and recognizable dance in a quintessential scenario of lo mexicano. And this is precisely the point I would like to emphasize: there is a *kinesthetic identification* with El jarabe tapatío that the movie invites the spectator to witness and performatively participate in, for the film does not appeal only via sonic rhythms, it also foregrounds localized forms of bodily movement and comportment as kinesthetic statements of an imagined national community at home and abroad. The Mexican embodied sociality rendered through the viewing of folklórico dance in film during the sequence of El jarabe tapatío encodes and simultaneously enacts a Mexican cultural poetics. After all, this cinematic sequence positions El jarabe tapatío as part and parcel of Mexican nationalism, as had been done since the turn of the century through revista performances, public education programs, civic festivals, and other official commemorations, particularly the centennial celebrations discussed in chapter 2.

The dancing scene of El jarabe tapatío captures diegetically how a sense of lo mexicano was unified and homogenized not only musically but also kinesthetically. The inclusion of this traditional dance scene in *Allá en el Rancho Grande* documented the role of dance and its public display as part of the emergence of a shared corporeal background, of an embodied imagined sociality. Dance performances in public spaces had been a common scene for decades, as illustrated by Pavlova's dance shows in bullrings and the Campobellos' performances, discussed in the previous chapter. Unlike the transnational aural and rhythmic identification that went on to become a cultural marker of a Latin American identity, as D'Lugo and Lopez suggest, the kinesthetic sense of belonging and relating promoted through dance remained clearly national and regional. It interpellated mainly Mexican nationals at home and abroad. This kinesthetic sense of identification never became a symbol of transnationality; instead, it remained an affirmation of Mexican and Mexican American diasporic communities. Unlike rumba, *danzón*, other Caribbean rhythms, and even tango, which were symbols of the urban and the modern, Mexican traditional dances always remained regional and affiliated with a long-gone era. And yet, as I have shown throughout this book, Mexican regional dance played a key part in the integration and consolidation of a modern Mexico.

The normative renditions of the Mexican couple via dance are clearly conservative, and yet they reveal the contradictions of a rapidly changing nation. The scene ultimately indexes the kind of national audience that such public displays of nationalism summoned as well as the scenarios of nationalism that invited viewers to choreographically experience it. The shots, the position of the camera, the close-ups of faces, and the dancing feet gesture toward the contemporaneity of a past that still lingers in the present. The scene reminded national and international audiences of the conflicting and contradictory ways modernization changed how people related to one another and what they imagined that relationship to be, a topic I explore in the last section of this chapter.

Kinesthetic Blackness and Gender Performativity in *La reina del trópico*

More than a radical break with the cinematic narratives of the time, Raúl de Anda's *La reina del trópico* (The queen of the tropics, 1946) encapsulates a timely portrayal of the ongoing shifts that were taking place in a rapidly modernizing nation.[105] Starring the iconic Cuban dancer María Antonieta Pons as a young woman who migrates from rural Veracruz to

Mexico City, the film features what would become a common cinematic narrative of wronged, fallen young women who were forced to migrate from rural towns to increasingly modern cities.[106] The movie begins in a town in Veracruz, El Naranjal, and captures the cultural, symbolic, and material transition between the Gulf of Mexico, from a typical, rural celebration of music and dance, a fandango, to the urban Caribbean rhythms of a cabaret associated with Mexico City. While the presence of a rumba dancer alongside Afro-Cuban musicians cinematically marks an urban form of Mexican modernity, the incorporation of La bamba (Mexico's foremost dance and music style with Afro-mestizo roots) nostalgically frames Mexico's ethnoracial diversity as anchored in the past. *La reina del trópico* renders Blackness kinesthetically (through movement and the body's awareness of its movement and position), which radically contrasts with a stylized version of an Afro-Indigenous Mexico through music and dance. The body of the Cuban María Antonieta Pons therefore summons a Caribbean imaginary sonically, visually, and rhythmically and mobilizes a sense of displaced Blackness, conjuring a mode of transnational belonging through movement. Analyzing the major dance scenes in the film, I argue that the circulation of the sounds and images of dancing bodies on the screen reveals that the bodies that aim to materialize lo mexicano also enact its undoing. As ambivalent sites and sights of a modernizing Mexico, the cultural performances of Afro-diasporic and Afro-Indigenous dances in *La reina del trópico* ultimately enabled the formation and circulation of contradictory renditions of a modern mestizo nation.

The emergence of the tropical as a trope to mark an urban Mexican modernity allowed certain expressions of Blackness to be acknowledged and even encouraged as long as they were Caribbean as well as Mexican. As Laura G. Gutiérrez has astutely argued, the cinematic rendition of a tropicalized sense of Blackness via visual, sonic, and (I would add) kinesthetic assemblages made it possible for filmmakers and spectators to reframe their "racialized anxieties" around Blackness in Mexico. This cinematic genre, commonly known as *cine de rumberas* (woman rumba dancer cinema), featured Black performers (musicians and backstage dancers) and white female dancers, usually from Cuba, repackaging Blackness to be consumed by Mexican spectators, turning the audience's racialized fears into admiration of the sexual exoticism of white bodies. According to Gutiérrez, the cine de rumberas "depended heavily on Afrodiasporic sounds and corporeal movements to register two opposing and irreconcilable ideas regarding blackness: a desire to flirt and experiment with exoticism to approximate *a notion* of modernity and cosmopolitanism, while simultaneously condemning the ways in which blackness . . . was a threat to the nation and its alleged sanctified traditions."[107] The experience of Afro-diasporic sounds and movements therefore became constitutive of the experience of a cosmopolitan modernity in mid-twentieth-century Mexico.

La reina del trópico became one of the first iterations of the cine de rumberas to reproduce the melodramatic cinematic story of the wronged fallen woman.[108] María Antonieta Pons plays the role of an orphaned woman, María Antonia, who falls in love with the son of a well-respected local family, Esteban (Carlos López Moctezuma), with whom she grew up. Esteban has just returned from the city where he has been studying to become a lawyer. He betrays María Antonia, seducing her and then leaving her. After Esteban's father falls ill and faces economic hardship, María Antonia travels to Mexico City to try to convince him to return to their town and support his sick father, but she fails. In an act of sacrifice, María Antonia decides to stay in the city, working as a waitress and sending money to Esteban's family on his behalf. One day, María Antonia suddenly becomes a famous exotic rumba dancer, as the musician Andrés Rosas (Luis Aguilar), who has helped her find a job and a place to stay, realizes that she is a very talented performer and launches her career.

The film begins with a folkloric and nostalgic depiction of a family house and a local fiesta that signals the end of the agricultural cycle and gestures toward the end of a way of life. One of the first opening sequences takes the viewer to the celebration of a fandango after Esteban's return to El Naranjal, his hometown, from Mexico City. A fandango enacts a popular festive space, a transculturated site where Afro-Indigenous and Hispanic traditions sonically, discursively, materially, and kinesthetically create a culturally mestizo universe. [109] Although certain musical, choreographic, and rhythmic aspects derive from Indigenous elements, I concur with B. Christine Arce that this festive space clearly marks an "Afromestizo universe."[110] The call-and-response structure of the vocals, the improvisation, and the syncopated nature of the stomps, slides, shuffles, and zapateado, in addition to the histories of some of the sones such as "El Chuchumbé," mark the aural and kinesthetic cartographies of the Black imaginaries in the region. The emergence of a *"jarocho* identity" was "founded on resistance to the colonial regime" and cannot be disassociated from the musical genres and dances typical of the Afro-mestizo communities that performed them and that led to the establishment of "música tropical" in the region.[111] The fandango unfolds around a *tarima*, a wooden platform around which dancers, signers, and spectators congregate. Characterized by local dancers and musical ensembles with stringed and percussive instruments, fandangos showcase the verbal, musical, and poetic improvisation skills of a particular community.

If the opening scene transports the viewer to a tropical landscape where lush greenery and palm trees dominate the terrain, the cinematic rendition of a fandango, a word originally from West Africa that literally means fiesta, symbolically marks the rural and circum-Caribbean interconnections of such a performative, festive diasporic space.[112] The fandango celebrates the harvest, the coming together of the whole town to rejoice over the year's work. It also represents the perfect opportunity to map out who is part of the community and offers a way to render musically and kinesthetically legible the bonds that make the community what it is. The sequence at the fandango maps out the festive celebration, the local people, and the cultural landscape, inviting the viewers to participate in the celebration, not unlike what we see in Eisenstein's scene of "Sandunga."

The first dance sequence begins with the performance of La bamba, by then a widely recognized son jarocho, proper to this Afro-mestizo universe and specific to these geographic coordinates.[113] Son jarocho is a multimedia "art form," according to Christine Arce, that incorporates dance, music, and poetry; its contested origins go back to Spanish *tonadillas* (popular theatrical pieces) and African and Afro-Cuban expressive cultures and performative repertoires.[114] The dance scene first goes from a close-up of the musicians to a panning shot of the dance space, the enramada and the tarima, where several couples are dancing or sitting down. Then there is a full shot of María Antonia and Esteban's parents, sitting down and surrounded by other members of the community, in a tropical mise-en-scène. The camera then goes back to a close-up of the musicians singing the most famous stanza of La bamba: "Para cantar 'La bamba'" (To sing "La bamba"). From there, there is a 2/3 shot of the dancers, which then becomes a full shot from which the audience can see their footwork. The dancers perform a choreography of La bamba played by Andrés Huesca and his musical ensemble and performed by Federico Ruíz's folklórico group (see fig. 4.5). Throughout the dance scene, the audience observes variations of basic steps, usually performed in groupings of three: flat right, flat left, and flat right and vice versa; shuffles changing the body weight from the right leg to the left and back to the right; and even at times typical *carretillas*, combinations of heel/flat right, heel/flat left, and heel/flat right, changing the body weight). This is a simplified version of the traditional dance, which the viewers see in the several close-ups of the footwork of the dancers, but the core movements or kinesthetic textualities remain the same. For the rest of the sequence, as the dancers execute a combination of circular choreographic figures and lines, the viewers see shots ranging from close-ups of musicians to full and 2/3 shots of the dancers and full shots from the position of the attendees. The effect is to make spectators part of the fandango from a distance and from the point of view of people sitting down or standing around the enramada. Even though this is not a representation of a traditional choreography, the dance ensemble performs some of the traditional steps, allowing local and national viewers to aurally and kinesthetically recognize and perhaps even identify with this traditional son jarocho and its concomitant movement vocabulary, as a distinct Afro-Mexican marker of lo mexicano. This, too, is not a balleticized version of the dance. The dancers' bodies remain flexed throughout the scene. However, unlike in El jarabe tapatío in de Fuentes's film, rarely do we hear the footwork that certainly characterizes the zapateado jarocho style, in which the footwork functions as another percussive instrument.[115]

This opening dance scene underscores the ambivalent ties of local jarocho imaginaries to those of the nation. Whereas a clearly folkloric

Figure 4.5. "La bamba," *La reina del trópico* (1946). Screen capture from film.

and nostalgic representation of the countryside is at stake, a tension exists between this otherwise nationalistic representation of the nation and a dis/placed portrayal of the Mexican Caribbean and thus African/Black imaginaries that the song of "La bamba" readily evokes. In fact, as the cultural historian Gabriela Pulido Llano notes, the verses of "La bamba" immediately make reference to Cuba: "De La Habana han llegado muchos fuereños / que se casen las viejas con los costeños" (From Havana many foreigners have arrived / let the women marry the coastal men).[116] Musically speaking, "La bamba" takes the audience to a Caribbean cartography. Though its verses and musical arrangement can be traced back to colonial times, by the turn of the twentieth century, particularly with the arrival of danzón and other tropical Caribbean rhythms, "La bamba" had become a site for and of a dis/placed Afro-Mexico.

The dance marks the beginning of a transitional period whose shift is not just generational but also cultural. The danzón that immediately follows La bamba emphasizes that this is a contemporary celebration, not simply one that is nostalgically anchored in the past. As the danzón starts, María Antonia is invited to dance. She gladly accepts, and while she dances with another man, she invites Esteban to the tarima with her gaze and hip movements. The full, 2/3, and medium shots of the tarima and the people dancing reveal the communal nature of the event as well as the corporeal engagements with this Afro-mestizo cultural imaginary. All members of the community, including the older couples, participate in this dance, which unfolds around the enramada. The slow movements, like a slow-paced tropical waltz but with a differentiated rhythm that showcases the cadences, pauses, and flow, allow the viewers to pay attention to the rocking and swinging of the dancers' bodies as they dance in small circles. Their slow lateral and circular movements, back and forth around the same space, also highlight María Antonia's *cachondería*, or her subtle but marked sensuality that seduces Esteban onto the dance floor.[117] María Antonia's sensually distinct way of moving her hips distinguishes her from the rest of the women, allowing her to kinesthetically embody Caribbean textualities and imaginaries beyond the rural space where the action takes place.

As part of a larger and increasingly popular genre of musical rhythms, the danzón traces the long and complex history of Mexican exchanges with its Caribbean neighbors, particularly Cuba in the second part of the nineteenth century. It also foreshadows what would become a common cinematic narrative in Mexican film historiography: the rumbera film of a modernizing Mexico, as discussed later in this chapter.[118] The danzón, then, alludes to the entanglements of the complicated history of Cuban cultural production. In this context, it is important to understand danzón as a "performance complex" that organizes the creation and dissemination of racialized cultural meanings. The ethnomusicologists Alejandro L. Madrid and Robin D. Moore contend that, as a performance complex, danzón allows us to ask questions about colonialism and local reinterpretations that range from social control and emancipation to the experience of pleasure and lived practices of African diasporic culture, particularly in Mexico, where constructions of lo mexicano have historically excluded Blackness.[119] Danzones, as much as son jarocho, function as localized reinterpretations of European musical traditions, "linked to the Atlantic slave trade through particular melodic/rhythmic figures, instruments, and/or styles of performance."[120] In this sense, La bamba and Veracruz in general and son jarocho music and dance in particular became a synecdoche of dis/placed Mexican Blackness.

Unlike the sensual and exaggerated hip movement of the rumbera dancer that becomes the center of the film, this cinematic rendition of La bamba and the danzón that immediately follows it showcases the way Mexican bodies literally contain and restrain such tropical and sensual corporeal expressions. And yet the movements and musical arrangements of the son jarocho, with its call-and-response structure, situate the spectator within a circum-Caribbean space of cultural exchanges for the rest of the film. Kinesthetically, there is a shift that allows different audience members to create a sense of identification not with what is marked as distinctly Mexican in *La reina del trópico*, such as the Indigenous dances performed later in the film, but with the dances that can be identified as Caribbean and therefore "tropical" in nature. In this sense, the kinesthetic identification with Mexican dances remains more regional than those of the danzón and eventually the rumba and conga rhythms, which mark a more cosmopolitan affiliation and later, as D'Lugo and López have noted, a more aural/rhythmic Latin American mode of identification. Blackness is therefore marked more in terms of form than in terms of content, and yet it remains predominantly a form of embodied expression, as the character of María Antonia performed by María Antonieta Pons reveals.

Halfway through the film, a significant transformation occurs in María Antonia's embodied expressions and movement vocabulary. After María Antonia has been working as a waitress at a local bar/café where Andrés and his group play, she suddenly encounters distinct Afro-diasporic rhythms. Andrés, who rescued María Antonia after she was robbed soon after arriving in the city, manages to get her an audition at a prestigious cabaret. The viewer unexpectedly finds out that Andrés is the son of a respected composer; he has written an original piece that he shares with his father's friend, a well-connected producer. Right away he and his group start rehearsing for the long-awaited audition, hoping to leave the local bar/café where they play orchestral and jazz-inspired tunes. Here is where María Antonia comes to terms with her "inner mulata." The sequence centers on the musicians' rehearsal for the audition while María Antonia helps Doña Gumersinda (Emma Roldán) put up curtains in the other room. The musicians, led by the Cuban Kiko Mendive, are visually and linguistically marked as Black Cubans, from their racialized bodies and accents to the instruments they play, particularly the bongos and maracas. As soon as Andrés and the other musicians start playing what is clearly a Cuban rumba, a medium long shot captures María Antonia in the background, moving, improvising dance steps and choreographic movements, and responding to the tropical percussive sounds. Andrés even begins with the following stanza as if to summon María Antonia as the queen of the tropics:

¿Qué tienes tú mi negrita?
¿qué tienes tú por ahí?
que la sangre se me agita
cuando estás junto de mí.

¿Qué tienes tú mi negrita?
¿qué tienes tú por ahí?
que al menear tu cinturita
no sé qué pasa por mí"

(What do you have, my *negrita* [little Black girl]?[121]
What do you have there?
That my blood stirs
when you are next to me.

What do you have, my *negrita*?
What do you have there?
That when you move your little waist
I don't know what goes through me).

The more the musicians improvise and allow the Caribbean rhythms to dominate the soundscape, the more deeply María Antonia falls into a trance. At one point, the viewers are left with the sound of the bongos and María Antonia's exotic moves in the background, characterized by frenetic corporeal outbursts and improvised sensual movements of her hips. The sounds conjure a sense of exoticness, foreignness, and Caribbean Blackness, contrasting with the seemingly contained and choreographed movements of the first dance scene and the various scenes of people dancing to orchestral and jazzlike music, particularly at the bar/café.

María Antonia's kinesthetic transformation is surprisingly complex. Until this point, she has remained a displaced member of a Mexican rural population from Veracruz, a jarocha. Though she no longer wears *campesina* (peasant) attire with long braids to signal her bond to a rural community, as she did when she first arrived in the city, her demeanor marks her as someone who is not from the city. She remains committed to supporting her benefactors so that they do not find out about Esteban's abandonment and the disdain he feels for their rural life. This situation reinforces the dichotomy between rural imaginaries, where a sense of nostalgia permeates the values that revolve around family ties, a strict moral code, and a sense of commitment, and the urban imaginaries that have corrupted Esteban, who now represents vice, corruption, and the lack of a moral compass.[122] The most interesting aspect of this scene is that María Antonia has always remained a somewhat foreign player. Let us not forget that María Antonia is an orphan, and therefore her origins are mysterious. Although she has adopted the demeanor of a jarocha from the countryside, the conga and bongo sounds have awakened the inner mulata who has always been inside her white body. Her "mulata soul," to use the phrase of Gabriela Pulido Llano,[123] suddenly takes over her body, transmitting through her sensual and abrupt hip movements the latent Blackness that has thus far remained dormant and static. It is her kinesthesia that leads her to recognize the mulata she has always been.

This solo dance scene in the middle of the film contrasts drastically with the danzón at the beginning of the film, where the viewer sees María Antonia dance for the first time on screen. The danzón, a dance form that is known for its sensuousness and *cachondeo*, looks like a controlled and restrained dance compared to this sequence, when María Antonia loses herself in a dancing ecstasy. In this latter scene, her unruly body reveals at once the threat of Blackness and the exotic, tropicalized embodiment of cosmopolitanism and modernity. When Andrés inquires where she has learned how to dance this way, she simply replies that she learned it in her town, El Naranjal. The opening dance sequence suggests some of her sensuous movements. Yet the kinetic language of the Sotavento region that the film cites did not necessarily display the Afro-Caribbean rhythms and movement vocabulary she somehow has always inherently known. These sounds and kinesthetic rhythms and textualities are marked as neither Mexican nor European or American. Rather, their marked Blackness invites Mexican audiences to identify them with a modernity in which Mexico occupies a central place as producer of such imaginaries and a promoter of such embodied cultural expressions.

The last part of the film reveals more this modern rhythmic equation as we return to the final dancing sequences. Here we encounter three kinds of dances: La bamba, but staged, choreographed, and performed at a cabaret; María Antonia's debut as a transnational rumbera; and balleticized and stylized Indigenous dances from the state of Michoacán. This time around, however, the Afro-Indigenous dances no longer create a nostalgic depiction of the countryside but rather emphasize dance as a spectacle to be consumed, one that grants the aura of authenticity and cosmopolitanism to the entertainment offered by the cabaret.

The cinematic rendition of the cabaret posits music and dance as diegetically central to a sense of cosmopolitanism, modernity, and exoticism.[124] It also captures the concomitant shifts in gender roles brought about by urbanization, migration, and modernization.[125] After all, the cinematic cabaret of the rumbera films represented a break from and a transformation of the Porfirian moral order. As Ana M. López contends, "Idealized, independent, and extravagantly sexual, the exotic *rumbera* was a social fantasy, but one through which *other* subjectivities could be envisioned, other psychosexual and social identities forged."[126] The cinematic transition to the cabaret in *La reina del trópico* is a movement from a popular, rural fandango to a cosmopolitan scenario that interpellates and materializes other forms of subjectivity. The last dancing scenes, then, capture the visual, aural, and kinesthetic rendition of a modern, cosmopolitan Mexico and the transformation of María Antonia into the exotic, extravagant, and sensual rumbera she has always been destined to become.

Through a series of musical and dance performances at the cabaret, this last part of the film conjures various sonic and kinesthetic gendered and racialized imaginaries. The first dance sequence starts when Andrés sings "Delirio" (Delirium) accompanied by an orchestra, which sonically connects the viewers to the beginning of the film, when the audience first heard it as a danzón. This is a part of the entertainment at the cabaret introduced as a "Mexican scene" with dances by Enrique Pastor's Pan-American Ballet. As soon as the song begins, the women slowly rise from their bent positions and begin waltzing and sliding across the dance floor, moving with cadence and rhythm in steps of three to the tune of a danzón. Then there is an abrupt change of rhythm and a literal change of stage as the musicians' stage rotates to reveal the jarocho ensemble we first saw in the opening of the film. The transition physically and symbolically suggests a literal and metaphorical continuum of the musical traditions on stage. We go from a nightclub orchestra to a traditional jarocho musical ensemble from Veracruz. The dancers on stage perform, just as in the opening dance scene, a choreographed rendition of La bamba. But before they do that, they execute part of the famous zapateado jarocho. This is a crucial transition before the stylized version of La bamba. The elaborate and pattered footwork in the zapateado becomes the kinesthetic and sonic referent of Blackness in Mexico. The zapateado jarocho is not displaced to an imagined and real Caribbean kinesthetic and aural landscape; rather, it is attached to a landscape that is distinctly Mexican. The zapateado's significance derives from the complex set of sonic and movement combinations executed by the dancers as if their feet were instruments, complementing the tropical soundscape in preparation for La bamba that is about to be performed in anticipation of the rumba, María Antonia's debut. Even though the zapateado jarocho is not balleticized per se, it is stylized. This is a significant difference, one that captures the distinct movement vocabulary of the region: the first series of alternating flats shifting the body weight, the carretillas, and the *guachapeados,* or alternating shuffles, conjure an immediate kinesthetic jarocho imaginary. This time around, the zapateado is heard loud and clear.

The dances are staged as a variety for the cabaret clientele, part of a larger cultural matrix of urban and modern Mexican nightlife. In contrast to the opening sequence at the beginning of the film, here the dance sequence is staged for the public to observe from a distance. After this initial percussive rhythmic transition comes La bamba. La bamba too is staged to be consumed and admired from afar, as the camera positions the spectators with a vertical view on top or with close-ups of the dancers' steps or 2/3 and full shots. Only seven couples are on the stage, and only one is left at the end. This is also a shorter version of La bamba. Unlike the panning camera in the opening dance scene that invited the viewers to participate in the celebrations, the camera here rechoreographs the dance to position the viewer as a spectator, like the rest of the patrons of the cabaret.

The costumes of the dancers also accentuate an Afro-mestizo sense of belonging; they gesture toward specific geographical coordinates, citing tropical imaginaries. The woman of the last remaining couple wears what has come to be recognized as a typical and stylized jarocho outfit, unlike the other six female dancers, who wear a simpler version of the dress that they wear at the beginning of the film. All of them, however, wear some of the sartorial elements characteristic of a jarocho outfit: the shawl on the shoulders, the long skirt (most with floral designs typical of a campesina outfit), the *mandil,* or apron, in front, and of course, the cameo on their chests. Most of the men wear traditional male jarocho attire: white pants and white shirt but with a small Panama hat in place of the jarocho hat. On stage, there is a tense relationship between a sense of jarocho belonging, one that is associated with the coast of Veracruz, materialized in terms of attire, music, and movement vocabulary by the dancers and musicians, and the tropical belonging associated with María Antonia, whose racial makeup could be considered Mexican but who cites decidedly different kinesthetic referents with her body in movement.

Immediately after La bamba, María Antonia makes her debut, singing, dancing, and transforming the stage into a tropical space. The sartorial, vocal, and kinesthetic referents signal an exotic configuration of a differentiated cultural space, one focused on the cosmopolitan, exotic singularity of María Antonia as opposed to the jarocha outfits, which point to a rural collectivity. She first moves around the stage singing, offering mangoes, and showcasing her sensual attire as she mesmerizes the audience with her body and rhythmic cadence. She carries a platter full of mangoes, and mangoes also hang around her flowing dress (see figure 4.6). The camera zooms in to highlight her sensual walk, focusing on her hips, her elaborate dress, and her attractively long, white legs. As she goes around the stage and the bongo beats increase, her pelvic thrusts and corporeal outbursts captivate the audience, particularly the men. The rumba does not include the patterned footwork or zapateado that characterizes Mexican traditional and regional dances; instead, it is all about María Antonia's cadence and the sound of her singing voice, complemented by the orchestra.

María Antonia cites Blackness and yet displaces it. The tropical ambience is created sonically and kinesthetically through her hypnotizing performance. The dance scholar Melissa Blanco Borelli challenges us to read the dancing of a rumbera "as a way for her to make an embodied statement of self-pleasure, resistance, and autonomy, [even when] her corporeality's history renders her a spectacle within the narrative structure of the scene."[127] Whereas Blanco Borelli's subject is a Cuban Black mulata, María Antonia is only a mulata kinesthetically speaking in this film. Corporeally and cinematically, she is a "white Hispanic performer," to borrow the term used by Laura G. Gutiérrez in her analysis of rumba dancers in Mexican films.[128] These Mexican films privilege white Cuban dancers and Afro-Cuban musicians as the embodiments of Caribbean difference. It is this version of the Caribbean that became a staple of Mexican rumbera films of the mid-twentieth century. The Caribbean imaginary, with its dancing rhythms and complex sonic referents that showcase the significant presence of Blackness, conjured a sense of transnational belonging.

This particular staging of Blackness, never quite Mexican and yet distinctly so, highlights the stereotypical presence of the Black male musicians and the "white-as-mulata" dancer or rumbera that characterized this cinematic genre.[129] Here, though, María Antonia enters the stage singing, not just dancing. The camera focuses on her body from afar, but the viewers also see close-ups of her exposed legs and wide hips through the open skirt of her flowing tropical dress. It is evident that she is no longer performing Mexican footwork. She transitions visually and kinesthetically from a rural jarocha to an urban mulata. Her debut captures this transition; it emphasizes that María Antonia, as an orphan jarocha, has always been a mulata. Consistent with the trend in representations of Indigenous people in Mexican films of the era ("white-as-Indigenous"), María Antonia is also not portrayed as visibly Black; after all, as Gabriela Pulido Llano claims, it is her soul that is mulata.[130] Her movements and attire are those of a mulata as well, movements that would become regulated just as they had been during colonial times.[131] The musicians, in contrast, are distinctively Afro-Cuban, as demonstrated by their accents in Spanish and the instruments they play, particularly the bongos. Kiko Mendive also dances rhythmically to the beat of the rumba, showcasing his racialized body, corporeal movements, and voice.[132] And yet the musicians conjure a sense of cosmopolitan belonging in which the foreign elements are incorporated to a nationalistic end but nevertheless marked as exotic.

Furthermore, the musical and dance numbers characteristic of cine de rumberas expanded the imaginaries of lo mexicano (usually reduced to notions of mestizaje and indigeneity) to incorporate Blackness and to broaden and destabilize ideas about women and the role of movement in the performance of sanctioned forms of femininity. By rendering Blackness "palatable" and "consumable" as a modern and cosmopolitan form of entertainment, as Laura G. Gutiérrez contends, these films appealed to a "tropicalized desire via Afrodiasporic sounds and dancing bodies [which] was able to disrupt a rigid Mexican gendered and sexual system of desire" while promoting "racialized and gendered stereotypes of the Caribbean."[133] The dancing bodies of white rumberas entrapped and seduced the spectators, functioning at once as repositories of desires and as containers of Black fears.[134] Indeed, the specter of Blackness was always repackaged in "racially palatable ways." The white bodies of rumbera films, then, helped to contain the racialized anxieties around Blackness, enabling Mexican spectators to consume representations of Blackness as an exotic other and portraying contact with dancing rumberas as an experience of cosmopolitan modernity. Therefore, the assemblages of tropicalized imaginaries "re-mediated" the experience of Blackness and, as I have shown, helped to develop a sense of kinesthetic identification, making Afro-diasporic movements and rhythms the markers of a pan-Latinx identity. The same did not occur for the performance of local Mexican kinetic languages, movements, and footwork. In fact, these tropicalized textualities and movement vocabulary went on to become part and parcel of Mexican social dancing and musical repertoires, continuing to shape an embodied Mexican sociality.

In this sense, the figure of the rumbera embodied the contradictions of changing social models for women, particularly in urban and modern centers. But in the early 1940s, as Maricruz Castro Ricalde observes, the cabaret was not yet associated with sexual work.[135] As a result, the reward for the wronged protagonists was marriage. Although alternative visions of femininity circulated through rumbera films (usually associated with an urban nocturnal life, excess, sexual work, and sin), the personal narratives discursively constructed by Cuban-born rumberas presented a model of decent, familial femininity that was consistent with the moral conservatism and Catholic sensual decorum of the time.[136] Despite these narratives, the public tended to conflate the rumberas' fictional roles with their real lives. María Antonia's name, which is almost identical to that of the cabaretera star who interprets her, María Antonieta, invites such conflation. After all, the rumberas featured in these films, such as María Antonieta Pons or Ninón Sevilla, were public figures.[137]

Films such as *La reina del trópico*, therefore, portrayed models of femininity that challenged national and traditional stereotypes of women. The sensual dancing bodies of the rumbera set in motion a modality of agency and independence that did not depend on the masculine gaze, signaling a freedom that threatened to destabilize the social order. Their performances enabled "momentary interruptions" in order to produce alternative corporeal meanings and the "possibility for different social, cultural, and national identities" to be rehearsed and experienced.[138] In short, the tropical imaginaries associated with the Cuban rumberas mobilized an unrestricted world. The dancing scenes, costumes, and staging of the rumba numbers allowed these rumberas to fuse their bodies with their emotions despite the policing mechanisms in place. Bringing to the screen a kinesthetic understanding of their protagonist roles, rumberas such as María Antonia invited the audience to experience and rehearse new subjectivities. In this way, the rumba numbers enabled the emergence of modalities of femininity that transcended, albeit temporarily, the moral dichotomies and cultural nationalism of the time.[139]

In the final dance sequences of *La reina del trópico*, Andrés and María Antonia sign a contract to tour in South America as a group of dancers begin their number. The music and attire of the dancers that set the scene mark these performances as Indigenous from Michoacán, though it is clear that they are performers, especially the women, whose postures are straight and not flexed (see fig. 4.6). The women performed balleticized renditions of Michoacán dances. Their arms extend with grace, and the steps imitate ballet as they go around the stage. The men maintain a straight posture, but they are less balleticized.

Figure 4.6. *La reina del trópico.* Courtesy of Colección Filmoteca UNAM.

The viewers see these Indigenous dances in pieces as the drama unfolds between the main characters. During this dance scene, Andrés chastises María Antonia for not sharing the whole truth with him regarding Esteban's betrayal. Meanwhile, the public at the cabaret sees part of a son from Michoacán with the presence of a performer from *La danza de los viejitos* (Dance of the old men).[140] The women and the viejito performer dance in two lines from right to left in waltz-like steps, although the male viejito dancer is clearly using his cane as a support, a typical marker of this dance from Michoacán. Except for the main female dancer, the rest of the dancers recede to the back as the viejito showcases some of his zapateado. One of the key components of this dance scene is his elaborate footwork, which includes stamping and tapping the floor, alternating feet while rotating in circles with the main female dancer. The focus shifts from his body to his feet, alternating between a medium long shot and a high-angle shot. The viejito dancer interprets the dance and complements the music with his zapateado, particularly in the finale, when he executes a combination of flats and heels, elevating them as if he were kicking with the back of his heels, interchanging feet and rotating in circles while the rest of the dancers return to the stage. Like the *Danza del venado* (Yaqui deer dance), La danza de los viejitos operates as a national and transnational marker of indigeneity in modern Mexico. The finale, therefore, stands in dramatic contrast to the balleticized rendition of the Indigenous dances by women in terms of the footwork, posture, skirt work, and even stylized dresses. Nevertheless, these dances are a key cultural referent in the slippery kinesthetic identifications of the film and the cartography they summon: the Mexican dances, Afro-Indigenous or not, remain distinctly local, pointing toward a nostalgic and noncoeval Mexico.

For the grand finale, there is a transition from an Indigenous Mexico to a modern, tropical one; that is, from the bodies of the musicians to the body of the white-as-mulata dancer. María Antonia makes her final entrance right after the opening musical sequence by Andrés, who begins singing in Spanish "siete negros vestidos de blanco" (seven Black men dressed in white). The camera immediately turns to seven Black men dressed in white suits, the seven Black musicians with tropical instruments, who are not on the main stage but on a balcony. This positioning serves as a literal distancing of such musical referents and embodied enactments. It is a performance of a tropical Blackness to be consumed as part of an imagined Caribbean that is specifically Afro-Cuban. There is a *contrapunteo* (counterpoint), to borrow Fernando Ortiz's concept, of images between Andrés and the Afro-Cuban musicians, and then between María Antonia and Kiko Mendive and his group, who are racially and musically marked as Black. The grand entrance of María Antonia as a rumbera actualizes the paradoxical gesture of citing Blackness to mark a modern, urban sense of tropicality while portraying it as foreign. The processes of becoming and "unbecoming" Black are at play in this film and the rest of the cine de rumberas.[141] On the one hand, rumba dancers significantly contributed to the representation of Cuba as a racialized "exotic otherness," depicting Afro-Cuban culture as "a visually wild and sensual display of erotic excess," thereby "associating blackness with Cuban difference" and erasing/denying Afro-Mexican culture.[142] On the other hand, white Hispanic rumba dancers needed to continuously "unbecome" Black, to borrow Antonio López's concept, in order to mark the distance between the mulata cabareteras they usually played and their private, honorable, and morally conservative lives.

I am interested in emphasizing how Blackness is kinesthetically rendered and contrasted with a stylized version of Mexicanness, though one that still incorporates a distinctive kinesthetic register of Afro-Indigenous dances, such as La bamba and sones from Michoacán. At the sonic level, Blackness occupies a central space. It enables the creation of a site of belonging, identification, and socialization. The sonic rendition of Afro-Caribbeanness conjures a kind of a modern aural identity, thereby enabling the clients of the cabaret to develop a shared sense of cosmopolitanism and urban imaginaries that characterize Mexican modernity: one where Blackness is consumed and marked as foreign, and yet distinctly Mexican first and eventually Latin American. The sound of the bongos and maracas, including the voice and gestures of Afro-Cuban musicians, grant this rendition of Blackness a certain "authenticity." Mexico too can partake of modernity and progress. The dancing, though distinctly gendered, also incorporates the Black male body into the cinematic sequence. Unlike the sensual movement of the rumbera María Antonia, whose white-as-mulata embodiment and attire cite Afro-Caribbeanness and tropicality, the body of the male signer and dancer kinesthetically congeals a sense of Cuban Blackness, one that is easily recognized and monitored. His attire signals refinement and containment, and yet his body undoes this connotation through his flexed movements, rhythmic hips, and hand gestures, conjuring an impression of cubanidad (Cubanness) that authenticates the spectacle at the cabaret as uniquely cosmopolitan.

The cabaret here, as mentioned, is not yet a place of vice, prostitution, and unrestrained sexuality, at least not in its cinematic rendition. Instead, it is a site that references Mexico's arrival at modernity; it represents global cosmopolitanism. This sense of glamour and refinement was soon lost, as this was a space where the bodies of women were consumed and objectivized. The cinematic cabaret became a key referent of an urban Mexico that materialized the corruption of modern times. The cabaret also served as a tropical space in the middle of the city, particularly Mexico City. The dances and the space of the cabaret enabled a kind of limited permissiveness that was crucial at the time. These instances, if only temporary, revealed the fractures of patriarchy and the fissures of cultural nationalism. At a moment when women had not yet become full citizens (they would not win the right to vote until 1953), these performances allowed them to choreograph themselves as social actors.

Paradoxically, Mexico was already seeing the development of staged productions of what would later become *ballet folklórico*, with the creation of competing renditions of Mexican dance that contrasted with and challenged that of the Escuela Nacional de Danza led by the Campobello sisters. Even though these first iterations of regional and Indigenous dances were supposed to serve as nostalgic reminders of rural Mexico, they were surprisingly contemporary. They reflected the reality that regional and Indigenous dances were part of a modernizing Mexico. These performances were avant-garde and contemporary, a form of choreo-politics that forced the mestizo state to grapple with the movement of others. And these embodied choreographies of Mexico remain today, not as markers of a long-gone past but rather as slippery instances of a living and uncomfortable presence in contemporary Mexico.

Ambivalent Images of a Festive Mexico

I conclude this chapter by returning to Eisenstein's film. As mentioned, the "Epilogue" is the best known and perhaps the most circulated fragment of *¡Que viva México!* It dialectically brings the film from its static, motion-less but animate beginning to a state of constant movement, mutability, and change. Its continuous moving references and the juxtapositions that it privileges establish a curvilinearity that at once closes and reopens the possibility of renewal. The images of life and death and the scenes of the dancing *calaveras* (skeletons) foreground the importance of dance for the aesthetic rendition of continuous change. The "Epilogue" circulated the now famous and iconic celebration of the "Day of the Dead," which had captivated Eisenstein for over a decade when he first heard about it.

The opening and closing sequences tell a story of regeneration. As Masha Salazkina contends, the dialects of life and death are constantly at play in this last novella: between the embedded revolutionary temporality of the death of all forms of domination and the birth of a rapidly modernizing nation represented by the image of a young child at the end, the epitome of a mestizo Mexico.[143] The body of the child in the last shot of the film is the site where these contradictions and tensions are negotiated. We will never know how Eisenstein would have edited this film, but the notion of rehearsal as a primary and critical mode can help us understand the unfinished nature of the film, a montage and a dialectics of the visual, the sonic, the discursive, and the kinesthetic.

Sonic and visual imagery of a modernizing Mexico dominated the description of the "Epilogue." The original idea was to film a modern Mexico, according to Eisenstein's notes: "Mexico of today on the ways of peace, prosperity and civilization. Factories, railroads, harbors with enormous boats; Chapultepec, castle, parks, museums, schools, sports-grounds. The people of today. Leaders of the country. . . . Builders of new Mexico. And Children—the future people of future Mexico." He went on to add, "Modern . . . Civilized . . . Industrial Mexico appears on the screen. Highways, dams, railways. . . . The bustle of a big city. New machinery. New houses. New people."[144] The imagery alludes to a political, cultural, and industrial revolution, materialized by the rapid modernization of the urban landscape. Newspaper articles from the time documented Eisenstein's interest in modern Mexico. On December 24, 1931, for instance, *El Universal Ilustrado* published a few pictures of Agustín Jiménez with Eisenstein at the Tolteca Cement Company,[145] a drastic change from the previous pictures referencing Indigenous peoples and rural landscapes, which I discussed at the beginning of this chapter. And while the initial focus is on the celebrations of the Day of the Dead, less on the altars than on the people and their rituals of remembrance, the "Epilogue" also pays homage to José Guadalupe Posada's *grabados* (engravings) of dancing calaveras.[146]

Instead of a cinematic rendition of a Mexican traditional dance, however, the viewers encounter the bodies of rumba dancers wearing calavera masks and moving to the sound of El jarabe tapatío, as described in the introduction. The first cinematic sequence of rumberas in the history of Mexican cinema is captured by Eisenstein and incorporated as part of his portrayal of a dynamic modernizing Mexico. Unlike *La reina del trópico*, where boundaries are clearly demarcated, the traditional tunes of El jarabe tapatío were kinesthetically interrupted by the dancing bodies referencing with their movements a Caribbean Blackness, which may never have been as foreign as it is implied to be. This contrast is paramount. The music of El jarabe tapatío, by then a symbol of Mexican nationalism, signals the relevance of marking sonically a sense of national belonging. But dancing to its beat gestures toward the dynamic (though often ignored) roles Mexican dance has played in the creation and circulation of social imaginaries of the nation. The festive image of Mexico cannot be complete without this dancing sequence. It is also a sequence that privileges movement as a primary means of conveying a sense of relatedness and mutual belonging. Even though Eisenstein did not capture the traditional choreography often associated with El jarabe tapatío, the dancing skeletons and rumba dancers certainly cite through their repetitive movements the slippery normative scripts for performing the nation.

The dancing sequences of the "Epilogue" emphasize the pelvic motion of the male dancers via close-ups of their moving hips. Although

Figure 4.7. "Epílogo," *¡Que viva México!* (1932). Screen capture from film.

women's bodies and faces are also featured, men's hips literally become the frame of this cinematic sequence. As shown in figure 4.7, the viewers observe flexed male bodies, whose sensuous cadence serves as an extended frame to capture more dancing calaveras. The dancing corporeally cites and enacts other modes of belonging, ones that kinesthetically fracture and transcend local modes of relating, thereby citing a sense of Afro-Caribbean intimacies. Ultimately, this sequence cinematically renders the intersection between kinesthetic Blackness, Afro-Caribbean imaginaries, and Mexican modernity.

The rumba scene was particularly vibrant in this period. Eisenstein was familiar with this scene from the dancing halls in Mexico City and probably included actual rumba dancers in the shooting of his film. Karetnikova included in her work an article in which Eisenstein describes a dancing hall that he and the American pilot Jimmy Collins visited. Eisenstein carefully sets the scene of the dancing hall:

> The music—from a distance—is fainter. The "Danson" [*sic*] is under way, that amazing dance, in which from time to time, in the midst of the most sharp motion, a couple suddenly, for several beats, freezes completely motionless, facing one another, and stands as if rooted, until they again continue the tormenting sensuality, or the quick tempo of rhythmic body movements. Just as motionlessly, their bodies barely touching, they stand—long and longingly—in the dark streets, under each tree, along the endless walls of the city hospital or in the side alleys of the "alameda"—the city park. Here they stand still in the dance. At such moments, the dance hall is frightening: it seems like a stiffened corpse, still trembling inside to the beat of the orchestra's screaming rhythm. In the semidarkness, the figures come to life and float away.[147]

In this passage, Eisenstein draws attention to the tension between kinesis and stillness, the continuous sensual tension between the bodies' movement and their stasis. But what this description also makes clear is the tension between the life and death forces that dancing seems to conjure, from a motionless corpse to a rhythmic body that comes to life and floats away. The dialectics of pleasure and the stiffening of death are both at play. Eisenstein's description of the danzón neatly captures the notion of cachondería, that sense of "tormenting sensuality," to use his phrase. As mentioned, cachondería in danzón refers to the experience of "subdued lust, subtle sensuality," oscillating between "uncritical pleasure" and a kind of pleasure that leads to the "subject's momentary repossession of his or her body beyond the constraints of disciplining discourses."[148] Eisenstein describes it as an oscillation that is frightening, intimidating, and tormenting. And yet it turns stiffened corpses into lively figures that float away to the beat of the orchestra's "screaming rhythm." The danzón, and likely other Afro-Cuban rhythms, certainly dominated the urban scene in Mexico City at the time.

The sonic and the kinesthetic complemented and interrupted each other continuously throughout Eisenstein's unfinished film. Though Eisenstein did not have a final say over the music selection, studies of the origin and creation of the film, particularly those by de los Reyes and Salazkina, make it clear that music was always an important component of the film, at times defined as symphonic.[149] Best Maugard, in fact, described the film as "symphonic cinema."[150] The film was going to be organized first around a Mexican orchestra of sorts and then around different instruments from diverse Mexican regions. As the previous descriptions reveal, sound, "natural" sounds, and the soundscape of modern Mexico were crucial at the literal transition between silent and sound cinema. Music, as in the case of *Battleship Potemkin*, was vital to the narrative of the film, in many ways becoming part of a sonic/visual montage.

Eisenstein's Mexican film also anticipated what would later become a staple of Mexican cinematic production: the creation of cinematic narratives derived from popular or classic songs. These musical narratives produced and reproduced a "sonic imaginary" that, as Deb Vargas claims, constitutes a "musically sounded/sonic field where people come to understand, relate, and connect to notions of belonging, history, place, and cultural sensibilities."[151] This sonic imaginary soon came to be deemed distinctively Mexican, and it had a tremendous impact on the creation of Latin American social imaginaries, particularly in relation to its Hollywood and European counterparts. Mexican sonic imaginaries not only reflected but also mediated the way Mexican nationals and eventually international audiences related to a sense of a shared Latinx and Latin American contemporaneity.

In this sense, Eisenstein's film functioned as a cinematic symphony of images and sounds. But it was more than that. It also foregrounded, perhaps inadvertently, the significance of kinesthetic imaginaries for the configuration of a shared sense of identification. Dance and movement became intimately related to the creation and circulation of slippery social imaginaries of the nation. And whether it was Eisenstein's intention or not, "Sandunga" and "El jarabe tapatío," two major musical scores used in the main and completed novellas, have become iconic song/dances of a Mexican sonic imaginary, together with "La bamba." The music and dances associated with each one of these songs symbolically, sonically, and kinesthetically complemented the visual and discursive narrative in Eisenstein's film. Though the 1979 version of the film may not encompass all that Eisenstein intended, for we will never know how he would have incorporated music and edited the visual and sonic montages, it is the version that has become standard and that, as Salazkina observes, best captures the original ideas for the film.[152]

If "Sandunga" encompassed both a sense of a moving, dynamic indigeneity and the gendered tensions and contradictions that accompany such representations, "El jarabe tapatío" in its role as the non-diegetic musical score for the "Epilogue" certainly congeals the kind of mestizo aesthetics that characterized state-sponsored Mexican cultural production. The lasting impact of the cinematic sequences of dance during the Day of the Dead festivities cannot be overlooked. The rumba dancers that appear in the "Epilogue" perform some of the rhythmic patterns easily identified with Caribbean Blackness, such as the "paso montuno" (montuno), resembling the two-beat of the claves. However, sonically, El jarabe tapatío reclaims such movements for an imaginary of the nation. And this is where I would like to conclude: both El jarabe tapatío and the rumba paradoxically became at once kinesthetic and sonic markers of Mexican modernity and nationalism.

The images projected on the silver screen were much more ambiguous than we normally recognize. To understand the symbolic and aesthetic potential of these moving images, it is imperative that we go beyond complicit and resistant models of cultural nationalism. Some of these moving images may allude to other intimate, albeit slippery, configurations. We must go beyond the idea that official and institutionalized cultural production becomes legible only through resistance and complicity models to recognize that such representations are often contradictory and much more complex than is generally acknowledged. The exclusive focus on the visual displaces and makes invisible other markers of ethnic, racial, and sexual difference that are present in Eisenstein's, de Fuentes's, and de Anda's cinematic worlds. One must interrogate the kind of pueblo that Eisenstein, Figueroa, and de Anda depicted through their moving images and the kinds of imaginaries that are summoned via their bodies in movement. When cinematic faces bring Mexican nationals out of anonymity, what kind of agency—if any—is left to modify the landscape, cinematic or otherwise, that constitutes them? Despite the contradictory nature of the configuration of a mestizo subject/landscape, *¡Que viva México!, Allá en el Rancho Grande,* and *La reina del trópico* continue to serve as visual, sonic, kinesthetic, and epistemic referents of nationalistic representations of Mexico.

Queering Mexico's Archive: Ephemerality, Movement, and Kinesthetic Imaginings

Llevamos la historia en nuestros cuerpos
(We carry history in our bodies)
MARGARITA TORTAJADA QUIROZ

On April 10 and 11, 2015, Duniya Dance and Drum Company and Ensambles Ballet Folklórico de San Francisco staged "Half and Halves: A Dance Exploration of the Punjabi-Mexican Communities of California" at the San Francisco Jewish Community Center's Kanbar Hall. Featuring thirty-five dancers and live music, the production highlighted the little-known history and the cultural and artistic legacy of the Punjabi-Mexican communities established in California in the early part of the twentieth century. Duniya's choreographer, Joti Singh, and Ensambles' choreographer, Zenón Barrón, drew from testimonies and oral histories, historical records, and dance and musical traditions from both regions to create a complex cultural representation of the Punjabi and Mexican diasporas in California. Bringing together Punjabi Bhangra and Mexican folklórico music and dance, this vibrant performance offered a kinesthetic exploration of migration, farming life, intermarriage, ethnoracial tensions and discrimination, and, perhaps more important, brown intimacies, as rendered in figure 5.1.

"Half and Halves" refers to the term used to describe Punjabi-Mexican individuals ("half and half"), usually the children of a Punjabi father and a Mexican mother. In the early 1900s, thousands of Punjabi men (most of them Sikhs) migrated to central California and formed biethnic families with young Mexican women working in the fields. The Punjab is a border region alongside the Indian and Pakistani border. The arrival of Punjabi men coincided with the Mexican Revolution, which increased the number of Mexican women in the fields. According to Karen Isaksen Leonard, about 378 such marriages were registered in the state of California, and thousands of Punjabi-Mexican couples were found throughout the Southwest in the United States. At the time, antimiscegenation laws and anti-immigration laws (such as the Asian exclusion legislation) prohibited interracial marriages. Labeled "brown" and unable to fit easily within US racial categories, most of these biethnic families lived in the Imperial and Central Valleys of California.[1] They planted fruit trees, particularly peach and plum orchards, and other crops, benefiting from agrarian credits, strong community networks, and their vast agricultural knowledge and experience. Mexican women and Punjabi men already had several things in common: farming, strong familial ties, a love of spicy food, and a vibrant expressive and material culture, as well as ethnoracial resemblances. Their Punjabi-Mexican families were numerous, averaging between five to six children. Needless to say, the Punjabi-Mexican community was not homogenous. They were usually labeled as Mexican-Hindus, and many of the children identified as Hindu.[2] But as these children grew older, most were mainly assimilated by the greater Indian community of California, which increased significantly after a 1946 bill granting citizenship to individuals of Asian and Indian origin.

Figure 5.1. *Half and Halves.* Kanbar Hall. April 2015. Courtesy of Duniya Dance and Drum Company and Ensambles Ballet Folklórico de San Francisco. Photo by Vijay Rakhra.

When I joined Ensambles Ballet Folklórico de San Francisco in 2011, I had no idea that it would bring me to a kinesthetic encounter with the Punjab. *Half and Halves* had premiered on November 13–14, 2010, at the Brava Theater in San Francisco. I first participated in its restaging in Fresno in November 2011, shortly after joining Ensambles. Like the Punjabi-Mexican children whose testimonies were featured throughout the ninety-minute production, I too grew up in a large immediate family, in my case in the small rural town of Loma Chica in the state of Chihuahua, Mexico, picking crops during the summer. In the summer of 2000, however, I migrated to Los Angeles, a move that radically upended my life. But as I discussed in the preface, one thing remained the same: dancing folklórico. Dancing and teaching folklórico in California enabled me to create a community and articulate my identity, drawing from corporeal cultures that were shared across the border. This pursuit is what eventually led me to join Ensambles Ballet Folklórico de San Francisco, where I first learned about the Punjabi-Mexican communities, and soon enough I found myself dancing bhangra.

The kinesthetic encounters and imaginings produced by folklórico dance bring to the fore the complex ways we carry history in our bodies (*llevamos la historia en nuestros cuerpos*, as the dance scholar Margarita Tortajada Quiroz once told me). As an embodied sociality, popular performance practice, and established discipline and technique, folklórico functions not just as a corporeal pedagogy but also as a means of articulating and interpellating a communal identity. Dancing, as a world-making practice, expands our ways of relating to others, activating other modes of being in the world. When I first learned to dance bhangra, I experienced the encounter as a *choque corporal*, a corporeal clash, to borrow the words of the dance scholar and choreographer Juan Carlos Palma Velasco. Compared to Mexican folklórico, bhangra requires significantly more hand movements and simultaneous bouncing of the shoulders. Although folklórico dance demands complex patterns of footwork and polyrhythmic and syncopated stomping, as I described in the last chapter, the men rarely use their arms and hands other than when dancing in couples or using a handkerchief, a rope, a whip, or machetes, depending on the region. I and my folklórico peers experienced a choque corporal, but so did our fellow bhangra dancers as they learned folklórico. Our strength was in our hands or in our feet, depending on the dance style we had mastered. And yet learning a different dance style to tell a little-known story required us to approach the other with our bodies. Each style demanded that we go beyond the materiality of the dance to include other affective, symbolic regimes. Dancing together asked us to occupy the position of the other. This kinesthetic encounter made us reconsider our corporeality.[3]

In bringing our own lived experiences to the dance floor in order to perform something that moved the other, each one of us attempted to instantiate a kind of performative translation, overcoming differences through our corporeal motions. Juan Carlos Palma Velasco invites us to dwell on that feeling of strangeness, divergence, discomfort, or initial distancing that occupying the position of the other engenders in order to productively engage the choque corporal. When the archive with which we grapple is the lived body of the other, he claims, "es necesario centrar la mirada en el encuentro, en el acontecimiento corporal que construye una alteridad de naturaleza performática, configurando a su vez un territorio (en términos de espacio-tiempo) liminal en el cual se producen transacciones y desplazamientos afectivos y de significaciones que colocan a ambos, el traductor y hablante, entre 'el uno y el otro' " (it is necessary to center the gaze on that encounter, on the corporeal event that brings about an alterity of performative nature, configuring at once a liminal territory [in terms of space-time] where affective and signifying transactions and displacements position both, the translator and speaker, between "one and the other").[4] Signaling the importance of working toward a kind of performative translation, Palma Velasco invites us to enact an embodied territory in which we can dwell simultaneously on "one and the other." What results is the rehearsal of a kinesthetic empathy. By creating alternative spaces in which to experience other forms of storytelling, *Half and Halves* allowed us to engender intercommunal and intersubjective solidarities. By dancing bhangra and folklórico, dancers, musicians, and spectators were invited to imagine and inhabit the world in new ways.[5]

Here, as in the preface, I gesture toward a form of performance ethnography to conceive of movement as a site of cultural memory that can potentially set in motion an intercultural dialogue and strategic solidarities. With the term *performance ethnography*, I refer to both Dwight Conquergood's theorization of the ethnography of performance as "co-performative witnesses" and Ramón H. Rivera-Servera's "theories in practice." Conquergood conceptualizes the ethnographic act as a performance event in order to attend to our affective, intellectual, and embodied participation.[6] Rivera-Servera invites us to critically engage with the vernacular theories derived from Latinx expressive practices. By grappling with the generative world-making power of performance, he asks us to consider the "situated forms of knowing that emerge from live embodied contexts . . . [that is,] the enfleshments and experiences produced in laboring together in the shared time-space of performance."[7] Like Rivera-Servera, I bring to my analysis the performative practices that I have learned, lived, and felt in my own body.[8] I have danced the nation for the past three decades, and in so doing, I have embodied a sense of belonging and community identity, first in Mexico and now as part of the Mexican diaspora in the United States, as captured in figure 5.2. Throughout my academic journey, my background in Mexican folklórico dance has shaped my approach to scholarship and teaching. This unique trajectory, from the fields of rural Mexico to community college, graduate school, and university teaching, has taught me the value and the necessity of creating new ways to produce and circulate knowledge. It also encouraged me to create the community spaces that I wanted to inhabit through dance. As a scholar of cultural, performance, dance, and queer studies, I recognize how important it is to depart from an understanding of knowledge based purely on the written.[9] Trained in Latin American and Mexican cultural and literary studies, I seek to advance scholarship that critically engages and promotes collaboration with individuals whose knowledge cannot be reduced to the academy.

In this book, I grapple with the challenges and generative questions of folklórico dance, which has often been dismissed as noncritical and complicit with hegemonic formulations of Mexican nationalism, even though it has played an evolving and vital role in Mexico and among the Mexican diaspora in the United States.[10] In fact, I contend that the integral and continuous presence of folklórico as a dance practice in Mexico in recent years cannot be separated from the increasing number of folklórico groups, festivals, competitions, conferences, and associations in the United States, which normally convene a large number of Mexican folklórico instructors throughout the United States.[11] Yet both Mexican cultural studies and Latinx performance studies suffer from a lacuna regarding this complex form of expressive culture. Unlike salsa, which has become a dynamic diasporic kinesthetic and sonic language for Latinx communities, folklórico has received scant critical attention.[12]

I have recast folklórico dance as a critical site of knowledge circulation and a vital world-making practice. In pointing toward the archiving potentiality of our bodies, the performance of Mexican folklórico can be seen to uncover the cultural historicity linked to our movements, and more important, reveal how power dynamics condition and enable profound affective and political forms of bodily expression and communal exchanges in times of forced displacement and precarity. By queering the archive of Mexican nationalism through folklórico dance, this project attends to the ephemera, histories, and embodied gestures of lo mexicano and to its productive engagement with regional diasporic communities. The queer excess—what remains and lingers—highlights the importance of bodily practices for the configuration of strategic alliances and embodied solidarities across Latinx and other minoritized communities in the United States.

One of the central questions that has animated my work and that I address through these chapters is what counts as evidence: evidence of what and for whom? As this illustrates, the process of archiving is intimately related to power. The power manifested in the physical location that houses the archives, as Achille Mbembe reminds us, literally delimits the evidence that can be retrieved and accessed, if it exists.[13] The process of accessing and retrieving (the rituals associated with it) implies or presupposes different forms of reading, some that are legitimate and others that ought to be. In assembling *Choreographing Mexico*, I recognized the need to embrace a generative approach in the way we relate to archives and therefore produce evidence. Throughout the writing of this book, I have faced the challenge of counteracting the coloniality that produces

Figure 5.2. "El palomo y la paloma," *The Golden Era: A Homage to Mexican Cinema*, March 2016. Featuring Manuel R. Cuellar and Lupe Flores Aguilera. Marine's Memorial Theatre. Photo by Alberto Morales.

and organizes our disciplines and the production and circulation of knowledge, or, as Aníbal Quijano argues, the Eurocentric, modern, and colonial "rationality" and the impact it has on "'the colonization of cognitive [and I would add affective and embodied] perspectives, modes of producing and giving meaning, the results of material existence, the imaginary, the universe of intersubjective relations with the world: in short, the culture."[14] In this sense, this project grapples with the accountability of knowledge production.

The queer Latinx authors that have guided my journey, particularly José Esteban Muñoz and Juana María Rodríguez, invite us to queer our methods for indexing memory, the idea of history as a register of the past, and the notion of the archive as the locus of truth. We are also invited to queer the way we relate to the archive: how we give an account of the archive, how we are connected to it, and how we discuss and identify or disidentify with the archive and our own personal, intellectual, and affective investments: *nuestro senti-pensar*.[15] Muñoz and Rodríguez call us to engage in/with processes of knowledge production that go beyond our training, cannot be reduced to academia, and involve our bodies, imagination, affects, and senses. In other words, we must continuously interrogate how meaning is created and can be produced and sensed in the archive.

Searching the archive for the ephemera of Mexican folklórico dance has led me to ponder the absences, silences, refusals, losses, and failures of the archive. How can we locate ephemeral traces of corporeal movement? Corporeal motions are impossible to completely textualize, and yet they can be felt or sensed, in line with José Esteban Muñoz's notion of ephemera as an alternate modality to index traces of lived experience. Looking for ephemera, then, leads us to think about how evidence is constructed and what is accomplished in the production of archives, evidence, and the knowledge they generate.[16] What does it mean that I too have danced time and again El jarabe tapatío just like Pavlova and the Campobello sisters? And what is at stake? According to Muñoz, "although we cannot simply conserve a person or a performance through documentation, we can perhaps begin to summon up, through the auspices of memory, the acts and gestures that meant so much to us."[17] The act of archiving is a site where unrealized possibilities survive as potentialities that might come to fruition in a utopic time that is neither fully of the past nor fully of the future. The archive's queer potentiality is, as Muñoz argues of queer futurity, all the more poignant and enduring for "being visible only in the horizon" as another time and space that always haunts the here and now.

As someone engaged in literary, cultural, performance, and queer studies, I am seduced by the idea of envisioning decolonial futures and knowledges and perhaps even rehearsing them, as some of the authors I have discussed do. Certainly, I participate in the uneven circulation of knowledge. Yet I also believe in the critical and generative potential of relating to archives as spaces of "ch'ixi," of "creative dialogue in a process of exchanging knowledges, aesthetics, and ethics," that offer a glimpse of decolonization and realize it at the same time, to cite Silvia Rivera Cusicanqui.[18] I am aware of the limitations and contradictions of looking for the traces of lived experience in historical documents, photographs, interviews, and even extant footage. But I embrace the chance to examine the kinesthetic work of the performance of tradition in Mexican dance and the potential imaginings of past and future subjectivities it engenders.

Dancing as an ephemeral practice complicates our understandings of temporality and memory vis-à-vis embodiments and representations. Through an examination of the embodied practices and knowledge associated with Mexican dance, I have considered the various historical discourses inscribed on racially and sexually marked bodies. To what extent can corporeal motions help us understand the body as a historical and historicizing entity? In what ways can moving bodies signal diasporic trajectories that have historically been negated, erased, and excluded? What is at stake when we privilege kinesthetic epistemologies?

Choreographing Mexico has involved rethinking and reexamining the epistemological tools that I use to write history. Susan Buck-Morss insists that each conceptual tool, category, and mode of thinking "comes to us full of residues of the past, containing the sedimented history of utopian dreams and cultural blind spots, political struggles and power effects. Historically inherited concepts form the collective consciousness of actors who, in turn, create history."[19] In writing this book, my hope has been to contemplate the political struggles and collective consciousness negotiated through Mexican dance. The dancing histories of Mexico offer the possibility of accessing and performing the past otherwise, of imagining other Mexicos, and, in so doing, of embodying unrealized potential. Dance, after all, produces and is produced by the cultural knowledges that we carry in our bodies and perform onstage: *llevamos la historia en nuestros cuerpos*. My background in Mexican folklórico, with all its residues of the past, utopian dreams, and cultural blind spots, led me to explore dance's role in Mexican national identity, indigeneity, gender, and queerness, examining the role of dancing bodies in public spaces and arguing for the significance of movement as a critical site for citizen formation and national belonging. But like Nellie Campobello, who first inspired my work as a writer and dancer, I have always longed above all to rehearse different modes of being and understanding the world in order to inhabit the here and now otherwise.

Notes

Preface

1. Palma Velasco, "Reposición, apropiación y download. Rutas sobre el proceso de creación de la otra propuesta: memoria e identidad en la danza folclórica contemporánea" (lecture, Instituto de Artes, UAEH, June 8, 2021. https://www.youtube.com/watch?v=Jng4L7QL23Q&t=58s).
2. Martínez, "Archives, Bodies, and Imagination," 172.
3. Hamera, *Dancing Communities*, 1–3.

Introduction

1. Anna Pavlova was born in Saint Petersburg, Russia, in 1882, attended the Imperial School of Ballet, and eventually became the prima ballerina of the Marynski Theater. In 1907, Pavlova left Russia to tour the world and never returned. She died in Holland in 1931. For a description of the impact of Pavolova's visit to Mexico, see Dallal, "Anna Pavlova en México;" and Lavalle, "Anna Pavlova." For an excellent analysis of Pavlova's impact on the consolidation of an embodied Mexican modernity, see Reynoso, "Choreographing Modern Mexico," and his forthcoming book tentatively titled *Dancing Mestizo Modernisms*. I thank José Luis Reynoso for sharing with me part of his manuscript.
2. Dallal, "Anna Pavlova en México," 166.
3. Rodríguez, "La fantasía mexicana." Lavalle notes that although other Mexican regional dances were performed as part of *Fantasía mexicana*, they remain unknown. She does mention that they were likely adapted by Pavlova herself and her assistant, the ballet master Mieczyslaw Pianowski. The premier of *Fantasía mexicana* at the Teatro Arbeu, however, was in honor of Alexandre Volinine, the leading dancer of Pavlova's company. Lavalle, "Anna Pavlova," 644–655.
4. With "modernist dance," I refer to the choreographic practices and movement vocabulary of expressivity and aesthetics at the turn of the twentieth century that were particularly associated with Isadora Duncan. The dance scholar Mark Franko notes that aesthetic modernism was characterized by "a split between emotion and expression"; dance modernism was also characterized

by a "defamiliarization of bodily emotion," "movement innovation and the return of expression." Franko, *Dancing Modernism/Performing Politics*, x–xi. In *Dancing Modernism/Performing Politics*, Franko discusses the history of modern dance and its relationship to modernism and politics. By reading the ebbs and flows of European and US expressions of modern dance vocabularies, Ramsay Burt similarly explores how dancing bodies grappled with the experience of modernity and urban dwelling. Whereas modernism has been reduced to abstractionism and at times conflated with modernity, Burt insists on understanding modernist aesthetics as a form of consciousness, one that rejected traditional ideologies of national identity and that deconstructed outmoded aesthetic conventions and traditions (15). See Burt, *Alien Bodies*. For an insightful analysis of Pavlova's distinct engagements with these modernist expressions and balleticized renditions of Mexican traditional practices, see Reynoso, "Choreographing Modern Mexico."

5. Lavalle, "Anna Pavlova," 644–645; Tortajada Quiroz, *La danza escénica de la Revolución Mexicana*, 12. Manuel Castro Padilla likely based his selection of the nine *sones* (traditional Mexican tunes) on a 1905 adaptation that was popular at the time in local venues and revues. Lavalle, "Anna Pavlova," 645.

6. It is beyond the scope of this study to trace the mythicized origins of the figure of the china poblana. Scholars, however, have pointed out that the legends alternatively refer to the mystic Indian princess, Catarina de San Juan, abducted by Portuguese corsairs and sold into slavery in the Philippines to a military officer from Puebla in the seventeenth century or to peasant women from the nineteenth century, whose beauty, attire, and demeanor were captured in painting, poetry, and literature similar to the Spanish *manolas* and whose traditional attire consisted of a white blouse embroidered with floral designs, a skirt decorated with sequins and beads, and a traditional shawl or *rebozo*. See Tibón, "Las dos chinas," and Pérez Montfort, "La china poblana," for a brief introduction. See also Pérez Montfort, "La china poblana. Notas y breve crónica sobre la construcción del estereotipo nacional," in *Expresiones populares y estereotipos culturales en México*, for a historical discussion.

7. Tortajada Quiroz, *La danza escénica*, 13. An article in *Revista de Revistas* (March 30, 1919) shows Pianowski dancing the charro with Pavlova. He probably alternated with Voliline, whom several programs of the time name as the leading dancer when *Fantasía mexicana* was performed. See Roberto *El Diablo*, "Después de Medio Siglo." For a description of the charro and charrería, see Palomar Verea, "La charrería."

8. Rodríguez, "La fantasía mexicana," 10. Unless otherwise indicated, all translations from Spanish are my own.

9. Reynoso, "Choreographing Modern Mexico," 82. My reading of Pavlova's balleticization of Mexican traditional dances is aligned with José Reynoso's discussion of Pavlova's "eliticization" of and engagement with Mexican regional dances. Reynoso astutely argues that "the resulting mestizo dance practices combining ballet, and then modern dance, with Mexican folk expressive cultures represented a challenge to notions of Western modernity that assumed an exclusive link between whiteness and universality."

10. For a detailed account of the construction of the National Stadium and its material and symbolic impact, see Gallo, *Mexican Modernity*, 201–226.

11. "Con un grandioso festival se inauguró ayer el Estadio Nacional," 1.

12. "Con un grandioso festival se inauguró ayer el Estadio Nacional"; "La Brillante Inauguración del Estadio Nacional."

13. Vasconcelos, "El Estadio Nacional."

14. Rubén Gallo criticizes Vasconcelos for using the stadium "to propagate his profoundly unmodern racial theories." Gallo, *Mexican Modernity*, 27. Gallo claims that such massive events were spectacles that rendered "individual bodies as expendable materials," numbed "the masses' critical judgment" and reduced them to "human ornaments," and operated as "vehicles for the propagation of fascist ideology (most notably by facilitating the anesthetization of political events)." Gallo, 216, 225. I complicate this view in chapter 3 by insisting on the ways bodies in movement, in choreographies like those performed by Nellie Campobello, often exceed and performatively undo the ideologies they purport to represent. See also Townsend, *Unfinished Art of Theater*, 27–62, for a discussion of the performative and ideological rehearsals at play in Vasconcelos's cultural program.

15. Vasconcelos, "El Estadio Nacional."

16. Guss, *Festive State*, 3–12.

17. For crucial theorizations of Mexicanness, see Gutiérrez, *Performing Mexicanidad*; and Hellier-Tinoco, *Embodying Mexico*. Both Gutiérrez and Hellier-Tinoco inform my discussions of lo mexicano as an embodied performance critical for examining how Mexican nationalism was experienced. I discuss this notion at greater length later in this introduction.

18. As my work engages with Indigenous imaginaries, practices that may not be reduced to the notion of the modern, and are hence nonmodern, are summoned. In this sense, I also understand "elsewhere" following José Rabasa's definition of it as instances that signal "spaces and temporalities that define a world that remains exterior to the spatio-temporal location of any given observer. . . . They consist of forms of affect, knowledge, and perception underlying what a given individual in a given culture can *say* and *show* about the world . . . *elsewheres* that disrupt the assumption that Western thought exhausts what can be said and thought—or, by extension, what must remain unsaid and unthought—about the experience humans may have of the world." Rabasa, *Tell Me the Story*, 1 (emphasis in the original). This definition becomes particularly evident in Sergei Eisenstein's interaction with and filming of Indigenous groups; see chapter 4.

19. Tenenbaum, "Street History," 140–141.

20. Tenenbaum, 143, 147.

21. Following Peter Wade's theorization, I use the term "ethnoracial" to refer simultaneously to the cultural spatialization of a group and the characteristics associated with it. According to Wade, ethnicity signals "cultural differentiation, but it tends to use a language of *place* (rather than wealth, sex, or inherited phenotype). . . . On a more practical level, if ethnicity invokes location in a cultural geography, it may be the case that the phenotypical

traits used in racial discourse are distributed across that geography." Wade, *Race and Ethnicity in Latin America*, 18, 21.

22. David Dalton claims that technology functioned as the mechanism through which Mexican Indigenous populations were modernized and hence racialized into mestizo bodies and individuals. Mixed-race identity, therefore, meant the consolidation of a version of modernity in postrevolutionary Mexico. See Dalton, *Mestizo Modernity*. See also Knight, "Racism, Revolution, and *Indigenismo*" for a discussion of the racial dynamics at play in this formative period in Mexican history.

23. For important work on the historical complexity of ethnoracial configurations in Mexico, see Schwaller, *Géneros de Gente*; Vinson, *Before Mestizaje*; Seijas, *Asian Slaves in Colonial Mexico*.

24. Sánchez Prado, *Naciones intelectuales,* 22. Rick López reminds us that contrary to the presumption that Hispanophobia dominated Mexican cultural politics, particularly immediately after the Revolution, elite and middle-class Mexicans, especially in Mexico City, still centered their attention on the Spanish colonial heritage, which was the mainstream perspective. López, *Crafting Mexico*, 68.

25. Gamio, *Forjando patria*, 96–98.

26. Vasconcelos, *La raza cósmica*, 98–99.

27. Knight, "Racism, Revolution, and *Indigenismo*," 83.

28. Alonso, "El 'mestizaje' en el espacio público," 173, 176. See also Varner, *La Raza Cosmética*. Varner insightfully frames the consolidation of mestizaje as a project of settler colonialism. She focuses particularly on the emergence of a visual economy that rendered Indigenous material and social realities as part of the past and their mestizo iterations as the future.

29. Monsiváis, *Historia mínima*, 96–97.

30. A discussion of Mexican muralism is beyond the scope of this study; however, for excellent analyses of the impact, development, and significance of muralism, see Anreus, Greely, and Folgarait, *Mexican Muralism*; Coffey, *How a Revolutionary Art Became Official Culture*; Folgarait, *Mural Painting and Social Revolution in Mexico*; Flores, *Mexico's Revolutionary Avant-Gardes*.

31. With *pueblo*, I refer to the peasants, Indigenous, and marginal groups that fought during the Mexican Revolution and to those who had previously been displaced and disenfranchised by the Porfirian regime. As Ricardo Pérez Montfort reminds us, however, el pueblo became less of an actual, concrete reference and more of a mythicized abstraction. Pérez Montfort, *Expresiones populares*, 123. In the process, it became increasingly associated with expressions of popular culture. In fact, as Juan Flores asserts, popular culture "is energized in 'moments of freedom,' specific, local plays of power and flashes of collective imagination. It is 'popular' because it is the culture of 'the people,' the common folk, the poor and the powerless who make up the majority of society. The creative subject of popular culture is the 'popular classes,' and its content the traditions and everyday life of communities and their resistance to social domination." Flores, *From Bomba to Hip-Hop*, 17.

32. I follow Lauren Berlant's and Michael Warner's definition of heteronormativity as "the institutions, structures of understanding, and practical orientations

that make heterosexuality seem not only coherent—that is, organized as a sexuality—but also privileged. Its coherence is always provisional, and its privilege can take several (sometimes contradictory) forms." Berlant and Warner, "Sex in Public," 548.

33. Franco, *Plotting Women*, 102.

34. Parra, *Writing Pancho Villa's Revolution*, 16.

35. Parra, 16. Benjamin Cowan warns us against the use of *machismo* as a shorthand for racialized and ethnicized negative hypermasculinity, which has come to be associated "simultaneously with retrograde patriarchy and unarticulated stereotypes of Latinity" as if it marked a form of "cultural essence" from Iberia or Latin America. See Benjamin Arthur Cowan, "How *Machismo* Got Its Spurs—in English."

36. According to Irwin, the arrest of the transvestites in 1901 "introduced male effeminacy and homosexuality as both the other that would define a macho heterosexual national model and an other that in fact was itself intrinsically Mexican, and that from that moment on would be viewed, albeit reluctantly by many, as an undeniable element of national culture." Irwin, *Mexican Masculinities*, xii.

37. Ramos, *El perfil del hombre y la cultura en México*, 119.

38. Paz, *El laberinto de la soledad*, 85. See Cervantes-Gómez, "Paz's *Pasivo*" for an insightful critique and reading of Paz's text, arguing for a "pasivo ethics" that centers gay sexual practices as foundational for a nationalistic narrative.

39. Here I draw from Joshua Lund's theorization of the mestizo state to rethink the cultural history of Mexico. For Lund, the mestizo state names "Mexico's institutions of sovereignty," "resonates symbolically as a way of indicating a 'state of being' that can define a national subjectivity and a national family," and "resonates materially as a historical-political process of state formation and capitalist penetration . . . , by drawing on a discourse of race." Lund, *Mestizo State*, xv.

40. Although the following is not an exhaustive list, some key titles include Pérez Montfort, *Estampas de nacionalismo popular mexicano* and *Avatares del nacionalismo cultural*; Bartra, *La jaula de la melancolía*; Lomnitz-Adler, *Exits from the Labyrinth* and *Deep Mexico, Silent Mexico*; López, *Crafting Mexico*; Vaughan and Lewis, *Eagle and the Virgin*; Olcott, Vaughan, and Cano, *Sex in Revolution*; Palou, *El fracaso del mestizo*; Legrás, *Culture and Revolution*; Arce, *México's Nobodies*; Varner, *La Raza Cosmética*; Cohen, *Finding Afro-Mexico*.

41. Palou, *El fracaso del mestizo*, 13.

42. Palou, *El fracaso del mestizo*, 20. Here I also draw from Palou's recasting of "habitus" as a generating practice: "El *habitus* no solo es un sentido del juego, o un sentido práctico, sino una serie de disposiciones que generan prácticas y percepciones, incorporando las propias condiciones sociales, objetivas, de su inculpación o reproducción" (The *habitus* is not a feeling of play or practicality but rather a series of dispositions that generate practices and perceptions. Current social conditions are incorporated into the *habitus* and then instilled and reproduced in society over time). Palou, *Mestizo Failure(s)*, 27.

43. See Williams, *Mexican Exception.*
44. Arce, 23.
45. Arce, 18.
46. Arce, 22. According to Arce, "the iterative nature of these figures [soldaderas, mulatas, runaway slaves, mothers] in the arts in conjunction with artists who reproduce their images time and again, and the audience who consumes them, constitutes a kind of knowledge and inserts these people, however negatively, back into the historical imaginary."
47. Siebers, *Disability Aesthetics,* 1.
48. Siebers, 3. Siebers even goes on to claim that "Aesthetics is the human activity most identifiable with the human because it defines the process by which human beings attempt to modify themselves, by which they imagine their feelings, forms, and futures in radically different ways, and by which they bestow upon these feelings, forms, and futures real appearances in the world."
49. Hewitt, *Social Choreography,* 2, 4.
50. Pérez Montfort, *Avatares del nacionalismo cultural,* 121–122.
51. Pérez Montfort, 123.
52. López, *Crafting Mexico,* 7.
53. López, 7.
54. Arce, *México's Nobodies,* 15–16. My formulation of slipperiness is aligned with and indebted to Arce's theorization of the "slippery word." Arce astutely conceives of the slippery word as an "interpretative mode that ascribes a slippery knowledge or way of comprehending social change and rupture to the arts." She contends that "In the form of a slippery word, image, or sound [and embodiment, I would add], the aesthetic realm in its manifolds forms can reveal what is oftentimes beyond historical language; it conceals at the same time it exposes, confuses as it illuminates," enacting a kind of "disruptive knowledge."
55. See Maffie, *Aztec Philosophy,* for a discussion of the cosmic, metaphysical, and vital role of movement.
56. The ethnohistorian James Lockhart highlights, for instance, the Nahuas' "general lack of clearly drawn polarities, seen above all in a disinclination to distinguish systematically between private and public." Lockhart, *Nahuas After the Conquest,* 440. For comparative studies of the festive celebrations of the Nahua Indigenous communities prior to their colonization and immediately after, see Toriz Proenza, *La fiesta prehispánica* and Brylak, "En busca del espectáculo prehispánico nahua." For a discussion of the complex ways embodied performances functioned as crucial sites of encounter, resistance, memory, and cultural transformation, see also Scolieri, *Dancing the New World;* Ybarra, *Performing Conquest.*
57. Taylor and Townsend, "Introduction," 3–4 (emphasis in the original).
58. Here I allude to James Lockhart's theorization of the notion of "double mistaken identity" and Mary Louise Pratt's "contact zone." Lockhart contends that both the Spanish and Nahuas often assumed the existence and transfer of analogous concepts between their cultures, engaging the world according to their respective principles, what he termed a "double mistaken identity."

Pratt proposes to think of the "contact zone" as the colonial space of uneven cross-cultural encounters and transculturation. See Lockhart, *Nahuas After the Conquest*; Pratt, *Imperial Eyes*.

59. Marino and Cuellar, "Fiesta Performance as Epistemology," 129. Angela Marino and Manuel Cuellar analyze how fiestas have functioned as an embodied alternative form of epistemology and meaning-making practice in the Americas. For a historical analysis of festive practices in Mexico, see Florescano and Santana Rocha, *La fiesta mexicana. Tomo I* and *La fiesta mexicana. Tomo II*.

60. Beezley, Martin, and French, *Rituals of Rule, Rituals of Resistance*, xiii. See also Curcio, *Great Festivals of Colonial Mexico City*, for a discussion of how public rituals operated as contested sites of colonial governance.

61. Van Young, "Conclusion," 345, 353–354.

62. Taylor and Townsend, "Introduction," 25, 15.

63. Van Young, "Conclusion," 344. I follow Eric Van Young's definition of "local knowledges" as "the contingent, historical, and even personalized understandings that groups of people and communities bring to ideas and cultural complexes shared in a general way with other groups."

64. Lomnitz-Adler, *Deep Mexico, Silent Mexico*, 153–155.

65. Lomnitz-Adler, 162–163.

66. Similar to Carlos Alonso's discussion of the rhetorical deployments of "autochthony" as a necessary marker of Latin American modernity (32), *Choreographing Mexico* studies how cultural discourses about the configuration of Mexican dance have emphasized the existence of an irreducible difference to mark a corporeal experience of Mexican modernity, particularly in the twentieth century. See Alonso, *Spanish American Regional Novel*. José Reynoso astutely examines the intersection between mestizo dance choreographies and the emergence and consolidation of modernist aesthetics, discourses, and practices. In particular, Reynoso attends to the various processes of subjectification and to the ways quotidian and specialized dance choreographies become important sites for negotiating sociopolitical values and practices, i.e., the experience of modernity and mestizaje. I thank José Luis Reynoso for allowing me to read part of his manuscript under review tentatively titled, *Dancing Mestizo Modernisms*, and for discussing with me his critical project on Mexican dance, modernity, and mestizaje prior to and after the Mexican Revolution.

67. Nájera-Ramírez, "Staging Autheticity," 290. Olga Nájera-Ramírez similarly theorizes folklórico dance as a cultural performance. She centers her discussion on the development of the genre in Mexico and the United States with a focus on the notion of authenticity. Nájera-Ramírez invites us to consider not only the ways folklórico is produced and consumed but also how it is "a complex and vital cultural expression" on both sides of the border, attending to the "power and potential of dance as a creative act of cultural representation."

68. Guss, *Festive State*, 3, 7. Among the various characteristics of a cultural performance, Guss emphasizes four. First, a cultural performance is a discrete

event, taking place at a particular time and place. Although each event is porous, it can be separated from other events of daily life. Second, cultural performances are "dramatizations" that allow individuals to engage with, disrupt, and even alter the worlds that they inhabit, adding a self-reflexive quality. Third, a cultural performance is "a profoundly discursive form of behavior" in which events are used to negotiate and challenge social imaginaries. As a result, they are dialogical and polyphonic. Each cultural performance enacts a field of action that allows different individuals to participate actively. Finally, a cultural performance offers the chance "to produce new meanings and relations." Guss, *Festive State*, 8–11.

69. Guss, 12, 15.
70. Taylor, *Archive and the Repertoire*, 2.
71. Taylor, *Performance*, 24.
72. For important work on performance and the nation in Mexico, see also Diéguez Caballero, *Escenarios liminales*; Fediuk and Prieto Stambaugh, *Corporalidades escénicas*; Ward, *Shared Truth*; Tenorio, "Queer Nightscapes" and "Broken Records."
73. Desmond, "Introduction," 12. As she goes on to claim, "the complexity of writing selves with and through the body is always framed by the social formations within which the work and its reception takes place."
74. I draw here from Elaine Peña's excellent theorization of "border scaffolding" as the symbolic and material infrastructure that upholds and maintains the meaning-making practices of "border enactments." See Peña, *¡Viva George!*
75. Nájera-Ramírez, Cantú, and Romero, *Dancing across Borders*, xiv.
76. My understanding of kinesthesia draws from Susan L. Foster's formulation to refer to the sensations of seeing others move, Carrie Noland's theorization of it as an awareness of one's own bodily motion, and SanSan Kwan's reinterpretation of the previous two to allude to the awareness of one's own movement and the sensing of that from others. See Foster, *Choreographing Empathy*; Noland, *Agency and Embodiment*; Kwan, *Kinesthetic City*.
77. Foster calls for an understanding of kinesthetic empathy, which she defines as "a process through which one experience[s] muscularly as well as psychically the dynamics of what [is] being witnessed." Foster, *Choreographing Empathy*, 177. Deidre Sklar similarly theorizes "empathic kinesthetic perception" as the ability to experience the movement of others by imagining their movements in one's own body, "feeling oneself to be in the other's body, moving." Sklar, *Dancing with the Virgin*, 32. Sklar further defines kinesthetic empathy as "the capacity to participate with another's movement or another's sensory experience of movement." Sklar, "Can Bodylore Be Brought to Its Senses?" 15. Judith Hamera has expanded my thinking about the affective micropractices that enact an intimate form of sociality across communities. For Hamera, intimacies are both the "condition for and the by-product of" sustained "physical and affective engagements" that create dancing communities. She casts technique as that which animates daily practice and as an interpretative strategy that enables communication and community. In other words, Hamera invites us to consider dance technique

as a "relational infrastructure": as a set of "communicative and interpretative conventions shared by performers and audiences who, both separately and in concert, produce and consume the dancing body." Hamera, *Dancing Communities*, 20.

78. See Foster, *Choreographing Empathy*, for a discussion of the historical development of the term.

79. Kwan, *Kinesthetic City*, 4.

80. Hewitt, *Social Choreography*, 11 (emphasis in the original).

81. Hewitt, 13.

82. Kwan, 5.

83. A historical overview of Mexican dance is beyond the scope of this study. For key historiographical studies of Mexican dance, see Tortajada Quiroz, *Danza y poder* and *Frutos de mujer*; Dallal, *La danza en México en el siglo XX*; Aulestia, *Despertar de la república dancística mexicana* and *Historias alucinantes de un mundo ecléctico*; Parga, *Cuerpo vestido de nación*; Nájera-Ramírez, Cantú, and Romero, *Dancing across Borders*. Fellow contemporaries of Mexican dance studies include Guerrero, *Dance and the Arts in Mexico*; Snow, *Revolution in Movement*; Reynoso, "Choreographing Politics, Dancing Modernity;" Adalpe Muñoz, "Choreotopias."

84. Blanco Borelli, *She Is Cuba*, 14.

85. Ramos Smith, *Teatro musical y danza en el México de la Belle Époque*, 44, 30. See also Ramos Smith, *El ballet en México*. For a discussion of the dance scene in colonial Mexico, see Ramos Smith, *La danza en México* and *La danza teatral en México*.

86. Dallal, *La danza en México*, 35. See Pérez Montfort, "El reino de las tehuanas. Apuntes sobre la creación de un estereotipo femenino regional" in *Expresiones populares y estereotipos culturales en México*, for a discussion of the consolidation of the Tehuana as a national figure of Mexican femininity. See also *La Tehuana* in *Artes de México*.

87. Tortajada Quiroz, *La danza escénica de la revolución mexicana*, 62.

88. Roger Bartra has argued that the creation of a people, el pueblo, was shaped by the emergence of a spectacle of a national culture that would allow el pueblo to see itself reproduced in its staging, as a prolongation or "transposition" of their reality. Bartra, *La jaula de la melancolía*, 228.

89. Critical studies that have analyzed the historical development of key national dances and musical genres in Latin America include Vianna, *Mystery of Samba*; Browning, *Samba*; Savigliano, *Tango and the Political Economy of Passion*; Austerlitz, *Merengue*; Quintero Rivera, *¡Salsa, sabor y control!*; Madrid and Moore, *Danzón*; Chasteen, *National Rhythms, African Roots*; Mendoza, *Shaping Society through Dance*. For recent critical scholarship that powerfully advances the cultural and political impact of concert, modern, and popular dance practices, see Fortuna, *Moving Otherwise*; Rosa, *Brazilian Bodies*; Höfling, *Staging Brazil*; Schwall, *Dancing with the Revolution*. For excellent work on dance and modernism, see Clayton, "Modernism's Moving Bodies"; Clayton, "Touring History"; Reynoso, "Racialized Dance Modernisms."

90. In her insightful analysis of contemporary Argentinian dance, Victoria Fortuna maintains that contemporary dance practices cannot be reduced to US and European formulations of cultural production; instead, they should be understood as the result of site-specific and localized responses to global circulation of ideas, bodies, and practices. See Fortuna, *Moving Otherwise*. José Reynoso astutely contends that Anna Pavlova's incorporation of Mexican dances into her repertoire challenged the supposed universality of Western referents. He goes on to claim that "the resulting *mestizo* dance practices combining ballet, and then modern dance, with Mexican folk expressive cultures represented a challenge to notions of Western modernity that assumed an exclusive link between whiteness and universality." Reynoso, "Choreographing Modern Mexico," 82.

91. Recent scholarly works in the US that critically trace the development and impact of dance in Mexico include Guerrero, *Dance and the Arts in Mexico*; Snow, *Revolution in Movement*; and Reynoso, *Mestizo and Other Danced Modernities*. Hellier-Tinoco, *Embodying Mexico*, is a notable exception to this.

92. Hamera, *Dancing Communities*, 1.

93. Here, I also draw from Elaine Peña's theorization of border infrastructure. In her cross-border ritual study, Peña invites us to reconsider the intricate ways "border enactments" or embodied cultural performances repurpose border infrastructure and in so doing the cultural and physical borderland geography. See Peña, ¡*Viva George!*

94. Legras, *Culture and Revolution*, 50.

95. Legras, 48.

96. Rodríguez, *Sexual Futures*, 6.

97. Rodríguez, 5.

98. Noland, *Agency and Embodiment*, 2.

99. Noland, 2.

100. Even though it is beyond the scope of this introduction, I want to call attention to the fact that the kinesthetic experience of El jarabe tapatío involved not only the dancers but also the public that witnessed it. I think of the role of the public as both spectators and actors. In this sense, each spectator experienced El jarabe tapatío corporeally and symbolically in different ways when partaking in a performance by Pavlova versus by the Mexican dancer María Cristina Pereda, the prima ballerina during the events of La Noche Mexicana, which I analyze in chapter 2. Both instances, however, corporeally summoned audiences as Mexicans.

101. Noland maintains that the awareness of one's own movement opens up the possibility for experimentation, modification, and even rejection of it. Noland, *Agency and Embodiment*, 3. She also reminds us that the sensations of our bodies executing a gesture must be mediated by culture in order for individuals to process them as an experience. She states,

> The kinesthetic body sense, then, is vulnerable to the intervention of culture at every moment when the situated subject must make propositional sense (meaning) of what she feels. That is, it is precisely

when sensations produced by holding a posture or executing a gesture become available to "introspection," or conscious awareness, that they must be mediated by language or by equally culture-specific systems of visual imagery. The intervention of culture is necessary to transform the inarticulate workings of the nervous system into the *experience* of a particular subject. (10)

102. Noland, *Agency and Embodiment*, 9. My understanding of embodiment follows Noland's definition of it as "the process whereby collective behaviors and beliefs, acquired through acculturation, are rendered individual and 'lived' at the level of the body."
103. Noland, 212 (emphasis in the original).
104. Puar, *Terrorist Assemblages*, 215.
105. Puar, 205. Although it is extremely important to continue to signal the significant work of analyzing the oppositional and alternative modalities to hegemonic cultural identity formations, it is as vital to recognize other modalities that suggest how embodied gestures can and do operate as contingent and complicit with dominant formations, as Puar asserts: "Queerness as an assemblage moves away from excavation work, deprivileges a binary opposition between queer and not-queer subjects, and, instead of retaining queerness exclusively as dissenting, resistant, and alternative (all of which queerness importantly is and does), it underscores contingency and complicity with dominant formations."
106. Puar, 212.
107. Here my work takes inspiration from Deborah R. Vargas's examination of the musical and cultural legacy of Chicana singers, particularly the figure of Rosita Fernández, and Elaine Peña's discussion of George Washington's birthday celebrations at the US-Mexico border. See Vargas, *Dissonant Divas in Chicana Music the Limits of La Onda*; Peña, ¡*Viva George!*
108. Rodríguez, *Sexual Futures, Queer Gestures, and Other Latina Longings*, 155. As Juana María Rodríguez discusses in regard to sexual practices, one can say that lo mexicano, like other forms of cultural production, "emerges in a social context wherein preexisting narratives circulate around available forms of representation, forms that must be legible in order to acquire social meaning."
109. Butler, *Undoing Gender*, 28.
110. Rodríguez, *Sexual Futures*, 26.
111. Taylor, "History and/as Performance," 69.
112. In this sense, my methodological approach is aligned with dance scholars' critical theorizations of embodied archival encounters and the impact of corporeal knowledge and imagination in choreographic reconstructions. See Foster, "Introduction"; Fortuna, *Moving Otherwise*, 23–25; Reynoso, "Choreographing Modern Mexico," 91, 97, and especially note 23.
113. See Martínez, "Archives, Bodies, and Imagination," which discusses the case of Juana Aguilar, an intersex individual in Guatemala in the late seventeenth century and the early eighteenth century. Martínez analyzes not only the performative, fictional, and imaginative components of history as

a craft and discipline but also the importance of understanding history as a process that engages our imagination and our embodied and experiential knowledge.

114. Martínez, "Archives, Bodies, and Imagination," 171–172.
115. I address the recent turn to queer evidence in the epilogue.
116. Gopinath, *Unruly Visions*, 9.
117. In the preface and epilogue, I discuss my experience as a folklórico dancer and analyze its impact on my scholarly work.

Chapter 1: Rehearsals of a Cosmopolitan Modernity

1. The ruling families of Tenochtitlan, the Mexica, and their allies from Texcoco and Tlacopan controlled the region. Commonly known as Aztecs, the ethnic groups that dominated the region called themselves Nahuas, sharing linguistic, cultural, political, and religious views. *Nahua* names the native speakers of the Nahuatl language still spoken today by more than 1.5 million Mexicans. See Lockhart, *Nahuas After the Conquest*, and Townsend, *Fifth Sun*, for a revised history of the Nahuas, privileging Indigenous sources and viewpoints. See Nichols and Rodríguez-Alegría, *Oxford Handbook of the Aztecs*, for a discussion of the term "Aztec" (1–17).
2. Pardo Bazán, *Al pie de la torre Eiffel*, 159. Throughout this project, I have respected the original spelling and grammatical conventions of all the documents consulted. Unless otherwise indicated, the translations are also my own.
3. Pardo Bazán, 159.
4. Martí, *La edad de oro*, 152–153.
5. Martí, 151.
6. Tenorio-Trillo, *Mexico at the World's Fairs*, 9.
7. Uslenghi, *Latin America at Fin-de-Siècle Universal Exhibitions*, 2.
8. See Uslenghi, *Latin America at Fin-de-Siècle Universal Exhibitions*, for a discussion of universal exhibitions as sites of spectacles, the emergence of a "commodified visuality," and the participation of Latin American nations in the world's fairs.
9. Yúdice, *Expediency of Culture*, 29. Here I draw from George Yúdice's theorization of conceiving of culture as a means.
10. Garrigan, *Collecting Mexico*, 147, 21.
11. Garrigan, *Collecting Mexico*, 3. According to Shelly E. Garrigan, when a collected object is introduced into the public sphere, it shifts into a "new economy of meaning—one that foregrounds the collective over the individual and the current act of meaning over the transmission of original contexts."
12. Tenorio-Trillo, *Mexico at the World's Fairs*, 64.
13. Garrigan, *Collecting Mexico*, 138; Tenorio-Trillo, *Mexico at the World's Fairs*, 71. Tenorio-Trillo claims that "cosmopolitanism was considered an attribute of the adventurous and tolerant, the conquest and appreciation of the exotic," while imposing European values as modern. Tenorio-Trillo, *Mexico at the World's Fairs*, 71.

14. Peñafiel, *Explication de l'édifice Mexicain*, 27–28. The description appeared in French, English, and Spanish. I cite the English version.
15. Peñafiel, 27–28.
16. Peñafiel, 34–36, 40–47.
17. Peñafiel, 33.
18. Tenorio-Trillo, *Mexico at the World's Fairs*, 108. Tenorio-Trillo thoroughly analyzes the symbolism of these Aztec figures and deities as well as the interior and exterior of the Aztec Palace. *Mexico at the World's Fairs*, 96–124. See also Ramírez, "Dioses, héroes y reyes mexicanos" for an essay on the cosmopolitan rendering of a nationalist indigeneity.
19. Tenorio-Trillo, *Mexico at the World's Fairs*, 66. Tenorio-Trillo also notes that the first comprehensive volume of Mexican history, *México a través de los siglos*, was simultaneously completed in 1889.
20. Tenorio-Trillo, *Mexico at the World's Fairs*, 85, 100. Charnay had been commissioned by Napoleon III in 1857 to explore southeast Mexico. His *Album fotográfico mexicano* (1858) produced for the Louvre Museum played a critical role in positioning Mexico's pre-Hispanic past as a foundational element of an emergent discourse of lo mexicano. Mraz, *Looking for Mexico*, 29.
21. See Garrigan, *Collecting Mexico*, 147. Like Uslenghi, I resist the "abstract closures and symbolic appropriations" that render objects and images on display at the world's fairs "dead objects of pure imagination" and instead reactivate "the core potential in the images [and objects], the collective desires, and the multiple narratives" of these fairs, thereby "grasping their meaning in their many, unfolding metonymies," particularly as this relates to embodied iterations of indigeneity. Uslenghi, *Latin America at Fin-de-Siècle Universal Exhibitions*, 10.
22. Tenorio-Trillo, *Mexico at the World's Fairs*, 64.
23. Tenorio-Trillo, 85–87.
24. Townsend, *Unfinished Art of Theater*, 6. As Townsend stresses, it is imperative to consider the significance of "working against deterministic views of history and elaborating a relational understanding of art." She also alludes to the notion of ensayo as a rehearsal, "a performance still in development and incomplete," and also as an essay, "a text conceived not as a finished object, but as an exploratory trial or attempt." Townsend, *Unfinished Art of Theater*, 4, 31. My use of the term here primarily mobilizes its references to a performance practice, including the material, discursive, symbolic, and embodied elements its staging prompts.
25. As Tenorio-Trillo observes, Mexico's exhibit incorporated, besides scientific treaties and studies of antiques, actual studies of "Indian customs." After all, there was an "anthropological focus" at the world's fair, centering it as a field of knowledge (including ethnography and archeology). Tenorio-Trillo, *Mexico at the World's Fairs*, 84–85.
26. Santoscoy, *La fiesta de los tastoanes*. Biblioteca Miguel Lerdo de Tejada (05. Box 12. Pamphlet 4). I thank Lydia Ortiz for her assistance locating this item.
27. Santoscoy, *La fiesta de los tastoanes*, 1. See Nájera-Ramírez, *La Fiesta de los Tastoanes,* for a discussion of the contemporary iteration of such Indigenous festivity.

28. Santoscoy, 2. I transcribed the Spanish respecting the original orthography.
29. Santoscoy, 22.
30. Santoscoy, 40.
31. Taylor, "History and/as Performance," 68. Leo Cabranes-Grant similarly describes the reenactment of such foundational scenes as part of a "performative genealogy" mobilized to "reconvene, solidify, or transform their history." Cabranes-Grant, *From Scenarios to Networks*, xi.
32. Taylor, "History and/as Performance," 70. Emphasis in the original. Or one can argue, as does Rabasa, "without history," referring to both its lack and its being outside history. See Rabasa, *Without History*.
33. Santoscoy, *La fiesta de los tastoanes*, 1–2.
34. Santoscoy, 26–27.
35. Santoscoy, 40.
36. Santoscoy, 40.
37. I further engage with the concept of *indigenismo* in the next chapter. See Tarica, *The Inner Life of Mestizo Nationalism*, for a theoretical and historical discussion of the term in Latin America, xi–xxx, 1–29.
38. Santoscoy, 41.
39. Tenorio-Trillo, *Mexico at the World's Fairs*, 97; Garrigan, *Collecting Mexico*, 138.
40. Tenorio-Trillo, *Mexico at the World's Fairs*, 124.
41. Tenorio-Trillo, "1910 Mexico City," 78.
42. Siskind, *Cosmopolitan Desires*, 21–22.
43. Antonio A. de Medina y Ormaechea, an influential lawyer and founder of the *Sociedad Mexicana de Consumo*, published a series of articles in the newspaper *El Faro* in 1889 and eventually a book in 1893, advocating for the realization of a universal exhibition for the centennial festivities in Mexico, which would attract foreign investors and European migrants, improve Mexico's infrastructure and economy, and help to modernize peasants and Indigenous communities. For a discussion of this and other related initiatives, see Gonzales, "Imagining Mexico in 1910"; Tenorio-Trillo, "1910 Mexico City."
44. The other nations sent either special envoys (Cuba, Guatemala, El Salvador, Honduras, Costa Rica, Panama, Bolivia, Peru, Brazil, Chile, Argentina, Uruguay, Russia, Austria, Holland, Portugal, Belgium, and Norway) or were represented by foreign nationals residing in Mexico (Colombia, Venezuela, and Switzerland). Because of the death of King Edward VII, Great Britain did not send an envoy, and Nicaragua did not send one because of a coup d'état, though the poet Rubén Darío was treated as a "guest of honor" by Mexican officials and intellectuals. See García, *Crónica oficial*, 1–32; Tenorio-Trillo, "1910 Mexico City," 90 n47; Gonzales, "Imagining Mexico in 1910," 511 n38.
45. Gonzales, "Imagining Mexico in 1910," 510.
46. Gonzales, 496.
47. A detailed description of the events is beyond the scope of this study; however, official historians covered the numerous celebrations of the Centenario, led by Genaro García. See García, *Crónica oficial*. For three excellent

analyses of the centennial festivities, see Garner, "Reflexiones sobre la historia patria"; Gonzales, "Imagining Mexico in 1910"; Tenorio-Trillo, "1910 Mexico City."

48. Gonzales, 502; Tenorio-Trillo, "1910 Mexico City," 76.
49. García, *Crónica oficial,* 59, 62, 82.
50. See García for a detailed description of each one of these events.
51. Tenenbaum, "Street History," 147.
52. Tenenbaum, 140.
53. Tenorio-Trillo, "1910 Mexico City," 86.
54. Tenorio-Trillo, 95–96; Gonzales, "Imagining Mexico in 1910," 528–529.
55. Gonzales, "Imagining Mexico in 1910," 529.
56. Taylor, *Archive and the Repertoire,* 28.
57. See García's description of both events in the *Crónica oficial* (182–186 and 70–76, respectively). See also Gonzales, "Imagining Mexico in 1910," 519–520, for a discussion of the emphasis on Morelos as a mestizo national hero and the reframing of mestizos as necessary for Mexico's development and modernity.
58. García, *Crónica oficial,* 70. This sense of mestizaje, of course, did not contemplate the Afro-descendant legacy of Morelos or Vicente Guerrero, which continued to be erased and denied for most of the twentieth century.
59. Gonzales, "Imagining Mexico in 1910," 497.
60. See Beezley and Lorey, ¡*Viva Mexico! ¡Viva La Independencia!* for a discussion of the impact and historical development of Independence Day festivities. See Martínez, *Performance in the Zócalo,* for an analysis of Independence Day festivities at Mexico's main stage, the city's center square known as the Zócalo (81–93).
61. Lempérière, "Los dos centenarios de la independencia mexicana," 322. Similarly, Gillingham claims that the past "is a universal tactical resource," departing from Appadurai's formulation of the past (6). Gillingham examines the ways in which Cuauhtémoc became a symbol of nationalism and the attendant material and figurative manipulation of Mexico's past. See Gillingham, *Cuauhtémoc's Bones.*
62. My understanding here follows Krista Brune's theorization of translation as a critical means to foreground the generative potential and utility of translation as a linguistic, cultural, and epistemological process to interrogate the place of Brazil in the Americas. See Brune, *Creative Transformations.*
63. Tenorio-Trillo notes that this is precisely how the Porfirian elite understood modernity: as the "harmonious and peaceful economic development, progress and science" that was materialized by a modern city that was at once "sanitary, comfortable and beautiful." Tenorio-Trillo, "1910 Mexico City," 78–79.
64. Here I draw from Debord's classic definition of spectacle as a series of social relations mediated by images. See Debord, *Society of the Spectacle.*
65. Mraz, *Looking for Mexico,* 54.
66. Kwan, *Kinesthetic City,* 22.
67. Kwan, 15–16.

68. García, *Crónica oficial,* 138.
69. See García, *Crónica oficial,* 140; Garner, "Reflexiones sobre la historia patria," 136; Gonzales, "Imagining Mexico in 1910," 513.
70. For a detailed description of the parade with several photographs from the event, see García, *Crónica oficial,* 138–141; "Vimos pasar ayer una época de historia nacional," 1, 6; "El Desfile Histórico del día 15," 1, 20–201. See also Gonzales, "Imagining Mexico in 1910," 512–515; Tenorio-Trillo, "1910 Mexico City," 98–99, for a discussion of the way the Desfile promoted a liberal vision of Mexico and an accurate, authentic rendition of Mexican history, respectively. In her insightful analysis of the Desfile, Ana Martínez discusses the repurposing of religious and popular rituals to promote patriotism and documents the elaborate preparations and the description of the numbers and participation of hundreds of performers in the creation of a "monumental and realistic narrative" by José Casarín. See Martínez, *Performance in the Zócalo,* 102–115.
71. García, *Crónica oficial,* 138.
72. See Martínez, *Performance in the Zócalo,* 50–80, for a discussion of the colonial commemorations of the conquest and its repurposing of El Paseo del Pendón to signal loyalty to the Spanish Crown.
73. García, *Crónica oficial,* 139. García notes that 288 people participated, but Tenorio-Trillo observes that the original plan included 800.
74. Gonzales, "Imagining Mexico in 1910," 512–513.
75. García, *Crónica oficial,* 139.
76. García, 141.
77. García, *Crónica oficial,* 140.
78. "Vimos pasar ayer una época de historia nacional," 1.
79. For an insightful study of the historical encounter between Moctezuma and Cortés, see Restall, *When Montezuma Met Cortés.*
80. "El Gran Desfile Histórico."
81. Tenorio-Trillo, "1910 Mexico City," 99; Gonzales, "Imagining Mexico in 1910," 514.
82. This was not unlike the demands imposed by the state's cultural project in the 1920s and 1930s to perform indigeneity in very specific ways, which I discuss in chapters 2 and 3. See also Varner, *La Raza Cosmética.*
83. "El Desfile Histórico del día 15," 2.
84. Johns, *City of Mexico in the Age of Díaz,* 53–57; Gonzales, "Imagining Mexico in 1910," 510, 513; Tenorio-Trillo, "1910 Mexico City," 91.
85. See Johns, *City of Mexico in the Age of Díaz,* for a discussion of the sociopolitical, cultural, and economic tensions at play in Mexico's transitioning capital at the turn of the century. As Knight notes, it is difficult to separate Indigenous from peasant populations in this period of transformation and ethnoracial shifting paradigms. Knight, "Racism, Revolution, and *Indigenismo*," 71–74.
86. Tenorio-Trillo, "1910 Mexico City," 98.
87. Gonzales, "Imagining Mexico in 1910," 526; Martínez, *Performance in the Zócalo,* 104.

88. For a description of the luxurious Garden Party, which was attended by more than fifty thousand people, see "El Garden Party en Chapultepec," 1. María de las Nieves Rodríguez observes the parallelism between the Garden Party and La Noche Mexicana, which I discuss in the next chapter. Rodríguez, "La 'noche mexicana,'" 64–65 n17.
89. "Vimos pasar ayer una época," 6.
90. García, *Crónica oficial*, 140.
91. Martínez, *Performance in the Zócalo*, 110. Ana Martínez similarly notes that Porfirian intellectuals and artists "mythologized the Indian past and aestheticized it in a neoclassical fashion, even as they negated the conditions of their Indian present."
92. Tenorio-Trillo, "1910 Mexico City," 99; Gonzales, "Imagining Mexico in 1910," 523, 525.
93. Kwan, *Kinesthetic City*, 11.
94. Muñoz, *Cruising Utopia,* 65.
95. Cabranes-Grant, *From Scenarios to Networks*, 11–13. Here I am in dialogue with Leo Cabranes-Grant's theorization of intercultural practices, scenarios, and networks in colonial Mexico as critical sites where "the twice-behaved becomes something *other* than what it was before through creative repetition, innovation, and networking," experienced in the present tense as a convergence of objects, peoples, and materials at a particular time and place. See also the insightful work of Ana Martínez, who explores the complex interplay between rituals, historical performances, and national celebrations at Mexico's Zócalo. Martínez, *Performance in the Zócalo*, 81–115.
96. See Leal, Barraza, and Jablonska, *Vistas que no se ven*, for a discussion and explanation of the films made during the Porfiriato in general and the Centenario in particular. Thirty-five films of the 370 total were produced in 1910. As the footage reveals, the filmmakers would normally leave the camera in a given spot to record whatever came across it, e.g., the Desfile (10, 12, 115–116). I thank Mónica García-Blizzard for bringing this archival source to my attention.
97. See Johns, *City of Mexico in the Age of Díaz,* for a description of the dress and activities of lower-class Mexicans, particularly his section on "Peasants and *Pelados*" (53–57).
98. García, *Crónica oficial*, "Apéndice. Número 160," 124.
99. For a discussion of Porfirian indigenismo and treatment of Indigenous populations at the various congresses, particularly the Americanist and Indianista congresses, see Garner, "Reflexiones sobre la historia patria," 136–144; Gonzales, "Imagining Mexico in 1910," 512–526; Tenorio-Trillo, "1910 Mexico City," 99–101.
100. Monsiváis, "Crónica del Centenario," xix.
101. Garner has similarly pointed out how some scholars such as Tenorio-Trillo and Lomnitz have reduced the Porfirian ideal of the nation to a mere fiction or a fetish, asking that we engage the Porfiriato in more generative terms. Garner, "Reflexiones sobre la historia patria," 129, 145.
102. Garner, "Reflexiones sobre la historia patria," 127.

Chapter 2: La Noche Mexicana and the Staging of a Festive Mexico

1. "La Noche Mexicana en el Bosque de Chapultepec," *El Universal*. September 6, 1921. Unless otherwise indicated, all translations are my own.
2. Pérez Montfort, *Estampas de nacionalismo popular mexicano*, 118. Pérez Montfort observes that it would take several years, most of the 1920s, for figures of the china and the charro to be consolidated as the indisputable symbols of Mexican nationalism, particularly due to the popularization of El jarabe tapatío as a distinct musical genre and national dance, which I will address in the next chapters. Accordingly, in the first years after the Revolution, particularly in the 1920s, figures from different regions of the country, such as *norteños* from northern México, *yucatecos* from Southern Mexico, and *jarochos* from the Gulf of Mexico, were considered as typically Mexican as the Indigenous peoples and the charros.
3. "La Noche Mexicana en el Bosque de Chapultepec."
4. "La 'Noche Mexicana' congregó en Chapultepec ayer." I follow the use of capital letters in the original.
5. See Palou, *El fracaso del mestizo* for an insightful and succinct analysis of the figure of the mestizo as the political embodiment of the state project of Mexicanness. I engage Palou's analysis on the construction of the mestizo in the introduction.
6. With *cosmopolitan*, I refer to Siskind's understanding of cosmopolitanism as "deseo de mundo" (desire for the world). Siskind contends that cosmopolitanism encompasses an imaginary discourse that fails to inscribe the particularities of Latin America with a universal purpose and yet "widens the margins of cultural and political agency and illuminates new meanings by reinscribing cultural particularities in larger, transcultural networks of signification." Siskind, *Cosmopolitan Desires,* 21–22. I elaborate on cosmopolitanism in chapter 1.
7. As Clayton reminds us, artistic expressions at the beginning of the twentieth century often blurred the boundaries between languages, disciplines, and spatiotemporal frames of reference. See Clayton, "Modernism's Moving Bodies," for a discussion of the porosity and mixing of languages of various artforms at the turn of the twentieth century as a crucial characteristic of cultural modernity.
8. In her insightful analysis, the historian Annick Lempérière looks at the commemorations of independence in Mexico in 1910 and 1921 as two related yet dissimilar instances in which discourses about memory and history operated as sites for the legitimization of state power. See Lempérière, "Los dos centenarios de la independencia mexicana."
9. See Díaz y de Ovando, "Las fiestas," for a thorough description of all the festivities that took place during the centennial celebrations.
10. The historian Michael Gonzales provides an excellent synthesis and analysis of the plethora of centennial activities that took place in 1921 in Mexico City, emphasizing the uses of historical memory, public policy, and the

press to promote a new cultural vision. See Gonzales, "Imagining Mexico in 1921." For a comparative treatment of the 1910 and 1921 centenaries, see Gonzales, "Modernity and the indigenous."

11. For an excellent synthesis of the complexity of this historical juncture in Mexico, see Knight, "Racism, Revolution, and *Indigenismo.*"

12. The Díaz regime certainly privileged the celebrations of Mexican Independence on the 15th and 16th of September. Coincidentally, Díaz's birthday was on the 15th of September. Surprisingly, Agustín de Iturbide's birthday, Mexico's first president and later emperor, was on the 27th. Iturbide was featured prominently in periodicals during the centennial celebrations of 1921. For a historical analysis of the celebrations of Mexican Independence, see Beezley and Lorey, ¡*Viva Mexico!* ¡*Viva La Independencia!*

13. Gonzales, "Imagining Mexico in 1921," 251.

14. Gonzales, 250.

15. "Serán populares las fiestas del Centenario."

16. "El pueblo tendrá acceso," 1, 12.

17. "El pueblo tendrá acceso." For a thorough analysis of the Exposición de Arte Popular, see López, *Crafting Mexico*. López summarizes the objectives of the exhibition, which intended to display an "aesthetic foundation" of popular art and promote it as a marker of Mexicanness (not as a sign of Indigenous "backwardness") to be possessed by the middle and upper classes. If the patrons and visitors were willing to pay for high-quality popular art, the organizers hoped to "bring economic uplift to the countryside and assure the survival of these arts, while at the same time fostering mutual understanding among the different sectors of society" (79).

18. López, *Crafting Mexico*, 15.

19. López, 15.

20. López, 20.

21. "El pueblo tendrá acceso," 12. In the introduction, I address the legacy and influence of Vasconcelos's cultural policies. For an insightful recent analysis of Vasconcelos's cultural work and impact, see Townsend, "Rehearsals of the Tragi-Co(s)mic Race," in *Unfinished Art of Theater*. Snow further emphasizes Vasconcelos's insistence on the role of the aesthetics for the production and dissemination of knowledge. See Snow, *Revolution in Movement*, 22–25, 78–80.

22. "El pueblo tendrá acceso," 12.

23. Later in the chapter, I address how some of these events circulated through the print media. For a detailed analysis of the contest and the racial and gender implications of this staging of a nationalistic embodied indigeneity, see Varner, *La Raza Cosmética*. Varner discusses how Indigenous women reproduced, appropriated, and even resisted the idealization of Indigenous femininity, i.e., the *India Bonita* (beautiful Indian) trope, in the consolidation of a national identity in postrevolutionary Mexico (Varner, *La Raza Cosmética*, 24–48). See also López, *Crafting Mexico*, especially "Ethnicizing the Nation: The India Bonita Contest of 1921."

24. I build on García Canclini's theorization of the staging of the popular as a scenario to understand how it is the result of both transnational and national

historical processes that rendered lo mexicano coherent and symbolically foundational during the postrevolutionary period. This operation reveals how such a staging became a political force as the postrevolutionary government culturally constructed the idea of the nation. The symbolic operation that took place to reach a sense of "verisimilitude," according to García Canclini, "was achieved *historically* through ritualization operations of essentialized patrimonies." Garcia Canclini, *Hybrid Cultures*, 273. Emphasis in the original.

25. Taylor, *Archive and the Repertoire*, 29.
26. Taylor, 28.
27. Rodríguez, "La 'noche mexicana,'" 65.
28. For an insightful analysis of these two state-sponsored events, La Noche Mexicana and Exposición de Arte Popular, see López's *Crafting Mexico*, 65–94.
29. López, *Crafting Mexico*, 68.
30. López, 74. López refers to this process as "ethnicization" to address the ambivalence with which artists and intellectuals engaged "Indigenousness" as a crucial element of the national identity and yet continued to hold prejudices against Indigenous people and to erase the contributions of Asians and Afro-Mexicans (9).
31. As discussed in the introduction, theorizing lo mexicano as an assemblage draws attention to the ways such an ideation functions as a contingent spatial, temporal, and corporeal convergence, following Puar's theorization of assemblage. Puar, *Terrorist Assemblages*, 204.
32. López notes that there were two duplicate performances in September and October, one of which was for a select audience (71). For the purpose of my argument, highlighting the popular and massive character of the event, I will thus limit my analysis to the September performance that was free and open to the public. On October 3, 1921, *El Demócrata* published the article, "La tercera Noche Mexicana fue muy animada y concurrida," describing the event from the night before as spectacular as the first one, free and open to the public, unlike the second one that was characterized as "sosa" (bland).
33. *El Demócrata* published a series of editorials denouncing the limited access to a select group of people and demanding free entrance to the park. When the committee announced the event would be free and open to the public, *El Demócrata* took credit for this decision. See Gonzales, "Imagining Mexico in 1921," 263–264, for a discussion of the newspaper's role in this controversy.
34. "Fiestas del Centenario."
35. Rodríguez, "La 'noche mexicana,'" 67.
36. Snow further elaborates on Best Maugard's experience with Pavlova's *Fantasía mexicana*. See Snow, *Revolution in Movement*, 57–69.
37. Tortajada Quiroz, *La danza escénica*, 13. According to Tortajada, Jaime Martínez del Río wrote the script; Eva Pérez Caro was the choreographer; Manuel Castro Padilla was in charge of the music; and Adolfo Best Maugard designed the scenography. Tortajada Quiroz, 12. I will discuss the significance of El jarabe tapatío in the following two chapters.
38. López, *Crafting Mexico*, 69.

39. It was in the 1920s that Best Maugard's influence became crucial for the emergence of a visual grammar through the circulation of his *Método de dibujo: Tradición, resurgimiento y evolución del arte mexicano*, which was published in 1922 and distributed nationwide to thousands of students. It advanced the implementation of seven primary elements of the "aboriginal arts" found in traditional Mexican art and in most, if not all, other cultures: the zigzag, the S-curve, the spiral, the half circle, the circle, the wavy line, and the straight line. Best Maugard's idea was to foster "a collective form of national expression." Flores, *Mexico's Revolutionary Avant-Gardes*, 165. For an introduction to Best Maugard's *Método*, see Velázquez, "Best Maugard Drawing Method" and Cordero, "Para devolver su inocencia a la nación." See Flores, *Mexico's Revolutionary Avant-Gardes*, for a critical contextualization of the visual and aesthetic innovations of the period.

40. I offer the entire program description, following the original spelling and use of capital letters, in order to give a complete sense of how this national feria was described and represented for the people in attendance:

A las 7.30 p.m., NOCHE MEXICANA EN EL BOSQUE DE CHAPULTEPEC.—Los carruajes llegarán por la Calzada de la Reforma, descendiendo el público de ellos en el Restaurant Chapultepec, donde bifurca la calzada de la Gran Avenida hasta la entrada de la NOCHE MEXICANA; los vehículos seguirán por la Calzada de circunvalación y la Avenida de la Exposición.—A la hora citada dará inicio la jamica, combate floral y de confetti, bailes música y cantos regionales.—Los puestos donde se venderán flores, confetti y platillos mexicanos, estarán atendidos por hermosas señoritas.—Habrá tres escenarios donde continuamente habrá representaciones típicamente mexicanas.—A las 8.30 p.m., se anunciarán con siete cohetes detonantes los fuegos sobre el Lago Grande.—Concluido este número seguirá la kermesse.—A las 9 p.m., bailable en el escenario grande del lago (grupo de tehuanas).—A las 9.30 p.m. fuegos artificiales, erupción del Popocatepetl, se simulará la erupción con cohetes de colores.—10 p.m., bailable en el escenario grande del lago (grupo de chinas y charros).—Saldrán comparsas en trajineras, dando la vuelta al lago y desembarcando en el escenario donde continuará el bailable.—A continuación, grandes fuegos artificiales.—A las 10.30 p.m., bailable final en el escenario grande del lago.—Himno Nacional cantado por todos los concurrentes y desfile de antorchas, tomando parte los charros y bandas de música.—Cada número en el escenario del lago será anunciado con cohetes detonantes, con el objeto de que el público que se halle en la kermesse acuda a la orilla del lago.—Las señoritas que atenderán los puestos, se hallarán vestidas de chinas poblanas y se invita a las damas a concurrir a esta fiesta, vistiendo trajes típicos nacionales; igual invitación se hace a los caballeros.—Una vez terminado el programa, seguirá la iluminación del Bosque.—Esta fiesta tendrá un carácter esencialmente mexicanista y estará hecha totalmente con elementos mexicanos de las distintas artes nacionales.—Una banda de música compuesta de 350 profesores pertenecientes a varias músicas del Ejército dirigida por el profesor Melquiades Campo, tocará composiciones del compositor mexicano Manuel Castro Padilla—bailable de las tehuanas y bailable de chinas y charros—y del profesor Manuel Ponce el bailable final.—Concurrirán también a esta fiesta la Orquesta Típica del Centenario dirigida por el maestro Miguel Lerdo de Tejada y la Orquesta de Trovadores Yucatecos y la Regional Yucateca, con su grupo de cantantes y bailarines.—El cuerpo de baile está formado por elementos exclusivamente mexicanos, siendo la PRIMERA BAILARINA MARIA CRISTINA PEREDA. Los fuegos artificiales han sido hechos en México bajo la dirección del señor Pereyra. PROYECTO LA FIESTA EL DIRECTOR GENERAL DE ELLA, SEÑOR ADOLFO BEST MAUGARD. LA ENTRADA A LA "NOCHE MEXICANA", ES ENTERAMENTE LIBRE (3).

(At 7:30 p.m., MEXICAN NIGHT AT CHAPULTEPEC PARK.— The carriages will arrive through *Calzada de la Reforma* [Reforma Avenue], letting people off at Chapultepec Restaurant, where the road diverges from the *Gran Avenida* [Grand Avenue] to the entrance to the MEXICAN NIGHT; the vehicles will follow the *Calzada de circunvalación* [Bypass Road] and the *Avenida de la Exposición* [Exposition Avenue].—At the designated starting time the jamaica, floral combat and confetti, regional dances, music, and songs will commence.—The stands where flowers, confetti, and Mexican dishes will be sold will be staffed by pretty young ladies.—There will be three stages where there will be continuous traditional Mexican performances.—At 8:30 p.m., seven explosive rockets will announce the fireworks at the *Lago Grande* [Grand Lake].—After this act, the kermis will follow.—At 9 p.m., dance on the main stage at the lake (the Tehuanas group).—At 9:30 p.m. fireworks, eruption of the Popocatepetl, the eruption will be simulated by colorful rockets.—10 p.m., dance on the main stage at the lake (the group of chinas and charros).—Groups of performers will circle around in the lake in trajineras [traditional decorated boats from Xochimilco] and will arrive at the main stage, where the dance will continue.—A large fireworks show will follow.—At 10:30 p.m., final dance on the main stage at the lake.—National Anthem sung by all the audience and a torch parade, with participation of the charros and the musical bands.—Each act on the main stage at the lake will be announced with explosive rockets, so that the public partaking in the kermis can gather by the shore of the lake.—The young ladies that will run the stands will be dressed as chinas poblanas and ladies are invited to attend this fiesta wearing typical national costumes; the gentlemen are invited to do the same.—Once the program ends, the illumination of [Chapultepec] Forest will take place.—This fiesta will have an essentially Mexicanist character and will be made up of Mexican elements from different national arts.—A musical ensemble consisting of 350 professors from various military bands and directed by the professor Melquiades Campo, will play compositions by the Mexican composer Manuel Castro Padilla—dance of the Tehuanas and dance of the chinas and charros—and by the professor Manuel Ponce the final dance.—The *Orquesta Típica del Centenario* [Folk Orchestra of the Centenary] directed by the maestro Miguel Lerdo de Tejada will also be present in this fiesta and the *Orquesta de Trovadores Yucatecos* [Orchestra of Troubadours from Yucatán] and the *Regional Yucateca* [Regional Orchestra from Yucatán], with its group of singers and dancers.—The dance troupe is exclusively composed by Mexicans, with MARIA CRISTINA PINEDA as the PRIMA BALLERINA. The fireworks have been made in Mexico under the direction of Mr. Pereyra. THE FIESTA WAS DESIGNED BY ITS GENERAL DIRECTOR, MR. ADOLFO BEST MAUGARD. ENTRANCE TO THE "MEXICAN NIGHT" IS ENTIRELY FREE.)

41. Warner, *Publics and Counterpublics*, 12, 67, 91.
42. Lomnitz-Adler, *Deep Mexico, Silent Mexico*, 12–13.
43. Bartra, *La jaula de la melancolía*, 228.
44. *Noche Mexicana*.
45. *Noche Mexicana*.
46. Snow, *Revolution in Movement*, 36–54.
47. Dance modernisms responded to and engaged with the experience of modernity in culturally specific ways across the globe. They also grappled with the emergence of mass culture and popular entertainment while attending to avant-garde sensibilities. In this way, they resulted from the interchange between peoples, ideas, dance practices, and aesthetic sensibilities, across continents and borders (Burt and Huxley, *Dance, Modernism, and Modernity*, 55). For a recent discussion of the interplay between dance practices, the experience of modernity, and modernisms, see Burt and Huxley, *Dance, Modernism, and Modernity*.
48. Cordero, "Para devolver su inocencia a la nación," 17. Cordero explains that the elements of Japonism derive from José Juan Tablada's influence; Tablada was residing in New York City at the time and was a close friend of Best Maugard (17). The influences of Best Maugard require further analysis that is beyond the scope of this chapter. For a discussion of the presence and impact of Mexican artists in New York, see Martínez, "Estéticas del desplazamiento." I thank Lisa Lipinski for the point about Matisse.
49. The art historian María de las Nieves Rodríguez points out that the designs featured in the decorations during the event offered a "mestizo" aestheticized version of Mexican nature and graphic stylizations of popular art, which together introduced a nationalistic visual conception of Mexico that went along with and, as I argue, was materialized by the dance and musical interventions at La Noche Mexicana. Rodríguez, "La 'noche mexicana,'" 65, 68.
50. Roberto *El Diablo*, "En Pleno Centenario."
51. Sluis, *Deco Body, Deco City*, 15–16.

52. Here, I follow Mark Franko's understanding of the role of spectators as "formative," contradicting "presuppositions about the body's purity and autonomy of presence, the tenets of modernist dance history." Public spaces of movement are constituted through the collaboration and conflict between dancers and spectators (Franko, *Dancing Modernism/Performing Politics*, xii).

53. Burt, *Alien Bodies*, 55. By reading the ebbs and flows of European and US expressions of modern dance vocabularies, Burt explores how dancing bodies grappled with the experience of modernity and urban dwelling. Whereas modernism has been reduced to abstractionism and at times conflated with modernity, Burt insists on understanding modernist aesthetics as a form of consciousness, one that rejected traditional ideologies of national identity and that deconstructed outmoded aesthetic conventions and traditions (Burt, 15). Modern dancing then captured the experience of alienation brought about by modernity: "By calling modern dancing bodies 'alien bodies' I am drawing attention to the fact that, where modernity undermined ideologies of national identity, it created needs for new definitions of origins that, during the 1920s and 1930s, were partially satisfied through the appreciation of primitivism in the arts" (Burt, 17).

54. For a discussion of how the dancing of the Tiller Girls rendered the experience of fragmentation, alienation, uniformity, and modernity, see Burt, *Alien Bodies,* 84–100.

55. Pérez Montfort, *Estampas de nacionalismo popular mexicano*, 114. See Sluis, *Deco Body, Deco City*, 61–99, for a discussion of the Mexicanization and copycat productions of the French variety show, its media coverage, and the embodiment of new female subjectivities.

56. For an excellent analysis of how images circulated throughout the nation in this period and how a visual culture emerged in Mexico, see Mraz, *Looking for Mexico*. For a gender analysis of the visual culture in this period, particularly of the modern woman, see Hershfield, *Imagining la Chica Moderna*.

57. "La Noche Mexicana fue aplazada para hoy."

58. Palavicini, "La Noche Mexicana en Chapultepec," 2.

59. Palavicini, 2.

60. Castro Ricalde, "Opacidad y transparencia," 131, 133.

61. According to the art historian Tatiana Flores, unlike European modernism, which referenced "primitivism" to romanticize "preindustrial cultures, whether exotic or local folk traditions," and reject "industrial mechanization," Mexican artists and their production "referenced and criticized European engagements with 'primitivism' and proposed instead a reading of modernism as an autochthonous and spontaneously occurring element of their own culture." She goes on to say that artists "sought to bridge the gaps between native traditions and modernity, the urban and the rural, and high and low culture" (161). Palavicini's reference also signals a kind of Mexican orientalism: a tendency, characteristic of Latin American intellectuals of the time, to describe the unknown and unfamiliar in the language of Otherness that was most legible on a global scale. See Altamirano, *Ensayos argentinos,* for a discussion of the orientalist gestures evident in Sarmiento's oeuvre.

62. Foster, *Choreographing Empathy*, 177.
63. Although a discussion of "indigenismo" is beyond the scope of this chapter, I would like to point out that indigenismo as a cultural and political discourse has paradoxically allowed for the simultaneous denial and recognition of Indigenous communities throughout Latin America. Indigenismo has promoted the subordination of Indigenous communities to the state in an effort to "civilize" them. Estelle Tarica contends that indigenismo has systematically operated through state institutions and discourses, from Christian evangelization campaigns to nationalist movements, and yet "indigenismo has set itself the task of humanizing Indians and rendering them familiars, and therefore of transforming the cultural and racial self-conception of Latin American subjects" (xiii). See Tarica, *Inner Life of Mestizo Nationalism,* for a thorough discussion of the impact of indigenismo on the formation of Latin American mestizo nations.
64 Tarica, *Inner Life of Mestizo Nationalism*, 1–2.
65. For an insightful analysis of the representation of Yaqui Indians in Mexican and Mexican American cultural production, see Tumbaga, *Yaqui Indigeneity.*
66. As the case of the jaraneros illustrate, they were described either as "yucatecos" or "indígenas mayas bailando danzas regionales" (Mayan Indians performing regional dances).
67. Castro Ricalde, "Opacidad y transparencia," 129, 135.
68. "La 'Noche Mexicana,' " 26.
69. "La 'Noche Mexicana,' " 26.
70. See Velázquez Becerril, "Intelectuales y poder en el porfiriato," for a discussion of the role of a nationalistic culture and Mexican intellectuals.
71. "La 'Noche Mexicana,' " 26.
72. Rodríguez, *Sexual Futures*, 126.
73. The extant historical footage at the Filmoteca, UNAM, of the centennial festivities, with a glimpse of La Noche Mexicana, corroborates this. I would like to thank dance historian Claudia Carbajal for this reference.
74. I would like to thank art historian María de las Nieves Rodríguez for sharing this reference with me.
75. "Ecos del Centenario," 6. I follow the spelling as it appeared on the original article to capture the imagined verbal expression of el pueblo. As it is impossible to reproduce the wordplay, contractions, and spelling changes, I opted to convey the general meaning of the phrases in the following examples and quotations.
76. Gonzales, for instance, documents that *El Demócrata* received numerous complaints from workers denouncing that people wearing frock coats were favored over those wearing huaraches at film screenings organized at the Centennial. Gonzales, "Imagining Mexico in 1921," 263.
77. "Ecos del Centenario," 6. The second iteration of La Noche Mexicana was not free; ticket sales were announced in *El Universal.*
78. In her insightful analysis of the gender politics of the India Bonita pageant, Varner discusses how this pageant served as a platform to advance a postrevolutionary ideation of Indigenous "authenticity" that erased Indigenous cultures while repositioning mestizos as the ultimate Mexican race. See

"La reina de la raza: The Making of the *India Bonita"* in Varner, *La Raza Cosmética*.

79. Rodríguez, *Sexual Futures*, 100.

Chapter 3: Nellie Campobello

1. Coignard, "El valor efectivo de ballet mexicano," 33. Unless otherwise indicated, all translations from Spanish are my own.
2. Vargas Valdés and García Rufino, *Nellie Campobello*, 163; Matthews, *Nellie Campobello*, 49–50.
3. "Artistas nuestros que triunfan en el extranjero," 14.
4. Del Río, "Nellie y Gloria Campobello," 29.
5. For a discussion of folklórico dance as an important cultural practice across the Mexico-US border, see Nájera-Ramírez, Cantú, and Romero, *Dancing across Borders*.
6. For an excellent contextualization of Nellie Campobello's literary work, see the prologue of Aguilar Mora, "El silencio de Nellie Campobello," and Arce's analysis of her work in *México's Nobodies*. For a discussion of her written and dance works, see Matthews, *Nellie Campobello*; Bidault de la Calle, *Nellie Campobello*; Tortajada Quiroz, *Frutos de mujer*.
7. For an insightful discussion and contextualization in English of the tensions between ballet, modern dance, and Mexican dance, see Snow, *Revolution in Movement*, particularly 116–198. See also Tortajada Quiroz, *Frutos de mujer*, and Reynoso, "Choreographing Politics, Dancing Modernity."
8. Ramos Villalobos, *Una mirada a la formación dancística mexicana*, 51.
9. Dallal, *La danza en México*, 27–28.
10. With *transculturation*, I use Ortiz's term that names the performative, transitional, and transformational process of the acquisition of foreign cultural forms, the loss or removal of local ones, and the consequent creation of new ones (260). See Ortiz, *Contrapunteo cubano del tabaco y el azúcar*.
11. Dallal, *La danza en México*, 18–19.
12. I expand on this discussion of the Porfirian regime in chapter 1. Here, suffice it to say that the emphasis on performance that characterized the postrevolutionary period had its explicit origins during the Díaz regime, but it can be traced back to precolonial and colonial times, as discussed in the introduction.
13. As I discuss in the introduction, with the term *postrevolutionary aesthetics,* I allude to the "mestizo aesthetics" and its concomitant policies, characterized by a visually Indigenous culture.
14. Clayton, "Touring History," 30.
15. Monsiváis argues that, in this period, teaching acquired a messianic character and that education itself gained a new status (*Historia mínima*, 116). See Marín, *La importancia de la danza tradicional mexicana en el Sistema Educativo Nacional*, for a critical study of the history of *misiones culturales* in Mexico.
16. Tortajada Quiroz, *Danza y poder*, 40.

17. As addressed in the introduction, I follow Van Young's definition of "local knowledges" as "the contingent, historical, and even personalized understandings that groups of people and communities bring to ideas and cultural complexes shared in a general way with other groups." Van Young, "Conclusion," 344. Such forms of knowledge shape local understandings about the sociocultural, political, and economic processes at play in the configuration of a given community.

18. Pratt, "Mi cigarro, mi Singer y la revolución mexicana," 268.

19. Townsend, *Unfinished Art of Theater*, 56.

20. López, *Crafting Mexico*, 9–10. In her excellent analysis on the institutionalization of postrevolutionary politics through federal educational policy, particularly in rural communities, Mary Kay Vaughan similarly notes that "the result was a nationalization of popular culture as Nahuatl-speaking children in Tlaxcala learned the Yaqui Deer Dance and Tarahumara children learned the criollo *jarabe* of Jalisco. This notion of the national, popular culture rested heavily on the achievements of the Indian past and contemporary Indian aesthetics, which were nationalized as symbols, objects, and artifacts. The SEP appropriated them out of their daily context in order to build a common culture. Never abandoned was the notion that although being Mexican rested on strong indigenous cultural foundations, being Mexican meant becoming modern; adopting urban, Western behavior and culture." Vaughan, *Cultural Politics in Revolution*, 46.

21. Tortajada Quiroz, *Danza y poder*, 54.

22. Burt, *Alien Bodies*, 104. Mexico established its Department of Physical Education in 1922. Its numerous activities, such as massive displays of gymnastics, physical culture, sports, and dances, helped to choreograph a sense of nationalism, revealing the interconnection between eugenics and calisthenics. The moving body symbolized "una nueva polis, joven, sana, natural y moderna" (a new polis, young, healthy, natural, and modern). Bidault de la Calle, *Nellie Campobello*, 117–118.

23. Burt, 109.

24. For an excellent and recent analysis of cultural displays of nationalism, including massive spectacles at the National Stadium, Condesa, and Teotihuacán and monumental choreographies of folklórico, gymnastics, and even Greek dance, see Claudia Carbajal Segura, "Los espectáculos masivos y las coreografías monumentales."

25. Kaplan rightly observes that during and after the Revolution, women experienced significant changes in their sanctioned roles. Mexican women often occupied contradictory positions, "simultaneously cast as dependent and nurturers"; nevertheless, and regardless of their class background, they enlisted in brigades and schools, claiming an active presence in the public sphere (Kaplan, "Final Reflections," 271). O'Malley also points out that despite the contribution of women during the Revolution, especially in their role as *soldaderas* (women soldiers), the "glorification of revolutionaries' manliness" dominated the public scene in postrevolutionary Mexico. O'Malley, *Myth of the Revolution*, 136.

26. Olcott, *Revolutionary Women in Postrevolutionary Mexico*, 199.

27. Here is important to keep in mind the ways female bodies were meant to signify and enact citizenship as part of a "civic body," which translated their actions as part of a larger matrix of inclusion and exclusion, of subordination and/or resistance. Moallem advances the notion of the "civic body" as a site for the intersection between "sexed corporeality, cultural nationalism and gendered citizenship" (319) in order to examine the gendered, classed, sexed, and political engagements within the nation-state. According to Moallem, the civic body generates and conditions "racialized and gendered citizenship" ("Universalization of Particulars," 320).

28. Dance became part of an orchestrated effort to interpellate Mexican subjects. Townsend, for example, mentions one example of the SEP's cultural series from 1935: a memo with the program for an open-air festival in the working-class neighborhood of Colonia Morelos, which featured a mariachi band, three short plays, and a jarabe by the Campobello sisters. This example illustrates the scope of such open-air programs, which, according to Townsend, seem to have been broadcast on the radio with the help of microphones and amplifiers (Townsend, *Unfinished Art of Theater*, 273 n85).

29. For a discussion of the dance trajectory and legacy of Miss Lettie Carroll, see Aulestia, *Las "chicas bien" de Miss Carroll*.

30. Matthews, *Nellie Campobello*, 48–51; Tortajada Quiroz, *Frutos de mujer*, 305–307. For a biographical study of the life and work of Nellie Campobello, see Matthews, *Nellie Campobello*. Published amidst the public outcry regarding Nellie's forced disappearance and death, Matthew's study denounces the lack of recognition of Campobello's work as well as the lack of accountability for her disappearance. The study traces Campobello's participation in the institutionalization of dance in Mexico as well as the publication of her fictional and nonfictional work. See also Vargas Valdés and García Rufino, *Nellie Campobello*, the most recent and thorough biographical account of Campobello's life.

31. Aulestia and Campobello, "Entrevista con Nellie Campobello." Transcription by Felipe Segura; my translation. I found out about the existence of the interview via rumors and hearsay, and Margarita Tortajada Quiroz confirmed its existence. I managed to get a transcription from the historian Jesús Vargas, who has published the most extensive work documenting Nellie's life, and eventually obtained a digital copy at the historical archive of the Escuela Nacional de Danza de Nellie y Gloria Campobello, Fondo Nellie Campobello. The interview had been transcribed by Felipe Segura on February 19, 1990. I thank Jesús Vargas, Flor García, and Dafne Dominguez for helping me access these materials.

32. Muñoz, *Cruising Utopia*, 65. By thinking about the voice as a site of embodied memory, I attend to the "ephemeral" legacy of Campobello's dance career. Its queer potentiality is, as Muñoz argues of queer futurity, all the more poignant and enduring for "being visible only in the horizon" as another time and space that always haunts the here and now in order to access and assess her legacy (Muñoz, 11).

33. In an unpublished short essay, the literary scholar Sandra Cypess recounts her encounter with Nellie Campobello in 1975, when Campobello danced

for Cypess and her husband the steps and movements of various Indigenous groups in Mexico. It is in moments like these that a kinesthetic memory of Campobello is conjured and literally set in motion. Emmanuel Carballo introduced them to Nellie Campobello (personal communication with Cypess). Carmen Madrigal evokes a similar instance in a short interview published in 1938. See Madrigal, "La charla y la danza."

34. Vargas Valdés and García Rufino, *Nellie Campobello*, 73. Her mother was Rafaela Luna, who maintained a romantic relationship with her nephew, Felipe de Jesús Moya (possibly Nellie's real father). Throughout her life, Nellie suggested different dates for her birthday, including November 7, 1909, in her well-known interview with Emmanuel Carballo in 1965. Carballo, *Protagonistas de la literatura mexicana*, 378.

35. Vargas Valdés and García Rufino, *Nellie Campobello*, 84. Nellie claimed that Gloria's father was a British or American doctor named Ernest Stephen Campbell Reed. Tortajada Quiroz, *Frutos de mujer*, 303.

36. "Aplaudidos en el Centro Asturiano anoche Los Charros de Mondragón."

37. "Las hermanas Campobello." I thank Roman Santillan for helping me locate these periodicals and sharing them with me.

38. Campobello, *Mis libros*, 29.

39. Matthews, *Nellie Campobello*, 72.

40. Bidault de la Calle, *Nellie Campobello*, 125.

41. Bidault de la Calle, 125–126.

42. Carballo, *Protagonistas de la literatura mexicana*, 381.

43. In an interview published in 1938 in *Hoy*, Nellie Campobello emphatically refused to be adorned as a doll with makeup, clothes, and jewelry. She perceived herself as a combative, cultural revolutionary ready to serve her country, with a strengthened body and a courageous spirit. See Madrigal, "La charla y la danza."

44. Tortajada Quiroz, *Danza y poder*, 44.

45. Del Río, "Nellie y Gloria Campobello," 29.

46. Snow, *Revolution in Movement*, 67–68. See also Toor, "Old and New Jarabe," 26, 34.

47. Snow, *Revolution in Movement*, 178.

48. Fiol-Matta, *Queer Mother for the Nation*, xv.

49. Festivals became essential to mobilizing communities and families in support of the nation. Teachers, as Mary Kay Vaughan observes, "excelled in festival-related skills: teaching dances, oratory, making costumes, staging skits," instilling values and teaching new skills. Vaughan, *Cultural Politics in Revolution*, 99.

50. It has nevertheless been neglected in historical studies of the period; Mary Louise Pratt speculates that this may be in part the result of the ephemeral quality of dance, especially during the period prior to video recording, and the fact that it was the only artistic field dominated by women. Pratt, "Mi cigarro," 268.

51. Vaughan, "Introduction," 23.

52. I discuss the inauguration of the National Stadium in the introduction. In the 1920s, Vasconcelos divided the SEP (Ministry of Education) into three

major departments: schools, libraries and archives, and fine arts. His pedagogical and cultural project, as explained previously, was meant to educate
the general public, including those living in the countryside and Indigenous
communities, while popularizing the arts, with an emphasis on performance
arts. It aimed to democratize Mexico. According to Matthews, it served a
triple purpose: literary, artistic, and pedagogical. Matthews, *Nellie Campobello*, 70. Nellie Campobello embodied all three purposes.

53. Carbajal Segura, "El nacionalismo en transición," 137.
54. The Mexican dance scholar Sophie Bidault similarly considers the foundational role of public displays of dance to showcase a nationalist understanding of citizen formation. She reads these massive nationalist demonstrations
and collective enterprises as a "*gestus*": "Los espectáculos masivos nacieron
de la necesidad de crear ritos, gestos y formas; en términos brechtianos, un
gestus social y teatral que fuera la manifestación visible de un orden cósmico
superior alcanzado por la nación" (The massive spectacles were born out
of the necessity to create rites, gestures, and forms; in Brechtian terms, a
theatrical and social *gestus* as the visible manifestation of a superior cosmic
order reached by the nation). Bidault de la Calle, *Nellie Campobello*, 130.
55. Bidault de la Calle, *Nellie Campobello*, 133. For a thorough and recent
analysis of such massive choreographies and spectacles in Mexico, see
Carbajal Segura, "Los espectáculos masivos." To my knowledge, Carbajal's
work is the only such study ever done on the subject.
56. Bidault de la Calle, *Nellie Campobello*, 107. The influence of foreign cultural
models of femininity, particularly from the United States and Europe, led to
the constant policing of female sexuality and racialized gender roles. Some
of the titles that explore the cultural shifts in views of femininity, women's
bodies, and gender performance in postrevolutionary Mexico include Hershfield, *Imagining la Chica Moderna*; Sluis, *Deco Body, Deco City*; Varner,
La Raza Cosmética; and the critical volume edited by Olcott, Vaughan, and
Cano, *Sex in Revolution*.
57. See Parra, *Writing Pancho Villa's Revolution,* for a discussion of the literary
representation of Villa and his influence on Mexican literary production,
including the work of Campobello. For a thorough historical discussion of
the life and legacy of Pancho Villa, see Katz, *Life and Times of Pancho Villa.*
58. Tortajada Quiroz, *Frutos de mujer*, 315.
59. Aulestia and Campobello, "Entrevista con Nellie Campobello."
60. It is notable that the "Marcha de Zacatecas" was the opening number of
the Mexican show by the Charros de Mondragón in Cuba, where Nellie
and Gloria Campobello debuted abroad as dancers in July 1929. For the
complete program, listing the numbers interpreted by the Campobellos, see
"Aplaudidos en el Centro Asturiano."
61. This is almost certainly a reference to the US dancers and choreographers
Anna Sokolow and Waldeen Falkenstein, who arrived in Mexico in 1939
invited by Celestino Gorostiza, chief of the Departamento de Bellas Artes, to
perform and then promote modern dance in Mexico. Carlos Mérida advocated for the expansion of the Graham technique to foster the development
of Mexican theatrical dance and the consolidation of a socially engaged

choreography. In contrast to modern dance and the Graham technique, the Campobellos embraced ballet and Mexican regional and traditional dances. For two excellent studies of the impact of Sokolow's and Falkenstein's work in the establishment and dissemination of Mexican modern dance, see Tortajada Quiroz, *Frutos de mujer*, 383–474, and Snow, *Revolution in Movement*, 142–170. See also Reynoso, "Choreographing Politics, Dancing Modernity."

62. Hamera, *Dancing Communities*, 20.
63. See Vaughan, *Cultural Politics in Revolution*, for a thorough study of the role that rural schools and teachers played in state efforts to modernize communities by translating policies into sets of embodied behaviors, values, and skills.
64. Martínez, "Archives, Bodies, and Imagination," 172. Here I build on María Elena Martínez's invitation to attend to "the experiential knowledge lodged in our bodies and minds" while grappling with archival work.
65. Guerrero, *Dance and the Arts in Mexico*, 102.
66. Tortajada Quiroz, *Frutos de mujer*, 317.
67. Carbajal Segura, "El nacionalismo en transición," 187–190. In fact, the civic celebration of the *Día del Soldado* (Soldiers Day) was inaugurated in 1935. Having been part of the military himself, Cárdenas maintained good relationships with the armed forces and incorporated them into his public agenda. Women also saw an increased mobilization to promote women's suffrage during his presidency, and Cárdenas integrated some women's movements as part of the restructuring of his political party, the Partido Nacional Revolucionario (PNR).
68. Burt, *Alien Bodies*, 106–112; Carbajal Segura, "El nacionalismo en transición," 173–178. Both Burt and Carbajal allude to the "aestheticizing" of politics and the deployment of art for propagandistic purposes, citing Walter Benjamin. A discussion of such a complex process is beyond the scope of this chapter. However, Burt asks us not to readily discard or reduce such forms of body culture and embodied performances as propagandistic art. Instead, he suggests that we reframe the "continuities between the subjective experience of embodiment and politics as ethics" in order to better understand the social construction and material experience of embodiment (Burt, *Alien Bodies*, 105).
69. Hewitt, *Social Choreography*, 12.
70. Quoted in Segura, *Gloria Campobello*, 23.
71. Reynoso, "Choreographing Politics, Dancing Modernity," 194. In his insightful analysis of the *30–30*, Reynoso emphasizes how the mass ballet sought to embody revolutionary ideals, produce modern subjects, and mobilize peasants and workers in the context of universal industrialization and modernity.
72. Hamera, *Dancing Communities*, 19–20. Here I draw from Hamera's generative theorization of dance technique as a "relational infrastructure," "template for sociality," and "communicative and interpretative convention" to render the dancing body "intelligible" within a particular community.

73. Aulestia and Campobello, "Entrevista con Nellie Campobello."
74. Tortajada Quiroz, *Frutos de mujer*, 317.
75. Ramos Villalobos, *Una mirada a la formación dancística mexicana*, 74.
76. Quoted in Ramos, *Una mirada a la formación dancística mexicana*, 74–75.
77. Tortajada Quiroz, *Danza y poder*, 67.
78. Tortajada Quiroz, 69. See also Carbajal Segura, "El nacionalismo en transición," for an abbreviated history of the creation of the Escuela de Plástica Dinámica, Escuela de Danza, and the Escuela Nacional de Danza, including the decision to name the painter Carlos Mérida as its first director due to the supposed lack of technical and administrative skills of dancers. Snow similarly presents an abbreviated history of the emergence and consolidation of a Mexican school of dance. *Revolution in Movement*, 116–141.
79. Mérida, *Escritos de Carlos Mérida sobre el arte*, 130. Judith Sierra-Rivera discusses the role of Carlos Mérida and his influence on the development of a Mexican aesthetics, material culture, indigeneity, and art. Sierra-Rivera, "Carlos Mérida's 'Goce Emocional.'"
80. Mérida, *Escritos de Carlos Mérida sobre el arte*, 130.
81. Mérida, 140.
82. Mérida, 142.
83. Snow, *Revolution in Movement*, 130; Carbajal Segura, "El nacionalismo en transición," 105–106.
84. Snow, *Revolution in Movement*, 136.
85. Mérida, *Escritos de Carlos Mérida sobre el arte*, 53–63; Carbajal Segura, "El nacionalismo en transición," 111–122. Snow mentions that around seventy dances were documented during Mérida's tenure. Together with Francisco Domínguez, Mérida created the Laboratorio de Ritmos Plásticos (Laboratory of Plastic Rhythms) to "create a mixture of indigenous forms and contemporary expressions" (Snow, *Revolution in Movement*, 132). Domínguez was also working with Carlos Chávez to record Mexico's musical repertoire.
86. Tortajada Quiroz, *Frutos de mujer*, 325; Snow, *Revolution in Movement*, 135.
87. Ramos Villalobos, *Una mirada a la formación dancística mexicana*, 120–126.
88. Tortajada Quiroz, *Frutos de mujer*, 330.
89. See the official school records written on July 8, 1937, *Archivo Histórico de la Escuela Nacional de Danza Nellie y Gloria Campobello (AHENDGyNC). Fondo Nellie Campobello*. I thank Fernando Aragón, former director at the Escuela Nacional de Danza Nellie y Gloria Campobello, for allowing me to consult the official records at the school and Dafne Domínguez for helping me locate this official letter and other important documents describing Nellie's tenure as its director.
90. Ramos Villalobos, *Una mirada a la formación dancística mexicana*, 138. For a detailed account of the emergence and development of a Mexican school of dance, its curricular reforms, and key players, see Ramos Villalobos.
91. Desmond, "Introduction," 2.
92. Desmond, 19.
93. For a critical analysis of Sokolow and Falkenstein's contribution to the development of Mexican dance, see Tortajada Quiroz, *Frutos de mujer*. See also

Snow, *Revolution in Movement*, and Reynoso, "Choreographing Politics, Dancing Modernity."

94. Tortajada Quiroz, *Frutos de mujer*, 339.
95. Campobello and Campobello, *Ritmos indígenas de Mexico*, 7.
96. Campobello and Campobello, 8.
97. Snow, *Revolution in Movement*, 119. Snow contends that in the case of the Laban method, decades passed before Mexican dancers and choreographers were properly trained to use it. Kirstein's *Ballet Alphabet* similarly included drawings by Paul Cadmus, illustrating ballet positions and pirouettes. Given that it was published in late 1939, I doubt that the Campobellos were able to familiarize themselves with it. I concur with Snow and Carbajal Segura that *Ritmos indígenas* responded to and evolved from the choreographic research and documentation of Indigenous and mestizo dances launched by Mérida and the misiones culturales (Snow, 32; Carbajal Segura, "El nacionalismo en transición," 155). For a recent and excellent analysis of the legacy of Lincoln Kirstein in the development of modern American dance and arts and the circulation of Latin American artistic works in the United States, see Friedman and Hauptman, *Lincoln Kirstein's Modern*.
98. Campobello and Campobello, *Ritmos indígenas de Mexico*, 10.
99. Bidault de la Calle, *Nellie Campobello*, 156–158.
100. Campobello and Campobello, *Ritmos indígenas de Mexico*, 12.
101. Campobello and Campobello, 12. In the same interview with Patricia Aulestia, Nellie reflects further on the creation of their dances and choreographies based on Indigenous rhythms. She affirms that she strategically mobilized her knowledge of Mexican Indigenous kinesis to police artistic creation and creators. Nellie also affirms that she is the embodiment of dance technique. Aulestia and Campobello, "Entrevista con Nellie Campobello."
102. Bidault de la Calle, *Nellie Campobello*, 123–126, 129.
103. Campobello and Campobello, *Ritmos indígenas de Mexico*, 8.
104. Tarica, *Inner Life of Mestizo Nationalism*, 139.
105. Tarica, 180–181. "Indigeneity" as a shared marker of nationalism became the dominant trope in narrating the nation. Tarica refers to this sense of indigeneity as "the whole symbolic complex erected by modernizing intellectuals who established that nationality is a form of nativism, of being native to the land, yet constructed that land as a site of barbarity that exerts a negative force on its habitants [which] must be tamed and civilized if they are to become properly national" (*Inner Life of Mestizo Nationalism*, 148).
106. Campobello and Campobello, *Ritmos indígenas de Mexico*, 12.
107. Tortajada Quiroz, *Frutos de mujer*, 340.
108. Campobello and Campobello, *Ritmos indígenas de Mexico*, 13.
109. This is not unlike what Richard Schechner would propose years later, asking to pay attention not only to the cognitive and experiential but also to the kinesthetic when conducting ethnographic work: "How about emphasizing not only the cognitive and experiential aspects of the ethnographies

enacted but also the kinesthetic—how the body is handled, held, restrained, released? This would put into the bodies of the student performers a living sense of what it is to move 'as if' one were the other" (Schechner, *Between Theater and Anthropology*, 31).

110. With *performance ethnography*, I refer to Conquergood's engagement with performance events and fieldwork as a "performative co-witness" in order to "focus on issues of embodiment and the body itself as sources and sites of meaning in ethnographic field research and as a way to privilege performance as a legitimate and *ethical* method." Johnson, "Introduction," 8, emphasis in original.

111. Noland, *Agency and Embodiment*, 190.

112. Campobello and Campobello, *Ritmos indígenas de Mexico*, 157, 159.

113. After all, the analysis of the Yaqui deer dance by Schechner was crucial to the emergence of performance studies. I thank my anonymous reviewer for bringing this matter to my attention. Schechner used the Yaqui dance to theorize the multiple and ambivalent identities at play—the "contingent existence" or even coexistence of selves—that lead to the "transformation of being and/or consciousness" during a performance/ritual event. Schechner, *Between Theater and Anthropology*, 4–7, 12–14.

114. It is unclear who made the musical notations.

115. Campobello, *Mis libros*, 261.

116. Campobello, 39.

117. Castro Ricalde reads Campobello's dance career more in line with social trends of the period, which led to the attenuation of the literary "radical transformations" and "transgressiveness" of her work. She claims that Campobello's career served to illustrate how women writers, particularly María Luisa Ocampo and Nellie Campobello, bring to the fore "the rejection of their transgressivenes in the world of literature, among other issues, and their relegation to agreed symbolic spaces where public recognition served to reinforce dominant morals such as the existence of 'modern,' educated and educating women." Castro Ricalde, "Women Writers in the Revolution: Regional Socialist Realism," 223. However, as I demonstrate in this chapter, I read Mexican dance and Nellie's contribution to this cultural field as contested terrain.

118. For a concise article on the forced disappearance and death of Nellie Campobello, see Manzanos, "La historia de terror." See also Vargas Valdés and García Rufino, *Nellie Campobello*; Poniatowska, *Las siete cabritas*. In her article, Manzanos states that Claudio Fuentes was sentenced to twenty-seven years in prison in 1999, along with Enrique Fuentes León. However, they were both released in 2001 by Mexico City's District Court. María Cristina Belmont became a fugitive and has not been located since.

Chapter 4: Cinematic Renditions of a Dancing Mexico

1. A.F.B. are the initials of Adolfo Fernández Bustamante, who wrote regularly for the weekly *El Ilustrado* or *El Universal Ilustrado*, as it is more commonly

known. Fernández Bustamante first documented Eisenstein's work in Mexico in a series of articles published in June 1931, which also included "Lo que en México hace Einsenstein [sic]" (What Eisenstein Does in Mexico) and "Los indios del señor Einsenstein [sic]" (The Indians of Mister Eisenstein). He later denounced the poor management of Hunter S. Kimbrough and the intention of Upton Sinclair, the principal financial sponsor of the film, to sell it in fragments, unfinished, and unedited by Eisenstein.

2. Fernández Bustamante, "Einsenstein, el magnífico," 25, 47.

3. Schroeder Rodríguez, *Latin American Cinema*, 44. For Paul A. Schroeder Rodríguez, it is precisely the documentary quality of the silent period of Latin American cinema that helped to consolidate "national cinematic landscapes."

4. Serna, *Making Cinelandia*, 2.

5. Serna, 14. For a thorough discussion of moviegoing practices, exhibition, and American cinema in Mexico during the 1920s, see Serna.

6. Salazkina, *In Excess*, 139.

7. Karetnikova and Steinmetz, *Mexico according to Eisenstein*, 137.

8. Karetnikova and Steinmetz, *Mexico according to Eisenstein*, 138.

9. Arce, *México's Nobodies*, 257–272.

10. Some of the titles include Irwin and Ricalde, *Global Mexican Cinema*; Hershfield, *Mexican Cinema/Mexican Woman*; Maciel and Hershfield, *Mexico's Cinema*; de la Mora, *Cinemachismo*; Mora, *Mexican Cinema*; Dever, *Celluloid Nationalism*; Avila, *Cinesonidos*; García Riera, *Historia documental del cine mexicano;* Ayala Blanco, *La aventura del cine mexicano;* de los Reyes, *Medio siglo de cine mexicano;* Monsiváis and Bonfil, *A través del espejo*; García Blizzard, *White Indians of Mexican Cinema*.

11. See Irwin and Ricalde, *Global Mexican Cinema*; Noriega, Ricci, and UCLA Film and Television Archive, *Mexican Cinema Project,* particularly López, "Cinema for the Continent." Schroeder Rodríguez, *Latin American Cinema*, offers a comparative analysis of the emergence, development, and impact of cinema in the region, with particular attention to Mexico, Brazil, and Argentina vis-à-vis Hollywood and Europe.

12. For a concise and insightful account of the impact of cinema in Mexico, its status as a "continuation of everyday life," and its relationship with the increasing urbanization, modernization, and circulation of popular culture, see Monsiváis, "Mexican Cinema."

13. Noble, *Mexican National Cinema*, 11.

14. For an excellent analysis on the significance of the sensorium, embodied cognition, perception, and politics through "sense work" in Latin America, see Masiello, *Senses of Democracy*.

15. In *Struggles for Recognition*, Juan Sebastián Ospina León charts the development of contingent and multiple modernities in Latin America and the concomitant role that melodrama as a visual regime played in capturing and negotiating the ever-changing experience of the modern. See Ospina León, *Struggles for Recognition*.

16. Ospina León, 9.

17. Burt and Huxley, *Dance, Modernism, and Modernity*, 6. See also Armstrong, *Modernism, Technology, and the Body*, for a discussion of how technology

at once enhanced and fragmented the body vis-à-vis its experience of modernity and its concomitant modernist representations through literary and cultural production.

18. See Folgarait, *Mural Painting and Social Revolution in Mexico*, and Coffey, *How a Revolutionary Art Became Official Culture*, for a discussion of the emergence, circulation, and impact of mural painting in Mexico. See also Haskell, *Vida Americana*, for an excellent analysis of the impact Mexican muralism had in the United States.

19. For a thorough analysis of the intricate connection between graphics, calendar production, and the Mexican Golden Age cinema, see Castro Ricalde, "Préstamos e intercambios"; see Serna, *Making Cinelandia*, for a description of exhibition practices outside Mexico City during the 1920s.

20. Noble, *Mexican National Cinema*, 133.

21. According to Carlos Monsiváis, Eisenstein's unfinished film became an "obligatory model" for Mexican filmmakers (*Historia mínima de la cultura mexicana*, 315). In some ways, Eisenstein's film circulated as a sort of "mythical point of origin" of Mexico's cinematography (Noble, *Mexican National Cinema*, 127). This is particularly true for what eventually became known as the Mexicanist school of cinema, *escuela mexicana*, which "synthesized Hollywood melodrama and Mexican muralism [via Eisenstein's unfinished film] into an indigenist national mythology" characteristic of the films of Emilio Fernández and Gabriel Figueroa. For film scholar Paul A. Schroeder Rodríguez, from Eisenstein, "whose rushes and stills from *¡Que viva México!* Fernández and Figueroa closely studied, the team adopted the framing of indigenous subjects as organic elements of the natural landscape, though not the film's dialectical montage within and between shots, or its Marxist historiography" (*Latin American Cinema*, 103).

22. Aurelio de los Reyes carefully traces Eisenstein's relationship with Mexico in *El nacimiento de ¡Que viva México!* De los Reyes documents Eisenstein's interest in Mexico prior to his encounter with Diego Rivera in Moscow in 1927 as it had been reported. He claims that the Russian director probably became intrigued with Mexico after reading about the Day of the Dead in a German magazine between 1926 and 1927 (41), even though he had already participated in the production of Jack London's *The Mexican*. According to de los Reyes, Eisenstein maintained that it was the Day of the Dead or rather "lo que yo sabía sobre él, lo que en mis años adultos me llenó de pasión mucho antes de haber tenido la oportunidad de visitar México" (what I knew about it, which during my adult years filled me with passion long before I had the opportunity to visit Mexico) (qtd. in de los Reyes 39).

23. De los Reyes, *El nacimiento de ¡Que viva México!,* 321. *Thunder Over Mexico* was sponsored by Upton Sinclair, allegedly based on Eisenstein's script, but was vehemently denounced by the editors of *Experimental Cinema* in the United States and by Agustín Aragón Leiva in Mexico.

24. Aragón Leiva, "Eisenstein's Film on Mexico," 6.

25. For a series of the various reports Adolfo Best Maugard sent to José Manuel Puig y Casaurranc, in charge of the Ministry of Public Education, see de los

Reyes, "Informes de Adolfo Best Maugard"; de los Reyes, *El nacimiento de ¡Que viva México!* Best Maugard too published his own description of the film in 1932 after traveling with Eisenstein for several months, titled "Mexico into Cinema." He contended that Eisenstein was "making the first cinema story of that country encompassing thousands of years of Mexican life from one end of Mexico to the other." Due to the innovative cinematic techniques, Best Maugard went on to describe it as "symphonic cinema." Best Maugard, "Mexico Into Cinema," 926–927.

26. De los Reyes, "Informes de Adolfo Best Maugard," 166.
27. Kahlo's intimist and self-referential work could not contrast more profoundly with the kind of *typages* that dominated the work of the Russian film producer. Karetnikova and Steinmetz, *Mexico according to Eisenstein*, 13.
28. Karetnikova and Steinmetz, 13.
29. Karetnikova and Steinmetz, 13.
30. In her excellent analysis of postrevolutionary Mexican art, Tatiana Flores recasts the Mexican avant-garde beyond expressions of nationalism and social realism in order to consider how Mexican artists and intellectuals defined, engaged, and challenged hegemonic constructions of Western modernism and modernity. See Flores, *Mexico's Revolutionary Avant-Gardes.*
31. Salazkina, *In Excess*, 6.
32. De los Reyes, *El nacimiento de ¡Que viva México!*, 36.
33. Salazkina, *In Excess*, 7.
34. Salazkina, 7.
35. De los Reyes reminds us that while in Mexico he published "The Cinematographic Principle and Japanese Culture with a Digression on Montage and the Shot." De los Reyes, *El nacimiento de ¡Que viva México!*, 36.
36. In "A Dialectic Approach to Film Form," Eisenstein describes one of the most iconic film sequences of an intellectual montage in his acclaimed film *October* (1927), where he set out to capture the conflict between the concept of God and its symbolic rendition. The film sequence showcases a series of images that denoted God or the divine, attempting "to achieve a purely intellectual resolution, resulting from a conflict between a preconception and a *gradual discrediting of it in purposeful steps.*" Eisenstein, *Film Form*, 62.
37. Eisenstein theorizes his intellectual montage as the result of a double movement: the representation of something "graphically unrepresentable" and, perhaps more important than the final product, the process through which such an operation took place. He destabilizes the concrete references to the divine, i.e., its "representable." In gesturing toward an "intellectual resolution" of the undoing of the concept of the divine via an intellectual montage, Eisenstein invites the audience to re/configure such a notion. For a critical study of Eisenstein's cinematic theory and practice, see Bordwell, *Cinema of Eisenstein*; Salazkina, *In Excess,* for an insightful discussion of his work in Mexico.
38. Karetnikova and Steinmetz, *Mexico according to Eisenstein,* 39. For the voice-over, I use the text in English reprinted by Karetnikova and Steinmetz, *Mexico according to Eisenstein.*
39. Karetnikova and Steinmetz, *Mexico according to Eisenstein,* 39.

40. Eisenstein, *Film Form*, 30. Eisenstein's theorization of the ideogram as the product of two "representables" that transcended the referents from which it was created to gesture toward another reality played a key role in his cinematographic praxis. His description of this procedure captures what is at play and at stake for the Russian director: "It is exactly what we do in cinema, combining shots that are *depictive*, single in meaning, neutral in content—into *intellectual* contexts and series. This is a means and method inevitable in any cinematographic exposition. And, in a condensed and purified form, the starting point for the 'intellectual cinema.'"
41. Karetnikova and Steinmetz, *Mexico according to Eisenstein*, 39.
42. Salazkina, *In Excess*, 39.
43. Quoted in Karetnikova and Steinmetz, *Mexico according to Eisenstein*, 19.
44. See Snow's discussion of the configuration of Mexican aesthetics vis-à-vis indigeneity and indigenismo, particularly the section "How Indigenous Should a Modern Nationalist Culture Be?" Snow, *Revolution in Movement*, 25–35.
45. Avila, *Cinesonidos*, 122–123.
46. Podalsky, "Patterns of the Primitive," 29.
47. Podalsky, 34–35.
48. See Maffie, *Aztec Philosophy*, for a discussion of the role of movement or motion in Mesoamerican thought. See also Toriz Proenza, *La fiesta prehispánica*, for a comparative study of Mesoamerican Indigenous festivities.
49. Salazkina, *In Excess*, 52.
50. Salazkina, 52.
51. Fernández Bustamante, "Lo que en México hace Einsenstein," 25.
52. De los Reyes, "Informes de Adolfo Best Maugard," 167–168.
53. Salazkina contends that, just like "Sandunga," "Soldadera" would have been sonically framed by the traditional revolutionary song of "La Adelita" at the suggestion of Best Maugard. Salazkina, *In Excess*, 33. I am also inclined to support this argument based on Best Maugard's reports of his travels with Eisenstein. Furthermore, as discussed in chapter 2, Best Maugard had already privileged and praised the figure of the Tehuana as an icon of Mexican Indigenous femininity.
54. See García Blizzard, *White Indians of Mexican Cinema*, for an astute analysis of the depiction of white actors as Indigenous Mexicans in film during the Golden Age of Mexican cinema.
55. For an ethnographic and historical study of the muxes, see Mirandé, *Behind the Mask*.
56. Salazkina similarly advances that the centrality of this novella lies on women's bodies (65), which is also true for the "Epilogue." And yet she soon drops the emphasis on the body and racialized kinesis, which are central to my argument, particularly in the "Epilogue," which incorporates Afro-Cuban dancing and which I discuss later in this chapter. See Salazkina, *In Excess*, and de los Reyes, *El nacimiento de ¡Que viva México!*, which provide acute analyses of Eisenstein's unfinished work.
57. Podalsky, "Patterns of the Primitive," 32–33.
58. De los Reyes, *El nacimiento de ¡Que viva México!*, 167–169.

59. De los Reyes, "Informes de Adolfo Best Maugard," 167.
60. De los Reyes, 168.
61. In fact, Hunter Kimbrough, executive producer of the film, in a letter to Upton Sinclair, his brother-in-law, shared that the crew members were threatened by men who thought the movie cameras could allow them to see through women's clothing. Geduld and Gottesman, *Sergei Eisenstein and Upton Sinclair*, 53.
62. Hershfield, "Paradise Regained," 57. Avila similarly describes Eisenstein's film as a "fictional ethnography," whose film form "borders on pseudo-documentary with a fictional narrative structure" (Avila, *Cinesonidos*, 122–123).
63. Salazkina, *In Excess*, 63. Eisenstein was certainly in dialogue with ethnodocumentary filmmaking. In fact, it was the ethnodocumentarian Robert Flaherty himself, director of *Nanook of the North*, who encouraged Eisenstein to make a movie about Mexico. According to de los Reyes, Flaherty had visited Mexico in 1928 and established a connection with no other than Adolfo Best Maugard. He even gave a letter of recommendation to Eisenstein to present to Best Maugard. De los Reyes, *El nacimiento de ¡Que viva México! de Serguei Eisenstein*, 80–82.
64. De los Reyes, "Informes de Adolfo Best Maugard," 166–168. For a thorough description of the itinerary and inclusion of other reports and correspondence between Eisenstein and Upton Sinclair, see Geduld and Gottesman, *Sergei Eisenstein and Upton Sinclair*.
65. Blanco Borelli, *She Is Cuba*, 14.
66. Covarrubias, *Mexico South*, 258–262.
67. Salazkina, *In Excess*, 65.
68. Eisenstein and Alexandroff, "Que Viva Mexico!," 6.
69. Varner, *La Raza Cosmética*, 48.
70. Eisenstein and Alexandroff, "¡Que Viva Mexico!," 6.
71. Salazkina, *In Excess*, 56, 62.
72. Salazkina, 66.
73. Varner, *La Raza Cosmética*, 87.
74. Noble, *Mexican National Cinema*, 134.
75. Avila, *Cinesonidos*, 158. The *revista* genre incorporated several theatrical and popular traditions, such as Spanish zarzuela, burlesque, and the French revue. As Jacqueline Avila has demonstrated, revistas provided the theatrical language and narrative framework for early sound film, including folkloric elements, popular characters like the china poblana and charro, musical elements, and traditional backdrops or scenarios. See Avila, "El Espectáculo" for a discussion of the impact and influence of revistas in popular culture, early sound film, and conflicting representations of the nation and Mexican identity at home and abroad. I thank Juan Sebastián Ospina León for pointing out these connections.
76. A notable exception to this reading is Paul A. Schroeder Rodríguez, who reads the reactionary politics of the film as an example of corporative values or "corporatism that favors capital over labor and the preservation of class, race, and gender hierarchies." Schroeder Rodríguez, *Latin American Cinema*, 91.

77. For two excellent brief articles contextualizing *Allá en el Rancho Grande* within the national and transnational film industries and cinematic cultures, see López, "Cinema for the Continent"; D'Lugo, "Aural Identity." See also the introduction to Irwin and Ricalde, *Global Mexican Cinema*. For a discussion of the 170 films produced in Spanish in Hollywood at the time and the attendant "Latino audiovisual culture that reflected these films' places of production," see Jarvinen, "Mass Market for Spanish-Language Films."

78. D'Lugo, "Aural Identity," 172. D'Lugo traces the patriarchal and traditionalist theme back to the Argentinian and Spanish silent films *Nobleza gaucha* (Gaucho chivalry, 1915) and *Nobleza baturra* (Rustic chivalry, 1925, 1936), respectively.

79. Schroeder Rodríguez, *Latin American Cinema*, 82–87; Mora, *Mexican Cinema*, 47.

80. Ruy Sánchez, "El arte de Gabriel Figueroa," 7.

81. Here, I follow Mraz's definition of modern visual culture "as that produced by technical images and sounds: photography and cinema" (3). See his critical study on the consolidation of Mexico's visual modernity, from the circulation of *cartes de visite* and postcards to the configuration of a post-revolutionary visual culture through photography and cinema and their role in the production of a Mexican identity.

82. Gabara notes that portraiture and landscape were two important visual genres of modernism in Latin America. In fact, she goes on to claim that the "ethos of modernism is embodied as much as it is located: it pictures the ethics of inhabiting a place. These two concepts—locale and subjectivity—have been at the center of discourses of modernity, in claims of cosmopolitanism and regionalism as well as civilization and primitivism" (Gabara, *Errant Modernism*, 7). Rather than approaching modernist aesthetics through the lens of artistic purity and formalism, Gabara reframes them as a means of "formal intervention into the forms of everyday life" (6).

83. Legrás, *Culture and Revolution*, 144. For Legrás, photography adopted an "ontological function," as it "has to claim that reality is stable enough to be photographed while contributing to its stabilization" (Legrás, 147). In presenting the revolution as an "organizable" event, photography also introduced the popular body as a subject in its own right. See Legrás, *Culture and Revolution*.

84. Perhaps the most iconic film of the fusion between the landscape and the subject/rostro and the primacy of the image is *María Candelaria*, which portrays the story of an image of an Indigenous woman and the attendant "looking relations" that "alternately promote identification with the characters on the screen and prevent such identification from taking place," as Andrea Noble perceptively describes it. Noble, *Mexican National Cinema*, 88.

85. Mitchell, "Imperial Landscape," 2. For Mitchell, a landscape "naturalizes a cultural and social construction, representing an artificial world as if it were simply given and inevitable, and it also makes that representation operational by interpellating its beholder in some more or less determinate relation to its givenness as sight and site."

86. In his excellent study of modern visual culture in Mexico, Mraz characterizes Figueroa's cinematography as the combination of "extreme low-angle takes" with a "curvilinear perspective, deep-field focus, and infrared filters to produced what became known internationally as 'Figueroa's skies.'" Mraz, *Looking for Mexico*, 111.

87. Monsiváis, "Gabriel Figueroa," 45.

88. Fuentes, "Una flor carnivora," 15.

89. Fuentes, 15.

90. By aural identity, D'Lugo refers to "the chain of transformations, hybridizations and the general deterritorialization of songs and musical rhythms during the crucial first two decades of the sound period" of cinema. D'Lugo, "Aural Identity," 165.

91. D'Lugo, 164.

92. For a concise but detailed discussion of how the jarabe became popularized after Pavolova's interpretation in 1919 and its eventual incorporation as part of school curriculum and festivals, see Snow, *Revolution in Movement*, 65–69. See also Saldívar, *El Jarabe*, for a study of its history at the time and Vaughan, *Cultural Politics in Revolution*, for an analysis of the promotion of a national culture through folk dance, educational policy, and festivals. Avila traces the folkloric themes and performative elements in the revistas, which were eventually incorporated into synchronized sound film; see "El Espectáculo." Peña documents how "tapatío" dancers served to mark a sense of lo mexicano during the celebration of George Washington's birthday at the US-Mexico border. See "Playing Mexican," in Peña, *¡Viva George!*

93. López, "Of Rhythms and Borders," 312.

94. López, 340.

95. López, 312.

96. López, 310.

97. For an analysis on the reception of *Allá en el Rancho Grande* among the Mexican diaspora in the United States, see Garcia, "'Soul of a People.'"

98. See Avila for an excellent analysis of the musical duel between the two trios. Avila, *Cinesonidos*, 170–171.

99. See Ruiz for a discussion of how the zapateado has evolved, using this film sequence as one case study and translating it to Labanotation. Ruiz, "Writing Down the *Jarabe Tapatío*, from Tradition to Academia." I thank Mitchell Snow for sharing this reference with me.

100. Limón, *Dancing with the Devil*, 14.

101. Avila, *Cinesonidos*, 172.

102. Monsiváis and Bonfil, *A través del espejo*, 32.

103. I thank Juan Sebastián Ospina León for bringing this to my attention.

104. Popular entertainment was socially but not necessarily sexually diverse until the arrival of sound cinema, as López observes (López, "Tears and Desire," 152).

105. Raúl de Anda was a Mexican director, producer, screenwriter, and actor. He appeared in the productions of *Santa* (Moreno 1932) and *Águilas frente al sol* (Moreno 1932), two pioneering films of Mexican sound cinema, as

well as in de Fuentes's *El prisionero 13* (1933) and ¡*Vámonos con Pancho Villa!* (1935). He then debuted as a director with *La tierra del mariachi* (1937). *El charro negro* (1940) was one of his first major hits, a film he wrote, directed, and starred.

106. López proposes to consider the consolidation of melodrama and the gendered social positioning it promoted and disseminated, particularly through the figure of the "prostitute" as the "emblem of desire, necessary evil, and mother of the nation," i.e., an "idealized fallen woman" (López, "Tears and Desire," 159). See Avila's "The Prostitute and the Cinematic Cabaret: Musicalizing the 'Fallen Woman' and Mexico City's Nightlife" for a discussion of the cinematic development of the melodramatic trope of fallen woman that inaugurated synchronized-sound cinema, *Santa* (Antonio Moreno, 1932). Avila, *Cinesonidos*. For an excellent analysis of melodrama and prostitution, see also " 'Midnight Virgin:' Melodramas of Prostitution in Literature and Film," in de la Mora, *Cinemachismo*.

107. Gutiérrez, "Afrodiasporic Visual and Sonic Assemblages," 3. Emphasis in the original.

108. For an excellent analysis of this film and the broader context of the cine de rumberas, see Pulido Llano, *Mulatas y negros cubanos*, and Castro Ricalde, "Rumba Caliente Beats Foxtrot"; see also Gutiérrez, "Afrodiasporic Visual and Sonic Assemblages," for an astute analysis of rumba dancers in Mexican films.

109. For a concise description of the fandango as a mestizo, circum-Caribbean, festive celebration, see "El fandango veracruzano y las fiestas del Caribe" in Pérez Montfort, *Estampas de nacionalismo cultural mexicano*. See also "The Music of the Afro-Mexican Universe and the Dialectics of *Son*" for a discussion of Afromestizo musical imaginaries, particularly the son jarocho, in Arce, *México's Nobodies*.

110. Arce, *México's Nobodies*, 236.

111. Arce, 235.

112. Pérez Montfort claims that the word *fandango* derives from the Mandinka language *fanda* that means fiesta and also notes that others have argued that it comes from a Guinea word that also means fiesta. *Estampas de nacionalismo*, 34, 41.

113. In *Finding Afro-Mexico*, Cohen discusses the "Africanization of 'La bamba,' " from its Indigenous and Spanish origins to the acquisition of Black melodies, harmonies, and rhythms and its sonic associations with the Caribbean, particularly in the 1940s and 1950s. See "Africanizing 'La bamba,' " in Cohen, *Finding Afro-Mexico*. See also "El 'negro' y la negritud en la formación del estereotipo del jarocho durante los siglos XIX y XX" in Pérez Montfort, *Expresiones populares y estereotipos culturales en México*, for a historical discussion of the emergence and consolidation of a jarocho identity and its attendant popular expressions.

114. Arce, *México's Nobodies*, 238.

115. For a critical reflection about how *zapateado fandanguero* and jarocho continue to be a predominant element of the expressive cultures of the

Mexican diaspora and Chicanx popular performance, see González, "*Zapateado* Afro-Chicana *Fandango* Style."

116. Pulido Llano, *Mulatas y negros cubanos*, 123.
117. Here I draw from Madrid and Moore's definition of *cachondería*, which they define as "an experience of subdued lust, subtle sensuality" that oscillates between "uncritical pleasure" and "an experience of pleasure that allows for the subject's momentary repossession of his or her body beyond the constraints of disciplining discourses." Madrid and Moore, *Danzón*, 19. This experience of pleasure will be crucial later as María Antonia asserts her individuality and reclaims her body and bodily expressions.
118. Avila analyzes the literary and musical references to the danzón and its associations to the tropical, the exotic, and the sexualized and seductive power in the literary and cinematic adaptations of *Santa*; see "Danzón dedicated to Santita, the most beautiful woman in Mexico" in Avila, *Cinesonidos*, 44–49.
119. Madrid and Moore, *Danzón*, 5.
120. Madrid and Moore, 7.
121. *Negrita* (little Black girl) is meant as a term of endearment, though one that is racialized.
122. Pulido Llano, *Mulatas y negros cubanos*, 124.
123. Pulido Llano, 124.
124. In "Bad Neighbors: Pérez Prado, Cinema, and the Politics of Mambo," Borge notes that rumbera or *cabaretera* films did more than disseminate Spanish Caribbean music and dance. Combining the Hollywood musical with the Mexican melodrama, these films oscillated between the marks of Afro-Caribbean authenticity and US mass culture. Analyzing the critical role of cinematic mambo as a symbol of "new hybridity, social conflict, and even corruption," he contends that these performances capture the "(North) Americanization of Latin American cultural production" as well as the "temptation" and exoticism of transnational modernity, serving as a "refuge from the rigidity of conservative, insular models of Mexican identity" (276–277).
125. For an insightful and concise analysis of the role of the melodramatic in the configuration of Mexican cinema and its impact on gendered social formations, see López, "Tears and Desire." See also "The Prostitute and the Cinematic Cabaret" for a discussion of how on-screen cabarets reframe the social, cultural, and gender dynamics of off-screen cabaret and urban spaces from the time. Avila, *Cinesonidos*, 49–53.
126. López, "Tears and Desire," 160.
127. Blanco Borelli, *She Is Cuba*, 156. In her critical analysis of the mulata body, *She Is Cuba: A Genealogy of the Mulata Body*, Blanco Borelli theorizes the notion of "hip(g)nosis" to account for the ways mulatas produce and articulate knowledge through "embodied activity" to "contest the historical objectification while at the same time acknowledging the power and pleasure involved in wielding one's hips." Blanco Borelli, *She Is Cuba*, 13. The term combines and calls for the notion of hips, hypnotism, and gnosis.

128. Gutiérrez, "Afrodiasporic Visual and Sonic Assemblages," 3.
129. My use of "white-as-mulata" is indebted to Mónica García Blizzard's analysis of indigeneity in Mexican films. García Blizzard's construction of "white-as-indigenous" points toward the racialized representation of whiteness-as-indigeneity in order to create characters on screen who must be desired by audience members while upholding and maintaining whiteness as an unquestioned, racialized construct. See García Blizzard, *White Indians of Mexican Cinema*.
130. Pulido Llano, *Mulatas y negros cubanos*, 124.
131. Monsiváis, "Tongolele y el enriquecimiento de las buenas costumbres"; Arce, *México's Nobodies*, 231–235.
132. It is important to note that the musicians and singers that started to appear in these productions, such as Kiko Mendive himself, were already established and recognized in the nightlife of Mexico and Cuba. Borge discusses the case of Pérez Prado; see Borge, "Bad Neighbors."
133. Gutiérrez, "Afrodiasporic Visual and Sonic Assemblages," 3–4.
134. Gutiérrez, 13–15.
135. Castro Ricalde, "Rumberas, pero decentes," 73. Avila discusses the relationship between sexual work, the figure of the "prostitute," and their associations with cabarets. Avila, *Cinesonidos*, 24–30. I concur with Castro Ricalde's analysis that María Antonia in *La reina del trópico* is not portrayed as a "prostitute," nor is the cabaret associated with sexual work.
136. Castro Ricalde, "Rumberas, pero decentes," 85–86.
137. See Castro Ricalde, "Rumberas pero decentes," for an excellent analysis of the discursive and visual strategies rumba dancers María Antonieta Pons and Ninón Sevilla deployed to influence public opinion about their modern, exotic, and sensual cinematic personas in Mexico.
138. Gutiérrez, *Performing Mexicanidad*, 114.
139. Gutiérrez, "Afrodiasporic Visual and Sonic Assemblages"; Castro Ricalde, "Rumberas, pero decentes."
140. For an insightful and thorough study of La danza de los viejitos as a local, national, and transnational performative icon of lo mexicano and indigeneity, see Hellier-Tinoco, *Embodying Mexico*.
141. In López, *Unbecoming Blackness*, the author proposes the notion of "unbecoming" to refer to the process by which Afro-Cubans reconfigured their Black identities, once in the United States, by undoing their Cuban identity in order to become Afro-Latino. López, *Unbecoming Blackness*, 8. I follow López's theorization to refer to the complex process by which "white" Cuban rumberas engaged with and simultaneously disavowed their fraught relation to an Afro-Cuban identity in Mexico.
142. Castro Ricalde, "Rumba Caliente Beats Foxtrot," 57.
143. Salazkina, *In Excess*, 167–172.
144. Karetnikova and Steinmetz, *Mexico according to Eisenstein*, 137.
145. "Un gran artista," *El Universal Ilustrado*, December 24, 1931.
146. Salazkina, *In Excess*, 141.

147. "Dance Hall in Mexico City," in Karetnikova and Steinmetz, *Mexico according to Eisenstein*, 170.
148. Madrid and Moore, *Danzón*, 19.
149. Salazkina, *In Excess*; de los Reyes, *El nacimiento de ¡Que viva México!*.
150. Best Maugard, "Mexico into Cinema," 926–927.
151. Vargas, *Dissonant Divas*, x.
152. Salazkina, *In Excess*, 2.

Epilogue

1. Leonard, *Making Ethnic Choices*, 10, 112. In *Making Ethnic Choices*, Leonard discusses how Punjabi-Mexican families negotiated a biethnic identity with other communities of the Indian and Mexican diaspora and within their families, as well as the regional, generational, gender, and class differences. For a brief article discussing the history of this community, see Gottlieb, "Punjabi Sikh-Mexican American Community Fading into History."
2. Leonard, 214.
3. Blanco Borelli, *She Is Cuba*, 14. Here, I refer once again to Blanco Borelli's theorization of the term to "read the body along the social, cultural, and historical processes that shape it," that is, as "a lived body with experiences in the material world."
4. Palma Velasco, "El otro que no soy yo," 68. Palma Velasco builds on the work on "performative translation" by the Mexican dance scholar Hilda Islas. See Islas, *El juego de acercarse y alejarse*.
5. For a short article about *Half and Halves*, see Dirks, "Punjabi-Mexicans in California." For a short clip of the performance, see KQED Arts, "Dancers Honor California's Mexican-Punjabi Heritage."
6. See Conquergood, "Rethinking Ethnography."
7. Rivera-Servera, *Performing Queer Latinidad*, 18.
8. See Cuellar, "Manuel Cuellar on Dancing as Community Building," for a brief discussion of my intellectual and dance trajectories and how my scholarship combines both.
9. See Marino and Cuellar, "Fiesta Performance as Epistemology," for a discussion of this kind of work.
10. The recent realization of the *Cátedra Patrimonial Margarita Tortajada Quiroz*, "La composición coreográfica y la danza folclórica escenificada: abordajes y aproximaxiones," at the Universidad Autónoma del Estado de Hidalgo, Instituto de Artes, in June 2021, offered an excellent forum in which to learn and discuss the emergence, evolution, conceptualization, classification, practices, and choreographic production of Mexican folklórico, *danza folclórica escénica*. See Margarita Tortajada Quiroz, "Trazos de la obra coreográfica de Amalia Hernández" (lecture, Instituto de Artes, UAEH, June 7, 2021, youtube.com/watch?v=7EvBoCL0TiA&t=7s), for a discussion of the foundational role of Amalia Hernández in the consolidation of folklórico dance. See also Raúl Valdovinos García, "Conceptos, clasificaciones y categorías

aplicadas a la danza folclórica" (lecture, Instituto de Artes, UAEH, June, 7, 2021, youtube.com/watch?v=qcCaVJNynA8), and Carlos Jesús Nieves Ixtla, "Recuento histórico de la producción coreográfica de la danza folclórica escénica" (lecture, Instituto de Artes, UAEH, June 8, 2021, youtube.com /watch?v=1qWsPRaKFKg&t=239s), for two insightful analyses of the trajectory and approaches to folclórico, particularly in the second half of the twentieth century. An analysis of the foundational role of Amalia Hernández in the development of Mexican dance starting in the 1950s is beyond the scope of this work. See Jiménez et al., *Homenaje Una vida en la danza. Amalia Hernández.*

11. Some of the most prominent examples include the annual Danzantes Unidos Festival (danzantes.org); the Asociación Nacional de Grupos Folklóricos-ANGF Conference (ANGFdance.com); and the regular master classes in various states (CA, NY, IL, OK, UT) taught by Amalia Viviana Basanta Hernández, artistic director of the renowned Ballet Folklórico de México de Amalia Hernández (balletmx.com). In addition, there are hundreds of folklórico groups at local high schools, community colleges, and universities throughout the United States.

12. See, for example, the critical work of García, *Salsa Crossings*; Aparicio, *Listening to Salsa*; Flores, *Salsa Rising*; Quintero Rivera, *¡Salsa, sabor y control!*; and Quintero-Herencia, *La máquina de la salsa.*

13. See Mbembe, "Power of the Archive and Its Limits."

14. Quijano, "Coloniality of Power, Eurocentrism, and Latin America," 541.

15. Muñoz, *Cruising Utopia*, 65. As mentioned in chapter 1, Muñoz defines "queer evidence" as the "evidence that has been queered in relation to the laws of what counts as proof."

16. Muñoz, 9. For Muñoz, "unlike a possibility, a thing that simply might happen, a potentiality is a certain mode of nonbeing that is eminent, a thing that is present but not actually existing in the present tense."

17. Muñoz, 71–72.

18. Rivera Cusicanqui, "Ch'ixinakax utxiwa," 106, 96.

19. Buck-Morss, *Hegel, Haiti, and Universal History*, 110.

Bibliography

Adalpe Muñoz, Juan Manuel. "Choreotopias: Performance, State Violence, and the Near Past." PhD diss., University of California, Berkeley, 2020. escholarship.org/uc/item/08b9x7tp.

Aguilar Mora, Jorge. "El silencio de Nellie Campobello." In *Cartucho: Relatos de la lucha en el Norte de México*, by Nellie Campobello, 9–43. Mexico City: Ediciones Era, 2000.

Alonso, Ana M. "El 'mestizaje' en el espacio público: estatismo estético en el México posrevolucionario." In *Formaciones de indianidad: Articulaciones raciales, mestizaje y nación en América Latina*, edited by Marisol de la Cadena, 173–196. Bogotá, Colombia: Envión, 2007.

Alonso, Carlos J. *The Spanish American Regional Novel: Modernity and Autochthony*. Cambridge: Cambridge University Press, 1990.

Altamirano, Carlos. *Ensayos argentinos: de Sarmiento a la vanguardia*. Buenos Aires: Ariel, 1997.

Anda, Raúl de. *La reina del trópico*. 1946; Mexico City: Producciones Raúl de Anda, n.d. DVD.

"Anna Pavlowa." *El Universal* (Mexico City), March 27, 1919.

Anreus, Alejandro, Robin Adèle Greeley, and Leonard Folgarait. *Mexican Muralism: A Critical History*. Berkeley: University of California Press, 2012.

Aparicio, Frances R. *Listening to Salsa: Gender, Latin Popular Music, and Puerto Rican Cultures*. Middletown, CT: Wesleyan University Press, 2010.

"Aplaudidos en el Centro Asturiano anoche Los Charros de Mondragón." *Diario de la Marina* (Havana), July 31, 1929.

Appadurai, Arjun. *Modernity at Large: Cultural Dimensions of Globalization*. Minneapolis: University of Minnesota Press, 1996.

Appelbaum, Nancy P., Anne S. Macpherson, and Karin Alejandra Rosemblatt. *Race and Nation in Modern Latin America*. Chapel Hill: University of North Carolina Press, 2003.

Aragón Leiva, Agustín. "Eisenstein's Film on Mexico." *Experimental Cinema* 4 (1933): 5–6.

Arce, B. Christine. *México's Nobodies: The Cultural Legacy of the Soldadera and Afro-Mexican Women*. Albany, NY: SUNY Press, 2017.

Archivo Histórico de la Escuela Nacional de Danza Nellie y Gloria Campobello (AHENDGyNC). Fondo Nellie Campobello. Mexico City.

Armstrong, Tim. *Modernism, Technology, and the Body: A Cultural Study.* Cambridge: Cambridge University Press, 1998.

"Artistas nuestros que triunfan en el extranjero." *Revista de Revistas* (Mexico City), May 4, 1930.

Asad, Talal. "The Concept of Cultural Translation in British Social Anthropology." In *Writing Culture: The Poetics and Politics of Ethnography*, edited by James Clifford and George E. Marcus, 141–164. Berkeley: University of California Press, 1986.

Aulestia, Patricia. *Despertar de la república dancística mexicana.* Mexico City: Ríos de tinta, 2012.

———. *Historias alucinantes de un mundo ecléctico. La danza en México, 1910–1939.* Mexico City: Impresos Chávez, 2013.

———. *Las "chicas bien" de Miss Carroll: Estudio y Ballet Carroll (1923–1964).* Mexico City: Instituto Nacional de Bellas Artes y Literatura/Centro Nacional de Investigación, 2003.

Aulestia, Patricia, and Nellie Campobello. "Entrevista con Nellie Campobello," January 4, 1972. Archivo Histórico de la Escuela Nacional de Danza de Nellie y Gloria Campobello. Fondo Nellie Campobello. Mexico City.

Austerlitz, Paul. *Merengue: Dominican Music and Dominican Identity.* Philadelphia, PA: Temple University Press, 1997.

Avila, Jacqueline. *Cinesonidos: Film Music and National Identity During Mexico's Época de Oro.* New York: Oxford University Press, 2019.

———. "*El Espectáculo*: The Culture of the *Revistas* in Mexico City and Los Angeles, 1900–1940." In *Cinema between Latin America and Los Angeles: Origins to 1960*, edited by Colin Gunckel, Jan-Christopher Horak, and Lisa Jarvinen, 31–50. New Brunswick, NJ: Rutgers University Press, 2019.

Ayala Blanco, Jorge. *La aventura del cine mexicano: en la época de oro y después.* Mexico City: Editorial Grijalbo, 1993.

Bardas, Nicolás Isidro. "Impresiones sobre la pintura de Adolfo Best Maugard." *El Universal Ilustrado* (Mexico City), October 27, 1921.

Bartra, Roger, ed. *Anatomía del mexicano.* Mexico City: Random House Mondadori, 2006.

———. *La jaula de la melancolía. Identidad y metamorfosis del mexicano.* Mexico City: Random House Mondadori, 2007.

Beezley, William H., and David E. Lorey. ¡*Viva Mexico!* ¡*Viva La Independencia!: Celebrations of September 16.* Wilmington, DE: SR Books, 2001.

Beezley, William H., Cheryl English Martin, and William E. French. *Rituals of Rule, Rituals of Resistance: Public Celebrations and Popular Culture in Mexico.* Wilmington, DE: SR Books, 1994.

Berg, Charles Ramírez. *Cinema of Solitude: A Critical Study of Mexican Film, 1967–1983.* Austin: University of Texas Press, 1992.

Berlant, Lauren, and Michael Warner. "Sex in Public." *Critical Inquiry* 24, no. 2 (1998): 547–566.

Bermann, Sandra. *Nation, Language, and the Ethics of Translation.* Princeton, NJ: Princeton University Press, 2005.

Best Maugard, Adolfo. "Mexico into Cinema." *Theatre Arts Monthly* 16, no. 11 (November 1932): 926–933.

Beverley, John. *Subalternity and Representation: Arguments in Cultural Theory.* Durham, NC: Duke University Press, 1999.

Bhabha, Homi K. *The Location of Culture.* London: Routledge, 1994.

———. *Nation and Narration.* London: Routledge, 1990.

Bidault de la Calle, Sophie. *Nellie Campobello: Una escritura salida del cuerpo.* Mexico City: Instituto Nacional de Bellas Artes y Literatura, 2013.

Blanco Borelli, Melissa. *She Is Cuba: A Genealogy of the Mulata Body.* New York: Oxford University Press, 2016.

Bordwell, David. *The Cinema of Eisenstein.* New York: Taylor and Francis, 2020.

Borge, Jason. "Bad Neighbors: Pérez Prado, Cinema, and the Politics of Mambo." In *Cosmopolitan Film Cultures in Latin America, 1896–1960*, edited by Rielle Navitski and Nicolas Poppe, 269–292. Bloomington: Indiana University Press, 2017.

Brenner, Anita. *Idols Behind Altars.* New York: Paysón and Clark, 1929.

Browning, Barbara. *Samba: Resistance in Motion.* Bloomington: Indiana University Press, 1995.

Brune, Krista. *Creative Transformations: Travels and Translations of Brazil in the Americas.* Albany, NY: SUNY Press, 2020.

Brylak, Agnieska. "En busca del espectáculo prehispánico nahua en fiestas y representaciones teatrales coloniales." *Politeja* 6, no. 38 (2015): 17–34.

Buck-Morss, Susan. *Hegel, Haiti, and Universal History.* Pittsburgh, PA: University of Pittsburgh Press, 2009.

Burgett, Bruce, and Glenn Hendler. *Keywords for American Cultural Studies.* New York: New York University Press, 2007.

Burt, Ramsay. *Alien Bodies: Representations of Modernity, "Race" and Nation in Early Modern Dance.* London: Routledge, 1998.

Burt, Ramsay, and Michael Huxley. *Dance, Modernism, and Modernity.* New York: Routledge, Taylor and Francis, 2020.

Butler, Judith. *Bodies That Matter: On the Discursive Limits of "Sex."* New York: Routledge, 1993.

———. *The Psychic Life of Power: Theories in Subjection.* Stanford, CA: Stanford University Press, 1997.

———. *Undoing Gender.* New York: Routledge, 2004.

Cabranes-Grant, Leo. *From Scenarios to Networks: Performing the Intercultural in Colonial Mexico.* Evanston, IL: Northwestern University Press, 2016.

Campobello, Nellie. *Cartucho: Relatos de la lucha en el Norte de México.* Mexico City: Ediciones Era, 2000.

———. *Mis libros.* Chihuahua, Mexico: Secretaría de Educación y Cultura/Gobierno del Estado de Chihuahua, 2004.

Campobello, Nellie, and Gloria Campobello. *Ritmos indígenas de México.* Mexico City: Editora Popular, 1940.

Carbajal Segura, Claudia. "El nacionalismo en transición. La institucionalización de la danza de concierto en México. Debates ideológicos, artísticos y vínculos políticos." MA thesis, Universidad Nacional Autónoma de México, 2015.

———. "Los espectáculos masivos y las coreografías monumentales en la posrevolución mexicana 1924–1940." PhD diss., Universidad Nacional Autónoma de México, 2020.

Carballo, Emmanuel. *Protagonistas de la literatura mexicana*. Mexico City: Editorial Porrúa, 2003.

Carson, Margaret, Diana Taylor, and Sarah J. Townsend. *Stages of Conflict: A Critical Anthology of Latin American Theater and Performance*. Ann Arbor: University of Michigan Press, 2008.

Castro-Gómez, Santiago, and Edgardo Lander. *La colonialidad del saber: eurocentrismo y ciencias sociales: perspectivas latinoamericanas*. Buenos Aires: Consejo Latinoamericano de Ciencias Sociales-CLACSO, 2000.

Castro Ricalde, Maricruz. "Opacidad y transparencia del Caribe en las representaciones de Yucatán. Dos casos de cultura visual." *Historia Caribe* 15, no. 37 (2020): 119–150.

———. "Préstamos e intercambios: el cine de la Época de Oro en la gráfica popular mexicana." In *Mexican Transnational Cinema and Literature*, edited by Maricruz Castro Ricalde, Mauricio Díaz Calderón, and James Ramey, 103–121. Oxford, UK: Peter Lang, 2017.

———. "Rumba Caliente Beats Foxtrot: Cinematic Cultural Exchanges between Mexico and Cuba." In *Global Mexican Cinema: Its Golden Age: "el Cine Mexicano Se Impone,"* edited by Robert McKee Irwin and Maricruz Castro Ricalde, 35–64. London: Palgrave Macmillan, 2013.

———. "Rumberas, pero decentes: Intérpretes cubanas en el cine mexicano de la edad dorada." *Hispanic Research Journal* 21, no. 1 (2020): 70–89.

———. "Women Writers in the Revolution: Regional Socialist Realism." In *History of Latin American Women's Literature*, edited by Mónica Szurmuk and Ileana Rodríguez, 211–227. New York: Cambridge University Press, 2016.

Castro Ricalde, Maricruz, Mauricio Díaz Calderón, and James Ramey. *Mexican Transnational Cinema and Literature*. Oxford, UK: Peter Lang, 2017.

Certeau, Michel de. *The Practice of Everyday Life*. Berkeley: University of California Press, 1984.

Cervantes-Gómez, Xiomara Verenice. "*Paz's Pasivo*: Thinking Mexicanness from the Bottom." *Journal of Latin American Cultural Studies* 29, no. 3 (2020): 333–347.

Chasteen, John Charles. *National Rhythms, African Roots: The Deep History of Latin American Popular Dance*. Albuquerque: University of New Mexico Press, 2004.

Chávez, Alex E. *Sounds of Crossing: Music, Migration, and the Aural Poetics of Huapango Arribeño*. Durham, NC: Duke University Press, 2017.

Clayton, Michelle. "Modernism's Moving Bodies." *Modernist Cultures* 9, no. 1 (2014): 27–45.

———. "Touring History: Tórtola Valencia between Europe and the Americas." *Dance Research Journal* 44, no. 1 (2012): 28–49.

Coffey, Mary K. *How a Revolutionary Art Became Official Culture: Murals, Museums, and the Mexican State*. Durham, NC: Duke University Press, 2012.

Cohen, Theodore W. *Finding Afro-Mexico: Race and Nation after the Revolution*. Cambridge: Cambridge University Press, 2020.

Coignard, Jerónimo. "El valor efectivo de ballet mexicano." *El Universal Ilustrado* (Mexico City), October 20, 1921.

"Con un grandioso festival se inauguró ayer el Estadio Nacional." *El Universal* (Mexico City), May 6, 1924.

Conquergood, Dwight. *Cultural Struggles: Performance, Ethnography, Praxis.* Ann Arbor: University of Michigan Press, 2013.

———. "Rethinking Ethnography: Towards a Critical Cultural Politics." *Communication Monographs* 58, no. 2 (1991): 179–194.

Cordero, Karen. "Para devolver su inocencia a la nación. (Origen y desarrollo del Método Best Maugard)." In *Abraham Angel y su tiempo*, 9–21. Mexico City: Museo Nacional de San Carlos, 1985.

Covarrubias, Miguel. *Mexico South: The Isthmus of Tehuantepec.* New York: Knopf, 1947.

Cowan, Benjamin Arthur. "How *Machismo* Got Its Spurs—in English: Social Science, Cold War Imperialism, and the Ethnicization of Hypermasculinity." *Latin American Research Review* 52, no. 4 (2017): 606–622.

Craib, Raymond B. *Cartographic Mexico: A History of State Fixations and Fugitive Landscapes.* Durham, NC: Duke University Press, 2004.

Cuellar, Manuel R. "Imagine Otherwise: Manuel Cuellar on Dancing as Community Building." Interview by Cathy Hannabach. *Ideas on Fire*, April 4, 2018. ideasonfire.net/60-manuel-cuellar/.

———. "La escenificación de lo mexicano y la interpelación de un público nacional: la Noche Mexicana de 1921." In *Mexican Transnational Cinema and Literature*, edited by Maricruz Castro Ricalde, Mauricio Díaz Calderón, and James Ramey, 123–140. Oxford, UK: Peter Lang, 2017.

Curcio, Linda Ann. *The Great Festivals of Colonial Mexico City: Performing Power and Identity.* Albuquerque: University of New Mexico Press, 2004.

Dallal, Alberto. "Anna Pavlova en México." *Anales del Instituto de Investigaciones Estéticas* 15, no. 60 (1989): 163–178.

———. *La danza en México en el siglo XX.* Mexico City: Consejo Nacional para la Cultura y las Artes, 1994.

Dalton, David S. *Mestizo Modernity: Race, Technology, and the Body in Postrevolutionary Mexico.* Gainesville: University of Florida Press, 2018.

Debord, Guy. *The Society of the Spectacle.* Berkeley, CA: Bureau of Public Secrets, 2014.

de la Cadena, Marisol, and Orin Starn, eds. *Indigenous Experience Today.* Oxford, UK: Berg, 2007.

de la Mora, Sergio. *Cinemachismo: Masculinities and Sexuality in Mexican Film.* Austin: University of Texas Press, 2006.

de los Reyes, Aurelio. *El nacimiento de ¡Que viva México!* Mexico City: Universidad Nacional Autónoma de México, 2006.

———. "Informes de Adolfo Best Maugard al jefe del Departamento de Bellas Artes de la Secretaría de Educación Pública, sobre su trabajo de supervisión y censura a Sergei Eisenstein, durante el rodaje de ¡Que viva México! en 1930." *Anales del Instituto de Investigaciones Estéticas*, no. 81 (2002): 161–172.

———. *Medio siglo de cine mexicano (1896–1947).* Mexico City: Trillas, 1991.

del Río, Carlos. "Nellie y Gloria Campobello, creadoras de la danza." *Nellie Campobello. Cuadernos del CID Danza*, vol. 15: 29–30 (1987).

Derrida, Jacques. *Archive Fever: A Freudian Impression*, translated by Eric Prenowitz. Chicago: University of Chicago Press, 1996.

Desmond, Jane C. "Introduction." In *Meaning in Motion: New Cultural Studies of Dance*, edited by Jane C. Desmond, 1–25. Durham, NC: Duke University Press, 1997.

Dever, Susan. *Celluloid Nationalism and Other Melodramas: From Post-Revolutionary Mexico to* fin de siglo Mexamérica. Albany, NY: SUNY Press, 2003.

Díaz y de Ovando, Clementina. "Las fiestas del 'Año del Centenario': 1921." In *México: Independencia y Soberanía*, 102–174. Mexico City: Secretaría de Gobernación/Archivo General de la Nación, 1999.

Diéguez Caballero, Ileana. *Escenarios liminales. Teatralidades, performatividades, políticas.* Madrid: Yorick, 2020.

Dils, Ann. *Moving History/Dancing Cultures: A Dance History Reader.* Middletown, CT: Wesleyan University Press, 2001.

Dirks, Sandhya. "Punjabi-Mexicans in California: A Story Told Through Dance." KALW. May 16, 2016. kalw.org/post/punjabi-mexicans-california-story -told-through-dance.

D'Lugo, Marvin. "Aural Identity, Genealogies of Sound Technologies, and Hispanic Transnationality on Screen." In *World Cinemas, Transnational Perspectives*, edited by Natasa Ďurovičová and Kathleen E. Newman, 160–185. New York: Routledge, 2009.

Ďurovičová, Natasa, and Kathleen E. Newman. *World Cinemas, Transnational Perspectives.* New York: Routledge, 2009.

"Ecos del Centenario." *El Universal Ilustrado* (Mexico City), October 13, 1921.

Eisenstein, Sergei. *Film Form: Essays in Film Theory.* Trans. and ed. by Jay Leyda. New York: Harcourt, 1949.

———. *¡Qué viva Mexico!* 1979; Mosfilm/Filmexport/Kino, 2001. DVD.

Eisenstein, S. M., and V. G. Alexandroff. "'Que Viva Mexico!'" *Experimental Cinema* 5 (1934): 5–13, 52.

"El Desfile Histórico del día 15." *Revista de Revistas* (Mexico City), September 18, 1910.

"El Garden Party en Chapultepec, fue una orgía de luz y de colores." *El Imparcial* (Mexico City), September 23, 1910.

"El Gran Desfile Histórico." *La Semana Ilustrada* (Mexico City), September 23, 1910.

"El pueblo tendrá acceso a todas las fiestas del Centenario." *El Universal* (Mexico City), June 2, 1921.

Eng, David. "What's Queer about Queer Studies Now?" *Social Text* 23, no. 3–4 (2005): 1–17.

Estrada, Oswaldo. *Ser mujer y estar presente: disidencias de género en la literatura mexicana contemporánea.* Mexico City: Universidad Nacional Autónoma de México, 2014.

Fabian, Johannes. *Time and the Other: How Anthropology Makes Its Object.* New York: Columbia University Press, 2002.

Fediuk, Elka, and Antonio Prieto Stambaugh. *Corporalidades escénicas: representaciones del cuerpo en el teatro, la danza y el performance*. Buenos Aires: Argus-a Artes y Humanidades, 2016.

Fein, Seth. "Myths of Cultural Imperialism and Nationalism in Golden Age Mexican Cinema." In *Fragments of a Golden Age: The Politics of Culture in Post-1940 Mexico*, edited by Gilbert Joseph, Anne Rubenstein, and Eric Zolov, 159–198. Durham, NC: Duke University Press, 2001.

Fernández Bustamante, Adolfo (A.F.B.). "Einsenstein, el magnífico." *El Ilustrado* (Mexico City), June 11, 1931.

———. "Einsenstein, orientador." *El Ilustrado* (Mexico City), July 16, 1931.

———. "Lo que en México hace Einsenstein." *El Ilustrado* (Mexico City), June 18, 1931.

———. "Los indios del señor Einsenstein." *El Ilustrado* (Mexico City), June 25, 1931.

Fernández, Emilio. *María Candelaria*. 1944; Mexico City: Films Mundiales. DVD.

Fernández l'Hoeste, Héctor D., and Juan Poblete. *Redrawing the Nation: National Identity in Latin/o American Comics*. New York: Palgrave Macmillan, 2009.

"Fiestas del Centenario. Domingo 25." *El Universal*, (Mexico City), September 25, 1921.

Fiol-Matta, Licia. *A Queer Mother for the Nation: The State and Gabriela Mistral*. Minneapolis: University of Minnesota Press, 2002.

Flores, Juan. *From Bomba to Hip-Hop: Puerto Rican Culture and Latino Identity*. New York: Columbia University Press, 2000.

———. *Salsa Rising: New York Latin Music of the Sixties Generation*. Oxford: Oxford University Press, 2016.

Flores, Tatiana. *Mexico's Revolutionary Avant-Gardes: From Estridentismo to ¡30–30!* New Haven, CT: Yale University Press, 2013.

Florescano, Enrique, and Bárbara Santana Rocha, coords. *La fiesta mexicana Tomo I*. Mexico City: Secretaría de Cultura/Fondo de Cultura Económica, 2016.

———. *La fiesta mexicana Tomo II*. Mexico City: Secretaría de Cultura/Fondo de Cultura Económica, 2016.

Folgarait, Leonard. *Mural Painting and Social Revolution in Mexico, 1920–1940: Art of the New Order*. Cambridge: Cambridge University Press, 1998.

Fortuna, Victoria. *Moving Otherwise: Dance, Violence, and Memory in Buenos Aires*. New York: Oxford University Press, 2019.

Foster, Susan Leigh. *Choreographing Empathy: Kinesthesia in Performance*. London: Routledge Press, 2010.

Franco, Jean. *Plotting Women: Gender and Representation in Mexico*. New York: Columbia University Press, 1989.

Franko, Mark. *Dancing Modernism/Performing Politics*. Bloomington: Indiana University Press, 1995.

Friedman, Samantha, and Jodi Hauptman. *Lincoln Kirstein's Modern*. New York: Museum of Modern Art, 2019.

Fuentes, Carlos. "Una flor carnivora." In *El arte de Gabriel Figueroa, Artes de México* 2, 13–21. Mexico City: Artes de México y del Mundo, 2006.

Fuentes, Fernando de, dir. *Allá en el Rancho Grande*. 1936; Mexico City: Lombardo Films/Cinemateca, 2007. DVD.

Gabara, Esther. *Errant Modernism: The Ethos of Photography in Mexico and Brazil*. Durham, NC: Duke University Press, 2008.

Galeana de Valadés, Patricia, Estela Guadalupe Jiménez Codinach, Clementina Diáz y de Ovando, and Archivo General de la Nación. *México: independencia y soberanía*. Mexico City: Secretaría de Gobernación/Archivo General de la Nación, 1996.

Gallo, Rubén. *Mexican Modernity: The Avant-Garde and the Technological Revolution*. Cambridge, MA: MIT Press, 2005.

Gamio, Manuel. *Forjando patria*. Mexico City: Editorial Porrúa, 1982.

García, Cindy. *Salsa Crossings: Dancing Latinidad in Los Angeles*. Durham, NC: Duke University Press, 2013.

Garcia, Desirée J. "'The Soul of a People': Mexican Spectatorship and the Transnational *Comedia Ranchera*." *Journal of American Ethnic History* 30, no. 1 (2010): 72–98.

García, Genaro. *Crónica oficial de las fiestas del primer centenario de la Independencia de México*. 1911. Mexico City: Talleres del Museo Nacional/Consejo Nacional para la Cultura y las Artes, 2011.

García Blizzard, Mónica. *The White Indians of Mexican Cinema: Racial Masquerade throughout the Golden Age*. Albany, NY: SUNY Press, 2022.

García Canclini, Néstor. *Culturas híbridas: estrategias para entrar y salir de la modernidad*. Mexico City: Debolsillo, 2009.

———. *Culturas populares en el capitalismo*. Mexico City: Grijalbo, 2002.

———. *Hybrid Cultures: Strategies for Entering and Leaving Modernity*. Translated by Christopher L. Chiappari and Silvia L. López. Minneapolis: University of Minnesota Press, 2005.

García Riera, Emilio. *Historia documental del cine mexicano*. Guadalajara, Mexico: Universidad de Guadalajara, 1993.

Garner, Paul. "Reflexiones sobre la historia patria y la construcción de la nación mestiza en el México porfiriano, o cómo interpretar las Fiestas del Centenario de 1910." *20/10 Memoria de las Revoluciones de México*, no. 1 (2008): 126–145.

Garrigan, Shelley E. *Collecting Mexico: Museums, Monuments, and the Creation of National Identity*. Minneapolis: University of Minnesota Press, 2012.

Geduld, Harry M., and Ronald Gottesman, eds. *Sergei Eisenstein and Upton Sinclair: The Making and Unmaking of* Que Viva Mexico! Bloomington: Indiana University Press, 1970.

Gilbert, Helen, and Charlotte Gleghorn. *Recasting Commodity and Spectacle in the Indigenous Americas*. London: Institute of Latin American Studies, 2014.

Gillingham, Paul. *Cuauhtémoc's Bones: Forging National Identity in Modern Mexico*. Albuquerque: University of New Mexico Press, 2011.

Gonzales, Michael J. "Imagining Mexico in 1910: Visions of the Patria in the Centennial Celebration in Mexico City." *Journal of Latin American Studies* 39, no. 3 (2007): 495–533.

———. "Imagining Mexico in 1921: Visions of the Revolutionary State and Society in the Centennial Celebration in Mexico City." *Mexican Studies/Estudios Mexicanos* 25, no. 2 (2009): 247–270.

———. "Modernity and the indigenous in centennial celebrations of indepen-dence in Mexico City, 1910 and 1921." In *Recasting Commodity and Spectacle in Indigenous Americas*, edited by Helen Gilbert and Charlotte Gleghorn, 37–54. London: Institute of Latin American Studies, 2014.

González, Martha. "*Zapateado* Afro-Chicana *Fandango* Style: Self-Reflective Moments in Zapateado." In *Dancing across Borders: Danzas y Bailes Mexicanos*, edited by Olga Nájera-Ramírez, Norma Cantú, and Brenda E. Romero, 359–378. Urbana: University of Illinois Press, 2009.

Gopinath, Gayatri. *Unruly Visions: The Aesthetic Practices of Queer Diaspora*. Durham, NC: Duke University Press, 2018.

Gottlieb, Benjamin. "Punjabi Sikh-Mexican American Community Fading into History." *Washington Post*, August 13, 2012. washingtonpost.com /national/on-faith/punjabi-sikh-mexican-american-community-fading -into-history/2012/08/13/cc6b7b98-e26b-11e1-98e7-89d659f9c106_story .html.

"Gráficas de la Conmemoración del Día del Soldado." *El Nacional* (Mexico City), April 23, 1935.

Graham, Richard, ed. *The Idea of Race in Latin America, 1870–1940*. Austin: University of Texas Press, 1990.

Grossberg, Lawrence. *Cultural Studies in the Future Tense*. Durham, NC: Duke University Press, 2010.

Guerrero, Ellie. *Dance and the Arts in Mexico, 1920–1950: The Cosmic Generation*. Cham, Switzerland: Palgrave Macmillan/Springer Nature Switzerland AG, 2018.

Gunckel, Colin, Jan-Christopher Horak, and Lisa Jarvinen, eds. *Cinema between Latin America and Los Angeles: Origins to 1960*. New Brunswick: Rutgers University Press, 2019.

Guss, David M. *The Festive State: Race, Ethnicity, and Nationalism as Cultural Performance*. Berkeley: University of California Press, 2000.

Gutiérrez, David. *The Columbia History of Latinos in the United States since 1960*. New York: Columbia University Press, 2004.

Gutiérrez, Laura G. "Afrodiasporic Visual and Sonic Assemblages: Racialized Anxieties and the Disruption of Mexicanidad in Cine de Rumberas." In *Decentering the Nation: Music, Mexicanidad, and Globalization*, edited by Jesús A. Ramos-Kittrell, 1–22. Lanham, MD: Lexington, 2020.

———. *Performing Mexicanidad: Vendidas y Cabareteras on the Transnational Stage*. Austin: University of Texas Press, 2010.

Gutiérrez, Natividad. *Nationalist Myths and Ethnic Identities: Indigenous Intellectuals and the Mexican State*. Lincoln: University of Nebraska Press, 1999.

Hamera, Judith. *Dancing Communities: Performance, Difference and Connection in the Global City*. Basingstoke, UK: Palgrave Macmillan, 2006.

Hames-Garcia, Michael Roy, and Ernesto Javier Martínez. *Gay Latino Studies: A Critical Reader*. Durham, NC: Duke University Press, 2011.

Haskell, Barbara. *Vida Americana: Mexican Muralists Remake American Art, 1925–1945*. New Haven, CT: Whitney Museum of American Art, 2020.

Hellier-Tinoco, Ruth. *Embodying Mexico: Tourism, Nationalism and Performance*. New York: Oxford University Press, 2011.

Helprin, Morris. "Eisenstein's New Film; Russian Director in Mexico at Work on 'Que Viva Mexico!'" *New York Times*, November 29, 1931.

Hershfield, Joanne. *Imagining la Chica Moderna: Women, Nation, and Visual Culture in Mexico, 1917–1936*. Durham, NC: Duke University Press, 2008.

———. *Mexican Cinema/Mexican Woman, 1940–1950*. Tucson: University of Arizona Press, 1996.

———. "Paradise Regained: Sergei Eisenstein's *Que Viva México!* As Ethnography." In *Documenting the Documentary: Close Readings of Documentary Film and Video*, edited by Barry Keith Grant and Jeannette Sloniowski, 55–69. Detroit, MI: Wayne State University Press, 1998.

Hewitt, Andrew. *Social Choreography: Ideology as Performance in Dance and Everyday Movement*. Durham, NC: Duke University Press, 2005.

Höfling, Ana Paula. *Staging Brazil: Choreographies of Capoeira*. Middletown, CT: Wesleyan University Press, 2019.

Homenaje Una vida en la danza. Amalia Hernández. Mexico City: Secretaría de Cultura/Instituto Nacional de Bellas Artes/Centro Nacional de Investigación, Documentación e Información de la Danza José Limón, 2017.

INtune (podcast). *Episode 12—LA PALOMA AT THE WALL—The Director's Salon*. Accessed March 11, 2020. soundcloud.com/inseries/intune-episode-12 -la-paloma-at-the-wall-the-directors-salon.

Irwin, Robert McKee. "Memín Pinguín: Líos Gordos con los Gringos." In *Redrawing the Nation: National Identity in Latin/o American Comics*, edited by Héctor Fernández L'Hoeste and Juan Poblete, 111–130. New York: Palgrave Macmillan, 2009.

———. *Mexican Masculinities*. Minneapolis: University of Minnesota Press, 2003.

Irwin, Robert McKee, and Maricruz Castro Ricalde. *Global Mexican Cinema: Its Golden Age: "el cine mexicano se impone."* Basingstoke, UK: Palgrave Macmillan, 2013.

Islas, Hilda. *El juego de acercarse y alejarse. Traducción performática de "otras" danzas*. Mexico City: Secretaría de Cultura/Instituto Nacional de Bellas Artes/ Centro Nacional de Investigación, Documentación e Información de la Danza José Limón, 2016.

Jarvinen, Lisa. "A Mass Market for Spanish-Language Films: Los Angeles, Hybridity, and the Emergence of Latino Audiovisual Media." In *Cinema between Latin America and Los Angeles: Origins to 1960*, edited by Colin Gunckel, Jan-Christopher Horak, and Lisa Jarvinen, 80–96. New Brunswick, NJ: Rutgers University Press, 2019.

Jáuregui, Jesús. *El Mariachi: símbolo musical de México*. Mexico City: Instituto Nacional de Antropología e Historia/Consejo Nacional para la Cultura y las Artes/Santillana, 2007.

Jenkins, Henry, Tara McPherson, and Jane Shattuc. *Hop on Pop: The Politics and Pleasures of Popular Culture*. Durham, NC: Duke University Press, 2002.

Jiménez, Enrique, et al. *Homenaje Una vida en la danza. Amalia Hernández*. Mexico City: Secretaría de Cultura/Instituto Nacional de Bellas Artes/Cenidi Danza, 2017.

Johns, Michael. *The City of Mexico in the Age of Díaz*. Austin: University of Texas Press, 1997.

Johnson, E. Patrick. "Introduction: 'Opening and Interpreting Lives.'" In *Cultural Struggles: Performance, Ethnography, Praxis*, by Dwight Conquerwood, 1–14. Ann Arbor: University of Michigan Press, 2013.

Joseph, G. M., and Daniel Nugent. *Everyday Forms of State Formation: Revolution and the Negotiation of Rule in Modern Mexico*. Durham, NC: Duke University Press, 1994.

Joseph, G. M., Anne Rubenstein, and Eric Zolov. *Fragments of a Golden Age: The Politics of Culture in Mexico since 1940*. Durham, NC: Duke University Press, 2001.

Kaplan, Temma. "Final Reflections: Gender, Chaos, and Authority in Revolutionary Times." In *Sex in Revolution: Gender, Politics, and Power in Modern Mexico*, edited by Jocelyn Olcott, Mary Kay Vaughan, and Gabriela Cano, 261–276. Durham, NC: Duke University Press, 2006.

Karetnikova, Inga, and Leon Steinmetz. *Mexico according to Eisenstein*. Albuquerque: University of New Mexico Press, 1991.

Katz, Friedrich. *The Life and Times of Pancho Villa*. Stanford, CA: Stanford University Press, 1998.

Knight, Alan. "Racism, Revolution, and *Indigenismo*: Mexico, 1910–1940." In *The Idea of Race in Latin America, 1870–1940*, edited by Richard Graham, 71–113. Austin: University of Texas Press, 1990.

KQED Arts. "Dancers Honor California's Mexican-Punjabi Heritage." April 10, 2015. youtube.com/watch?v=CzpgvCZQjkY.

Kwan, SanSan. *Kinesthetic City: Dance and Movement in Chinese Urban Spaces*. Oxford: Oxford University Press, 2013.

"La Brillante Inauguración del Estadio Nacional." *Revista de Revistas* (Mexico City), May 11, 1924.

"La 'Noche Mexicana' congregó en Chapultepec ayer, a muy cerca de quinientas mil personas." *El Demócrata* (Mexico City), September 28, 1921.

"La Noche Mexicana en el Bosque de Chapultepec." *El Universal* (Mexico City), September 6, 1921.

"La 'Noche Mexicana' en el Bosque de Chapultepec." *El Universal Ilustrado* (Mexico City), September 29, 1921.

"La Noche Mexicana en los Lagos del Bosque." *Excélsior* (Mexico City), August 21, 1921.

"La Noche Mexicana fue aplazada para hoy." *El Universal* (Mexico City), September 27, 1921.

La Tehuana. Artes de México 49. Mexico City: Artes de México y del Mundo, 2000.

"La tercera Noche Mexicana fue muy animada y concurrida." *El Demócrata* (Mexico City), October 3, 1921.

"Las hermanas Campobello." *Diario de La Marina* (Havana), January 26, 1930.

Lavalle, Josefina. "Anna Pavlova y el jarabe tapatío." In *La danza en México: Visiones de cinco siglos. Tomo I: Ensayos históricos y analíticos*, edited by Maya Ramos Smith and Patricia Cardona Lang, 635–650. Mexico City: Centro Nacional de Investigación, Documentación e Información de la Danza

José Limón/Consejo Nacional para la Cultura y las Artes/Instituto Nacional de Bellas Artes, 2002.

Leal, Juan Felipe, Eduardo Barraza, and Alejandra Jablonska. *Vistas que no se ven: filmografía mexicana 1896–1910*. Mexico City: Universidad Autónoma de México, 1993.

Legrás, Horacio. *Culture and Revolution: Violence, Memory, and the Making of Modern Mexico*. Austin: University of Texas Press, 2017.

Lempérière, Annick. "Los dos centenarios de la independencia mexicana (1910–1921): de la historia patria a la antropología cultural." *Historia Mexicana* 45, no. 2 (1995): 317–352.

Leonard, Karen Isaksen. *Making Ethnic Choices: California's Punjabi Mexican Americans*. Philadelphia: Temple University Press, 1992.

Limón, José E. *Dancing with the Devil: Society and Cultural Poetics in Mexican-American South Texas*. Madison: University of Wisconsin Press, 1994.

Lockhart, James. *The Nahuas After the Conquest: A Social and Cultural History of the Indians of Central Mexico, Sixteenth Through Eighteenth Centuries*. Stanford, CA: Stanford University Press, 1992.

Lomnitz-Adler, Claudio. *Death and the Idea of Mexico*. Brooklyn, NY: Zone, 2005.

———. *Deep Mexico, Silent Mexico: An Anthropology of Nationalism*. Minneapolis: University of Minnesota Press, 2001.

———. *Exits from the Labyrinth: Culture and Ideology in the Mexican National Space*. Berkeley: University of California Press, 1992.

López, Ana M. "A Cinema for the Continent." In *The Mexican Cinema Project*, edited by Chon A. Noriega and Steven Ricci, 7–12. Los Angeles: UCLA Film and Television Archive, 1994.

———. "Of Rhythms and Borders." In *Everynight Life: Culture and Dance in Latin/o America*, edited by Celeste Fraser Delgado and José Esteban Muñoz, 310–344. Durham, NC: Duke University Press, 1997.

———. "Tears and Desire: Women and Melodrama in the 'Old' Mexican Cinema." In *Mediating Two Worlds: Cinematic Encounters in the Americas*, edited by John King, Ana M. López, and Manuel Alvarado, 147–163. London: British Film Institute, 1993.

López, Antonio M. *Unbecoming Blackness: The Diaspora Cultures of Afro-Cuban America*. New York: University Press, 2012.

López, Rick Anthony. *Crafting Mexico: Intellectuals, Artisans, and the State after the Revolution*. Durham, NC: Duke University Press, 2010.

Loza, Steven Joseph, and Jack Bishop. *Musical Cultures of Latin America: Global Effects, Past and Present*. Los Angeles: Department of Ethnomusicology and Systematic Musicology, University of California, Los Angeles, 2003.

Lund, Joshua. "The Mestizo State: Colonization and Indianization in Liberal Mexico." *PMLA* 123, no. 5 (2008): 1418–1433.

———. *The Mestizo State: Reading Race in Modern Mexico*. Minneapolis: University of Minnesota Press, 2012.

Maciel, David R., and Joanne Hershfield. *Mexico's Cinema: A Century of Film and Filmmakers*. Lanham, MD: SR Books, 1999.

Mackay, Barbara. "Review: 'La Paloma at the Wall' by The In Series." *DC Metro Theater Arts*, March 24, 2019. dcmetrotheaterarts.com/2019/03/24/paloma -wall-in-series/.

Madrid, Alejandro L., and Robin D. Moore. *Danzón: Circum-Caribbean Dialogues in Music and Dance.* New York: Oxford University Press, 2013.

Madrigal, Carmen. "La charla y la danza." *Hoy* (Mexico City), April 23, 1938.

Maffie, James. *Aztec Philosophy: Understanding a World in Motion.* Boulder: University Press of Colorado, 2014.

Manzanos, Rosario. "La historia de terror del secuestro y muerte de Nellie Campobello." *Proceso*, December 1, 2002.

Marín, Noemí. *La importancia de la danza tradicional mexicana en el Sistema Educativo Nacional (1921–1938): Otra perspectiva de las misiones culturales.* Mexico City: Consejo Nacional para la Cultura y las Artes/Instituto Nacional de Bellas Artes/Centro Nacional de Investigación, Documentación e Información de la Danza José Limón, 2004.

Marino, Angela, and Manuel Cuellar. "Fiesta Performance as Epistemology." *Performance Research* 20, no. 1 (2015): 123–135.

Martí, José. *La edad de oro*, edited by Gonzalo de Quesada y Miranda. Rome: Casa editrice nazionale, 1905.

Martín-Barbero, Jesús. *De los medios a las mediaciones: comunicación, cultura y hegemonía.* Mexico City: Antropos, 2010.

Martínez, Ana. *Performance in the Zócalo: Constructing History, Race, and Identity in Mexico's Central Square from the Colonial Era to the Present.* Ann Arbor: University of Michigan Press, 2020.

Martínez, Marco Antonio. "Estéticas del desplazamiento: artistas mexicanos en Nueva York (1920–1940)." PhD diss., Princeton University, 2015. ProQuest (ATT 3729652).

Martínez, María Elena. "Archives, Bodies, and Imagination: The Case of Juana Aguilar and Queer Approaches to History, Sexuality, and Politics." *Radical History Review* 120 (2014): 159–182.

Masiello, Francine. *The Senses of Democracy: Perception, Politics, and Culture in Latin America.* Austin: University of Texas Press, 2018.

Matthews, Irene. *Nellie Campobello: la centaura del norte.* Mexico City: Cal y Arena, 1997.

Mbembe, Achille. "The Power of the Archive and Its Limits." In *Refiguring the Archive*, edited by Carolyn Hamilton, Verne Harris, Jane Taylor, Michele Pickover, Graeme Reid, and Razia Saleh, translated by Judith Inggs, 19–26. Boston: Kluwer, 2002.

Mendoza, Zoila S. *Shaping Society through Dance: Mestizo Ritual Performance in the Peruvian Andes.* Chicago: University of Chicago Press, 2000.

Mérida, Carlos. *Escritos de Carlos Mérida sobre el arte: La danza.* Mexico City: Instituto Nacional de Bellas Artes/Centro Nacional de Investigación y Documentación de Artes Plásticas, 1990.

Mirandé, Alfredo. *Behind the Mask: Gender Hybridity in a Zapotec Community.* Tucson: University of Arizona Press, 2017.

Mitchell, W. J. T. "Imperial Landscape." In *Landscape and Power*, edited by W. J. T. Mitchell, 5–34. Chicago: Chicago University Press, 2002.

Moallem, Minoo. "Universalization of Particulars: The Civic Body and Gendered Citizenship in Iran." *Citizenship Studies* 3, no. 3 (1999): 319–335.

Monsiváis, Carlos. "Crónica del Centenario: 'Detente un momento, eres tan bello.'" In *Crónica oficial de las fiestas del primer centenario de la independencia de México*, by Genaro García, ix–xx. Mexico City: Consejo Nacional para la Cultura y las Artes, 2011.

———. "Gabriel Figueroa: la institución del punto de vista." In *El arte de Gabriel Figueroa*, *Artes de México* 2, 41–49. Mexico City: Artes de México y del Mundo, 2006.

———. *Historia mínima de la cultura mexicana en el siglo XX*. Mexico City: El Colegio de México, 2010.

———. *Los rituales del caos*. Mexico City: Ediciones Era, 1995.

———. "Mexican Cinema: Of Myths and Demystifications." In *Mediating Two Worlds: Cinematic Encounters in the Americas*, edited by John King, Ana M. López, and Manuel Alvarado, 139–146. London: British Film Institute, 1993.

———. "Tongolele y el enriquecimiento de las buenas costumbres." In *No han matado a Tongolele*, edited by Arturo García Hernández, 11–19. Mexico City: La Jornada Ediciones, 1998.

Monsiváis, Carlos, and Carlos Bonfil, eds. *A través del espejo: el cine mexicano y su público*. Mexico City: Instituto Mexicano de Cinematografía, 1994.

Mora, Carl J. *Mexican Cinema: Reflections of a Society, 1896–2004*. Jefferson, NC: McFarland, 2005.

Mraz, John. *Looking for Mexico: Modern Visual Culture and National Identity*. Durham, NC: Duke University Press, 2009.

Mulvey, Laura. *Visual and Other Pleasures*. Bloomington: Indiana University Press, 1989.

Muñoz, José Esteban. *Cruising Utopia: The Then and There of Queer Futurity*. New York: New York University Press, 2009.

———. *Disidentifications: Queers of Color and the Performance of Politics*. Minneapolis: University of Minnesota Press, 1999.

Nájera-Ramírez, Olga. *La Fiesta de los Tastoanes: Critical Encounters in Mexican Festival Performance*. Albuquerque: University of New Mexico Press, 1997.

———. "Staging Autheticity: Theorizing the Development of Mexican Folklórico Dance." In *Dancing across Borders: Danzas y Bailes Mexicanos*, edited by Olga Nájera-Ramírez, Norma Cantú, and Brenda Romero, 277–292. Urbana: University of Illinois Press, 2009.

Nájera-Ramírez, Olga, Norma E. Cantú, and Brenda M. Romero. *Dancing across Borders: Danzas y Bailes Mexicanos*. Urbana: University of Illinois Press, 2009.

Navitski, Rielle, and Nicolas Poppe, eds. *Cosmopolitan Film Cultures in Latin America, 1896–1960*. Bloomington: Indiana University Press, 2017.

Nellie Campobello. In *Cuadernos del CID Danza*, vol. 15. Mexico City: Instituto Nacional de Bellas Artes/Centro de Investigación, Información y Documentación de la Danza, 1987.

Nichols, Deborah, and Enrique Rodríguez-Alegría, eds. *The Oxford Handbook of the Aztecs*. New York: Oxford University Press, 2017.

Noble, Andrea. *Mexican National Cinema*. London: Routledge, 2005.

Noche Mexicana en los lagos del Bosque de Chapultepec. Comité Ejecutivo de las Fiestas del Centenario. Mexico City: Talleres de Federico E. Graue, 1921.

Noland, Carrie. *Agency and Embodiment: Performing Gestures/Producing Culture.* Cambridge, MA: Harvard University Press, 2009.

Noriega, Chon A., Steven Ricci, and UCLA Film and Television Archive. *The Mexican Cinema Project.* Los Angeles: UCLA Film and Television Archive, 1994.

Noriega Hope, Carlos. "El ballet como nuevo sentido educacional." *El Universal Ilustrado* (Mexico City), June 16, 1927.

Olcott, Jocelyn. *Revolutionary Women in Postrevolutionary Mexico.* Durham, NC: Duke University Press, 2005.

Olcott, Jocelyn, Mary Kay Vaughan, and Gabriela Cano, eds. *Sex in Revolution: Gender, Politics, and Power in Modern Mexico.* Durham, NC: Duke University Press, 2006.

O'Malley, Ilene V. *The Myth of the Revolution: Hero Cults and the Institutionalization of the Mexican State, 1920–1940.* New York: Greenwood, 1986.

Ortiz, Fernando. *Contrapunteo cubano del tabaco y el azúcar: advertencia de sus contrastes agrarios, económicos, históricos y sociales, su etnografía y su tranculturación.* Madrid: Cátedra, 2002.

Ospina León, Juan Sebastián. *Struggles for Recognition: Melodrama and Visibility in Latin American Silent Film.* Berkeley: University of California Press, 2021.

"Otro éxito fue ayer la Noche Mexicana." *El Universal* (Mexico City), September 29, 1921, section 2.

Palavicini, Manuel. "La Noche Mexicana en Chapultepec." *El Universal* (Mexico City), September 28, 1921, section 1.

Palma Velasco, Juan Carlos. "El otro que no soy yo." *Tablas. Revista Cubana de Artes Escénicas* 111, nos. 3–4 (2017): 65–68.

Palomar Verea, Cristina. "La charrería en el imaginario nacional." In *Artes de México* 50, 8–20. Mexico City: Artes de México y del Mundo, 2000.

Palou, Pedro Ángel. *El fracaso del mestizo.* Mexico City: Ariel, 2014.

———. *Mestizo Failure(s): Race, Film and Literature in Twentieth Century Mexico.* Boston: Art Life Lab, 2016.

Pardo Bazán, Emilia. *Al pie de la torre Eiffel.* Madrid: Administración, 1900.

Parga, Pablo. *Cuerpo vestido de nación: danza folklórica y nacionalismo mexicano (1921–1939).* Puebla, Mexico: Consejo Nacional para la Cultura y las Artes/Fondo Nacional para la Cultura y las Artes, 2004.

Parr, Andrew. "Theatre Review: 'La Paloma at the Wall' at The In Series." *Maryland Theatre Guide,* April 2, 2019. mdtheatreguide.com/2019/04/theatre-review-la-paloma-at-the-wall-at-the-in-series/.

Parra, Max. *Writing Pancho Villa's Revolution: Rebels in the Literary Imagination of Mexico.* Austin: University of Texas Press, 2005.

Paz, Octavio. *El laberinto de la soledad; Postdata; Vuelta a El laberinto de la soledad.* Mexico City: Fondo de Cultura Económica, 2005.

Peña, Elaine. *¡Viva George! Celebrating Washington's Birthday at the US-Mexico Border.* Austin: University of Texas Press, 2020.

Peñafiel, Antonio. *Explication de l'édifice Mexicain à l'Exposition Internationale de Paris en 1889.* Barcelona: d'Espase et Cía, 1889.

Pérez Montfort, Ricardo. *Avatares del nacionalismo cultural. Cinco ensayos.* Mexico City: Centro de Investigación y Docencia en Humanidades del Estado de Morelos/Centro de Investigaciones y Estudios Superiores en Antropología Social, 2000.

———. *Estampas de nacionalismo popular mexicano. Ensayos sobre cultura popular y nacionalismo.* Mexico City: Centro de Investigaciones y Estudios Superiores en Antropología Social, 1994.

———. *Expresiones populares y estereotipos culturales en México. Siglos XIX y XX. Diez ensayos.* Mexico City: Centro de Investigaciones y Estudios Superiores en Antropología Social, 2007.

———. "La china poblana como emblema nacional." In *Artes de México* 66, 40–49. Mexico City: Artes de México y del Mundo, 2003.

Podalsky, Laura. "Patterns of the Primitive: Sergei Eisenstein's *Qué Viva México!*" In *Mediating Two Worlds: Cinematic Encounters in the Americas,* edited by John King, Ana M. López, and Manuel Alvarado, 25–39. London: British Film Institute, 1993.

Poniatowska, Elena. *Las siete cabritas.* Mexico City: Ediciones Era, 2001.

Portal, Marta. *Proceso narrativo de la revolución mexicana.* Selecciones Austral 75. Madrid: Espasa-Calpe, 1980.

Portilla, Jorge. *Fenomenología del relajo, y otros ensayos.* Mexico City: Ediciones Era, 1966.

Pratt, Mary Louise. *Imperial Eyes: Travel Writing and Transculturation.* London: Routledge, 2008.

———. "Mi cigarro, mi Singer y la revolución mexicana: la voz corporal de Nellie Campobello." *Revista Iberoamericana* 70, no. 206 (2004): 253–273.

Puar, Jasbir K. *Terrorist Assemblages: Homonationalism in Queer Times.* Durham, NC: Duke University Press, 2007.

Pulido Llano, Gabriela. *Mulatas y negros cubanos en la escena mexicana 1920–1950.* Mexico City: Instituto Nacional de Antropología e Historia, 2010.

Quijano, Anibal. "Coloniality of Power, Eurocentrism, and Latin America." Translated by Michael Ennis. *Nepantla: Views from South* 1, no. 3 (2000): 533–580.

Quintero-Herencia, Juan Carlos. *La máquina de la salsa: tránsitos del sabor.* San Juan: Ediciones Vértigo, 2005.

Quintero Rivera, Ángel G. *¡Salsa, sabor y control! sociología de la música "tropical."* Mexico City: Siglo Veintiuno Editores, 1998.

Rabasa, José. *Tell Me the Story of How I Conquered You: Elsewheres and Ethnosuicide in the Colonial Mesoamerican World.* Austin: University of Texas Press, 2011.

———. *Without History: Subaltern Studies, the Zapatista Insurgency, and the Specter of History.* Pittsburgh, PA: University of Pittsburgh Press, 2010.

Ramírez, Fausto. "Dioses, héroes y reyes mexicanos en París 1889." In *Historia, leyendas y mitos de México: Su expresión en el arte,* 201–253. Mexico City: Universidad Nacional Autónoma de México, 1988.

Ramos, Samuel. *El perfil del hombre y la cultura en México.* 4th ed. Mexico City: Universidad Nacional Autónoma de México, 1963.

Ramos Smith, Maya. *El ballet en México en el siglo XIX: De la Independencia al Segundo Imperio (1825–1867)*. Mexico City: Consejo Nacional para la Cultura y las Artes, 1991.

———. *La danza en México durante la época colonial*. Mexico Ciy: Consejo Nacional para la Cultura y las Artes, 1990.

———. *La danza teatral en México durante el virreinato (1521–1821)*. Mexico City: Escenología Ediciones, 2013.

———. *Teatro musical y danza en el México de la Belle Époque (1867–1910)*. Mexico City: Escenología Ediciones, 2013.

Ramos Villalobos, Roxana Guadalupe. *Una mirada a la formación dancística mexicana (CA.1919–1945)*. Mexico City: Fondo Nacional para la Cultura y las Artes/Instituto Nacional de Bellas Artes/Centro Nacional de Investigación/ Documentación e Información de la Danza José Limón, 2009.

Restall, Matthew. *When Montezuma Met Cortés: The True Story of the Meeting That Changed History*. New York: Ecco/HarperCollins, 2018.

Reynoso, Jose Luis. "Campobello, Nellie (1900–1986) and Campobello, Gloria (1911–1968)." In *Routledge Encyclopedia of Modernism*, edited by Stephen Ross and Allana C. Lindgren. Milton Park, UK: Routledge Taylor and Francis, 2016.

———. "Choreographing Modern Mexico: Anna Pavlova in Mexico City (1919)." *Modernist Cultures* 9, no. 1 (May 2014): 80–98.

———. "Choreographing Politics, Dancing Modernity: Ballet and Modern Dance in the Construction of Modern México (1919–1940)." PhD diss. University of California, Los Angeles, 2012. ProQuest (ATT 3516285).

———. "Racialized Dance Modernisms in Lusophone and Spanish-Speaking Latin America." In *The Modernist World*, edited by Stephen Ross and Allana C. Lindgrin, 392–400. London: Routledge, 2015.

Riggio, Milla Cozart, Angela Marino, and Paolo Vignolo. *Festive Devils of the Americas*. Enactments 31. London: Seagull, 2015.

Rivera Cusicanqui, Silvia. "Ch'ixinakax utxiwa: A Reflection on the Practices and Discourses of Decolonization." *South Atlantic Quarterly* 111, no. 1 (2012): 95–109.

Rivera-Servera, Ramón H. "Choreographies of Resistance: Latino Queer Dance and the Utopian Performative." In *Gay Latino Studies: A Critical Reader*, edited by Michael Hames-García and Ernesto Javier Martínez, 259–280. Durham, NC: Duke University Press, 2011.

———. *Performing Queer Latinidad: Dance, Sexuality, Politics*. Ann Arbor: University of Michigan Press, 2012.

Roberto *El Diablo*. "Después de Medio Siglo." *Revista de Revistas* (Mexico City), March 30, 1919.

———. "En Pleno Centenario." *Revista de Revistas* (Mexico City), September 18, 1921.

Rodríguez, Ileana, and Mónica Szurmuk. *The Cambridge History of Latin American Women's Literature*. New York: Cambridge University Press, 2016.

Rodríguez, Juana María. *Queer Latinidad: Identity Practices, Discursive Spaces*. New York: New York University Press, 2003.

————. *Sexual Futures, Queer Gestures, and Other Latina Longings*. New York: New York University Press, 2014.

Rodríguez, Luis. "La fantasía mexicana." *El Universal Ilustrado* (Mexico City), March 28, 1919.

Rodríguez, María de las Nieves. "La 'noche mexicana' como parte de los festejos de celebración de la Independencia de 1921." *Estudios: filosofía, historia, letras* 11, no. 105 (2013): 57.

Rosa, Cristina F. *Brazilian Bodies and Their Choreographies of Identification: Swing Nation*. Houndmills, UK: Palgrave Macmillan, 2015.

Ruiz, Raymundo. "Writing Down the *Jarabe Tapatío*, from Tradition to Academia." In *The Mystery of Movement: Studies in Honor of János Fügedi*, edited by Dóra Pál-Kovács and Vivien Szönyi, 349–362. Budapest: L'Harmattan, 2020.

Ruy Sánchez, Alberto. "El arte de Gabriel Figueroa." In *El arte de Gabriel Figueroa*, by *Artes de Mexico* 2, 5–7. Mexico City: Artes de México y del Mundo, 2006.

Salamon, Gayle. *The Life and Death of Latisha King: A Critical Phenomenology of Transphobia*. New York: New York University Press, 2018.

Salazkina, Masha. *In Excess: Sergei Eisenstein's Mexico*. Chicago: University of Chicago Press, 2009.

Saldívar, Gabriel. *El jarabe: Baile popular mexicano*. Mexico City: Talleres gráficos de la nación, 1937.

Sánchez, Carlos Alberto. *The Suspension of Seriousness: On the Phenomenology of Jorge Portilla*. Albany, NY: SUNY Press, 2012.

Sánchez Prado, Ignacio M. *Naciones intelectuales: las fundaciones de la modernidad literaria mexicana, 1917–1959*. West Lafayette, IN: Purdue University Press, 2009.

Santoscoy, Alberto. *La fiesta de los tastoanes. Estudio etnológico histórico*. Guadalajara: Tipografía del Gobierno, á cargo de J. G. Montenegro, 1889.

Savigliano, Marta. *Tango and the Political Economy of Passion*. Boulder, CO: Westview, 1995.

Schechner, Richard. *Between Theater and Anthropology*. Philadelphia: University of Pennsylvania Press, 1985.

————. *The Future of Ritual Writings on Culture and Performance*. London: Routledge, 1993.

Schroeder Rodríguez, Paul A. *Latin American Cinema: A Comparative History*. Oakland: University of California Press, 2016.

Schwall, Elizabeth B. *Dancing with the Revolution: Power, Politics, and Privilege in Cuba*. Chapel Hill: University of North Carolina Press, 2021.

Schwaller, Robert C. *Géneros de Gente in Early Colonial Mexico: Defining Racial Difference*. Norman: University of Oklahoma Press, 2017.

Scolieri, Paul A. *Dancing the New World: Aztecs, Spaniards, and the Choreography of Conquest*. Austin: University of Texas Press, 2013.

Segura, Felipe. *Gloria Campobello: la primera ballerina de México*. Mexico City: Instituto Nacional de Bellas Artes, 1991.

Seijas, Tatiana. *Asian Slaves in Colonial Mexico: From Chinos to Indians*. New York: Cambridge University Press, 2014.

"Serán populares las fiestas del Centenario." *El Universal* (Mexico City), May 15, 1921.

Serna, Laura Isabel. *Making Cinelandia: American Films and Mexican Film Culture Before the Golden Age*. Durham, NC: Duke University Press, 2014.

Sheehy, Daniel. "Fandango Without Borders." Smithsonian Center for Folklife and Cultural Heritage. *Folklife Digital Magazine* (blog), October 10, 2017. folklife.si.edu/talkstory/fandango-without-borders.

Siebers, Tobin. *Disability Aesthetics*. Ann Arbor: University of Michigan Press, 2010.

Sierra-Rivera, Judith. "Carlos Mérida's 'Goce Emocional': An Aesthetics Proposal Circumventing the Space of Catastrophe of Mexican Nationalism." *The Comparatist* 41, no. 1 (2017): 41–59.

Siskind, Mariano. *Cosmopolitan Desires: Global Modernity and World Literature in Latin America*. Evanston, IL: Northwestern University Press, 2014.

Sklar, Deidre. "Can Bodylore Be Brought to Its Senses?" *Journal of American Folklore* 107, no. 423 (1994): 9–22.

———. *Dancing with the Virgin: Body and Faith in the Fiesta of Tortugas, New Mexico*. Berkeley: University of California Press, 2001.

Sluis, Ageeth. *Deco Body, Deco City: Female Spectacle and Modernity in Mexico City, 1900–1939*. Lincoln: University of Nebraska Press, 2016.

Snow, K. Mitchell. *A Revolution in Movement: Dancers, Painters, and the Image of Modern Mexico*. Gainesville: University Press of Florida, 2020.

Sommer, Doris. *Proceed with Caution, When Engaged by Minority Writing in the Americas*. Cambridge, MA: Harvard University Press, 1999.

Stern, Seymour. "Introduction to Synopsis for 'Que Viva Mexico!'" *Experimental Cinema* 5 (1934): 3–4.

Storey, John. *Cultural Theory and Popular Culture: An Introduction*. Athens: University of Georgia Press, 2006.

Tarica, Estelle. *The Inner Life of Mestizo Nationalism*. Minneapolis: University of Minnesota Press, 2008.

Taylor, Diana. *The Archive and the Repertoire: Performing Cultural Memory in the Americas*. Durham, NC: Duke University Press, 2003.

———. "History and/as Performance." *Drama Review* 50, no. 1 (2006): 67–86.

———. *Performance*. Durham, NC: Duke University Press, 2016.

———. *¡Presente! The Politics of Presence*. Durham, NC: 2020.

———. "Scenes of Cognition: Performance and Conquest." *Theatre Journal* 56, no. 3 (2004): 353–372.

Taylor, Diana, and Sarah J. Townsend. "Introduction." In *Stages of Conflict: A Critical Anthology of Latin American Theater and Performance*, 1–28. Ann Arbor: University of Michigan Press, 2008.

Tenenbaum, Barbara A. "Street History: The Paseo de La Reforma and the Porfirian State, 1876–1910." In *Rituals of Rule, Rituals of Resistance: Public Celebrations and Popular Culture in Mexico*, edited by William H. Beezley, Cheryl English Martin, and William E. French, 127–150. Wilmington, DE: SR Books, 1994.

Tenorio, David. "Broken Records: Materiality, Temporality, and Queer Belonging in Mexican Drag Cabaret Performance." *Transmodernity* 9, no. 1 (2019): 55–79.

———. "Queer Nightscapes: Touching Nightlife in Neoliberal Mexico." In *The Routledge Companion to Gender and Affect*, edited by Todd W. Reeser. London: Routledge, forthcoming.

Tenorio-Trillo, Mauricio. *Mexico at the World's Fairs: Crafting a Modern Nation*. Berkeley: University of California Press, 1996.

———. "1910 Mexico City: Space and Nation in the City of the *Centenario*." *Journal of Latin American Studies* 28, no. 1 (1996): 75–104.

Tibón, Gutierre. "Las dos chinas: Catarina de San Juan y la atractiva mestiza." *Artes de México* 66, 8–16. Mexico City: Artes de México y del Mundo, 2003.

Toor, Frances. "The Old and New Jarabe." *Mexican Folkways* 6, no. 1 (1930): 26–37.

Toriz Proenza, Martha. *La fiesta prehispánica: un espectáculo teatral: comparación de las descripciones de cuatro fiestas hechas por Sahagún y Durán*. Mexico City: Instituto Nacional de Bellas Artes, 1993.

Tortajada Quiroz, Margarita. *Danza y poder*. Mexico City: Instituto Nacional de Bellas Artes/Centro Nacional de Investigación, Documentación e Información de la Danza José Limón, 1995.

———. *Frutos de mujer: las mujeres en la danza escénica*. Mexico City: Instituto Nacional de Bellas Artes y Literatura, 2012.

———. *La danza escénica de la Revolución Mexicana, nacionalista y vigorosa*. Mexico City: Instituto Nacional de Estudios Históricos de la Revolución Mexicana, 2000.

Toscano, Carmen, and Salvador Toscano. *Memorias de un mexicano*. Documentary. Mexico City: Archivo Salvador Toscano, 1950.

Toscano, Salvador. *Fin del Desfile Histórico*. 1910; Mexico City: Filmoteca UNAM.

Townsend, Camilla. *Fifth Sun: A New History of the Aztecs*. New York: Oxford University Press, 2019.

Townsend, Sarah J. *The Unfinished Art of Theater: Avant-Garde Intellectuals in Mexico and Brazil*. Evanston, IL: Northwestern University Press, 2018.

Tumbaga, Ariel Zatarain. *Yaqui Indigeneity: Epistemology, Diaspora, and the Construction of Yoeme Identity*. Tucson: University of Arizona Press, 2018.

Turner, Victor W. *The Ritual Process: Structure and Anti-Structure*. New York: Aldine/Transaction, 2009.

"Un gran artista." *El Universal Ilustrado* (Mexico City), December 24, 1931.

"Uno de los números que fueron más aplaudidos en el festival que ayer se ejecutó en el Estadio Nacional." *El Universal* (Mexico City), April 28, 1935.

Uslenghi, Alejandra. *Latin America at Fin-de-Siècle Universal Exhibitions: Modern Cultures of Visuality*. Houndmills, UK: Palgrave Macmillan, 2016.

Van Young, Eric. "Conclusion: The State as Vampire—Hegemonic Projects, Public Ritual, and Popular Culture in Mexico, 1600–1900." In *Rituals of Rule, Rituals of Resistance: Public Celebrations and Popular Culture in Mexico*, edited by William H. Beezley, Cheryl English Martin, and William E. French, 347–374. Wilmington, DE: SR Books, 1994.

Vargas, Deborah R. *Dissonant Divas in Chicana Music the Limits of La Onda*. Minneapolis: University of Minnesota Press, 2012.

Vargas Valdés, Jesús, and Flor García Rufino. *Nellie Campobello: Mujer de manos rojas*. Chihuahua, Mexico: Secretaría de Educación, Cultura y Deporte/ Gobierno del Estado de Chihuahua, 2013.

Varner, Natasha. *La Raza Cosmética: Beauty, Identity and Settler Colonialism in Postrevolutionary Mexico*. Tucson: University of Arizona Press, 2020.

Vasconcelos, José. "El Estadio Nacional." *El Universal* (Mexico City), May 5, 1924, section 2.

———. *La raza cósmica*. Mexico City: Porrúa, 2010.

Vaughan, Mary Kay. *Cultural Politics in Revolution: Teachers, Peasants, and Schools in Mexico, 1930–1940*. Tucson: University of Arizona Press, 1997.

———. "Introduction. Pancho Villa, the Daughters of Mary, and the Modern Woman: Gender in the Long Mexican Revolution." In *Sex in Revolution: Gender, Politics, and Power in Modern Mexico*, edited by Jocelyn Olcott, Mary Kay Vaughan, and Gabriela Cano, 21–32. Durham, NC: Duke University Press, 2006.

Vaughan, Mary Kay, and Stephen E. Lewis, eds. *The Eagle and the Virgin: Nation and Cultural Revolution in Mexico, 1920–1940*. Durham, NC: Duke University Press, 2006.

Velázquez, Mireida. "The Best Maugard Drawing Method and a New Generation of Artists." In *Paint the Revolution: Mexican Modernism, 1910–1950*, edited by Matthew Affron, Mark A. Castro, Dafne Cruz Porchini, and Renato González Mello, 291–299. Philadelphia: Philadelphia Museum of Art/Instituto Nacional de Bellas Artes, Museo del Palacio de Bellas Artes, 2016.

Velázquez Becerril, César Arturo. "Intelectuales y poder en el porfiriato. Una aproximación al grupo de los científicos, 1892–1911." *Revista fuentes humanísticas* 22, no. 41 (2010): 7–23.

Vianna, Hermano. *The Mystery of Samba: Popular Music and National Identity in Brazil*. Chapel Hill: University of North Carolina Press, 2000.

"Vimos pasar ayer una época de historia nacional." *El Imparcial* (Mexico City), September 16, 1910.

Vinson III, Ben. *Before Mestizaje: The Frontiers of Race and Caste in Colonial Mexico*. New York: Cambridge University Press, 2019.

Wade, Peter. *Race and Ethnicity in Latin America*. Chicago: Pluto, 1997.

Ward, Julie Ann. *A Shared Truth: The Theater of Lagartijas Tiradas al Sol*. Pittsburgh, PA: University of Pittsburgh Press, 2019.

Warner, Michael. *Publics and Counterpublics*. New York: Zone, 2002.

Williams, Gareth. *The Mexican Exception: Sovereignty, Police, and Democracy*. New York: Palgrave Macmillan, 2011.

Wilson, Edmund. "Eisenstein in Hollywood." *New Republic*, November 4, 1931, 320–322.

Ybarra, Patricia A. *Performing Conquest: Five Centuries of Theater, History, and Identity in Tlaxcala, Mexico*. Ann Arbor: University of Michigan Press, 2009.

Yúdice, George. *The Expediency of Culture: Uses of Culture in the Global Era*. Durham, NC: Duke University Press, 2003.

Zolov, Eric. *Refried Elvis: The Rise of the Mexican Counterculture*. Berkeley: University of California Press, 1999.

Index

Page numbers in italics refer to figures

1889 World's Fair in Paris. *See* Paris Universal Exposition (1889)

access to festivities: differentiated, 89, 111–112, 115; open, 79, 81–82, 86, 108; restricted to elites, 65–66, 252n33
Adamchevsky, Carol, 126
aestheticization: of Mexican national identity, 15, 85, 87, 96, 165, 249, 255; of politics, 263n68
affective investments, xii, xiv, 17, 48–49, 66, 163, 227–230, 240n77; of spectators, 14, 68, 71, 142, 169
Afro-Caribbean imaginaries, 166, 209, 215–216, 220–221, 275n124
Afro-Cuban music, 201, 203, 212, 215–216, 221
Afro-descendant populations, 9, 31, 33, 177, 247n58
Afro-diasporic dances, 166–167, 201–203, 206, 212–213
Afro-Indigenous dances, 22, 37, 201–202, 209, 215–216
Afro-Latino identity, 204–205, 215, 276n141. *See also* Blackness
Afro-mestizo identity, x, 167–168, 204, 205, 274n109; *jarocha/o* (Afro-mestizo Veracruz identity), 21, 202–204, 206, 208, 210–212, 250n2, 274n113. *See also mestizaje*
Afro-Mexican culture, 204–205, 215
Aguilar, Juana, 243n113
Aguilar, Luis, 202

ahuehuetes ("Moctezuma" cypress), 87
Alameda, 8, 56, 61, 63, 220
Alexandrov, Grigory: *¡Que viva México!*, 36, 165, 173
alien bodies, 97, 184, 256n53
Alonso, Carlos, 239n66
Alva Brothers (Hermanos Alva), 69
Anderson, Benedict, 88
Ángel de la Independencia (Winged Victory), 56, 59, 65–66
Anglada, Hermen, 94
anti-immigration laws (US), 225
antimiscegenation laws (US), 225
Appadurai, Arjun, 247n61
Aragón Leiva, Agustín, 171, 268n23
Arce, B. Christine, 202–203, 238n46, 238n54; *México's Nobodies*, 14
architectural design, 55, 59, 121–122, 175–176; of Aztec Palace in Paris, 39–40, 44–45, 47
archives, xi, 68, 71, 86; bodies as, 21, 27–28, 38, 151, 227, 263n64; and corporeality, 18, 27–28, 156, 180–181, 231, 243n112; dance as archival practice, 7–8, 25, 36–37, 50, 163, 243n112; Fondo Martín Luis Guzmán Franco, *88, 90, 92, 95, 107*; Fondo Nellie Campobello, *134, 145, 154, 162,* 260n31; queering of, 30–34, 69, 129, 227–232
Argentina, 39, 54, 242n90
Argüelles, Carlos, 79

Armendáriz, Pedro, 189
art nouveau, 95–96
Asian peoples, 17, 76, 158–159, 225;
    erasure from Mexican history, 9,
    177, 252n30. *See also* Japonism;
    orientalism
Asociación Nacional de Grupos
    Folklóricos (ANGFdance.com),
    278n11
assemblages, 201, 213; of Mexicanness,
    38, 47, 53, 85, 95, 101–102,
    252n31; of Mexicos, 89, 91,
    99–100; queer, 30–33, 243n105
Atlanta Exposition (1895), 48
attire, 47, 61–62, 67, 92, 104, 132,
    212, 257n76; in cinema, 198–199,
    208, 211, 214, 216; *mandil* (apron),
    211; *rebozos* (shawls), 69, 166, 195,
    198, 234n6; of spectators, 62, 67,
    104–105, 109, 111, 114, 198–199;
    tehuana, 164, 185; *ternos yucatecos*
    (traditional gala dresses), 104;
    traditional, 2, 62, 75, 104, 120,
    198–199, 208, 211, 234n6. *See also*
    costumes; footwear
Audiencias (Spanish courts), 61
Aulestia, Patricia, 127, 129, 138–139,
    265n101
aural identifications, 192, 195–197,
    200, 204, 206, 216, 273n90
aural landscapes, 175, 178, 202,
    209–210
authenticity, 20, 105–106, 111,
    152–153, 176–177, 197, 239n67,
    248n70; and Blackness, 209,
    216, 275n124; and Campobello's
    self-mythologizing, 121, 129,
    134–135, 140–141; and
    Indigeneity, 16, 60, 64, 68, 159,
    184, 257n78
autochthony, 44, 91, 148, 164,
    239n66, 256n61
Avila, Jacqueline, 271n62, 271n75,
    273n92, 275n118, 276n135
Ayuntamiento (town hall), 61
Aztec Empire (Tenochtitlan, Texcoco,
    and Tlacopan), 8, 17, 39, 46, 61,
    66, 109, 244n1
Aztec Palace, 9, 34, 39–48, 52–53, 55,

245n18. *See also* Paris Universal
    Exposition (1889)
Aztecs, 55, 60, 66–68, 244n1;
    referenced by Campobello sisters,
    119; represented by La India Bonita,
    109–110, 114

ballet, 24, 147–151, 217, 265n97;
    balleticization in *Allá en el Rancho
    Grande*, 195, 197; balleticization
    in *La Reina del Tropico*, 204,
    209–210, 214–215; *ballets masivos*
    (massive ballets), 19, 136–137,
    143; Campobellos' Mexicanization
    of, 119–122, 131, 133, 137–141,
    263n61; Pavlova's balleticization
    of Mexican dances, 1–3, 6–7, 23,
    28–29, 86, 95, 117–118, 233n3,
    234n4, 234n9, 242n90, 242n100
Ballet 30-30, 36, 136–143, 145–146,
    263n71
Ballet del Centenario, 117
Ballet Folklórico de México de Amalia
    Hernández (balletmx.com), 278n11
Ballets Russes, 94, 150
Ballu, Albert, 39
bamba. See *La bamba* (dance/song)
Barilli, Aldo, 126
Barricada, 136
Barrón, Zenón, 224
Bartra, Roger, 89, 241n88
bataclán (variety spectacle), 97
battle of Tetlán, 51
Belle Époque, 24, 94
Belmont, María Cristina, 162, 266n118
Benjamin, Walter, 263n68
Beristáin, Evelia, 146
Berlant, Lauren, 236n32
Berlin Film Festival, 188
Berlin Olympic Games (1936), 144
Best Maugard, Adolfo, 37, 255n48;
    designer of La Noche Mexicana
    (1921), 86–92, 94–96, 99, 101–102,
    104, 117, 253n40; and Eisenstein's
    film, 171, 178–180, 221, 268n25,
    271n63; *Método de dibujo*, 253n39;
    set designer on *Fantasía mexicana*,
    2, 86, 252n37; on the *Tehuana*, 186,
    270n53

bhangra, 224, 226–227
Bidault de la Calle, Sophie, 131, 153, 262n54
biethnic identities, 224–225, 277n1
Blackness, 26, 29, 100, 170, 275n121; Caribbean, 167, 200–201, 205–210, 212–216, 219–222, 274n113; disavowal of, 21, 201–202, 205–211, 216, 276n141; "unbecoming" Black, 216, 276n141
Blanco Borelli, Melissa, 24, 181, 211, 275n127, 277n3
Boaz, Franz, 55
Bonfil, Carlos, 197
border crossings, xi, 37–38, 99–100, 226, 239n67, 242n93, 243n107, 255n47, 258n5, 273n92
border enactments, 240n74, 242n93
Borge, Jason, 275n124
borrachos (drunken ones/footwork), 196
bourgeoisie, 111, 123, 191; *catrín* (bourgeois male), 108–110, 114; at Desfile Histórico, 65, 69; at La Noche Mexicana, 75, 89, 105, 107, 115; women of, 19, 74–75, 88–89, 94, 96, 108. *See also* class status
Brava Theatre, 226
Brenner, Anita: *Idols behind Altars*, 179
brown bodies, xii, 94, 100, 224–225
Brune, Krista, 247n62
Buck-Morss, Susan, 231
Buffalo Exposition (1901), 48
Burt, Ramsay, 97, 125, 233n4, 256n53, 263n68
Bustamante, Anastacio, 61
Butler, Judith, 32

cabaret, 201, 207, 209–210, 213, 215–217, 275n124–125, 276n135. *See also cine de rumberas* (woman rumba dancer cinema)
cabaretera films, 213, 275n124. *See also cine de rumberas* (woman rumba dancer cinema)
Cabranes-Grant, Leo, 246n31, 249n95
Cacama, 45–46

cachondería (sensuality), 205, 208, 220; definition, 275n117
Cadmus, Paul, 265n97
Cahuantzi, Próspero, 64
calaveras (skeletons) dancing, 217–220
California, USA, x, 37, 224–226
Calles, Plutarco Elías, 79
Camaxtli, 46
Campbell Reed, Ernest Stephen, 261n35
campesina (peasant attire), 208, 211
Campobello, Gloria, 126–130, 154, 162, 260n28, 262n60; *El Ballet 30–30*, 36, 136–143, 145–146, 263n71; and Escuela Nacional de Danza (END), 147, 150–151, 260n31, 264n89; parents of, 261n35; performing *El jarabe tapatío*, 20, 29, 118–120, 133–135, 141, 195, 230; *Ritmos indígenas de México* (Indigenous rhythms of Mexico), 36, 147, 152–160, 265n97
Campobello, Nellie, 22, 30, 130, 162, 162–163, 260n28, 260n33, 262n60, 266n117; *Cartucho*, 36, 138; *El Ballet 30–30*, 36, 136–143, 145, 146, 263n71; and Escuela Nacional de Danza (END), 36, 121, 137, 147, 150–151, 217, 260n31, 264n89; "Estadios" (Stadiums), 160–161; kidnapping of, 162, 260n30, 266n118; and masculinity, 126–128, 132, 134–136, 141, 261n43; and Mexicanization of ballet, 119–122, 131, 133, 137–141, 263n61; *Mis libros* (My Books), 129, 160; parents of, 261n34; performing *El jarabe tapatío*, 20, 26, 29, 31, 34, 118–120, 133–135, 141, 195, 230; *Ritmos indígenas de México* (Indigenous rhythms of Mexico), 36, 147, 152–160, 265n97; self-mythologizing, 127–129, 132–133, 142, 265n101
Campuzano, Fausto, 130
cancan, 24
Cannes Film Festival, 188

Cantú, Norma: *Dancing across Borders*, 22
capitalism, 8, 11, 43, 54–55, 97, 172, 237n39, 271n76
Carbajal Segura, Claudia, 125, 143, 263n68, 265n97
Carballo, Emmanuel, 129, 132, 260n33
Cárdenas, Guillermo, 56
Cárdenas, Lázaro, 143, 145, 147, 150, 188, 194, 263n67
Cardona, René, 199
Carranza, Venustriano, 1, 188
carretillas (folklórico footwork), 203, 210
Carroll Girls, 118, 127–130
Carroll, Miss Lettie H., 118, 126–130
Casa Azul (Blue House), 171
Casarín, José, 60, 64–65, 72, 248n70
Castellanos, Rosario, 154–155
Castle of Chapultepec, 56, 218
Castro Padilla, Manuel, 2, 177, 234n5, 252n37, 253n40
Castro Ricalde, Maricruz, 100, 104, 213, 266n117, 276n135
Cátedra Patrimonial Margarita Tortajada Quiroz, 277n10
Catholicism, 9, 61–62, 213
catrín (bourgeois male), 108–110, 114
celo civilizador (civilizing zeal), 51
Centenario (Centennial of 1910), 53–56, 58–60, 71–73, 117, 249n96, 253n40; "Ecos del Centenario," 108–109, 257n75
Centeotl, 46
Centro Nacional de Documentación, Información e Investigación de la Danza (CENIDI), 127
Chalchiuhtlicue, 46
Chapultepec Park, Mexico City, 35, 218; Garden Party in, 65, 84, 249n88; and La Noche Mexicana, 74–76, 78, 86–91, 98, 100, 102–103, 105, 117, 253n40; naming of Chapultepec Forest, 87
Charlot, Jean, 171
Charnay, Désiré: *Album fotográfico mexicano*, 245n20; *American Cities and Ruins*, 47
charros (traditional horsemen), 24,

74–76, 103, 105, 112–114, 250n2, 253n40, 271n75; in Anna Pavlova's performances, 2, 86, 234n7; attire of, 2, 120, 195–199; in María Cristina Pereda's performances, 90–91, 99; Nellie Campobello as, 20, 120, 134–135
Charros de Mondragón, 130, 262n60
Château Madrid, 130
Chávez, Carlos, 264n85
chicas modernas (modern girls), 96–97, 108. *See also* flappers
Chichén Itzá, 174
Chihuahua, ix, xi, 129, 226
children, 88, 122, 136, 185, 259n20; attending national celebrations, 69–71, 105; as dancers, 126, 129, 195; Declaration on the Rights of Children, 78; in Punjabi-Mexican families, 224–226; as symbolic of mestizo Mexico, 57, 166, 218
chinas poblanas (traditional feminine figure), 149, 234n6, 250n2, 253n40, 271n75; Ana Pavlova performing as, 2, 86; attire of, 24, 120, 195; Gloria Campobello performing as, 120, 134–135; at La Noche Mexicana, 74–76, 90, 98–99, 102–104, 108; schoolgirls as, 4, 7, 28
choque corporal (corporeal clash), 226–227
chorus line dancers, 96–97. *See also chicas modernas* (modern girls); Tiller Girl troupes
cine de rumberas (woman rumba dancer cinema), 166, 201–202, 212–214, 216, 218
citizen formation, 36, 58, 68, 168; and La Noche Mexicana, 76–82, 88–89, 111–112; and mestizaje, 72–73; and public displays, 4, 6, 78, 121–122, 161, 232, 262n54; and women, 125–126, 135–136, 142, 217, 260n27
Clarín, 136
class status, 58, 61, 67, 73, 111, 188, 194, 197–199, 259n25, 260n28, 271n76; lower-class status, 12,

69; middle-class status, 59, 69, 71, 122, 236n24; "popular" classes, 65, 68–69, 75, 78–81, 95, 105, 122–123, 236n31, 251n17; upper-class status, 59, 65, 69, 71, 80, 95, 109, 122, 251n17. *See also* bourgeoisie; elites; peasant populations
Clayton, Michelle, 123, 250n7
cockfights, 194, 197–199
Coignard, Jerónimo (Francisco Zamora), 117
Collins, Jimmy, 220
colonialism, 21, 50–51, 65, 111, 181, 206, 236n28, 238n58; resistance to, 18, 202, 229–231
colonization, xii, 10, 43–44, 155, 180, 238n56; colonizing gaze, 40; of knowledge, 229–230
Columbus, Christopher, 59
Communist Party of the Soviet Union, 143
Compañía de Baile de Pantomima, 126
Comte, Auguste, 53
Conquergood, Dwight, 227, 266n110
contact zones, 238n58
contrapunteo (counterpoint), 215
Contreras, Jesús, 45
Corazón Folklórico Dance Company, x
Cordero, Karen, 95, 255n48
corridos (Mexican ballads), 141
Cortés, Hernán, 46, 60–62, 66–67
cosmic race, 4-5
cosmopolitanism, 3, 28, 114, 118, 123, 132, 165, 175, 181, 244n13, 272n82; cosmopolitan modernity, 9, 41, 56, 58–59, 73, 213, 217; definition, 250n6; and La Noche Mexicana, 75–77, 85–87, 89, 97, 106, 109–111, 115; and *La reina del trópico*, 202, 206, 208–209, 211–212, 216–217; and Porfirian regime, 34–35, 39–40, 42–46, 53, 58–59, 64–65, 77–78, 87, 109
Costa, Amelia, 126
Costa, Linda, 126
costumes, 2, 24, 69, 125, 181, 261n49; in cinema, 194–195, 198–199, 210, 214; at La Noche Mexicana, 74,

89, 103–104, 108, 253n40. *See also* attire; footwear
Covarrubias, Miguel, 181
COVID-19 pandemic, xii–xiii
Cowan, Benjamin, 237n35
creole nationalism, 8, 55
criollos, 9, 259n20
Crónica Oficial, 61, 248n73
crónica viva (living chronicle), 49–50
Cuauhtémoc, 8, 46, 55–56, 109, 114, 247n61
Cuba, 1, 201, 205, 216, 276n132; Campobello sisters in, 118, 130–131, 133, 135, 138, 166, 262n60. *See also* Afro-Caribbean imaginaries; Afro-Cuban music
cubanidad (Cubanness), 216
Cuellar, Manuel, 239n59
Cuitláhuac, 45–46
cultural capital, 43–44, 124
curricula, ix, 124, 147–150, 192, 273n92
Cypess, Sandra, 260n33

Dalcroze eurythmics, 150
Dallal, Alberto, 24, 122
Dalton, David, 236n22
dance halls, 182–183, 203–205, 220
Danza del venado (Yaqui deer dance), 150, 215, 259n20, 266n113
Danzantes Unidos Festival (danzantes. org), 278n11
danzarinas técnicas (technical dancers), 154
danzón, 200, 205–206, 208–210, 220–221, 275n118
Darío, Rubén, 246n44
Day of the Dead, 218, 222, 268n22
de Anda, Raúl: *El charro negro*, 273n105; *La reina del trópico* (The Queen of the Tropics), 37, 167–168, 200–202, 204, 206, 209, 213–214, 219, 223, 276n135; *La tierra del mariachi*, 273n105
de Anza, Antonio, 41, 45, 47
de Basil, Wassily, 150
Debord, Guy, 247n64
de Cárdenas, Amalia S., 143
Declaration of the Rights of Children, 78

de Dios Bojorquez, Juan, 79, 143
de Fuentes, Fernando: *Allá en el Rancho Grande* (Out on the Big Ranch), 26, 37, 167–168, 187–188, 191–194, 200, 204, 222–223, 272n77; *El compadre Mendoza* (Godfather Mendoza), 188; *El prisionero 13* (Prisoner 13), 188, 273n105; *¡Vámonos con Pancho Villa!* (*Let's Go with Pancho Villa*), 188, 273n105
de Habsburgo, Maximilano, 56
de Iturbide, Agustín, 61, 251n12
de Jesús Moya, Felipe, 261n34
de la Huerta, Adolfo, 79
Delhort, Adria, 130
"Delirio" (Delirium), 209
de los Reyes, Aurelio, 221, 268n22, 269n35, 271n63
del Río, Carlos, 119–120, 133–135
del Río, Dolores, 189
de Medina y Ormaechea, Antonio A., 53, 246n43
Departamento de Bellas Artes (Department of Fine Arts), 143, 151, 262n61
Department of Physical Education, 259n22
derecho de pernada (droit du seigneur), 188
deseo de mundo (desire for the world), 250n6. *See also* cosmopolitanism
Desfile Histórico (Historical Parade) de 1910, 35, 59–60, 66–70, 248n70; documentation of, 61–65, 71, 249n96
Desmond, Jane, 21, 151, 240n73
Día del Soldado (Soldiers Day), 143–144, *144*, 263n67
Diaghilev, Serge, 94
Dirección de Misiones Culturales (Office of Cultural Missions), 125
disidentification, 135, 230
D'Lugo, Marvin, 192, 200, 206, 272n78, 273n90
Domínguez, Francisco, 136, 138, 150, 264n85
double mistaken identity, 238n58
"Ducanism" (Greek dance), 150

Duncan, Isadora, 233n4
Duniya Dance and Drum Company, 224, *225*

"Ecos del Centenario," 108–109, 257n75
education, 54–55, 259n25, 263n63; and author's positionality, ix–x, 228; and cinema, 169, 268n21; to create national identity, 4–5, 15, 65, 80–81, 85, 97, 117, 136–137, 193, 199, 259n20; performative, ix, xxi, 118, 120–128, 147–151, 233n1, 278n11; reforms, 11, 13, 72, 77–78, 123, 140–141, 258n15; and systematizing dance, 36, 131, 137, 147–148, 150–151, 264n78
Edward VII, King, 246n44
effeminacy (male), 12, 237n36
Eiffel Tower, 39–41
Eisenstein, Sergei, 164–165, 266n1, 269n27, 270n53; *Battleship Potemkin*, 175, 221; ideogram theorization, 172–174, 269n37, 270n40; *October*, 172–173, 175, 269n36; *¡Que viva México!*, 36, 92, 169–170, 188–191, 198, 220–221, 223, 268n21–23, 268n25, 271n63; *El jarabe tapatío* in, 166–167, 218–219, 222; "Epilogue," 166–167, 173, 217–219, 222, 270n56; "Prologue," 172–176; "Sandunga," 37, 168, 173, 177–187, 203, 270n53; "Soldadera," 173, 178, 270n53; *Thunder Over Mexico*, 171, 268n23
Ejército Trigarante (Army of the Three Guarantees), 60–61
"El Alabado" (The praised one), 177
El ballet simbólico 30–30 (The Symbolic Ballet 30–30), 36, 136–143, 145–146, 263n71
el chingón, 12
"El Chuchumbé," 202
El Demócrata, 75, 79, 86–87, 98, 252n32–33, 257n76
El Hemiciclo a Juárez, 56, 66
El Imparcial, 62

elites, 3, 10, 15–16, 30–31, 123, 132, 136, 171, 191, 236n24; at La Noche Mexicana, 76–80, 83–84, 89, 106–107; Porfirian, 8, 35, 53, 55, 57–58, 60, 68–69, 72, 247n63, 249n91. *See also* class status

El jarabe tapatío (Mexican hat dance/song), xi, 24, 130, 259n20, 273n92; in *Allá en el Rancho Grande*, 37, 168, 191–199, 204; balleticized by Anna Pavlova, 1–4, 6, 23, 26, 28–29, 86, 242n100; central to demonstrations of nationalism, 5, 7, 19, 133–136, 250n2; at La Noche Mexicana (Mexican Night), 28, 103, 117; in *¡Que viva México!*, 166–167, 218–219, 222; reclaimed by Campobello sisters, 20, 26, 29, 31, 34, 118–120, 133–135, 141, 195, 230

El Nacional, 143–144, *144*

"El palomo y la paloma," 229

El Paseo del Pendón, 60–61. *See also* Spanish conquest

el pelado, 12

El Universal Ilustrado, 2–5, 86–87, 90, 98, 105, 117, 143; Adolfo Fernández Bustamante (A.F.B.) writing for, 164, 266n1; "Ecos del Centenario," 108–109, 257n77; Eisenstein photos in, *165*, 218; "India Bonita" pageant in, 82, 109–110; "La 'Noche Mexicana' en el Bosque de Chapultepec," 74, 79, 102–103

empathy, 7; as kinesthetic, 23, 227, 240n77

en pointe (bailados en puntas), 1–2, 28–29, 86; resistance to, 117–120, 135

enramada (arbor), 182, 203–205

Ensambles Ballet Folklórico de San Francisco, x, 224–226

ephemerality, xi, 23, 30, 35–38, 69, 71, 85, 106, 108, 116, 142, 163, 229–231; of dance prior to video, 261n50; of voice, 128–129, 142, 163, 260n32

Escuela de Plástica Dinámica (School of Dynamic Plastic Arts), 131, 147–148, 156, 264n78

escuela mexicana (Mexicanist school of cinema), 268n21

Escuela Nacional de Danza (END), 36, 121, 134, 137, 147, 150–151, 154, 161–162, 217, 260n31, 264n78

Escuela Normal buildings, 54–55

Escuela Normal Rural "Ricardo Flores Magón," ix

escuelas del centenario (centennial schools), 78

Escuela Superior de Danza Folklórica Mexicana, ix

Estadio Nacional (National Stadium). *See* National Stadium (Estadio Nacional)

ethics, 17, 33, 231, 237n38, 263n68, 266n110

ethnicization, 124, 237n35, 252n30

ethnodocumentary filmmaking, 176, 180–181, 271n62–63

ethnography, 176, 181, 245n25, 265n109, 271n63; as fictional, 180, 271n62; performance, 37, 157, 227, 266n110

ethnoracial communities, 18, 21, 59, 73, 75, 191, 224–225; definition, 235n21; and diversity in Mexico, 9, 22, 37, 124, 168, 170, 199, 201

Experimental Cinema, 183, 185, 268n23

Exposición de Arte Popular, 80, 84, 251n17

Falcón, Olga, 195–196

Falkenstein, Waldeen, 152, 262n61

"famous 41" arrests, 12, 237n36

fandango, 201–204, 209, 274n112

Fantasía mexicana, 1–2, 86–87, 233n3, 234n7

fantasy, 31–32, 72, 117, 127, 209

Federico Ruíz's folklórico group, 203

Félix, María, 189

femininity, 7, 28, 96, 132, 262n56; and changing gender roles, 137, 145, 262n56; queer femininity, 31; and racialization, 212–214; and *Tehuanas*,

94, 96, 241n86, 251n23, 270n53.
See also chinas poblanas (traditional
feminine figure); effeminacy (male);
gender; girls; women
ferias (fairs), 35, 76, 84, 86, 253n40
Fernández Bustamante, Adolfo (A.F.B.),
164–165, 266n1
Fernández, Emilio, 188, 195–196,
268n21
fiestas escolares (school festivities), 122
Figueroa, Gabriel, 188–191, 222,
268n21, 273n86
Fiol-Matta, Licia, 135
Flaherty, Robert: *Nanook of the North*,
271n63
flâneur, Mexican, 109
flappers, 96–97, 108, 132, 137
Flores, Juan, 236n31
Flores, Tatiana, 256n61, 269n30
folklórico, 5, 18, 22, 31, 123, 136–137,
161, 239n67, 277n10; author's
practice of, ix–xiv, 33, 226–231; as
ballet folklórico, 217; definition,
19, 120; in films, 37, 163, 167,
193, 195, 199; groups, ix–x, 203,
224–225, 278n11
food traditions, 74–75, 225
footwear: huaraches, 29, 120, 133,
135, 257n76; lack of, 67, 107, 110,
140–141, 184; sandals, 63, 65, 67,
69, 132, 135, 184. *See also* attire;
costumes
footwork, 183–184, 215, 226;
borrachos (drunken ones/footwork),
196; *carretillas* (folklórico
footwork), 203–204, 210; of *El
jarabe tapatío* (Mexican hat dance/
song), 195–197; *en pointe (bailados
en puntas)*, 1–2, 28–29, 86;
guachapeados (alternating shuffles),
210; *guaguancó* (Afro-Cuban
dance), 166; of *jaraneros*, 35, 104;
of *rumberas*, 211–213. *See also*
rhythms; *zapateado* (footwork)
Fortuna, Victoria, 25, 242n90
Foster, Susan, 23, 101, 240n76–77
France: French aesthetics, 39–40, 47,
55–56, 87, 256n55, 271n75; French
Revolution, 42, 54, 143; Porfirio

seeking legitimation from, 8, 54. *See
also* Paris Universal Exposition (1889)
Franco, Jean, 11
Franko, Mark, 233n4, 256n52
Fuentes, Carlos, 190
Fuentes, Claudio, 162, 266n118
Fuentes León, Enrique, 162, 266n118

Gabara, Esther, 272n82
gachupines (people born in Spain), 64
Galé, Carmen, 126
Gallo, Rubén, 235n14
Gamio, Manuel, 11, 86, 101; *Forjando
Patria*, 9–10, 78
García Blizzard, Mónica, 178,
276n129
García Canclini, 251n24
García, Genaro, 54, 57, 60–61, 66,
246n47; *Crónica oficial*, 248n70,
248n73
Garden Party in Chapultepec Park, 65,
84, 249n88
Garner, Paul, 249n101
Garnier, Charles, 47
Garrigan, Shelly E., 244n11
gaze, 40, 169, 184, 190, 205, 213, 227.
See also spectatorship
gender, 7, 82, 92, 113–114, 123,
132–133, 135–136, 251n23,
257n78, 260n27; in cinema,
178–179, 181–182, 184, 209,
213, 216, 222, 272n76, 274n106;
women's changing roles, 96, 126,
137, 141–142, 146, 161, 259n25,
262n56. *See also* effeminacy (male);
femininity; girls; masculinity;
matriarchy; *muxes* (third
gender individuals); patriarchy;
transvestism; women
genealogies, 33, 57, 129; of Aztec
domination, 39, 45–46; of
movement, x, 8, 147, 158, 160;
performative, 246n31
German expressionist cinema, 188
gestus, 262n54
Gillingham, Paul, 247n61
girls, 107, 164, 183–184; Campobello
sisters as, 118–119; Carroll Girls,
118, 127–130; *chicas modernas*

(modern girls), 96–97, 108; flappers, 96–97, 108, 132, 137; *negrita* (little Black girl), 207, 275n121; schoolgirls performing, 4–7, 23, 28, 136–137; Tiller Girl troupes, 96–97, 256n54
Golden Age of Mexican cinema, 6, 7–8, 36, 163, 167, 188, 191
Gonzales, Michael, 56, 250n10, 257n76
González, Carlos, 138–140
Gopinath, Gayatri, 33
Gorostiza, Celestino, 147, 262n61
grabados (engravings), 218
Graham, Martha, 150, 262n61
Gran Canal del Desagüe extension, 55
Greek aesthetics, 46, 96, 119, 150
gringa/os, 127–128, 197–198
guachapeados (alternating shuffles), 210
Guadalajara, 19, 49, 51, 75
guaguancó (Afro-Cuban dance), 166
Guerrero, Vicente, 61, 247n58
Guízar, Tito, 191, 199
Gulf of Mexico, 201, 250n2
Guss, David, 6, 19–20, 239n68
Gutiérrez, Laura G., 201, 212, 235n17
Guzmán, Martín Luis, 79
gymnastics, 4, 125, 169, 259n22, 259n24

"Habitations of Humanity" exhibition, 47
habitus, 13, 237n42
Half and Halves, 37, 224, 226–227
Hamera, Judith, xiii, 25, 141, 240n77, 263n72
Haussmann, Georges-Eugène, 8, 55, 59
Havana, Cuba, 130, 205
Hellier-Tinoco, Ruth, 235n17, 242n91
Hermanos Alva (Alva Brothers), 69
Hernández, Amalia Viviana Basanta, 277n10, 278n11
Hershfield, Joanne, 180
hervidero (the masses), 111–112
heteronormativity, 11, 20, 22, 29, 116, 133, 135–136, 161, 237n36; definition, 236n32
heteropatriarchy, 30–31
Hewitt, Andrew, 23, 145
Hidalgo y Costilla, Guadalupe, 57

Hidalgo y Costilla, Miguel, 57, 62
hip(g)nosis, 275n127
Hispanophobia, 236n24
Hollywood, 198, 221, 267n11, 268n21, 272n77, 275n124; misrepresenting Mexicanness, 165, 187–188, 197
homosexuality (male), 12, 237n36. *See also* queerness
homosocial bonding (male), 12
huaraches, 29, 120, 133, 135, 257n76, 257n76. *See also* footwear
Huerta, Victoriano, 123, 188
Huesca, Andrés, 203
Human Rights Commission of Mexico City investigation, 162
hypermasculinity, 11–12, 36, 83, 120, 237n35

Iberian empires, 43
imperialism, xii, 8, 47, 55, 225
impuesto del centenario (tax), 79
"India Bonita," 110, 112–114, 251n23; pageant, 82, 109, 257n78. *See also* Uribe, María Bibiana
Indigeneity, xi, 29, 34, 102, 114, 121, 184, 264n79; and Blackness, 26, 212; embodied understanding of, 52, 155, 215, 232, 245n21, 251n23; erasure of, 160; exploitation of, 10, 65–66, 68, 248n82, 265n105; operationalized by Aztec Palace, 40–42, 44, 46–48, 55; and resistance to cosmopolitanism, 64, 251n23; resisting colonial tropes of, 175, 177, 180–181, 186–187; and whiteness, 276n129
Indigenismo, 51–52, 72, 101, 154–155, 180, 257n63, 270n44
Indigenista narratives, 101–102, 121, 155, 158, 160
Indigenous bodies, 67–68, 114–115, 155–156, 158–160, 272n84; in cinema, 170, 172–173, 181, 183–184, 186–187, 268n21
"Indigenous essence," 10, 84
Indigenous peasant populations, 70, 84, 166, 187, 236n31, 248n85. *See also* peasant populations; *pueblo* (people)

institutionalization of Mexican dance, 121, 137, 147, 169, 222, 260n30
Instituto Nacional de Bellas Artes y Literatura (INBAL), 162
insurrection at US Capitol, xii
International Congress of Americanists and Indianists, 55, 71, 249n99
intimacies, xiii, 15, 18, 166, 182–184, 191, 220, 222, 224, 240n77
Irwin, Robert McKee, 12, 237n36
Islas, Hilda, 277n4
Itzcoátl, 45–46

Jalisco, 48–49, 259n20
Japonism, 55, 94–95, 158–159, 255n48
jarabe tapatío. *See El jarabe tapatío* (Mexican hat dance/song)
jaranas yucatecas (dances from Yucatán), 35, 104, 137, 150
jaraneros (dancers from Yucatán), 35, 76, 99–102, 104, 257n66
jarocha/o (Afro-mestizo Veracruz identity), 21, 202–204, 206, 208, 210–212, 250n2, 274n113
jazz, 207–208
Jesusita en Chihuahua (dance/song), xi
Jiménez, Agustín, 218
Juárez, Benito, 56, 66

Kahlo, Frida, 92, 171, 269n27
Kaplan, Temma, 259n25
Karetnikova, Inga, 171, 220
Kimbrough, Hunter, 266n1, 271n61
kinesis, 152, 156, 159, 220, 265n101, 270n56
kinesthesia, 7, 22–23, 101, 151, 208, 240n76
kinesthetic empathy, 23, 101, 227, 240n77
kinesthetic identification, 23, 37, 146, 168, 192–196, 199–200, 204, 206, 213–216
kinesthetic memory, 7, 142, 192, 231, 261n33
Kirstein, Lincoln: *Ballet Alphabet*, 153, 265n97
Knight, Alan, 10, 248n85
Kórima dance group, ix
Kwan, SanSan, 23, 60, 68, 240n76

La bamba (dance/song), xi, 168, 203, 222, 274n113; in *La reina del trópico*, 37, 168, 201, 203–206, 209–211, 216
Laboratorio de Ritmos Plásticos (Laboratory of Plastic Rhythms), 264n85
"La Chaparrita," 4
La danza de los tastoanes (The dance of the tastoanes), 22, 50, 72
La danza de los viejitos (Dance of the old men), 150, 215
La División del Norte, 138
La fiesta de los tastoanes (The feast of the tastoanes), 49–51, 53, 245
Landa y Escandón, Guillermo, 54, 60
landscapes, 94, 268n21; aural, 210; cinematic, 166, 172, 175, 178, 185–191, 203, 223, 267n3, 272n84; definition, 272n85; sociopolitical, xiii, 25, 170, 203; urban, 55, 218
La Noche Mexicana (Mexican Night), 18, 22, 30, 35, 116, 249n88, 257n73; designs of Alberto Best Maugard, 86–92, 94–96, 99, 101–102, 104; *El jarabe tapatío* at, 28, 103, 117; illustrating social tensions, 74–77, 83–85, 87–89, 96, 101–102, 105–115, 252n32; newspaper coverage of, 74–75, 79, 86–87, 98–99, 102–106, 108–115, 252n32, 257n77; program description, 90–93, 253n40
"La Norteña," 4
"La Pajarera," 4
"La raspa," ix
Lavalle, Josefina, 233n3
Legrás, Horacio, 26, 272n83
Lempérière, Annick, 58, 250n8
Leonard, Karen Isaksend, 224–225, 277n1
Liceaga, David, 164
Limón, José, 127, 196
"L'Internationale," 143, 145
literacy rates, 11, 65, 79, 169
local knowledges, 18–19, 50–51, 124; definition, 239n63, 259n17
Lockhart, James, 238n56, 238n58

Lomnitz-Adler, Claudio, 18, 88–89, 249n101
London, Jack: *The Mexican*, 268n22
López, Ana M., 193, 209, 272n77, 273n104, 274n106
López, Antonio, 216, 276n141
López Figueroa, Emiliano, 79
López Minjarez, José Alfredo, ix
López Moctezuma, Carlos, 202
López, Rick, 16, 80, 84–86, 124, 236n24, 251n17, 252n30, 252n32
Luna, María Francisca, 129. *See also* Campobello, Nellie
Luna, Rafaela, 261n34
Luna, Soledad, 129. *See also* Campobello, Gloria
Lund, Joshua, 237n39

machismo. *See* hypermasculinity
Madrid, Alejandro, 206, 275n117
Madrigal, Carmen, 260n33
Malitzin (Doña Marina; Malinche), 60–61
Manicomio General La Castañeda building, 54
Manzanos, Rosario, 266n118
Marcha de Zacatecas (March of Zacatecas), 138–143, 262n60
María Candelaria, 272n84
Marino, Angela, 239n59
Marquis de Polavieja, 57
Martí, José, 39, 41
Martínez, Ana, 248n70, 249n91
Martínez del Río, Jaime, 2, 252n37
Martínez, María Elena, xi, 33, 243n113, 263n64
masculinity, 109, 213; hypermasculinity, 11–12, 36, 83, 120, 237n35; mestizo, 8, 12, 36, 83, 135; and national ideals, 11–12, 20, 126–127, 137; performed by Nellie Campobello, 126–128, 132, 134–136, 141
Matisse, Henri, 95
matriarchy, 37, 168, 178–180
Matthews, Irene, 260n30, 261n52
Mayans, 100, 104, 172–173, 257n66
Mbembe, Achille, 229

Mendive, Kiko, 207, 212, 216, 276n132
Mérida, Carlos, 94, 148–151, 262n61, 264n79, 264n85, 265n97
Mesoamerica, 16–17, 46, 176, 270n48
mestizaje, 9–13, 57, 71–73, 177, 212, 236n22, 236n28, 239n66, 247n58
mestizo aesthetics, 11, 15, 84, 120, 166, 170, 180, 222, 258n13; and dances, 35, 76, 104, 120–121, 150, 210, 234n9, 265n97, 274n109
mestizo habitus, 13–14, 237n42
mestizo state, 8–9, 12–13, 217–218, 237n39
methodology of book, xi, 7–15, 26–33, 69, 243n112; on translations, 244n2. *See also* ethnography
Mexican diasporas, 5–6, 19, 120; in United States, 37–38, 54, 194, 200, 224, 228–229, 231, 273n97, 277n1. *See also* Afro-diasporic dances
Mexican-Hindu families. *See* Punjabi-Mexican families
mexicanidad (Mexicanness), 11, 86, 197
Mexicanist school of cinema (*escuela mexicana*), 268n21
Mexican national anthem, 4, 89, 124, 253n40
Mexican Revolution, ix, 9–12, 15, 71, 73, 86, 126, 129, 188–189, 191, 194, 224, 236n31; and celebrations of independence, xi, 27, 35, 77–79, 136, 141–143, 178, 251n12; changes brought by, 24, 77, 96, 125, 136, 168, 259n25; novels of, 13, 29, 36, 120–121, 138
Mexican War of Independence, 61
Michoacán, 2, 61, 137, 158, 209, 214–216
Mier y Terán, Manuel, 61
migration, 43, 55, 191–192, 246n43; anti-immigration laws (US), 225; author's, x, 226; rural to urban, 77–78, 168, 200–201, 209, 224
Ministry of Defense building, 54

Ministry of Foreign Affairs building, 54
Ministry of Public Education (SEP),
11, 81, 123, 131, 178, 259n20,
261n52
misiones culturales (cultural missions),
123–125, 148, 150, 265n97
Miss Lettie H. Carroll's dance school,
118, 126–130
Mistral, Gabriela, 135
Mitchell, W. J. T., 272n85
mixed-race identity, 21, 236n22
Moallem, Minoo, 260n27
Moctezuma II, 60–62, 66–67, 70, 87
modern dance, xi, 125, 147, 149–150,
234n4, 234n9, 242n90, 256n53,
262n61
modernism, 1, 3, 39, 144, 239n66,
256nn52–53, 256n61, 272n82;
and Campobello sisters, 119, 121,
125, 135, 149–150, 152–153, 159;
influencing La Noche Mexicana, 76,
86, 89–90, 94, 100, 117; modernist
dance definition, 233n4. *See also*
modern dance
Monsiváis, Carlos, 11, 72, 190, 197,
258n15, 267n21
Montenegro, Roberto, 94, 171
monumentalization, 47, 55; of
Alexander von Humboldt, 54; of
Benito Juárez, 56, 66; of George
Washington, 54; of Louis Pasteur,
54; and Winged Victory sculpture,
56
Moore, Robin, 206, 275n117
Morelos y Pavón, José María, 57,
247n57–58
Moreno, Antonio: *Águilas frente al
sol*, 273n105; *Santa*, 177, 273n105,
274n106, 275n118
moros y cristianos (Moors and
Christians), 49
Mosaico Mexican Folk Ensemble, x
Moya, Mauro Rafael, 152, 160
Mraz, John, 272n81, 273n86
mulata bodies, 181, 211, 216, 238n46,
275n127. *See also* whiteness: white-
as-mulata performances
Muñoz, José Esteban, 38, 69, 129,
230–231, 260n32, 278nn15–16

muralism, 13, 29, 143, 148, 169–170,
172, 177, 236n30, 268n21; and
nationalist murals, 4, 11, 124, 171,
176
Murciélago trio, 195
muxes (third gender individuals), 179,
270n55

Nahua people, 16–17, 46–47, 238n56,
238n58, 244n1
Nahuatl (language), 87, 244n1, 259n20
Nájera-Ramírez, Olga, 239n67;
Dancing across Borders, 22
Nashville Exposition (1896), 48
National Ballet of Ecuador, 127
National Centennial Commission, 54
National Center for the Research and
Documentation of Dance, 127
National Congress of Elementary
Education, 55
National Congress of Students, 55
National Medical Congress, 55
National Museum of Anthropology, 174
National Museum of History,
Archeology, and Ethnology, 54
National Palace, 11, 62, 171
National Penitentiary, San Jerónimo
Atlixco, 55, 64–65
National School of Dance. *See* Escuela
Nacional de Danza (END)
National Stadium (Estadio Nacional),
3–7, 22–23, 28, 81, 125, 169,
235n14, 259n24; and Nellie
Campobello's choreography, 133,
136, 141, 143, 146
nativism, 265n105
negrita (little black girl), 207, 275n121
Nezahualcóyotl, 45–46
Noble, Andrea, 168, 272n84
Noche Mexicana. *See* La Noche
Mexicana (Mexican Night)
Noland, Carrie, 28–29, 158, 242n101,
243n102
nostalgia, 66, 70, 191–192, 194, 202,
205, 208–209, 215, 217
nuestro senti-pensar, 230

Obregón, Álvaro, 4, 11, 79, 86, 123, 142
Ocampo, María Luisa, 266n117

Olcott, Jocelyn, 126
O'Malley, Ilene, 259n25
orientalism, 24, 40–41, 76, 94–97, 106, 127, 172, 256n61. *See also* Japonism
Orlov, Nikita: *¡Que viva México!*, 36, 173
Orozco, José Clemente, 11, 171–172
Orquesta Mexicana de Charros de Mondragón, 130
Ortiz, Fernando, 215, 258n10
Ospina León, Juan Sebastián, 169; *Struggles for Recognition*, 267n15
Ottoman Empire, 40

Palacio de Bellas Artes (Palace of Fine Arts), 146, 150, 162
Palavicini, Manuel, 98–102, 104–105, 256n61
palenque (fighting ring), 197, 199
Palma Velasco, Juan Carlos, x, 226–227, 277n4
Palou, Pedro Ángel, 13, 237n42, 250n6
Pan-American Ballet, 209
Pani, Alberto, 79
Pardo Bazán, Emilia: *Al pie de la Torre Eiffel*, 39–40
Paris Universal Exposition (1889), 57, 170; Aztec Palace at, 9, 34, 39–48, 52–53, 55, 245n18; Latin American pavilions at, 39
Parra, Max, 12
Partido Nacional Revolucionario (PNR), 263n67
pascoleros (Yaqui dancers), 105
Paseo de la Reforma (Reforma Avenue), 8–9, 55–56, 59, 61, 87, 253n40
pasivo ethics, 237n38
paso montuno (montuno), 222
Pasteur, Louis, 54
pastiche, 40–41
Pastor, Enrique, 209
Patapovich, Stanislava Moll, 126
patriarchy, 30–31, 145, 217, 237n35, 272n78
Pátzcuaro Indians, 74–75
Pavlova, Anna, 26, 119–120, 126–128, 133–135, 200, 230, 233n1; balleticization of Mexican dances, 1–3, 6–7, 23, 28–29, 86, 95,

117–118, 233n3, 234n4, 234n9, 242n90, 242n100; and *Fantasía mexicana*, 1–3, 87, 233n3, 234n7, 252n36
Paz, Octavio: *El laberinto de la soledad*, 12, 237n38
peasant populations, 58, 65, 68–71, 89, 124, 131, 136, 177–178, 246n43; as also Indigenous, 70, 84, 166, 187, 236n31, 248n85. *See also* class status; *pueblo* (people)
Peña, Elaine, 240n74, 242n93, 243n107
Peñafiel, Antonio, 41; *Explication de l'édifice*, 45–47
Pereda, María Cristina, 91, 99, 242n100, 253n40
Pérez Caro, Eva, 2, 252n37
Pérez Montfort, Ricardo, 15, 97, 236n31, 250n2, 274n112
performance ethnography, 37, 157, 227, 266n110
performance studies, emergence of, 266n113
performative translation, 227, 277n4
photography, 42, 61, 63, 69, 86, 164, 170, 272n81, 272n83; of Gabriel Figueroa, 188–190; at La Noche Mexicana, 102–105, 107
Pianowski, Mieczyslaw, 2, 233n3, 234n7
Pitasio Bielas, Juan, 108, 110–111
plástica dinámica (dynamic plastic art), 148
Plaza de la Constitución, 61–62
Podalsky, Laura, 176, 179
Pons, María Antonieta, 200–202, 206, 213, 276n137
popular art, 80, 95, 146, 149, 251n17, 255n49
Porfirian regime (regime of Porfirio Díaz), 15, 77, 81, 83, 87, 109, 181, 209, 236n31, 249n101, 258n12; Belle Époque (1880–1910), 24; contradictions of, 10, 34–35, 42, 48, 60, 72; and Desfile Histórico (Historical Parade) de 1910, 59–60, 65, 68, 71–72, 249n96; elite classes, 8, 35, 53, 55, 57–58, 60, 68–69,

72, 247n63, 249n91; Garden
Party in Chapultepec Park, 65, 84,
249n88; and notions of progress, 8,
42, 53–55, 58–59, 65, 78, 80
Posada, José Guadalupe, 218
positionality of author, ix–x, 37–38,
225–232
positivism, 53
Pratt, Mary Louis, 124, 238n58,
261n50
pre-European past, 34, 39
pre-Hispanic past, 10–11, 86–87, 104,
172, 245n20; exoticization of, 47, 68
primitivism, 86, 94–95, 176, 179–180,
184, 256n53, 256n61, 272n82
"problema del Indio" (the Indian
Problem), 9
professionalization of dance, 148, 151
prostitute figure, 274n106, 276n135
Puar, Jasbir, 30–31, 243n105, 252n31
publics. *See* access to festivities
pueblo (people), 138–139, 146, 191,
197, 222; converging at La Noche
Mexicana, 75, 80–81, 99, 106–107,
111, 115, 257n75; definition,
236n31; mythification of, 11, 15,
89, 91–92, 241n88. *See also* peasant
populations
Pulido Llano, Gabriela, 205, 208, 212
Punjabi-Mexican families, 37,
224–226, 277n1

queerness, xi, xiii, 8, 36, 120, 232; as
assemblage, 29–33, 243n105. *See
also* homosexuality (male)
queer of color critique, 136; queer
evidence, 229–230, 278n15; queer
futurity, 230–231, 260n32; queering
the archive, 27, 30, 32–33, 38, 69,
129, 135, 229–231
queer studies/theory, 69, 228, 231
Quijano, Aníbal, 230
Quiroga, Pablo, 143

Rabasa, José, 235n18, 246n32
race. *See* Blackness; brown bodies;
ethnoracial communities; Indigenous
bodies; mixed-race identity; *mulata*
bodies; whiteness

Ramos, Samuel: *El perfil del hombre y
la cultura en México*, 12
Ramos Smith, Maya, 24
Ramos Villalobos, Roxana Guadalupe,
121–122, 147
Rancière, Jacques, 14
rebozos (shawls), 69, 166, 195, 198,
234n6
Reconquista (Spanish), 22, 49–50
Red and White Crosses, 74–75
Reflejos de México, x
Reforma Avenue. *See* Paseo de la
Reforma (Reforma Avenue)
relational infrastructure, 146, 159,
263n72
religion, 17, 45, 123. *See also*
Catholicism
Revista de Revistas, 119, 234n7
revista genre, 191, 271n75. See also
teatro de revistas (revue theater)
Reynoso, José Luis, 25, 146, 234n9,
239n66, 242n90, 263n71
rhythms, xi, 35, 119, 169, 195, 226;
Afro-diasporic, 166–167, 201–202,
206, 212–213; Caribbean, 200–201,
205–207, 209–212, 215–216,
220–222, 274n113, 275n124; as
cinematic signifiers, 193, 199–202,
220–222, 273n90; Indigenous,
152–153, 156, 158, 265n101; of
jaranas yucatecas, 100, 104; of
"Sandunga," 182, 184–185
Rivas Mercado, Antonio, 56
Rivera Cusicanqui, Silvia, 231
Rivera, Diego, 4, 11, 37, 92, 94, 155,
171, 179, 268n22
Rivera-Servera, Ramón, 38, 227–228
Rodríguez, Juana María, 27, 32, 38,
230, 243n108
Rodríguez, Luis A., 3
Rodríguez, María de las Nieves, 107,
115, 249n88, 255n49
Roldán, Emma, 207
Romero, Brenda: *Dancing across
Borders*, 22
rostros (faces), 99, 189–190, 193, 198,
272n84
rumba dancers, 166–167, 206,
209–214, 216, 218–220, 222,

276n141. *See also cine de rumberas* (woman rumba dancer cinema)

Russian Revolution, 189

Russian school of ballet, 147–148

"Sandunga" (dance/song), 37, 168, 178–187, 203, 222, 270n53

Salas, Ángel, 138

Salazkina, Masha, 172, 174–176, 180, 186, 218, 221–222, 270n53, 270n56

Sánchez Prado, Ignacio, 9

Sánchez Rivero, Manuel, 64

sandals, 63, 65, 67, 69, 132, 135, 184. *See also* footwear

San Francisco Jewish Community Center, 224

Santiago, Saint, 50–52

Santoscoy, Alberto, 49–52, 72

Schechner, Richard, 20, 265n109, 266n113

Schroeder Rodríguez, Paul A., 267n3, 267n11, 268n21, 271n76

Serna, Laura Isabel, 165

settler colonialism, 236n28

Sevilla, Ninón, 213, 276n137

sexuality. *See* heteronormativity; homosexuality (male); queerness

Siebers, Tobin, 15, 238n48

Sierra, Bolívar, 171

Sierra, Justo, 71–72, 122

Sierra-Rivera, Judith, 264n79

Simiente, 136

Sinclair, Mary Craig, 171

Sinclair, Upton, 171, 266n1, 268n23, 271n61

Singh, Joti, 224

Siqueiros, David Alfaro, 11, 171, 177; *Entierro de un obrero* (Burial of the sacrificed worker), 176

Siskind, Mariano, 53, 250n6

Sklar, Deidre, 240n77

slavery, 17, 206, 234n6, 238n46

Sluis, Ageeth, 96

Snow, Mitchell, 94, 134, 264n85, 265n97

socialism, 143, 188, 194

socialities, xii, 60, 146, 195, 199–200, 240n77, 263n72; alternative, xiv,

7, 23, 26, 68, 71, 73, 101, 213; and lo mexicano, xiii, 15, 22, 27, 76, 85, 89, 107–108, 116, 197; of the popular, 35, 37, 76, 89, 226; "stranger sociality," 88

Sociedad Mexicana de Consumo, 246n43

Sokolow, Anna, 152, 262n61

soldaderas (women soldiers), 166, 238n46, 259n25

sonajas (rattles), 105

son del atole (section of *El jarabe tapatío*), 196

Sonora, 35, 76, 99–100

sound, 37, 168, 271n75, 272n81, 273n90, 273n104–105, 274n106; in *Allá en el Rancho Grande*, 189, 191–192; in Eisenstein's films, 175, 177–178 , 182, 185, 221–222; in *El jarabe tapatío*, 166, 218, 273n92; in *La reina del trópico*, 201–202, 207–212, 216. *See also* rhythms

spaces, urban, 25, 55, 60, 65, 87, 256n52–53, 256n61; and cinema, 169, 188, 216, 275n125; migration to, 77–78, 168, 200–201, 209, 224; women in, 97, 125–126, 137, 217

Spanish conquest, 11, 17, 51–52, 60–61

Spanish Reconquista narrative, 22, 49–50

spectacle, 24, 53, 66, 75, 241n88, 262n54; Aztec Palace as, 40–42; dance as, 119, 122, 125, 130, 135, 137, 151, 209; definition, 247n64; of human sacrifice, 47; La Noche Mexicana as, 35, 84, 86, 89–90, 106; and modernity, 39, 43, 59, 89–90, 97; and National Stadium, 81–82, 125, 235n14, 259n24; women as, 96, 186, 211, 216

spectatorship, xiii, 4, 14, 23, 29, 97, 122, 124, 193, 227, 242n100, 256n52; in *Allá en el Rancho Grande*, 198–199; and Campobello sisters, 135–136, 159; and cinema, 168, 176, 182, 184, 187, 190–191,

195, 197; at Desfile Histórico, 59–64, 66, 68–70, 73; at La Noche Mexicana, 83, 104, 108–109; and racialized anxieties, 201, 203–204, 210, 213. *See also* access to festivities
stereotypes, 106, 155, 191, 237n35, 265n205; of the Caribbean, 212–213; of lo mexicano, 13–16, 161, 172, 194, 198, 269n27; of masculinity, 134, 141; of women, 96, 213, 274n106
St. Louis Exposition (1904), 48

Tablada, José Juan, 255n48
Tariácuris trio, 195
Tarica, Estelle, 101, 155, 257n63, 265n105
tastoanes (lords), 48, 51; *La danza de los tastoanes*, 22, 49–50, 72; *La fiesta de los tastoanes*, 49, 53
Taylor, Diana, 17, 20, 32–33, 50, 56, 83, 87, 158
"Taylorist" dancing, 97
Teatro Arbeu, 1, 117, 233n3
teatro de revistas (revue theater), 119, 187, 191, 199, 234n5, 271n75, 273n92
Teatro Iris, 96
Teatro Martí, 130
teatros de barriada (neighborhood theaters), 3
Tehuanas (women from the Isthmus of Tehuantepec, Oaxaca), 24, 74, 92–93, *162*, 241n86, 253n40, 270n53; women costumed as, 76, 90, 94–96, 98–99, 108, 153; in "Sandunga," 164, 178–181, 185–186
temporality, 17, 68, 83, 250n7, 252n31; displacing Indigeneity into the past, 10, 166, 170, 172–176, 179, 187, 235n18; and La Noche Mexicana, 87, 90–91, 93–94, 101, 115; and queerness, 30, 33
Tenenbaum, Barbara, 8, 55
Tenochtitlan, 17, 39, 46, 109, 244n1
Tenorio-Trillo, Mauricio, 41, 44, 48,

55, 244n13, 245n18–19, 245n25, 247n63, 249n101
teocalli (pyramidal temple), 34, 39, 109, 172–175
Teotihuacán, 86, 175
ternos yucatecos (traditional gala dresses), 104
Tetlapayac, 164, 171
Texcoco, 17, 39, 46, 60, 244n1
third gender (*muxes*), 179
Tiller Girl troupes, 54, 96–97, 256
Tissé, Edward, 164
Tlacopan, 17, 39, 46, 61, 244n1
tlahtoanih (lords), 47–48. *See also tastoanes* (lords)
Tlaloc, 46, 172
Tlaxcaltecan Indian warriors, 60–61, 64
Tolteca Cement Company, 218
Toor, Frances: *Mexican Folkways*, 134, 179
Tortajada Quiroz, Margarita, 24, 125, 148, 156, 224, 226, 252n37, 260n31; *Danza y poder*, 123
Toscano, Salvador, 69–70
Totoquihuatzin, 45–46
Townsend, Sarah, 17, 48, 245n24, 260n28
trajineras (decorated boats from Xochimilco), 75, 253n40
transculturation, 18, 238n58, 258n10
transgressiveness, 12, 266n117
transvestism, 12, 237n36. *See also* gender; queerness
Trejo y Lerdo de Tejada, Carlos, 131, 134
Triple Alliance (Aztec Empire), 17, 39, 46
Trump, Donald, xii
typages (Eisenstein), 172, 198, 269n27

"unbecoming" Black, 216, 276n141
United States Independence centennial (1876), 54
Universal Ilustrado. *See El Universal Ilustrado*
universalism, 10, 25, 39, 42–44, 52, 234n9, 242n90, 247n61, 250n6, 263n71

Universidad Autónoma del Estado de
Hidalgo: Instituto de Artes,
277n10
Universidad Nacional Autónoma de
México (UNAM), 123: Filmoteca
Nacional (National Film Library),
69, 257n73; Fondo Martín Luis
Guzmán Franco, Archivo Histórico,
107
unruly bodies, 105–106, 208
Uribe, María Bibiana, 82, 109, 113. See
also "India Bonita"
Usigli, Rodolfo, 147
Uslenghi, Alejandra, 245n21
utopianism, 43, 172, 178, 181,
186–187, 191, 231–232

Van Young, Eric, 17, 239n63,
259n17
vaquerías (festive celebrations in
Yucatán), 104
Vargas, Deborah, 221, 243n107
Vargas Valdés, Jesús, 260n31
Varner, Natasha, 186, 236n28, 251n23,
257n78
Vasconcelos, José, 13, 15, 81, 101,
123–124, 126, 136, 235n14,
251n21, 261n52; *La raza cósmica*
(*The Cosmic Race*), 10–11
Vaughan, Mary Kay, 259n20,
261n49
Venice Film Festival, 188
Veracruz, 1, 21, 61, 100, 181,
200–201, 206, 208, 210–211
Victoria, Guadalupe, 61
Villa, Francisco "Pancho," 138, 142,
188
Viollet-le-Duc, Eugène, 47
voice, 33, 68, 72, 108, 111, 121,
154–155, 211–212, 216; as
ephemera, 128–129, 142, 163,
260n32; narration in *¡Que viva
México!*, 166, 173–174, 182,
184–185, 269n38
Volinine, Alexandre, 2, 86, 233n3,
234n7
von Humboldt, Alexander, 54
von Laban, Rudolph, 153,
265n97

Wade, Peter, 235n21
Waldeen. *See* Falkenstein,
Waldeen
Warner, Michael, 88–89, 236n32
Washington, George, 54, 243n107,
273n92
whiteness, 65, 197, 201, 213, 234n9,
242n90; "white-as-Indigenous"
film representations, 178, 212,
270n54, 276n129; "white-as-mulata"
performances, 207–208, 211–212,
215–216, 276n129
white supremacy, xii
Williams, Gareth, 13
Winged Victory sculpture. *See* Ángel
de la Independencia (Winged
Victory)
women, 102–105, 119–120, 133,
201, 205, 214–215, 224; bodies
of, 82, 96, 121, 137, 146, 179,
260n27, 270n56, 271n61;
bourgeois, 19, 74–75, 88–89, 94,
96, 108; changing roles for, 20,
123, 125–126, 135–138, 141–146,
151, 154, 209, 212–213, 259n25,
262n56; and citizen formation,
125–126, 135–136, 142, 217,
260n27; as dominating dance,
261n50; Indigenous, 61, 63–64,
69–71, 88, 92–94, 109, 164, 166,
178–182, 184–187, 251n23;
marginalization of, 12, 31; rights of,
126, 263n67; teacher training for,
ix, 54–55. *See also chinas poblanas*
(traditional feminine figure); *cine
de rumberas* (woman rumba
dancer cinema); femininity; gender;
matriarchy; *Tehuanas* (women
from the Isthmus of Tehuantepec,
Oaxaca)
World War I, 189

Xochimilco, 75, 86, 253n40
Xochiquetzal, 46

Yacatecuhtli, 46
Yaqui deer dance (*Danza del
venado*), 150, 215, 259n20,
266n113

Yaqui Indians, 21, 30, 102, 158–160; dancers, 35, 76, 99–101, 104–105
Yucatán, 100, 130, 137, 171, 173, 253n40; *jaraneros* from, 35, 76, 90, 99, 104
Yúdice, George, 244n9

Zamora, Francisco, 117
Zapata, Emiliano, 142

zapateado (footwork), xi, 166, 195–197, 202, 204, 210–211, 215. *See also* footwork; rhythms
zarzuelas (operettas), 24
Zihua Temachtiani, x
Zócalo of Mexico City, 8, 55, 61–66, 247n60, 249n95
Zybin, Hipólito, 147–148, 150

Printed in the USA
CPSIA information can be obtained
at www.ICGtesting.com
LVHW050203200923
757466LV00004B/14/J